The Schenker Project

The Schenker Project

Culture, Race, and Music Theory
in Fin-de-siècle *Vienna*

NICHOLAS COOK

OXFORD
UNIVERSITY PRESS

2007

OXFORD

UNIVERSITY PRESS

Oxford University Press, Inc., publishes works that further
Oxford University's objective of excellence
in research, scholarship, and education.

Oxford   New York
Auckland   Cape Town   Dar es Salaam   Hong Kong   Karachi
Kuala Lumpur   Madrid   Melbourne   Mexico City   Nairobi
New Delhi   Shanghai   Taipei   Toronto

With offices in
Argentina   Austria   Brazil   Chile   Czech Republic   France   Greece
Guatemala   Hungary   Italy   Japan   Poland   Portugal   Singapore
South Korea   Switzerland   Thailand   Turkey   Ukraine   Vietnam

Copyright © 2007 by Oxford University Press

Published by Oxford University Press, Inc.
198 Madison Avenue, New York, New York 10016

www.oup.com

Oxford is a registered trademark of Oxford University Press

Library of Congress Cataloging-in-Publication Data
Cook, Nicholas, 1950–
The Schenker project : culture, race, and music theory in
fin-de-siècle Vienna / Nicholas Cook.
p.   cm.
Includes bibliographical references and index.
ISBN 978-0-19-517056-6
1. Schenker, Heinrich, 1868–1935—Criticism and interpretation. 2. Music
theory—Social aspects—Austria—Vienna. 3. Music theory—
Political aspects—Austria—Vienna. I. Title.
ML423.S33C66 2007
780.92—dc22   2006031704

1   3   5   7   9   8   6   4   2

Printed in the United States of America
on acid-free paper

Acknowledgments

Ideally this book would have been written by someone who combined deep knowledge of Schenkerian theory, German history and philosophy, and eastern European Jewish culture, not to mention the language skills demanded by Schenker's often convoluted German. Many people have helped me to overcome the gaps between ideal and reality. I aired this material in a tentative way during a series of seminars held in June 2002 at the Mannes Institute for Advanced Studies in Music Theory: my thanks—for giving me innumerable comments, criticisms, and pointers to further work, but mainly for not eating me alive—to Kofi Agawu, Wayne Alpern (who also directed the Institute), William Caplin, Thomas Christensen, Richard Cohn, Henry Klumpenhouwer, Patrick McCreless, William Pastille, Wayne Petty, Matthew Riley, William Rothstein, Janet Schmalfeldt, Hedi Siegel, and Peter Smith. The work reached a more developed form in a series of public lectures sponsored by Royal Holloway, University of London, and the Society for Music Analysis, to whom again my thanks. Julie Brown, William Drabkin, Patrick McCreless, Andrea Reiter, and William Rothstein commented on (and corrected) draft materials, while Suzannah Clark, William Drabkin, Ludwig Holtmeier, Lee Rothfarb, and Harry White let me see their prepublication work. Similarly, Wayne Alpern gave me access to his forthcoming thesis (it should be noted that the quoted passages are subject to final revision). Other debts are owed to Hedi Siegel and Patrick Miller, as well as to Georg Werkwerth, who took the photographs of Reisnerstrasse 38 (figs. 2.5–7). I am very grateful to William Pastille for not only allowing me to include his translation of Schenker's 'Der Geist der musikal-ischen Technik' (which originally appeared in *Theoria*) in this volume but also revising and updating it. Special thanks are due to Ian Bent, who read the first full draft of this book for the publishers and was more than generous with comments, suggestions, corrections, and new material, as well as allowing me access to unpublished writings; and to Lars Franke, who read a wide range of German-language material for me, not only summarising and providing translations where appropri-ate (all unattributed translations are by him) but also using his excel-lent academic judgment in directing me to passages relevant to this project. Finally, it is a pleasure to acknowledge a publication subven-tion from the Otto Kinkeldey Publication Endowment Fund of the American Musicological Society.

Contents

Abbreviations   ix

Introduction: Schenker's Contexts   3

Chapter 1   Foundations of the Schenker Project   29
Schenker and the Philosophers   29
Formalists against Formalism   48
Rehabilitating Musical Logic   63

Chapter 2   The Reluctant Modernist   89
Curlicues and Catastrophe   89
Ornamentation and Critique in Fin-de-Siècle *Vienna   97*
Modernists against Modernism   108
Reinventing the Classics   129

Chapter 3   The Conservative Tradition   140
Schenker's Politics   140
The Logic of Nostalgia   158
The Anachronistic City   175

Chapter 4   The Politics of Assimilation   199
Schenker's Project and Jewish Tradition   199
The Logic of Alterity   217
Schenker and Others   229

Chapter 5   Beyond Assimilation   246
             Schenker's Rosenhaus   246
             The Posthumous Schenker   269

Conclusion: Music Theory as Social Practice   307

Appendix: Heinrich Schenker, 'The Spirit of Musical Technique'
             (Der Geist der musikalischen Technik)
             Translated by William Pastille   319

References   333

Index   347

Abbreviations

Translations of Schenker's Writings

AP   *The Art of Performance,* ed. Heribert Esser, trans. Irene Schreier Scott. New York: Oxford University Press, 2000

BCFF   *J. S. Bach's Chromatic Fantasy and Fugue,* trans. Hedi Siegel. New York: Longman, 1984. [*Chromatische Phantasie und Fuge D-moll.* Vienna: Universal Edition, 1910]

BNS   *Beethoven's Ninth Symphony,* trans. and ed. John Rothgeb. New Haven: Yale University Press, 1992. [*Beethovens neunte Sinfonie.* Vienna: Universal Edition, 1912]

C1   *Counterpoint,* bk. 1 (*Cantus Firmus and Two-Voice Counterpoint*), ed. John Rothgeb, trans. John Rothgeb and Jürgen Thym. New York: Schirmer, 1987. [*Kontrapunkt: Cantus Firmus und Zweistimmiger Satz.* Stuttgart: Cotta, 1910]

C2   *Counterpoint,* bk. 2 (*Counterpoint in Three and More Voices, Bridges to Free Composition*), ed. John Rothgeb, trans. John Rothgeb and Jürgen Thym. New York: Schirmer, 1987. [*Kontrapunkt: Drei- und Mehrstimmiger Satz, Übergänge zum freien Satz.* Vienna: Universal Edition, 1922]

CSO   'A contribution to the study of ornamentation', trans. Hedi Siegel. *Music Forum* 2 (1976), 1–139. [*Ein Beitrag zur Ornamentik.* Vienna: Universal Edition, 1903]

DAC   'The decline of the art of composition: A technical-critical study', ed. and trans. William Drabkin. *Music Analysis* 24 (2005), 33–130

FC   *Free Composition (Der freie Satz)*, ed. and trans. Ernst Oster. 2 vols.
      New York: Longman, 1979. [*Der freie Satz*. Vienna: Universal
      Edition, 1935]

FGMA *Five Graphic Music Analyses*. New York: Dover, 1969. [*Fünf
      Urlinie-Tafeln*. Vienna: Universal Edition, 1932]

H   *Harmony*, ed. Oswald Jonas, trans. Elisabeth Mann Borgese.
      Chicago: University of Chicago Press, 1954. [*Harmonielehre*.
      Stuttgart: Cotta, 1906]

MM1   *The Masterwork in Music*, vol. 1, ed. William Drabkin, trans. Ian
      Bent et al. Cambridge: Cambridge University Press, 1994. [*Das
      Meisterwerk in der Musik: ein Jahrbuch von Heinrich Schenker*, vol.
      1. Munich: Drei Masken Verlag, 1925]

MM2   *The Masterwork in Music*, vol. 2, ed. William Drabkin, trans. Ian
      Bent et al. Cambridge: Cambridge University Press, 1996. [*Das
      Meisterwerk in der Musik: ein Jahrbuch von Heinrich Schenker*, vol.
      2. Munich: Drei Masken Verlag, 1926]

MM3   *The Masterwork in Music*, vol. 3, ed. William Drabkin, trans. Ian
      Bent et al. Cambridge: Cambridge University Press, 1997. [*Das
      Meisterwerk in der Musik: ein Jahrbuch von Heinrich Schenker*, vol.
      3. Munich: Drei Masken Verlag, 1930]

T1   *Der Tonwille: Pamphlets in Witness of the Immutable Laws of Music:
      Issues 1–5 (1921–1923)*, ed. William Drabkin, trans. Ian Bent et
      al. New York: Oxford University Press, 2004. [*Der Tonwille:
      Flugblätter zum Zeugnis unwandelbarer Gesetze der Tonkunst*, is-
      sues 1–5. Vienna: Tonwille Flugblätterverlag (i.e. Universal
      Edition), 1921–23]

T2   *Der Tonwille: Pamphlets/Quarterly Publication in Witness of the Im-
      mutable Laws of Music: Issues 6–10 (1923–1924)*, ed. William
      Drabkin, trans. Ian Bent et al. New York: Oxford University
      Press, 2005. [*Der Tonwille: Flugblätter zum Zeugnis unwandel-
      barer Gesetze der Tonkunst*, issues 6–10. Vienna: Tonwille Flug-
      blätterverlag (i.e. Universal Edition), 1923–24]

Hellmut Federhofer's Collection of Schenker's Writings
from 1891 to 1901

HSEK *Heinrich Schenker als Essayist und Kritiker. Gesammelte Aufsätze,
      Rezensionen und kleinere Berichte aus den Jahren 1891–1901*, ed.
      Hellmut Federhofer. Hildesheim: Georg Ohlms Verlag, 1990.

Archives

CA   Cotta-Archiv (Stiftung der Stuttgarter Zeitung), Schiller Na-
      tionalmuseum/Deutsches Literaturarchiv, Marbach

DLA   Schiller Nationalmuseum/Deutsches Literaturarchiv, Marbach

NMI   Nederlands Muziek Instituut, Den Haag

OC   Oster Collection, New York Public Library (referenced by file/item)

OJ   Oswald Jonas Memorial Collection, Special Collections, University of California, Riverside Libraries (referenced by box/folder)

WSLB   Wiener Stadt- und Landesbibliothek, Vienna

The Schenker Project

Introduction:
Schenker's Contexts

If Schenker's theory was the solution, what was the problem? In terms of the English-speaking academic environment within which Schenker's ideas became naturalised in the period after the Second World War, the answer is obvious: how to account for the coherence of Western 'art' music of the eighteenth and nineteenth centuries, how to make both musical and conceptual sense of it. But that answer only generates a further question: what role we should ascribe to 'that Pandora's box, hygienically referred to until now as his "polemics"', as Ian Bent calls it (*MM1* x), in other words the passionate and often colourful views on contemporary society, politics, German nationalism, and so forth which Schenker expressed at length in his music-theoretical writings—views that at first sight have little or nothing to do with either music or theory. Bent's opinion on this is straightforward: 'every utterance in his theoretical and analytical writings on music is saturated with his ideas in these other realms', he says, so that 'where his world of ideas is concerned, there are no margins: there is only a single, integrated network of thought'. If that is the case—and it is a view that has gained a great deal of ground in the past two decades—then we clearly need to draw the problem to which Schenker's theory is the solution in much broader terms.

That is the overall aim of this book, in which I set Schenker's work into a variety of contemporary contexts ranging from the artistic (music criticism, architectural modernism) to the broadly political (the tradition of German cultural conservatism, Schenker's position as a Jewish

3

immigrant to Vienna). In doing this I have a number of objectives: to
add depth to our reading of Schenker's music-theoretical writings; to
use them as a vantage point for exploring the world of *fin-de-siècle* Vienna; to consider the relationship between music theory and social
context; to gain critical purchase on ways of thinking about music that
remain influential today but have their origin in very different social,
cultural, and political circumstances. The last point is particularly
salient for musicologists and theorists of my generation, who trained at
a time when—in Britain at least—Schenkerian analysis had only recently become established in the programmes of the more progressive
university music departments. It was presented not as the cultural
product of a particular time and place, but rather as the best way to
understand how music is. It wasn't long before the 'New' musicology
put a stop to that. First we learned to think of Schenkerian analysis as
representing not the truth about music, not the truth about European
music of the eighteenth and nineteenth centuries, not even *a* truth
about European music of the eighteenth and nineteenth centuries, but
rather a particular way of making sense of music, an admittedly bulky
item in the analyst's toolkit to be used where it worked and set aside
where it didn't. Then we learned to think of the analytical project as itself the result of a particular set of historical contingencies, a means
through which a particular set of social and ideological values were
maintained under the guise of being just the way things are: it was
Joseph Kerman's book *Contemplating Music* (1985; British title *Musicology*) that made me realise for the first time how far my discipline was
itself a historical construction. And in the field of Schenkerian theory,
William Rothstein's seminal article 'The Americanization of Schenker'
(first published in the following year) played the same kind of role. It
was as if Schenkerian analysis had acquired an instant history.

Rothstein (1990a: 195) catalogued some of 'those elements of
Schenker's thought which clash most spectacularly with the American
mind', as he put it—Schenker's sometimes xenophobic nationalism, ab-
solutism, cult of German genius, condemnation of music after Brahms—
and demonstrated the extent to which Schenkerian theory, as promulgated on both sides of the Atlantic in the late twentieth century, was
the product of American postwar academia. In so doing, he opened up
the possibility of what might be termed historically informed Schenker
studies, by analogy with the historically informed performance movement at its zenith in the 1980s: the attempt to resituate Schenker's theory in its historical and geographical context, to de-Americanise it as it
were, or at least to recognise the differences between the Viennese
Schenker and the American one. Much work of this nature has been
done in the two decades since Rothstein's article first appeared. In some
cases it has taken the form of advocacy for the rich messiness of
Schenker's middle-period analytical practice as against the more sani-
tised, systematic, and scientific image of the Americanised theory (itself

based, though selectively, on Schenker's final formulation of his thought in *Der freie Satz*). More often it has taken the form of an attempt to delineate the conceptual threads that link Schenker's theorising to the broader thinking of his day, with an emphasis on the legacy of nineteenth-century German philosophical idealism: my own first attempt at this, an essay entitled 'Schenker's Theory of Music as Ethics' (1989c), originated in an attempt to focus on the polemical asides in the *Meisterwerk* volumes, on the pastry rather than the analytical plums contained within it—and of course my claim, like Bent's, was that the asides are not just asides but an integral part of the whole.

The work of writers like Leslie Blasius, Allan Keiler, Kevin Korsyn, William Pastille, Robert Snarrenberg, and many others has reinstated a great deal of the intellectual background that the founders of American Schenkerism—first-generation pupils such as Oswald Jonas and Felix Salzer, second-generation pupils such as Ernst Oster, William Mitchell, and John Rothgeb—had jettisoned in mid-Atlantic. (There is a sense in which, to borrow Adorno's phrase, the project of recontextualising Schenker is one of defending him against his devotees.) My own 1989 article looks decidedly primitive in light of work carried out since then. Yet I feel there is still unfinished business. At one level, Korsyn's demonstration of the affinities between Schenker and Kant, or Pastille's demonstration of the affinities between Schenker and Goethe, add crucially to our understanding of what Schenker wrote: if you don't pick up these resonances, then you won't understand the terms within which Schenker framed his thought. (More on this in chapter 1.) And Snarrenberg's book *Schenker's Interpretive Practice* (1997), with its emphasis on the linguistic fabric of Schenker's discourse, reveals something of the inner dynamic of Schenker's thought, the metaphorical complexity that underlies what look like straightforward analytical decisions, the multilayered meanings that emerge from his words in action. (As Snarrenberg [xvii] put it, the aim of his book is 'to reconstruct the structure and content of the musical experiences reported by Schenker'.) But all this still leaves unanswered questions about Schenker's motivation, the deep-seated beliefs—or prejudices—about music and society that fuelled not only his polemics but also, if I am right, his theoretical development. In one sense, the reason for the polemics is plain, for Schenker explained it himself: 'Polemic is the *classroom* in which the "people" learn! The rest they will not understand for a long time to come'.[1] Yet one is left wondering just *why* was Schenker so polemical, so angry, so passionate? Just what were the expectations that he found so blatantly unfulfilled in the social, cultural, and musical world around him? Just what power did he attribute to music in setting right the social and cultural ills that he diagnosed? Just what, to return to my

---

[1] Letter draft to Emil Hertzka (OC 52/589–90), dating from around 1922; translation from *TI* x.

opening formulation, was his problem, and in what way might his theory represent the solution to it?

In order to address these questions, we need to set Schenker into a broader period context than the philosophical or the linguistic, and in recent years there has been a developing tendency to factor the dimensions of cultural, political, and even legal history into the equation (as represented by the work of Ian Bent, Martin Eybl, Carl Schachter, or Wayne Alpern, in many cases based on Hellmut Federhofer's documentation of Schenker's letters and diaries). This book is, in a sense, the converse of Snarrenberg's: it focuses on the outer dynamic of Schenker's thought. Building on the work of all those I have named, and others, it sets Schenker and his work into a series of contrasted contexts, including those of Viennese modernism, which appears in an unfamiliar light when seen through the eyes of a musician whose reactionary views were tempered only by idiosyncrasy (chapter 2); German cultural conservatism, which proves to be the source of many of the most entrenched values in the work of Schenker and for that matter other music theorists (chapter 3); and the situation of a Galician Jewish immigrant to the city in which fully racialised anti-Semitism—and its mirror image, Zionism—developed during precisely the period when Schenker lived there (chapter 4). The book is motivated by the belief that basic aspects of Schenkerian theory—aspects which survived the journey across the Atlantic—arose out of these circumstances, and that without an understanding of this, one cannot really claim ownership of the agenda to which one works through the very act of doing Schenkerian analysis. The book is also motivated by the idea that Schenker's theory is not, or not simply, a theory in the way that music theorists today commonly understand that word, but an integral element in a much broader programme for artistic, social, and political change, and it is to convey this that I speak of the Schenker 'project' (a term I have borrowed from James Hepokoski's [1991] interpretation of the 'Dahlhaus project').

The idea that Schenkerian (or any other) theory needs to be understood in its period context is open to misconstrual. Following a brief discussion of Schenker's political views, Schachter writes that we should 'beware of making facile connections between the political ideology and the music theory. After all, Hugo Riemann also believed in German superiority, and his views on World War I were, as far as I know, not so different from Schenker's; but their music-theoretical ideas were mostly very far apart' (2001: 13). It might be worth pursuing the comparison a little further. There is, to take the most obvious example, nothing in Schenker remotely like Riemann's harmonic dualism, but there are some more basic affinities in conceptual approach. Thomas Christensen has emphasised the way in which both Riemann's functions and Schenker's *Stufen* (scale steps) embody a hierarchical conception of music: 'Polemics aside', Christensen says, 'there are undeniable overlappings in the theories of Riemann and Schenker' (1982: 37). Indeed, Riemann's early (1880) claim that 'the first stipulation and cardinal characteristic . . . of a musical art work is first and foremost the unity of the key',[2] which predates the development of his own theory, could serve equally well as a statement of Schenker's basic theoretical premise. But the more salient affinities have to do with the way theory is used and the meanings that are attached to it. For instance, Riemann's insistence on the principle of harmonic dualism despite the lack of accepted empirical verification might be compared with Schenker's insistence on the encompassing of complete movements within the *Urlinie* despite the lack of evidence that listeners ordinarily hear any such thing. Though their justifications were different (Riemann insisted that undertones were audible, Schenker dismissed the perceptions of 'dilettantes'), both saw their theories as psychological, as at core theories of musical listening—but in the sense of prescribing how music should be heard, what it would mean to hear it adequately, and not of describing how it is actually heard in the real world. When on this basis Alexander Rehding claims of Riemann that 'this implicit "ought" . . . is simply the flipside of his systematic and essentialising approach to music' (2003: 9), he might as well have been talking about Schenker.

Both theorists, then, thought prescriptively. Referencing Lydia Goehr's 1992 study, Rehding writes that 'Riemann could use his theoretical system as an admission pass to the "imaginary museum of musical works"' (2003: 94): the same can be said of Schenker. And following a tradition that goes back at least as far as Goethe, both Riemann and Schenker understand the canon as an embodiment of timeless values: the 1894 edition of Riemann's *Musik-Lexicon* defines 'classical' as 'a work of art which is resistant to the destructive power of time' (111), just as Schenker refers to the masterworks remaining 'removed from the generations and their times' (*MM2* 60). As Rehding says, this results in the atrophy of the historical dimension in Riemann's thinking ('classicism becomes an abstract concept in which the aspect of perfection is idolised at the expense of its historical position. The underlying syntactical model is elevated into the sphere of eternal truth')—which has long been one of the most frequently attacked features of Schenker's approach. It also leads both theorists to posit certain musical features as enduringly essential: Riemann 'saw the future of German music in an eternal regeneration of triadically based music' (137), while for Schenker 'music remains . . . from the beginning to the end of time, the composing out of a triad' (*MM1* 89). Both accordingly ridiculed contemporary composers' search for new forms, on the grounds that (as Riemann rhetorically asked) 'Do not the masterworks of past times

---

[2] Translated (from Riemann's *Handbuch der Harmonielehre*) in Christensen 1982: 40.

exist in all the arts as templates and ideals for all times, incapable of
ageing, let alone outdating?' (100). Both moreover drew on the conservative ideology that identified the traditional with the natural: as
Rehding says (91), 'nature is invoked as a category in Riemann's theoretical system because it invariably presents an argument that cannot
be contradicted', and—as will become clear from chapter 3—the same
might once more be said of Schenker. Finally, both saw music as bearing on issues of ethics at an individual and even a national level: Rehding (136) could just as well be talking about Schenker when he speaks
of 'Riemann's concern with "the moral regeneration of the national
community" that characterises cultural nationalism', and continues:
'Like other thinkers participating in the nationalist discourse, Riemann
raised his moral rhetoric at a time of social disorder, and drew on the
past in order to construct from the historical imagination a brighter
future'.

One should not then be misled by Schenker's characterisation of
Riemann as 'the most dangerous musical bacillus in Germany':[3] Schenker's and Riemann's systems may be significantly different, but they proceed from a largely shared diagnosis of the failings of both contemporary music and contemporary society. They propose different solutions
to the same problems, which in turn need to be understood in terms of
an at least partly shared historical context. But it goes further than this,
for at one point in his *Musikalische Syntaxis* (1877) Riemann denounces
the theorists Melchior Sachs, Albert Hahn, and Heinrich Vincent, using
what Rehding terms 'the bewildering epithet "Social Democrats"'
(2003: 63). (As it happens, Schenker once referred to Riemann himself
as a democrat [*T1* 92], a term whose negative connotations I shall discuss in chapter 3.) Riemann's epithet turns out to be not so bewildering when explained: all three theorists attempted to build a harmonic
system on the chromatic scale, so—in Riemann's view, which Schenker
would certainly have shared—subverting the natural foundations of
music in the overtone series. As Rehding continues, 'The common conservative reproaches against the political Social Democrats can indeed
be easily transferred to the music-theoretical realm: they promoted a
society without hierarchy'. This might of course be seen as an example
of the 'facile connection' between music theory and politics of which
Schachter complains: a few lines later, Schachter adds 'one does not
need to be a monarchist or a pan-German nationalist to perceive hierarchies'. But that, as I see it, is just where Schenker is different from
Riemann, or indeed from the many other theorists who have drawn

---

[3] Letter of 16 December 1907 to the publishers Cotta (CA 71); transcribed and translated by Ian Bent on the Schenker Correspondence Project website, http://mt.ccnmtl.
columbia.edu/schenker (accessed December 2006). Quotations from this website are
used by kind permission of Professor Bent. As well as letters to and from Schenker, in
German and English, this developing but already indispensable resource contains syn-
opses of Schenker's correspondents and acquaintances.

passing (and usually facile) parallels between music and politics. My claim in this book is that what might be described in a broad sense as the political is deeply thought into Schenker's theory. And in saying this I mean not that Schenker's theory was determined in any direct, cause-and-effect manner by the social and political circumstances within which he found himself—that is how to misconstrue the relationship between theory and context—but that Schenker's theory may be profitably understood as a discourse on the social and political at the same time that it is a discourse on the musical, and that in order to understand this discourse we need to place it in context.

Although it is the job of the book and not this introduction to make that argument, I can at least give some indication of what I am talking about through a consideration of Schenker's origins. Schenker moved to Vienna on a government scholarship in 1884, and lived there for the remainder of his life, but as I have already mentioned he came from Galicia, in the extreme northeast of the Habsburg empire, on what are nowadays the borders of Poland and Ukraine. This was perhaps the most backward region of the entire empire. From Vienna it was viewed as the back of beyond: Karl Kraus spoke dismissively of the 'mud puddle of Galician culture' (Berkley 1988: 116), and this metropolitan perspective is perhaps reflected in William McCagg's characterisation of it—which I quote in chapter 4—as 'a roadless, cold, foothills region leading nowhere'. But in reality nineteenth-century Galicia had a more developed cultural life than such comments might suggest, even if it was largely restricted to a small number of cities such as Lvov (in German Lemberg), where Schenker was sent away to school, and where from 1858 to 1884 Chopin's pupil Karol Mikuli (1821–97) directed the local conservatory. As Jolanta Pekacz explains (2002: 132), there was during the second half of the nineteenth century a Galician Music Society in Lvov, with a core professional orchestra supplemented by amateurs, playing a repertory of overtures or symphonies by Haydn, Mozart, Beethoven, Weber, and Mendelssohn, among others, as well some works by more local composers. The domestic piano was widespread in Galicia, too, though this trend developed later than elsewhere in Europe (150), while there were not insignificant local industries of instrument manufacture, publication and retailing of sheet music (predominantly easy waltzes, mazurkas, polonaises, and suchlike), as well as music teaching.

By any European benchmark, however, standards were low. Pekacz quotes an account by Emil Dunikowski of teaching at the secondary school he attended during the 1860s in Brzeżany, where as it happens Schenker moved from Lvov to complete his schooling some fifteen years later:

> After eight years of studying, we knew about as much about music as an Indian in southern Dakota. Instead of music, we could have been given a

cuneiform from the period of Saitefernes I. And yet we sang, and it happened in the following way: Waniak [Piotr Waniek, the music teacher] first
played on the violin the song we were to learn, and, with a ram-like voice,
he sang it through for us; then, angry, he beat our heads with his bow,
until we finally found a proper tone, melody, and a bit of rhythm. The only
thing we knew was that the higher a black spot is on that five-level ladder,
the higher one had to go with the voice; the spots at the bottom required
bowing the head forward and . . . droning like a duck on a Brzeżany lake.
(2002: 66–7)

And private teaching could be no better, perhaps reflecting a view of
piano playing as primarily a social accomplishment: in her memoirs,
published in 1889, Sabina Grzegorzewska wrote that 'about the setting
of hands, finger action, arpeggios and etudes, nobody had any idea. A
teacher would beat out the rhythm mechanically . . . without caring
whether a pupil, when left alone, would be able to apply this ever-
so-short music theory' (Pekacz 2002: 153). Of course the teaching
Schenker experienced will surely have been very different from this—
it is said that he took lessons from Mikuli (more on this later)—and
Grzegorzewska's account refers to a considerably earlier period. All the
same, the view of music as a social accomplishment rather than a serious art and the reliance on rote learning form a suggestive backdrop
to Schenker's later writings, as do the no doubt fortuitous resonances
with the quotations from Dunikowski and Grzegorzewska: in *Der freie
Satz* Schenker likened conventional analyses to 'unsuccessful decipherings of papyrus rolls', and inveighed against rapid results approaches to
music teaching ('Surely it is time to put a stop to the teaching of music
in condensed courses, as languages are taught for use in commerce' [*FC
I 9*, xxiii]).

But there is something about Pekacz's account of music in Galicia
which is suggestive at a rather deeper level. She sees Galicia as

> a cultural laboratory where a variety of forms, objects, and values repre-
> senting the local and the foreign, the urban and the rural, the elite and the
> popular, the traditional and the modern, and the cosmopolitan and the
> xenophobic, were being accepted, resisted, or—most frequently—
> modified and appropriated by the public that was diversified along social,
> political, ethnic, financial, and historical lines, to name just the major
> ones.[4]

Galicia, in other words, was a highly fragmented society, fissured along
multiple dimensions. If the Ruthenians (modern Ukrainians) and Jews
were marginalised in relation to the historically dominant Poles, the
Poles constructed their identity within the larger context of the Habsburg empire: as Pekacz says (2002: 181), 'The point of reference was
not Warsaw but Vienna, personified after 1848 by the Emperor Franz

---

[4] Pekacz 2002: 2.

Joseph' (who reigned until 1916). And music was one of the means by which this construction took place, with music from outside Galicia being—in one of Pekacz's key terms—appropriated in such a way as 'to maintain the traditional hierarchies' (205–6). She quotes the Polish musicologist Józef Reiss, who wrote in 1939 that in turn-of-the-century Cracow 'all forms of musical life were imitated. . . . One went to Vienna to study, and a diploma of the Viennese Music Conservatory was considered a mark of the highest artistic qualifications. Whatever E[douard] Hanslick published in the *Neue Freie Presse* was considered ultimate for the [music] reviewers in Cracow'. Indeed the last words of Pekacz's book are: 'For Galicia, the culture of Austria, Germany, or France was regarded as superior to its own, and examples provided by these countries were irresistible. Lwów and Cracow preferred to be seen as neglected outposts of Western Europe rather than capitals of Slavonic culture' (206).

All of this provides a fertile context within which to consider Schenker's going to Vienna to study, where he did indeed attend the Conservatory (though he never gained its diploma); the sense of being an outsider emerges from a letter Schenker wrote while still a student— probably in the first half of 1886—to the music critic Max Kalbeck, in which he referred to 'the strange "theory" and the masterworks about which I know only very, very little'.[5] Schenker's exceptionally thoroughgoing assimilation of German musical culture over the ensuing decades might in this way be seen as an act of appropriation—especially when he came close to claiming that culture as uniquely his, writing in the final volume of *Das Meisterwerk in der Musik,* at the age of sixty-two, that Vienna 'will, through my theory, for a second time assume the leadership in music' (*MM3* 9). In the following year, 1931, he even confided—thankfully only to his diary—that 'I am the *only* living musician'.[6]

Yet there is more to this than simple hubris, for the dialectic of insider and outsider, centre and periphery, penetrated deep into Habsburg culture. If Galicia was socially, politically, ethnically, financially, and historically fissured, then Vienna was all the more so. Until the First World War, the centrifugal elements were held together by the multinational or supranational construct of the Hapsburg empire: Marsha Rozenblit makes the point with specific reference to the empire's Jews when she explains that they

> did not have to abandon or submerge the ethnic component of Jewish identity as they modernized. Indeed, Jews could comfortably assume a tripartite identity in which they espoused a fervent loyalty to the state, adopted the culture of one or another people in whose midst they lived, and unconsciously behaved as a separate ethnic group. . . . [Jews] appre-

[5] Translated in Karnes 2001: 38; the letter is transcribed in Federhofer 1985: 8–9.
[6] Quoted in Jackson 2001: 109.

ciated the opportunity the multinational state gave them to be patriotic citizens, adherents of German, Czech, or Polish culture, and Jews all at the
same time. (2001: 23)

But it was not just a question of the Jews. In David Rechter's words
(2001: 27), 'As a supranational entity Austria was deemed uniquely
situated to be a force for reconciliation between nations and peoples,
to mediate between eastern and western Europe'. Although the overlapping of insider and outsider identities that coloured Viennese modernism is often seen as a specifically Jewish phenomenon (more on
this in chapter 4), it can be seen as reflecting migration within the empire more generally—though if so, it is still the Jews who were at the
sharp end.

And it is with the idea of reconciliation that we get to music theory. There was, as I shall argue in chapter 3, a longstanding Viennese,
or Habsburg, tradition (I trace it back to the seventeenth century) of associating music and social structure. A striking example of such thinking from Schenker's own time comes from Guido Adler, Hanslick's successor at the University of Vienna and by no means one of Schenker's
natural allies: 'as the customs of the Austrian peoples are interwoven
in the works of the classical composers of music', Adler wrote in 1906,
'as the motivic material is taken from the national stores, which the
artists . . . work up into classical structures, so may a higher statescraft
join the particularities of the peoples into a higher unity'.[7] To paraphrase this in Rechter's language, Adler is saying that music offers a
model for how the supranational empire can reconcile or mediate between its constituent cultures, nationalities, and ethnicities. The thought
is not far from Schenker's hope, expressed in the second volume of
Kontrapunkt, that mankind may be 'guided through the euphony of
art . . . to shape all institutions of his earthly existence, such as state,
marriage, love, and friendship' (*C2* 20); that in turn is reminiscent of
the suggestion by Simon Sechter, the foremost Viennese theorist of the
generation before Schenker's, that music (he is talking specifically
about enharmonic modulations) is 'the image of the world at large, in
which family life founders and disappointments often occur'.[8] And such
claims for music border on the idea, commonplace among German-
speaking aestheticians and music theorists of the nineteenth century
and into the twentieth, that music forms an analogue of emotional life,
so that—as Arnold Schering put it 1915—'we recognize in [tone con-

---

[7] Translated in Notley 1999: 52; this passage is taken from an article in the *Neue freie
Presse* (27 January 1906) purporting to be by a 'colleague' of Adler, but Notley (1999:
69n.) quotes evidence from Edward B. Reilly showing that the author was in fact Adler
himself.

[8] Translated from Sechter, *Die Grundsätze der musikalischen Komposition* (1853–54), in
Wason 1985: 58.

nections] the reflection of our own volitional life and moods'; this explains the resonances between Schenker's theory and the 'energetics' of Schering, Ernst Kurth, or August Halm (who corresponded with Schenker and wrote favourably about his work).[9]

Yet, as I shall argue in this book, there is in Viennese *fin-de-siècle* culture a persistent emphasis on not just the personal but the interpersonal, the social—an aspect of which is the emphasis on the idea of reconciliation or mediation to which I have just referred. Such terms of course invoke Theodor Adorno, himself briefly a resident of Vienna, whose views on Beethoven I present in chapter 3 as part of this same tradition of associating music and social structure. In Beethoven's music, Adorno said in his *Einleitung in die Musiksoziologie* (Introduction to the Sociology of Music),

> the essence of society . . . becomes the essence of music itself. Both are comprehensible in the interior of the works only, not in mere imagery. The central categories of artistic construction can be translated into social ones. . . . It is in fitting together under their own law, as becoming, negating, confirming themselves and the whole without looking outward, that his movements come to resemble the world whose forces move them. . . . What he calls thematic work is the mutual abrasion of the antitheses, the individual interests. . . . The motive kernels . . . are preshaped by the totality as much as the individual is in individualistic society. . . . Society recurs in great music: transfigured, criticized, and reconciled.[10]

My argument is that Schenker's theory articulates the way in which absolute instrumental music expresses such mutual abrasion or reconciliation between individual interests, or between the interests of individual and state—or to put it the other way round, that Schenker makes it possible to conceive, to imagine, such social values in musical terms. In other words, he transforms what in Adler and Adorno is at best a metaphor or aspiration into a working model. And the manner in which he does this bears further comparison with Adorno, whose musically obscure reference to Beethoven's movements 'becoming, negating, confirming themselves' has an obvious Hegelian resonance. In fact the passage in *Einleitung in die Musiksoziologie* from which I have been quoting teems with references to Hegel: at one point Adorno writes, 'It is exceedingly illuminating that Hegelian philosophy . . . can be applied without violence to every detail of a music that cannot possibly have been exposed to an Hegelian "influence" in terms of the history of ideas', while in his fragmentary book-length study of Beethoven he bluntly states that 'Beethoven's music is Hegelian philosophy'

---

[9] See Rothfarb 2002, where the quotation from Schering may be found (p. 945; I have deleted the word 'and' after 'volitional'). Rothfarb actually classifies Schenker as an energeticist, emphasising in particular the relationship between his and Halm's work (pp. 936–9).

[10] Adorno 1976/1962: 209–11.

(1998: 14). Although in this book I try to avoid the widespread error of turning Schenker into a philosopher (as will become clear in chapter 1, he was not above making philosophical howlers), I do see the Hegelian concept of sublation, the subsumption of opposed entities within a higher unity, as central to Schenker's thought. The point is that this idea is equally basic to Hegel's political philosophy and his aesthetics: in this way it provides a framework within which to make sense of Schenker's equation of musical and social structure. It is a key to understanding how Schenker's theory is not just a theory of music but a theory of society—or to put it another way, not just a theory but a project.

How are we to explain the comprehensiveness of Schenker's thinking together of the musical and the social? There are several answers, some of which I have already mentioned. One is the Viennese tradition of associating music and society. Another is Schenker's personal situation as an immigrant who lived through the collapse of the tripartite Jewish identity consequent upon that of the Habsburg empire itself. (The nation-states that took its place identified territory, ethnicity, and culture: hence the 'Jewish problem'.) But a particularly crucial factor—comprehensively explored in Wayne Alpern's forthcoming doctoral thesis—is likely to have been Schenker's legal training. As is well known, when Schenker travelled to Vienna on a government scholarship, it was not to study music: he took a law degree at the University of Vienna, while for a time taking classes at the Conservatory on the side. And as might be expected, issues of the relationship between state and individual, centre and periphery, whole and part occupied a prominent role on the agenda of the supranational empire's most prestigious law school; the influence of Hegel was also prominent, so that it is more than likely that Schenker acquired a basic knowledge of Hegel in the course of his legal studies (and probably at second hand). While this conjunction of historical circumstances may go far to explain the particular way in which Schenker thought together the musical and the social, however, I am not suggesting that it is *only* with Schenker that music theory acquires social meaning: my claim is that in Schenker's case the social dimension implicit in much if not all music theory is exceptionally well developed and explicit. There is to that extent a sense in which this is not simply a book about Schenker, but a book about music theory in which Schenker assumes the role of principal witness.

There is a further claim I would wish to advance. In an article entitled 'Cinderella; Or Music and the Human Sciences', Leon Botstein called for music to be understood as 'a species of fundamental social action' and its study enlisted 'as a primary vehicle for the reinterpretation of culture and society' (1992a: 128, 134). The prospect is mouthwatering: 'For the first time', Botstein writes (127), 'the study of music might lead the way in the human sciences'. But how, exactly? Botstein's examples are indicative rather than definitive: we could try and understand basic aspects of Wittgenstein's thought by analysis of his use of musical metaphors, he suggests; we might attempt to unravel Adorno's critical theory by focussing on his writings about music; we might use music as the basis for a general interpretation of the central European *fin de siècle*, to be confirmed or refined through examination of the visual and literary arts rather than the other way round. But there is a methodological issue similar to that encountered by the first-generation 'New' musicologists who, largely as a result of the arguably pernicious influence of Adorno, attempted to read social meaning straight off the music: Tia DeNora complains that Susan McClary 'treats musical compositions as if they are simply "waiting to be read"—that is, as if their meanings are located outside of situated contexts of reception' (1995: 127), and it is the assumption—Adorno's assumption—that social meaning is inherent in the music which is responsible for this. It would be better to say that social meaning is not inherent in music but constructed through the interpretation of music. Or to put it another way, to understand music's social meaning we need to understand the means of its interpretation at a given time and place.

And this has implications for the role played by music theory, which after all provides the foundation for any such interpretation, the means by which concepts are cross-mapped between music and other domains. One of the most fruitful aspects of Schenker's thinking is the idea that theory should be seen as an essential part of musical culture rather than an academic sideline: in 1916 he noted in his diary that 'art and theory are in essence a single, inseparable concept',[11] and this is why he claims in *Der freie Satz* that 'the flight from music which characterizes our time is in truth a flight from an erroneous method of instruction, one which renders impossible an effective approach to art' (*FC* I xxi). In the same way, I would argue that music theory represents more than an attempt to understand how music has meaning: it is the anvil on which music's meaning is forged, or at least the currency through which it is negotiated. Through the attempt to relate Schenker's theory to its social, cultural, and political context, then, I hope in this book to provide a snapshot of musical meaning in the making.

This book is not a biography of Schenker, but it is organised around his life as well as his publications. As the standard biography of Schenker (in Federhofer 1985) is not available in English, I now offer a brief overview of both for the convenience of readers. I have little new to say here, and Schenker experts may speedread the remainder of this introduction.

I said that Schenker came from small-town Galicia, not far from the regional capital, Lvov; he was born in 1868 and not, as at one time was thought, in 1867. (The reason for the confusion is that Schenker's fa-

---

[11] Diary entry for 29 December 1916, transcribed and translated by Bent and Lee Rothfarb, Schenker Correspondence Project website.

Figure I.1   Heinrich Schenker around 1900, with autograph inscription to Moriz Violin. Used by permission of Special Collections, University of California, Riverside Libraries, University of California, Riverside, California (OJ 72/14, no. 1).

ther falsified his date of birth in order to send him to school a year earlier.)[12] His family background was Jewish and professional: Schenker described his father as 'a poor but far and wide highly revered doctor'.[13] He was sent at a tender age to the Gymnasia (German-speaking schools which were practically the only route to the major universities) in Lvov and, later, Brzeżany; it was in 1884 that he won his government scholarship to the University of Vienna. However, the letter to Kalbeck which I have already quoted makes it clear that his heart was not in his legal studies: 'Late at night', Schenker writes, 'I often set aside the godly "Roman Law", and allow myself the purest joy of a little musical thought. Every night brings me an idea'.[14] According to Peter Drucker, work requirements in the law faculty were so undemanding that students were commonly asked 'Are you a real student or are you studying law?' (Berkley 1988: 20); at all events, Schenker found time to study in parallel at the Vienna Conservatory during the academic years 1887–88 and 1888–89, where he was taught by Ernst Ludwig (piano), Anton Bruckner (harmony and counterpoint), and Johann Nepomuk Fuchs (composition). The violinist Carl Flesch, a student at the Conservatory at this time, wrote in his memoirs that 'towering over all of us "duffers" was an emaciated university student who studied music on the side. It was Heinrich Schenker',[15] and the impression this conveys is accurate in two respects: first, Schenker's conservatory records show that he excelled in his studies, and second, he was impoverished—particularly following the death of his father in late 1887. At some point after this, his mother and other family members followed him to Vienna, and Schenker had to support them through giving piano lessons. It was possibly for this reason, though the conservatory records refer only to his doctoral studies at the University,[16] that he dropped out of the Conservatory in November 1889.

Following his graduation with a doctor of law degree from the University in February 1890, Schenker abandoned law and moved rapidly to establish himself in a three-pronged musical career: as a critic, composer, and performer. His earliest articles and reviews, dating from 1891–94, appeared in German journals (the Leipzig-based *Musikalisches*

---

[12] Federhofer 1985: 3, citing a letter of 29 December 1927 to Schenker's lifelong friend Moriz Violin. Information for which no source is stated in the remainder of the introduction may be found in chapter 1 of Federhofer 1985; I also draw on Kevin Karnes's 2001 thesis, which is a valuable source for Schenker's early career, particularly as a critic. A chronology of Schenker's life may be found in Benjamin Ayotte's (2004: 271–5) research guide.

[13] Letter of 17 January 1918 to August Halm, DLA 69.930/2; transcribed and translated by Rothfarb, Schenker Correspondence Project website.

[14] Translated in Karnes 2001: 38 (see note 5 above).

[15] Translated in Miller 1991: 179 from Federhofer 1985: 11.

[16] See Karnes 2001: 41n.; copies of Schenker's matriculation papers are in the Jonas Collection (OJ 35/1).

Wochenblatt and Berlin-based *Die Zukunft*), but from 1894 he also established himself in the Viennese press, writing for the *Neue Revue* and *Die
Zeit;* in all he had published exactly one hundred articles and reviews
in these journals by the time he gave up criticism in 1898, many of
them substantial essays on a wide range of musical topics. (The most
substantial, and the most closely related to his later theoretical writings,
is 'Der Geist der musikalischen Technik', published in 1895, on which
I focus in chapter 1.) As a composer, too, Schenker seems to have established himself quickly, with the publication in 1892 of his *Zwei
Clavierstücke* op. 1; there was then a six-year gap before the publication
of his *Fantasie* op. 2, *Sechs Lieder* op. 3, *Fünf Klavierstücke* op. 4, and *Zweistimmige Inventionen* op. 5, though his correspondence indicates that he
continued to be active as a composer during the intervening period. His
only other published compositions (apart from *Vorüber* for mixed cho-
rus, apparently published in an anthology)[17] were the *Ländler* op. 10,
published in 1899, and the unnumbered *Syrische Tänze* (Syrian Dances)
for piano four hands—also published in 1899, but known mainly for
having been orchestrated a few years later by Schoenberg. (This happened at the instigation of Busoni, resulting in one of the more unlikely
conjunctions in twentieth-century music history.)

Finally, Schenker was at least sporadically active as a pianist, particularly an accompanist, and as a conductor. The highlight of his performing career was his tour in 1899 with the Dutch baritone and Bach
specialist Johannes Messchaert, taking the place of the singer's regular
accompanist, Julius Röntgen (the concerts included some of Schenker's
own compositions, and one of the stops was Lvov). This seems to have
been one of the formative experiences of Schenker's life: nearly thirty
years later, he wrote that 'The concert tour with Messchaert furnished
me with insight into the utterly and uniquely subtle workshop of this
singer, whom I readily acknowledge to be the greatest singer of all
times and places'.[18] Indeed, the most impressive evidence of the seriousness with which Schenker pursued his career in the 1890s is the
range and quality of his professional contacts. Writing again to Kalbeck,
but this time in 1897, Schenker claimed that Brahms, Busoni, Eugen
d'Albert, and Karl Goldmark had all praised his compositions;[19] both
Busoni and d'Albert performed his music and helped him either financially or through recommendation, as did Julius Epstein and Max Brüll.
So indeed did Kalbeck, with whom Schenker corresponded until 1906,
and also Hanslick, with whom Schenker corresponded between 1894
and 1899.

---

[17] See Lang and Kunselman 1994: 68; C6 in Ayotte 2004.
[18] Letter of 29 April 1928 to Felix-Eberhard von Cube (von Cube family collection,
vC 14), transcribed and translated by William Drabkin, Schenker Correspondence Project website.
[19] Letter of 10 May 1897, transcribed in Federhofer 1985: 15–16.

But in the late 1890s there was a major shift in Schenker's activities. I said that he gave up music criticism in 1898; his last published compositions appeared in 1899 (though opp. 3 and 5 were reissued in 1901, the latter in an expanded edition); and the 1899 tour with Messchaert was his last intensive bout of performing, though there were sporadic public appearances up to 1911.[20] The question of why Schenker abandoned this developing career is one I pursue in chapter 1, but the overall pattern is clear: from now until the end of his life, Schenker essentially divided his time between private teaching, editorial work (from his 1902 edition of C. P. E. Bach's *Klavierwerke* to the 1928 edition of Beethoven's sonatas), and the series of theoretical and analytical works for which he is known today. Table I.1 summarizes his published output.

Given his impoverished background, one might wonder how Schenker made a living during these decades. The editorial work at least—all of which was published by the Vienna-based Universal Edition—was paid; Schenker's voluminous correspondence with Emil Hertzka, the director of Universal Edition from 1907, contains many disparaging references to the inadequacy of their rates of pay, sometimes laced with aspersions concerning the firm's business methods. Ian Bent's comprehensive study (2005) of this correspondence vividly illustrates how difficult Schenker could be to deal with: by turns bombastic, sarcastic, pernickety, and paranoid. Sometimes Schenker's behaviour seems plain peculiar, for example in the lengths to which he went to avoid face-to-face meetings, to the point of drafting and copying out a seven-page letter to Hertzka explaining that he is too busy to meet for a quarter of an hour (92). Hertzka's side of the correspondence shows how much effort he expended in maintaining a productive relationship with Schenker—at times one is reminded of Jaeger and Elgar—and so it is sad to record that in 1924–25 Schenker threatened and may have actually taken out a lawsuit against Universal Edition, alleging a list of misdemeanours so long that I am consigning it to a footnote.[21] Nobody with experience of the law will be surprised that there are 172

---

[20] Largely with Eduard Gärtner. For details of Schenker's concert activities see Federhofer 1985: 18–9; his concert programme and itineraries are in the Jonas Collection (OJ 35/5).

[21] In his thesis, Wayne Alpern, like Schenker a lawyer turned music theorist, lists the charges as 'asserting unauthorized editorial control over content without [Schenker's] approval or consent; unjust "terrorist censorship" over personal political and polemical matter; unfairly restricting the size and scope of the publication; failing to honor timely publication schedules; minimizing the number of published issues; using a pseudonymous and fictitious imprint to conceal the true source of the publication; failing to actively publicize, promote, display, and disseminate copies; stockpiling unsold copies; failing to publish scores of analyzed compositions; misrepresenting that published issues were not in print; failing to locate and produce copies when requested for purchase; misrepresenting that unfulfilled orders were fulfilled; failing to pay full royalties due; imposing false deductions; failing to provide fair, accurate, and timely accountings; and falsifying

Table I.1   Schenker's Published Works

Year(s)	Work(s)
1891	1 article
1892	4 articles
	Zwei Clavierstücke Op. 1 (Doblinger)
1893	7 articles
1894	19 articles
1895	20 articles (including 'Der Geist der musikalischen Technik')
1896	31 articles
1897	15 articles
1898	3 article
	Fantasie Op. 2 (Breitkopf)
	Sechs Lieder Op. 3 (Breitkopf, issued 1901)
	Funf Klavierstücke Op. 4 (Breitkopf)
	Zweistimmige Inventionen Op 5 (Breitkopf, reissued 1901)
1899	*Ländler Op 10* (Simrock)
	Syrische Tänze (Weinberger)
1901	1 article
1902–3	C. P. E. Bach, *Klavierwerke*, 2 vols. (Universal)
1903	*Ein Beitrag zur Ornamentik* (Universal, rev. ed. 1908)
1904	Handel, *Sechs Orgelkonzerte* arr. for piano 4 hands (Universal)
1905–6	*Über den Niedergang der Kompositionskunst* drafted (pub. 2005)
1906	NMTP 1: *Harmonielehre* (Cotta), published anonynously
1908	*Instumentations-Tabelle* (Universal), published pseudonymously
1910	NMTP 2/1: *Kontrapunkt I* (Cotta)
	J. S. Bach, *Chromatische Phantasie und Fuge* (Universal)
1911	*Die Kunst des Vortrags* drafted (pub. 2000)
1912	*Beethovens neunte Sinfonie* (Universal)
1913	*Die letzten fünf Sonaten*, Op 109 (Universal)
1914	*Die letzten fünf Sonaten*, Op 110 (Universal)
1915	*Die letzten fünf Sonaten*, Op 111 (Universal)
1916	1 article
1921	*Die letzten fünf Sonaten*, Op 101 (Universal)
	Beethoven, *Sonate op. 27/2*, facsimile of autograph and sketches (Universal)
1921–4	*Der Tonwille*, 10 issues ('Tonwille-Flugblätterverlag' = Universal)
1922	NMTP 2/2: *Kontrapunkt II* (Cotta in association with Universal)
	1 article
1923	Beethoven, *Samtliche Klaviersonaten*, 4 vols. (Universal)
	1 article
1925	1 article
	Beethovens fünfte Sinfonie (Gutman, repr. from *Der Tonwille*)
1925–30	*Das Meisterwerk in der Musik* (Drei Masken)
1927	1 article
1929	1 article
1931	2 articles

Year(s)	Work(s)
1932	1 article
	Fünf Urlinie-Tafeln (Universal)/*Five Analyses in Sketchform* (David Mannes School)
1933	2 articles
1934	Johannes Brahms, *Octaven und Quinten u.a.* (Universal)
1935	NMTP 3: *Der freie Satz* (Universal, posthumous)
1937	5 articles (posthumous)

surviving documents relating to the case, covering a period of some fifteen months.[22] An out-of-court settlement was eventually reached.

An essential element of Schenker's income, however, was his extensive roster of private teaching, practically a full-time commitment in itself; in a letter from 1908 he speaks of being 'tied to my music studio from 10.30 a.m. to 6.30 p.m. (or even later)', while in 1914 he writes that 'during the day I have to give lessons, which leave me only the evenings and nights for work'.[23] This is not a matter of piano lessons in the normal sense of the term. Piano performance featured as only one part of a comprehensive programme of musicianship, with analysis and in some cases composition taking a major place in it, and lessons could be highly intensive, with teaching on occasion lasting several hours or taking place on successive days (we know this from the lesson books for 1912–31).[24] Perhaps for this reason, they frequently resulted in lasting relationships. Schenker's wife (Jeanette Kornfeld, née Schiff, whom he married in 1919) was a former student, while a warmth of feeling and affection for Schenker as a teacher shines through the obituaries written by his pupils. And the strength of the musical relationship between Schenker and his students, or ex-students, is demonstrated both by the surviving correspondence and by the way Hans Weisse, Felix Salzer, and Oswald Jonas, in particular, proselytised for the Schenkerian cause even after emigrating to America: they became disciples, adherents to a common cause—rather like the followers of Freud, to anticipate a point I make in chapter 4. The fees for the lessons, as Federhofer expresses it (1985: 45), were not small, but many of Schenker's pupils

accounts'. The principal source of information on these proceedings is Bent and Drabkin's introduction to the second volume of their *Tonwille* translation (*T2* x–xii).

[22] OC 52/657–828.

[23] Letters to Emil Hertzka dated 14 October 1908 (WSLB 23) and 19 February 1914 (WSLB 200), transcribed and translated by Bent, Schenker Correspondence Project website.

[24] OC 3 and 16, with additional material in files 30 and 38.

were affluent. In fact, a number of them—including Angi Elias, Baron Alphons von Rothschild, and Anthony van Hoboken—offered their former teacher continuing financial support, while Sophie Deutsch left him a legacy of 5,000 kroner together with an annual payment of 2,000 kroner.[25] And that takes us to the third element in Schenker's income. It is well known that a number of his larger publications were sponsored by his supporters: for example, Rothschild contributed towards the production costs for both *Harmonielehre* and *Kontrapunkt,* and Wilhelm Furtwängler paid 3,000 marks towards the final volume of *Das Meisterwerk in der Musik,* while Hoboken subsidised both *Meisterwerk* and *Der freie Satz* (as well as funding the establishment in 1927, at Schenker's initiative, of an archive of photographic reproductions of composers' autographs at the Austrian National Library). But these were just the tip of the iceberg. Bent's study of the diaries has revealed a positive industry of money-raising for Schenker's projects, with just a single month in 1907 yielding references to a Mrs Thorsal ('What folly', Schenker complains, that she should spend so much on caring for septuagenerians while 'within her own circle <[?]> discarding a <still> very young artist who is suffering <so greatly> in body and talent!'), a Mrs T. M., who refuses him further support ('How childish', sniffs Schenker), a Baron Em. Ferstals, with whom 'the discussion . . . was long and arduous', and a Mrs Eissler, to whom Schenker had to write a follow-up letter ('since the first one surprisingly went unanswered') but who duly sent him 250 florins.[26] Bent notes that Schenker's donors appear to have been largely Jewish, and comments that 'Schenker, with his belief in monarchic and enlightened aristocratic rule, seems to have conceived patronage as the ideal mode of employment'—though he adds, 'as we see not infrequently in the diary, it had its irksome side' (Bent 2005: 97–8).

If Schenker's editorial work, teaching, and theoretical writing occupied almost the entire period from around the turn of the century to the end of his life, then how might one best tell the story of those years? One way would be in terms of larger historical events: this creates a picture of sometimes unimaginable turbulence and chaos. In the early years of the century, Austria was dominated by the Christian Socialists, in some ways a dry run for Hitler's National Socialists three decades later, with a wide variety of divergent interests fused largely through anti-Semitism; as I explain in chapter 3, opposition to the Christian Socialists made bedfellows of the affluent liberal classes now denied political representation, Jews of whatever socioeconomic status, and Franz Josef, whom many Habsburg Jews (whether in Vienna or Galicia) saw as their protector. The fissuring of Viennese society was

---

[25] Letter to Schenker from Fritz Mendel, dated 12 January 1917 (OJ 12/52).

[26] Bent 2005: 95–6; angle brackets show redraftings, while the reading 'T.M.' is uncertain. (Schenker's handwriting is usually difficult and sometimes impossible to read.)

only exacerbated by the First World War: huge numbers of displaced Jews from the eastern empire (*Ostjuden*) flocked to Vienna, adding further to anti-Semitic sentiment, and the empire itself fell to pieces as the war drew to its close. The Treaty of St Germain (1919), in effect the Austrian equivalent of Versailles, recognised the national autonomy of the various former Habsburg territories (thereby cutting away the basis of the tripartite Jewish identity to which I referred) and reduced Austria to an economically unsustainable rump with seven million inhabitants, of whom some 30 percent lived in Vienna—an imperial city without an empire. After a period of extreme economic hardship during the early 1920s, the Austrian economy began to revive, only to be devastated by the international depression that followed the Wall Street crash (1929). Meanwhile, political tensions between the Christian Socialists and Social Democrats (who dominated rural Austria and Vienna, respectively) grew steadily more unmanageable, with the appearance of private militias and a slide into civil war in 1934. At the time of Schenker's death in the following year, what is sometimes called the Austro-fascist government of Kurt Schuschnigg was trying, with decreasing success, to play off Hitler and Mussolini; Schenker did not live to see the Anschluss, that is to say Hitler's annexation of Austria in March 1938.

As will emerge in particular from chapter 3, many of these political events are reflected in Schenker's writings, not only in his diaries but also in his theoretical works. Yet it is hard to know how far the political chaos really permeated into the fabric of Schenker's existence. A second narrative of Schenker's later life, then, might be organised round his everyday affairs: his domestic circumstances, his professional disappointments, his successes. While his early years in Vienna were impoverished, by the time of his marriage he had achieved what Federhofer refers to as 'modest prosperity' (1985: 44), with regular holidays in the Tyrol (fig. I.2). Disappointments included his failure to obtain a teaching post at the Vienna Conservatory in 1908; Schenker's account in his diary of the 'difficult interview' in February that year arguably raises questions as to how capable he would have been of holding down the job, or even whether he really wanted it (Schenker told his interviewers that the truth of 'higher laws . . . is easier to grasp than the untruth of the nonsensical and faulty rules that are given out today', which is probably not what they wanted to hear from a prospective harmony teacher, especially if they themselves were in the business of giving out the nonsensical and faulty rules).[27] It is evident nevertheless that Schenker resented the lack of official recognition of his work in Vi-

---

[27] Transcribed in Federhofer 1985: 26, translated in Bent 2005: 140. Schenker seems to have been still thinking about this possible appointment nearly two years later, writing to the publishers Cotta that 'There is a plan to appoint me to this leading post with all the possible advantages of honor and remuneration' but going on to raise the question

Figure I.2   Jeanette and Heinrich beside a path above Galtür, ca. 1930.
Used by permission of Special Collections, University of California, Riverside
Libraries, University of California, Riverside, California (OJ 72/15, no. 6).

enna, and Bent (2005: 114) refers to his 'sense of being an "outsider" in Vienna's professional world'; the sense of being an outsider may have been a lifelong one, and in the later part of his career he repeatedly thought of leaving Vienna for a post in Germany, whether in Munich, Leipzig, or Berlin.

The successes on the other hand included a growing band of devoted pupils, some of whom obtained teaching posts within Schenker's lifetime, in Austria, Germany, and in the case of Hans Weisse the United States; the excerpts from articles and other sources in the scrapbook which Schenker maintained from 1902 to the end of his life show how carefully he followed the dissemination of his ideas, sometimes underlining explicit or what he took to be implied references to his theories.[28] What appears to have given him the greatest satisfaction, however, was the value attached to his theories by respected performers—and above all Furtwängler, who had encountered Schenker's monograph on Beethoven's Ninth Symphony shortly after it was published in 1912, and had been so impressed by it that he sought out Schenker and maintained a close professional relationship with him for the rest of his life. As Schenker wrote in a letter of 1934 to Rothschild, Furtwängler 'designates himself as my pupil, which fills me with no little pride. It is also to him that I owe the spreading of my name and work; he tirelessly proclaims my teachings to be the only route to the future wellbeing of music' (Federhofer 1985: 39–40). In the previous year, as part of a coordinated but ultimately fruitless attempt to increase recognition of Schenker, Furtwängler had written to the critic Ludwig Karpath, who had a position in the ministry of education in Vienna, saying it was a 'scandal' that Schenker had not been invited to offer lectures at the Conservatory, and enclosing a testimonial which read as follows:

> I consider Schenker the most important music theorist of the present day and am of the opinion that his music-theoretical work, which, while not yet completed, is nevertheless in existence to the extent that a judgement of it is possible, belongs among the great and most significant achievements of the present day. I can only express surprise that in his home town of Vienna no one takes any notice whatsoever of the fact that this man has long been active there. If anyone, it is he who in truth—as the future will show—has made a greater contribution to music than many a currently famous composer, and deserves honorary posts, honour, and recognition. (41–2)

Furtwängler copied his testimonial to Schenker, who in turn told his pupil Otto Vrieslander about the epithet 'the most important music

---

as to 'whether I shall ultimately be able to make up my mind to sacrifice my freedom' (letter of 2 December 1909 [CA 106–7], transcribed and translated by Bent, Schenker Correspondence Project website).

[28] OC 2.

theorist of the present day', and interpreted Furtwängler's final comment as a dig at Richard Strauss.

The third way of telling the story of Schenker's later life is, of course, in terms of the development of his theoretical thought. The traditional way of doing this—which has its roots in Schenker's pupils and even Schenker himself—is as a cumulative process in which the *Neue musikalische Theorien und Phantasien* ('New Musical Theories and Fantasies', the collective title he gave to *Harmonielehre*, the two volumes of *Kontrapunkt*, and *Der freie Satz*) form the core, with the other analytical works—the Ninth Symphony monograph, the *Erläuterungsausgaben* (critical editions with commentary of Beethoven's late piano sonatas), the *Tonwille* and *Meisterwerk* periodicals—being seen primarily as applications of the theory to the central items of the repertory (what in a letter to Hertzka Schenker once referred to as 'the principal fortresses of music').[29] Understood this way, to cram it into a nutshell, *Harmonielehre* sets out the basic concept of *Stufen*, the idea that subsidiary tonal areas are built on the scale degrees of a single, structural tonality, are in this sense phenomena of the musical surface; the first volume of *Kontrapunkt* introduces the idea of melodic fluency (a term which Schenker borrows from Fux [*C1* 302]), the conjunct linear motion that underlies the leaps and discontinuities of actual melodies. The second volume of *Kontrapunkt* develops this into the idea of an imaginary cantus firmus that might be seen as controlling the counterpoint,[30] which becomes a bridge to the theory of free composition (as developed through the *Tonwille* and *Meisterwerk* journals, as well as *Der freie Satz*), for this imaginary cantus firmus is in essence the *Urlinie*—a term that first appears in the op. 101 *Erläuterungsausgabe* (1921). Linked to the *Urlinie* is the conception of prolongation, according to which the musical surface is an elaboration of simpler, more primordial, underlying formations:[31] to explain a composition, then, means to derive it from these underlying formations, the principal means of which is the graphic analysis dividing the music into a number of layers arranged from the background to the foreground. What we think of today as the 'Schenker graph' appeared only in the 1920s, by which time Schenker was in his fifties: he initially developed this approach through work on a series of short keyboard pieces in successive issues of *Tonwille*, subsequently extending it on the one hand by applying it to increasingly long compositions (such as Mozart's G Minor Symphony) and on the other by penetrating deeper into the music, as it were, so that earlier graphs were sometimes

[29] Letter of 9 June 1912 (WSLB 120), transcribed and translated by Bent, Schenker Correspondence Project website.

[30] *C2* 176, 270–1; see also *T1* 105.

[31] To avoid confusion, it should be said that Schenker used this term earlier on, but in a different sense: the extension of theoretical rules or principles from their normal application to a new one (Alpern forthcoming).

reworked as middleground formations within a new, more comprehensive analysis.[32] There was also a parallel, but related, theoretical development, consisting of the refinement and codification of the technical categories employed in the analyses: the *Ursatz* (combination of
Urlinie and bass arpeggiation) in its three possible forms, the inter-
rupted *Ursatz*, the initial ascent, obligatory register, and so forth.

That story could, of course, be told in a less teleological manner. For
one thing, although it is very tempting to see the component parts of
Neue musikalische Theorien und Phantasien as adumbrated in the writings
of the 1890s (and I do so in chapter 1), Schenker's conception of these
core texts repeatedly changed: at various times he intended both what
ended up as the unpublished *Über den Niedergang der Kompositionskunst*
(Decline and fall of the art of composition) and the Ninth Symphony
monograph as part of *Neue musikalische Theorien und Phantasien*, while
Der freie Satz developed from a chapter originally intended for *Kontrapunkt* 2 (Drabkin 2005; Siegel 1999). Then again, there are theoretical
cul-de-sacs, ideas or in some cases publications that Schenker announces
for imminent completion, but which do not appear: the best known is
Die Kunst des Vortrags (The art of performance), a study of analytically
informed performance that Schenker largely drafted in 1911 and tin-
kered with for more than a decade thereafter without bringing it to
completion, but there are others, such as the theory of dynamics which
Schenker confidently announced in the first volume of *Meisterwerk*—
and even illustrated in analyses of two of Bach's works for solo violin—
but which was thereafter quietly forgotten.

And finally there is the broader question, much debated by
Schenkerians over the last decade, of how far it is appropriate to see *Der
freie Satz* as a summation of Schenker's achievement at all. Joseph
Lubben, in particular, has argued in favour of the kind of analysis that
Schenker practised in the 1920s—in *Tonwille* and *Meisterwerk*—where
the totalising framework of the *Urlinie* and *Ursatz* is not applied with
the rigour and consistency at which Schenker aimed in *Der freie Satz*,
and where analytical procedures tend accordingly to be more induc-
tive, flexible, even improvisatory. This might suggest that *Der freie Satz*
represents some kind of false turn. Alternatively, one might resist the
temptation to see Schenkerian theory as 'a theory' at all, instead understanding it as an indefinite number of divergent practices, at most di-
alects of a single theoretical language, each with its own particular
strengths and weaknesses as a means of representing music and opening it up to discursive negotiation. I will revisit these matters in chapter 5; for now, the point is that any story of the development of Schenker's theoretical thought is less a reflection of the facts of the matter than
a decision as to what the facts are. And so, in the end, even the kind of

[32] For an example of this, involving Schumann's *Träumerei* (from *Kinderszenen*, op.
15, no. 7), see *TI* 156n.

concise, factual summary I have tried to offer in the second part of this introduction turns out to be a matter of interpretation, and as such inseparable from the contexts within which Schenker brought his theoretical ideas into existence, and the contexts within which we interpret them today.

Schenker died on 14 January 1935, less than three weeks after he finished correcting the proofs of *Der freie Satz;* his last words were apparently 'something occurred to me from the St. Matthew Passsion'. Jeanette spent six months in Chile during 1936 but then returned to Vienna. She was deported to the Theresienstadt concentration camp in 1942, where she died on 8 January 1945.

1

Foundations of the Schenker Project

Schenker and the Philosophers

Whoever has once perceived the essence of a pure idea—whoever has fathomed its secrets—knows that such an idea remains ever the same, ever indestructible, as an element of an eternal order. Even if, after millennia, such an idea should finally desert mankind and vanish from the foreground of life—that foreground which we like to call chaos—it still partakes of God's cosmos, the background of all creation whence it originated. (*FC* I 161)

This passage comes from the infamous appendix 4 of *Free Composition,* the English translation of Schenker's final work, *Der freie Satz,* where the editors placed materials from the main text which they felt would not help the Schenkerian cause, and it is not hard to see why it ended up there. In itself the quotation is not overtly offensive in the manner of some of Schenker's xenophobic writings in the aftermath of the First World War, though it is actually the climax of an argument to the effect that Italian music can never be considered on the same level as German music: Italian music 'must be appraised as merely a preliminary first step toward the German', Schenker writes, an earlier stage in the same historical evolution, and so must be judged by the eternal standards of 'art as pure idea' (and that is where the quotation comes).

The larger argument is certainly objectionable from a present-day viewpoint, since we think it neither meaningful nor ethical to evaluate different cultures according to supposedly universal criteria, but that is not in itself a problem: we don't expect writers whose thinking was forged well before the First World War to have the same views as us. The idea that different cultures form part of a single historical development towards a point of perfection or culmination, so that to understand a culture is to place it within that development, was a commonplace of German idealist thought (particularly, but by no means exclusively, that of Hegel)—and if you think that, then the validity and perhaps necessity of making judgments of value across cultures follows as a matter of course. The difficulty for us comes rather in Schenker's extremely abstract, or metaphysical, conception of the pure, eternal idea, an idea that would exist even if there were nobody to conceive it, and the problem is made worse by the way in which Schenker goes on to link this on the one hand with his theory of music (he means 'foreground' and 'background' in the technical sense of his theory), and on the other hand with God: for us these are all elements of completely different discourses, so it is rather as if you were to mix together the elements of recipe book, mathematical treatise, and bedtime story. In the case of what might be termed Schenker's magazine-format publications (the *Tonwille* and *Meisterwerk* volumes) this generic mixture is visible on the printed page, not only in the use of *Fraktur* type—which was not normal for academic works—but also in the juxtaposition of sober music-theoretical prose, rhetorically heightened polemic, quotations, letters, and on occasion conversations. It is evident that the present-day genre of academic music theory is much more narrowly defined than Schenker's all-encompassing discourse, and this is just one of the many mismatches between Schenker's writings and the music-theoretical frameworks within which we habitually situate them.

It is common knowledge that there is a philosophical tradition of Platonic thought according to which ideas are timeless, not so much invented as discovered. We can cope with that tradition so long as we know we are doing philosophy. Schenker not only introduces it into his music-theoretical writing but also draws literal conclusions from it: with our modest faculties and short lifespan, Schenker continues after the quoted passage, how can we possibly 'hope to stumble upon the true meaning of life' for ourselves? Instead, he says, we must learn to understand the chaotic foreground of our lives in accordance with 'the universal order of the background . . . let us finally learn humbly to love and honor the chaos for the sake of the cosmos, which is God's own'. And then, in what might look like a bizarre non sequitur, Schenker's original text—before the offending passage was removed to appendix 4—continues by quoting a vocal melody by Hans Leo Hassler and considering the relationship between its text and tonal structure. Again this stimulates a kind of generic queasiness: we think of music theory as an ultimately empirical project where one seeks to understand real experiences in terms of explanatory principles, but Schenker's homily enjoins faith, the acceptance of established authority—attitudes that we might make sense of in the context of religion, but that seem completely out of place in music theory. The feeling becomes even more uncomfortable when we find Schenker advancing the same idea in a letter of May 1914 to his publisher, Emil Hertzka of Universal Edition ('My work is once-for-all and requires no supplements whatsoever as the centuries go by'), especially when it turns out that the purpose of the letter is to ask for money (' you might apply to the Ministry for a grant for the last two volumes in the collection').[1] From what kind of lofty viewpoint can it be that Schenker watches the centuries roll past? 'If I may be permitted to quote myself', Schenker writes in the fourth of his *Tonwille* pamphlets, referring back to something he had published more than twenty years earlier,[2] 'for mankind a Sebastian Bach will have more importance for all time than will a talent of the fortieth century' (*T1* 160). It is as if Schenker is surveying eternity from some remote seat, delivering with quasi-divine certainty judgments based on absolute standards (genius against mere talent, Bach against the ensuing twenty-two centuries of musicians), as if the entire potential for human culture was already mapped out, already known.

Actually there is no 'as if' about it, for just a few lines earlier Schenker has spelled it out: 'Just as Kant established these limits for human thought as a whole, so, too, did the great masters of Germanic composition establish the limits of specifically musical thought. . . . They have been not just ahead of their own time, but ahead of all times'. (In his more hubristic moments, Schenker claimed no less for his own work: in December 1914 he told Hertzka that 'the works of mine that you have published will, for all time to come, remain undisputedly the unique foundation of all disciplines. . . . I still have in mind publications of the greatest importance such as no one before me and no one after me, endowed with such eternal truth, has ever revealed to the world, nor ever will.')[3] And a few lines after the remark about Bach and the fortieth century, Schenker continues: 'Just as Plato lives on in what one may call the idea-made-flesh of his "ideas" . . . so, too, will the German masters of music, detached from the ages of human history, represent to all eternity the idea-made-flesh of music'. Kant, Plato, and the Bible in the space of three short paragraphs: it hardly comes as a surprise when, in the next paragraph, Schenker quotes Haydn's claim after completing *The Creation* that 'I did not write that: God did'. How is

---

[1] Letter of 5 May 1914 (WSLB 23), transcribed and translated by Ian Bent, Schenker Correspondence Project website.

[2] In 'Unpersönliche Musik' of 1897, Schenker (1988: 138) had written that 'the talent of the thirtieth century will be smaller than the genius of the eighteenth century'; the same idea also occurs in the unpublished *Über den Niedergang der Kompositionskunst* (*DAC* 35).

[3] Letter of 19 February 1914 (WSLB 200), transcribed and translated by Bent, Schenker Correspondence Project website.

one meant to find one's bearings in such a welter of cultural, philosophical, and religious references?

In this book I attempt to bridge what Stephen Peles has called 'the unbridgeable cultural chasm between our world and Schenker's' (2001: 177), or if that really is not possible then at least to provide a degree of orientation, by setting Schenker's work into a number of distinct historical contexts: these include Viennese modernism, cultural and political conservatism, and race, as well as the philosophical context on which attempts to situate Schenker's work to date have tended mainly to focus. This philosophical focus is not surprising, given the way in which Schenker litters his writings with references to the major philosophical writers of the German tradition, often in the most conspicuous places: to Kant in the inscription to the foreword of *Das Meisterwerk in der Musik*, Goethe (the inscription to chapter 1 of *Der freie Satz*), Hegel (the first sentence of the same chapter), and so forth. It is also worth noting the possible reflections in Schenker's thinking of more local traditions within the Austro-Hungarian empire where Schenker spent virtually his entire life, in particular the idealist tradition deriving from Leibniz, whom Schenker also mentions ('The Urlinie, to apply Leibniz's concept, is the pre-established harmony of the composition' [*MM1* 109]): this was transmitted through Bolzano to Robert Zimmermann, who taught the course on practical philosophy which Schenker took during the first year of his law degree at the University of Vienna (1884–85). In his encyclopedic survey *The Austrian Mind*, William Johnston writes that the 'notion that there exists a heaven of ideas, some of which come to be thought by man while others never enter a human mind, is one of the fundamental achievements of Austrian philosophy' (1972: 277). There is then an established context for Schenker's unfamiliar mode of thought when he characterises music as 'detached from the ages of human history', or when he speaks of the masterworks existing 'forever in the eternal heaven of the imagination' (*T2* 55) or refers to them as a 'paradise of unity'.[4]

It is however the mainstream tradition of German idealist philosophy on which commentators have focused, that is to say the tradition of eighteenth- and nineteenth-century thought that emphasises the formative activity of the mind in shaping experience and hence the world as we know it. (As Bryan Magee says in his lucid summary of German idealism [2001: 159], that doesn't mean reality is a product of our minds: it means that there is an unbridgeable gulf between the world as we know it and the world as it exists in itself.) Rather than attempting to summarise these commentaries in a general way, I shall focus my discussion around a key early text by Schenker: 'Der Geist der musikalischen Technik' (The spirit of musical technique), commonly

---

[4] Letter of 18 January 1920 to Halm (DLA 69.930/9), transcribed and translated by Lee Rothfarb, Schenker Correspondence Project website.

known as the *Geist* essay, which was published in the Leipzig-based periodical *Musikalisches Wochenblatt* in 1895 and subsequently issued as a pamphlet.[5] Offering the most sustained insight into Schenker's theoretical thinking in the 1890s—though the theory in question is arguably more aesthetic than musical in the conventional sense—this essay has attracted a variety of strikingly contradictory readings, with the contradictions resulting largely from the different period contexts against which different commentators have read it. The very title could hardly be more Hegelian, and the essay opens *in medias res:* the explanation for this may lie in a footnote provided by the editor of the *Musikalisches Wochenblatt,* saying that the text (which had been given as 'a lecture at the Philosophical Society of the University of Vienna') was extracted from 'a larger work still in manuscript' (Pastille 1984: 30). This could also explain the essay's equally abrupt ending, and its strange organisation into five parts, of which the last is virtually equal in length to all the others added together[6]—though having said that, its compact expression is hard to read as a fragment from a more extended work. All one can really say is that, if there was in fact such a larger work, then it is lost.

The essay begins with a discussion of music's origins in the spontaneous expressions of primitive peoples, which Schenker sees as subsequently evolving through the cultivation of singing for its own sake and the development of musical imagination; he goes on to discuss the principles of melody, repetition, and polyphony, and presents counterpoint as a historical means for developing both composers' imaginations and listeners' perceptions. This can be easily read within the context of the evolutionary debates that were sparked off by Darwin in the 1870s, and that continued well into the twentieth century—for example in the work of Carl Stumpf, whose *Die Anfänge der Musik* of 1911 not only assigned the same role to the voice in the development of music (in itself a commonplace idea) but also proposed a basic psychological mechanism, tone fusion, that he saw as codetermining its development: in this way, as Alexander Rehding puts it (2000: 353), Stumpf 'ascertained that the way music evolved was not arbitrary, but was led by the irresistible forces of nature', so that 'after primitive man discovered musical intervals, nature saw to it that he would never forget them'. Despite the date, the resonance between this and Schenker's essentially psychological approach to harmony and counterpoint is not misleading, for the idea that the development of music must be understood in psychological terms was in place well before the turn of the

---

[5] Reprinted in *HSEK* 135–54; a translation by William Pastille, originally published in *Theoria* 3 (1988), 86–104, but now completely revised, may be found in the appendix (to which page numbers in this volume refer). The essay was originally published in vol. 26 of the Leipzig *Musikalisches Wochenblatt,* 245–46, 257–59, 273–74, 279–80, 297–98, 309–10, and 325–26.

[6] And also a number of internal contradictions, as discussed by Pastille (1984: 30).

century. But its direct source as represented in the *Geist* essay is Hegelian history, understood as the unfolding of *Geist*, for which the direct
translation is 'Spirit', though Hegel's use of the word might be more
clearly rendered as 'consciousness'. When Schenker says that through
polyphony 'revolutionary changes began to insinuate themselves into
the realm of sensibility' (p. 322), he is presenting polyphony not as a
mere technique but rather as a mode of developing consciousness: the
history of music is at bottom the history of musical perception.

But more than this, it is the history of music unfolding itself. When
in the *Geist* essay Schenker says that 'music became an art only when a
series of tones arose that demanded to be understood and felt as a
whole, as a self-contained idea', his anthropomorphising language is
not simply a literary figure: it constitutes music as a historical subject.
(That is the conceptual basis underlying the chauvinism in Schenker's
unfavourable comparison between Italian and German music.) And if
human history is to be understood as the unfolding of *Geist*, so is the
temporal evolution of an individual piece of music. When Schenker
says that 'every succession of tones, every melody, carries its own harmonic credo within itself' (p. 325), he is already anticipating what he
said at the beginning of chapter 1 of *Der freie Satz*, 'The inner law of origin accompanies all development and is ultimately part of the present'—a statement that looks metaphysical but is actually, or also, a concise statement of Schenker's basic principle of prolongation. This
statement directly follows an explicit reference to Hegel ('Hegel defines
destiny as "the manifestation of the inborn, original predisposition of
each individual"'), while the idea of development as a process of unfolding is equally evident in the opening sentence of the *Geist* essay:
'Each organ of the human body strives on its own to perfect the particular characteristics of qualities bestowed on it'. In both his first theoretical work and his last, then, Schenker's basic construction of what it
might mean to understand music and its development—whether in
terms of the unfolding of an individual piece or that of musical history—is deeply impregnated with Hegelian thought, or at least with
German idealism. And the same might equally be said of Schenker's
other writings of the 1890s, such as the essay 'Das Hören in der Musik'
(Hearing in music) of 1894,[7] which again discusses the historical development of the ear, as well as such other topics—also featured in the
Geist essay—as the importance of repeated listenings in order to do justice to music, and the excess of compositional artifice over perceptual
ability. The ubiquity in Schenker's intellectual milieu of such idealist
thinking perhaps provides a better explanation of the way in which the
Geist essay apparently starts *in medias res* than the possibility that it was
excerpted from a larger text: the abrupt effect, that is to say, is a mea-

---

[7] *HSEK* 96–103.

sure of the distance between us and a nineteenth-century way of thinking that was understood as simply the way the world is.

While repetition and counterpoint are classic Schenkerian topics, the *Geist* essay is also notable for the prominence of topics that we don't generally associate with Schenker, such as the communication of emotions or moods to the listener. Schenker makes a striking analogy between the cycles of the musical tone and what he calls the repeated 'mood-waves' that are necessary if the effect is to be successfully conveyed to a listener (pp. 326–7): some of Beethoven's bagatelles, he adds, are too brief to do this. (Here is an unexpected source for the idea of prolongation so important for Schenker's later thought, though its meaning would change radically.) And just as he takes it for granted that the attempt to understand music is in some sense a psychological undertaking, so Schenker takes it for granted that the basic purpose of artistic music, and even of harmony and counterpoint, lies in the creation of such effects. But this is not a matter of signifying or representing emotions, in the manner of *Affektenlehre*. It is a matter of releasing qualities that already exist objectively in the music, that are literally composed into its melodies, harmony, and counterpoint. Schenker first makes this point in an inverted form: 'once all of the work's contrapuntal techniques have been fixed permanently,' he says, 'they become just as subjective as the work's emotional character' (p. 323). But then he turns the argument around (p. 324):

> Of course, the spirit of the mood hovers over the totality of the interests, but the composer's interest is demonstrable to everyone, whereas the mood appears to each according to his own taste. This is a very important distinction. Only after one has heard and understood all of the composer's interests and all of the objective materials in the artwork is it permissible— either at the same moment, or sometime later on—to submit the artwork to one's own sensibility for mood, and then to make a final 'judgment' about it.

Subjective qualities, in short, are inherent in music, but it is only on their objective dimension that a practical criticism of music may be based: as will become clear, this position has a quite specific source in Schenker's Vienna, and the position Schenker outlines in the *Geist* essay—it is no more than an outline—emerges out of the concern with the relationship between subjective and objective modes of description that Kevin Karnes has also identified in Schenker's earliest reviews (2001: chap. 2), from 1891 to 1892.

If, then, this reads like the beginnings of a rationale for practical criticism, the same applies to another major theme of the *Geist* essay: the relationship between music and language. After explaining the origins of music in spontaneous expression, Schenker claims that music came to be increasingly fashioned after language, while at the same time arguing that the basic principles of language and music are quite different: whereas a word is 'a sign for something', he says, a musical motive 'is only a sign for itself; or to put it more accurately, it is nothing more and nothing less than itself' (p. 321). In other words, whereas language borrows its structure from the external world it represents, music can 'solicit understanding' only through 'clarifying individual motives and tonal successions through repetition and imitation.' But at this point Schenker's argument takes a critical turn, for music's language-like properties, he says, represent a kind of deception: composers concealed artifice, they 'dressed it up, in order to keep the sensibilities entirely in that instinctive state which would be most likely to hear and accept the artificial whole as something generated naturally' (p. 328). (To put it another way, music is the artifice that disguises itself as nature—and when I said 'critical', I intended the Adornian resonance, which as we shall see belongs to a region of the intellectual universe rather less remote from Schenker than one might think.) Music, in short, created the *illusion* of an inherent musical logic: 'an illusory halo of rational logic began to shine over all the structures elaborated by the artificial designs of the imagination'. It is in order to articulate this sense of an inherent musical logic, Schenker adds, that we use the term 'organic' of those 'works to which we can listen without upsetting our own abilities, capacities, and enjoyment'.

And this is the basis of the claim for which the *Geist* essay has become famous. The 'simple analogy' between music and organism, Schenker explains, 'leads to errors, just as it originated in an error. . . . As a matter of fact, no musical content is organic. It lacks any principle of causation, and a contrived melody never has a determination so resolute that it can say, "Only that particular melody, and none other, may follow me"' (p. 328). Indeed, if the analogy were to be taken literally, Schenker continues, he could envisage only one circumstance in which music could be properly said to be 'organic':

> I find that the imagination, after it has generated a particular pattern, is positively besieged by many patterns similar in nature, and that the influence of these similar patterns on the composer is often so irresistible that he includes them in the developing content without having become aware at all of their similarity. Often—and one can discover this only by an extremely painstaking study of the artwork—the composer would have preferred to conjure up a completely different pattern, but behold! the imagination refuses to change its original direction, and compels him to accept a similar pattern instead. . . . A particular similarity has actually arisen *organically* in the imagination only inasmuch as the composer has *not intended* it.

Schenker's claim that there can in reality be no inherent logic in music is not restricted to the *Geist* essay. It appears in other publications of the same period, such as 'Die Musik von heute' (The music of today), in which Schenker writes that 'music is denied for ever the kind of logic that is peculiar to the world of ideas',[8] or 'Notizen zur Verdis Falstaff' (1893), where Schenker says that Wagnerian leitmotifs create 'an appearance of causality, of logic, I would like to say'.[9] (The term 'appearance'—*Schein*, a common antonym to 'reality'—is crucial here.) But the specific formulation of the claim in terms of organicism, as it appears in the *Geist* essay, has become well known as a result of William Pastille's article 'Heinrich Schenker, anti-organicist', which brought the essay for the first time to the attention of the Schenker-reading public. Pastille's basic argument is exactly what his title implies (1984: 31): 'The view of musical organicism presented in *Geist* is exactly the opposite of that expressed in Schenker's later works'. And so he attempts to trace the process by which 'the anti-organicist' became 'the arch-organicist' (32).

However, the next major commentator on the *Geist* essay, Allan Keiler (1989), rejects the whole idea that there was a fundamental change of view in Schenker's thinking. You get the impression he has been spending too much time with Schenker's polemics when he complains of the 'utter absurdity of the view that . . . Schenker moved gradually from anti-organicist to arch-organicist throughout the course of his writing' (Keiler 1989: 291), and puts Pastille's error down to his 'utter disregard of the complicated meaning of the essay from which the evidence is drawn . . . disregard of any other of Schenker's writing during this period, and . . . disregard of the many contemporary works of musical historical and theoretical scholarship that must have played a crucial role in Schenker's thinking' (275). As an example of Schenker's other writings from this period, Keiler (289) quotes from an article of 1894 in which Schenker characterises the playing of one of the pianists he most admired, Eugen d'Albert. By comparison to the subjective style of the also admirable Anton Rubinstein, Schenker says, d'Albert's playing is objective: it embodies a dimension of reflection, and in this way reproduces rather than reenacts the composer's original creative vision. It is in this context that Schenker refers to compositions being 'conceived and received in one stroke, and the whole fate of their creation, life, growth and end already designated in their first seed',[10] and having quoted this, Keiler concludes: 'We should be prepared to believe . . . that when Schenker is struck by the compelling coherence of a work, he attributes it to the organic character of its compositional origin'. So why, in the *Geist* essay, did Schenker insist that 'no musical content is organic. It lacks any principle of causation'? Keiler's explanation essentially comes in two halves, neither in my view entirely sat-

---

[8] *HSEK* 62–4, translated in Schenker 1988: 133–4 (p. 134).

[9] *HSEK* 46, translated in Keiler (1996: 184), where it is read—in my view wrongly—as a statement of the reality of musical causality and logic; also discussed in Karnes 2001: 140–1.

[10] 'Eine Lebenskizze—Eugen d'Albert', *HSEK* 115–21 (p. 117).

isfactory. First, Keiler says (289), Schenker does not mean to deny music's organicism in general: his comments are addressed to the specific context of the composer's conception, where 'it becomes hard for him to see the primacy of the musical materials unaffected by the more conscious reflection and will of the composer'. (But that is not what Schenker was saying, as is evident from the denials of musical logic and causality in 'Die Musik von heute' and the essay on *Falstaff*.) Second, Keiler continues, it is something that comes out of Schenker's particular engagement with the influential formalist aesthetics propounded by his older contemporary, then in his seventieth year, Eduard Hanslick: Schenker's 'anti-organicist position', Keiler claims, 'has to be seen as based on arguments that are constructed within a somewhat contrived and unsystematic framework, in order to stand in opposition to ideas of Hanslick and others'. I shall in due course offer a very different interpretation of this.

In the third of this series of articles, Kevin Korsyn (1993) begins where Keiler began, with the need for contextualisation. In fact, Korsyn more or less repeats Keiler's accusations against Pastille, except that now the accusations are directed against Keiler as well: both, Korsyn says (85), have largely overlooked 'the historical, philosophical, and biographical background to "Geist"', as well as emphasising German idealism at the expense of specifically Austrian thinking. (It's too bad it doesn't fit Irving Berlin's tune: anything you can contextualise, I can contextualise better.) Despite this last comment, however, Korsyn's interpretation is largely built on the foundation of an earlier article in which he had argued that 'Schenker's work is saturated with Kant' (Korsyn 1988: 2). He had focused in particular on Kant's idea of synthesis, the process of mental construction that gives rise to subjectivity, which Kant formulated as a response to Hume's empiricist critique of personal identity: as Korsyn explains (21),

> If the sequence of my mental states do not have causal connections, then I am merely, to quote Hume, 'a bundle or collection of different perceptions'. The self dissolves into a series of mental states without relation to a single identity. . . . Kant's problem, then, was to provide a theory of personal identity that would show how representations can be unified in a single consciousness. . . . Kant must prove that there are causal connections among mental states.

The argument is that, as revealed by Schenker's frequent use of the Kantian term 'synthesis', compositional unity is the musical embodiment of selfhood: as Korsyn puts it (24), 'for Schenker the organic composition becomes a surrogate for the soul'. It follows that there is a parallel between Schenker's sceptical view of organicism in the *Geist* essay (which Korsyn does not attempt to explain away) and Hume's empiricism: indeed Korsyn calls the resemblance 'uncanny' (47), though he stops short of suggesting that Schenker had read Hume. In this earlier article Korsyn does not, however, suggest why Schenker should have adopted, and later abandoned, this sceptical position, his purpose being—as he continues—'simply to show Schenker's keen understanding of the problems of causality'.

The purpose of Korsyn's later article is to explain what the earlier one left unexplained. After detours via Schopenhauer, Nietzsche, and Wagner, Korsyn draws a parallel between the views of Hume and the Austrian physicist Ernst Mach (1993: 110), who in the 1890s launched the so-called sensationalist critique of 'all hitherto accepted unities such as the ego, body, matter, and so on'. Mach's critique, which was based on the idea that experience is nothing but a construct of sensations and there can be no firm distinction between reality and appearances, certainly had a sensational influence: as Korsyn explains, it was taken up among artists and writers such as Hermann Bahr, the weather vane of Viennese modernism, for whom it epitomised the dissolution of bourgeois subjectivity. (Johnston's convenient term for this whole movement is Viennese 'impressionism' [1972: 185].) This means that, instead of drawing a historically implausible parallel with Hume, Korsyn (111) can now propose that 'Schenker's anti-organicism . . . could be considered an extension of Mach's anti-metaphysical critique'. Again, then, Korsyn gives us a philosophically sceptical Schenker, but now he goes further: 'Schenker's textual strategy', Korsyn claims (99), 'is one of deconstruction', for he destabilises conventional organicist ideology through insisting that 'a composition is always an "artifical whole" rather than "an apparently natural occurrence"'. (Korsyn does not bring Adorno into the argument, but he does cite some parallels between Schenker and Nietzsche.) Even the title of Schenker's essay, Korsyn argues (102), bears a deconstructive thrust, for it invokes the classical opposition between the organic and the inorganic, the former represented by *Geist* and the latter by technique: 'To speak of a spirit of musical technique is to deconstruct this opposition by inscribing each term within the other, destabilizing the hierarchy that privileges *Geist*'.

It would be hard to imagine two Schenkers more diametrically opposed than Keiler's and Korsyn's—the modernist and the postmodernist, as it were—even though both are generated from contextually informed readings of the same essay, and I shall pursue what this disparity might tell us about issues of interpretation and ascriptions of influence before returning to the *Geist* essay in the next section. Essentially Keiler and Korsyn follow the same approach. They invoke major German philosophers (like Hegel and Kant) with whose thought Schenker might reasonably be expected to have some familiarity, together with a selection of more local luminaries (Mach and Hanslick). They identify possibly significant parallels between their writings and Schenker's, and observe coincidences of dates. And in the case of Korsyn's linking of Schenker with Mach, it is possible to go further: '*Schenker and Mach were personally acquainted*', Korsyn writes (1993: 111), citing as evidence a postcard Mach sent to Schenker on 2 December 1896, which reads 'it seems to me that the views you have broached have a healthy kernel and deserve to be pursued. In any case the discussion will be beneficial and stimulating'.[11] At this point the search for affinities passes over into a clear ascription of influence: that is why it matters for Korsyn that Schenker and Mach were in personal contact. But is this really the smoking gun Korsyn's italics suggest? It is not, after all, as if Mach had said he was pleased that Schenker had rethought his position on organicism following their previous discussion; indeed it would be quite possible to read Mach's words as indicating polite disagreement (the 'healthy kernel' might suggest that Mach did not like the way Schenker elaborated his ideas, while the 'in any case' creates the impression of covering something up). The closer one gets to claiming direct influence, the more irredeemably speculative the argument becomes, as Korsyn (113) himself recognises when he says that 'Of course, a single postcard constitutes a slender basis for establishing influence'.

There is a real problem here. For Schenker's career as a whole there is an enormous quantity of documentation in the form of the Schenker *Nachlass:* Robert Kosovsky (1999: 9) refers to 'Schenker's seemingly compulsive drive to commit a thought or idea to paper . . . an almost maniacal desire to use what was at hand, grabbing whatever he could, whenever the moment'. (It is hard not to be reminded of Beethoven.)[12] With Jeanette's help, Schenker maintained an elaborate system of files in which these materials were kept. After Schenker's death, Jeanette passed the majority of the materials relating to his theoretical and analytical work on to Ernst Oster and the rest to Erwin Ratz, who in turn passed them on to Oswald Jonas. Both sets of material are now in the United States; the first being the Oster Collection at the New York Public Library, and the second part of the Oswald Jonas Memorial Collection at the University of California, Riverside.[13] (It is on the latter that Hellmut Federhofer based his documentary semibiography of Schenker.) But among this overwhelming mass of materials, the 1890s are underrepresented. The Jonas Collection contains some letters and, of course, postcards, many of them transcribed in Federhofer (1985), but these are unlikely to represent his complete correspondence from the period, and in any case Schenker's side of the correspondence exists only in the form of a few drafts. There is also Schenker's diary, again part of the

---

[11] OJ 12/47, transcribed in Federhofer 1985: 14–5, translation from Korsyn 1993: 112.

[12] The parallel seems to have been a conscious one: in his notes and sketches, Schenker sometimes made use of the same system of cross-references found in Beethoven's sketchbooks (for a discussion of this parallel see Helsby 2001: 2:54–5).

[13] There are published catalogues of both collections: Kosovsky 1990 and Lang and Kunselman 1994 (also accessible online at the Online Archive of California website: www.oac.cdlib.org/findaid/ark:/13030/tf4j49n9zc). The complete Oster Collection is available on microfilm. For further details of these and related collections see Berry 2005: 465–7.

Jonas Collection, which is normally said to begin in 1896. But up to 1902, it would be better called a notebook or commonplace book: the largest part of the entries, some but not all of which are dated, are on literature (classical drama, Shakespeare, Ibsen, Maeterlinck, Zola, Schnitzler), though there are also some entries on music (Bach's transcriptions, Mozart, Reger, Mahler) and the Dreyfus Affair, as well as aphorisms. Only occasionally is there anything that looks like a conventional diary entry.[14] And none of this casts significant light on Schenker's development as a theorist.

Then again, Schenker compiled voluminous collections of newspaper cuttings, quotations, and commentaries on whatever he had been reading, which demonstrate a strikingly broad range of interests from literature to politics to contemporary science, but the earliest of these (a scrapbook consisting primarily of reviews of Schenker's works) goes back only to 1902.[15] Schenker's library was dispersed after his death, and the only catalogue was compiled by the specialist dealer who bought his scores and books on music and theatre, so that books on other areas are excluded.[16] That leaves us with the published works, together with the unpublished ones to which I have already referred, but here we run into a further problem: Schenker was more than willing to criticise other writers, particularly music theorists, and that of course provides evidence of his reading, but it does not seem to have been his habit to record his intellectual debts. That may simply be because he would have seen it as irrelevant to his project; he was not after all a twenty-first-century academic. Or, as I have elsewhere suggested (Cook 1995), it may have been because of some urge to suppress the traces of such indebtedness. (Schenker's propensity to accuse others of plagiarising his ideas perhaps lends weight to this suggestion.)[17] But the

---

[14] Such as the entry for 31 May 1897 ('returned from Germany . . . nowhere [were there] new springs of art' (OJ 1/1, leaf 2b). As detailed in Lang and Kunselman (1994: 3), materials relating to this period are found in both series A and B of the manuscript diaries (OJ 1/1–3, 1/4): series A includes pages in Jeanette's hand consisting of selected, reordered, and recopied materials from elsewhere (including the 31 May 1897 entry), in some cases with corrections in Heinrich's hand. (I find it hard to know what the purpose was, unless to preserve his thoughts for posterity.) While some of these materials are in a diary-like format, arranged by date, it is only from 1902 (series B, leaf 9) that the materials can properly be said to constitute a diary.

[15] OC 2. Other large collections of such materials, which I have barely explored, include OJ 12 (the contents of which are much more heterogeneous than the headings in Kosovsky [1990] make them appear, ranging from cursory notes in Schenker's hand to newspaper clippings), OC C (which consists of clippings from the 1920s to 1930s), 'Das Leben als Lobgesang Gottes' (a miscellany of Schenker's thoughts and commentaries from 1917 to 1934, OJ 21/5), and OC 30, which consists of the materials on Schenker's desk at the time of his death.

[16] The dealer was Heinrich Hinterberger, and the catalogue is reproduced in Eybl 1995: 161–92.

[17] For example a letter to Cotta of 2 December 1909 accuses Rudolf Louis of purloining 'a concept that was first invented by myself along with the terminology belonging to it'

net effect of all this is that we can speculate about possible influences upon Schenker in the 1890s based on a combination of similarity and circumstance—the equivalent of the crime writer's motive and opportunity—but that proof generally lies beyond the available evidence. And yet these years, as I shall argue, represent the critical period in which the foundations of Schenker's project were laid.

Instead of beginning with the identification of similarities and attempting to correlate them with circumstantial evidence, it is of course possible to work the other way round: you identify figures with whom Schenker had some known connection, and look for similarities in their thinking. (I imagine that is what Korsyn did in the case of Mach.) The most fruitful example of this approach concerns Schenker's legal education at the University of Vienna, for the existence in the Oster Collection of his official transcript (*Meldungsbuch*) reveals exactly whose classes he attended.[18] Other than the philosopher Robert Zimmermann, of whom more later, the best known of Schenker's teachers was Georg Jellinek, whose classes in legal philosophy and international law Schenker took in spring 1886 and autumn 1887 respectively, and Wayne Alpern (1999, forthcoming) has identified compelling similarities between Jellinek's thinking and Schenker's. To cite just a few examples, Alpern draws a parallel between Schenker's belief that the principles of music are to be discovered through analysis of existing compositions and the basic scientific and historical orientation of Jellinek's approach to law, and compares Jellinek's concept of 'intervening spaces' (areas of personal freedom that surround the prescriptions of the law) with Schenker's concept of 'tonal space', which allows for the exercise of creativity within the framework of strictly defined principles. Alpern also stresses Jellinek's and Schenker's shared concern with reconciling the respective rights of the individual and the state, the part and the whole, a concern which led both to be highly critical of democracy, and I shall return to this in chapter 3. Enlightening as such tandem readings undoubtedly are, however, they are still problematic when viewed in terms of the ascription of influence. Alpern (forthcoming) spells out the reasons himself:

> The temporal priority of Schenker's legal studies in and of itself, of course, does not necessarily imply a causal connection. . . . The assertion of a meaningful relationship between Schenker's legal training and his later musical thought on the sole basis of temporal priority alone would constitute the inductive fallacy of *post hoc ergo propter hoc* were it not for the very substantial, and to some degree, overwhelming circumstantial evidence proffered here.

(CA 106–107, translated by Bent, Schenker Correspondence Project website), while Wason (1985: 186) quotes a diary entry dated 17 May 1913 which mentions 'Schoenberg, who derived his work from me!' (the reference is to Schoenberg's *Harmonielehre*).

[18] OC B/435 (reproduced in Alpern forthcoming).

What makes Alpern's case convincing is, as much as anything, the sheer cumulative weight of Schenker's employment of legal terminology for music-analytical purposes or his references to putative 'laws' of musical organisation.

There is the occasional smoking gun in Alpern's thesis, or at least something near to it. For instance, in the 1917 draft of what became *Der freie Satz* (intended, as I mentioned, as a chapter for *Kontrapunkt* 2), Schenker speaks of the *Urgesetz,* or primordial law, in more or less the same sense that he later speaks of the *Ursatz:* Alpern shows not only that this was a standard term for transcendent, divinely sanctioned law but also that Schenker encountered it in the courses on canon law he took with Joseph Zhismann. More often, however, circumstantial evidence of this kind suffers from the fundamental problem that ideas circulate widely and are not owned by individuals, a point that can be made simply by spending an hour or two reading Johnston's book *The Austrian Mind* with Schenker's *Meldungsbuch* in hand. To take a single example, in his final year (spring 1888) Schenker took a course in dispute resolution with Anton Menger, who in Johnston's words 'injected unwonted moral fervour into the Vienna Faculty of Law' through his insistence that judges place more weight on equity than on statute (1972: 93); such concerns were further pursued by Eugen Ehrlich, who did not teach Schenker but took his doctorate at the Vienna Faculty during the period when Schenker was studying there, and whose attacks on abstract legal formulae parallel the attacks on conventional music theory which Schenker was already making in the 1890s. Ehrlich instead developed a theory of 'living law' grounded in the functioning of actual communities, a move from the general to the particular that is immediately reminiscent of Schenker—and all the more so when one reads that 'By hypothesis, living law eludes theorists: it must be experienced . . . but not verbalized' (91). Seen in such a context, one might well understand Schenker's objective in the *Geist* essay, with its qualms about the relationship of language and music, as the scoping of a 'living theory' of music. Yet the parallel development of Ehrlich's and Schenker's theories, even supported by their simultaneous connection with the Faculty of Law at the University of Vienna, is not strong evidence for a direct relationship of influence between them, because both may have been developing ideas from a common source. And whereas Jellinek is in this case an obvious candidate for such a role,[19] many of the ideas Jellinek and Schenker have in common themselves come from earlier philosophers: the suspicion of democracy on the grounds that it represents the tyranny of the majority, for instance, comes straight from Hegel, as does the basic framework within which both

---

[19] Alpern (forthcoming), who briefly mentions Ehrlich, comments that he 'no doubt studied with Jellinek'. He also discusses Menger.

Jellinek and Schenker sought in their respective spheres to reconcile the interests of part and whole.[20]

Peles remarks ominously that 'I can think of no more perilous world, in the West at least, in which to search for influences, roots, and origins than the twilight world of the Habsburg empire' (2001: 178); later he comments that you cannot 'support a claim of influence simply by showing that a particular idea was "in the air"—at least not in Vienna, where just about *everything* was in the air' (184). In the end, then, the seeking out of meaningful comparisons becomes an exercise as interminable as it is exasperating: there is always one more parallel to be drawn, one more context to be adduced, and the result is that attempts to ascribe influence easily degenerate into free-floating speculation. Keiler expresses this exasperation when he writes that 'the search for patterns of similarity in intellectual history, not to mention influence (another matter altogether) tends towards superficiality and tendentious generality' (1989: 274). And a few lines later he spells out what he means:

> How loose is the connection between Schenker's work and its intellectual background can be seen in the literature from the endless points of comparison drawn between it and the history of (mostly) German thought. One study mentions Coleridge, Leibnitz, Kant, Hegel, the Gestalt psychologists; another, Goethe, Schopenhauer, and Bertalanffy. . . . The list could go on, and include, even more reasonably Herder, Schelling, the Schlegels and Humboldt, the group Dilthey named the 'poetic idealists'.

Yet the looseness of which Keiler complains—and which the disparity between his and Korsyn's readings of the *Geist* essay illustrates—may also reflect the nature of Schenker's philosophical thought. Keiler proceeds on the assumption, as he puts it (291), that Schenker 'knew in a fairly intimate way the works of Goethe, Kant, Hegel and Schiller and, of course, many others'. Korsyn quotes Allan Janik and Stephen Toulmin's (1973: 26) claim that in *fin-de-siècle* Vienna 'everyone in the educated world discussed philosophy and regarded the central issues in post-Kantian thought as bearing directly on his own interests, whether artistic or scientific, legal or political', and argues that 'Schenker expected his readers to have a broad cultural background . . . in literature and philosophy' (Korsyn 1988: 6); he cites an exchange of letters with the critic and composer August Halm in which Halm says he believes in the people, but 'perhaps in Kant's sense', while (as Korsyn puts it) Schenker's reply 'uses Kantian terminology with casual grace'. Korsyn even goes as far as to claim that 'Because he presupposed familiarity with Kant, Schenker often uses Kantian concepts without attribution'—a plausible yet dangerous argument which turns *lack* of mention of any given source into evidence of depth of influence.

---

[20] Byron Almén's (1996) study of the relationship between Schenker and Spengler illustrates the problem: it deduces direct links from features that both share with Hegel.

If at times *fin-de-siècle* Vienna is made to sound like the stereotypical Oxbridge college combination room, it fell to a doctoral candidate
to expose the emperor's new clothes. In a 1996 thesis, Bryce Rytting
suggested that Schenker's knowledge of Kant—and one would assume
the same applies to Schopenhauer, Hegel, and the rest—was not in fact
at the high level assumed by commentators like Keiler and Korsyn (and
many others whom I have not discussed).[21] He actually begins with the
same exchange of letters between Schenker and Halm, pointing out
that Schenker uses the term 'pure' reason in a quite un-Kantian sense,
as if it were the opposite of 'practical' reason (81–2). Next, Rytting
catches Schenker misapplying the Kantian concept of the categorical
imperative, and if that can be excused because it was only in Schenker's
diary, the following mistake comes from the 'Elucidations' section that
Schenker included in the last two issues of *Tonwille* and, with minor alterations, the first two volumes of *Meisterwerk* as a summary of his theory, surely as considered a piece of writing as any: here, Rytting says
(87), Schenker garbles Kant's central idea of a priori reason 'in such a
way as to suggest the reverse of Kant's position, and . . . gives no indication of being aware of the difference'.

And then Rytting comes in for the kill. Schenker 'mentions the
most famous works and the most famous ideas from each of those
works', Rytting says, but he deploys them decoratively, for their literary
resonance: 'he uses Kant's terminology as though he were not aware of
its technical meaning. His writing betrays no evidence of his ever having read Kant carefully or understood his philosophy with any sophistication. Quite the contrary, Schenker's knowledge of Kant appears to
be meager' (Rytting 1996: 88–9). This image of Schenker patching and
matching sometimes half-understood snippets fits very well with the
large numbers of miscellaneous quotations from prestigious philosophers and other writers that are scattered through the Oster and Jonas
collections—not to mention the highly eclectic miscellany of materials
piled high on Schenker's desk at the time of his death (there were an
astonishing 390 items). In retrospect, it's hard to see why we should
have expected anything else. Schenker's diaries and notes in the Oster
and Jonas collections show that he was more than well read in classical German literature (his notes on Goethe's *Wilhelm Meister* run to over
130 pages),[22] but there is no reason to believe that the same is true of
the more technical philosophical literature; in fact Federhofer specifically comments that, by comparison with literature, 'he had less interest in works of a philosophical content' (1985: 270). And after all, the
only formal training Schenker had in general (as opposed to legal) phi-

---

[21] But not Blasius (1996: 92n.), who comments inconspicuously in a footnote that
Schenker 'seems to have had for the most part only a second- or third-hand acquaintance
with the specifics of philosophy or aesthetics'.
[22] OJ 21/4.

losophy was the first-semester course in practical philosophy taught by Zimmermann.

As I said in the introduction, all this doesn't mean that you can understand Schenker without understanding something about the German idealist tradition. Rytting makes this point in terms of the deterministic concept of causality that Schenker puts forward in the *Geist* essay ('Only that particular melody, and none other, may follow me'), showing how this reflects Kant's distinction between the domains of nature, which is governed by laws of cause and effect, and of humanity ('a free agent not subject to the law of cause and effect'): art brings these domains into conjunction (Rytting 1996: 109). Unless you are aware of the idealistic background, you don't understand why the issue of causality presents itself to Schenker in the way it does, which means that you don't understand the problem he is trying to solve. However, what all this *does* mean is that in most cases the idealist background is present in Schenker's writing at a level of generality that is common to the different idealist philosophers. Not only the basic opposition of causality and freedom but also the idea of appearances being explained by underlying laws, the idea of a perceptual synthesis which constructs both subjectivity and world as we know it, of striving towards higher levels of organisation, of the dialectical relationship between part and whole, of genius: all of these are present to a lesser or greater degree in the works of Kant, Goethe, Schopenhauer, and Hegel, and often inextricably linked, since the philosophers influenced one another. In consequence, there is generally little to be gained by ascribing Schenker's views to the influence of one particular philosopher as against another: as Joseph Lubben says (1995: 46), many commentators 'have seemed too eager to link individual Schenkerian concepts exclusively to a single author or school'. And when Schenker *does* draw on recognisably different philosophical traditions (for instance the Leibnizian and Hegelian strains of idealism), what emerges is as often as not simply the inconsistency of his thought: Leibnizian assumptions about the unchanging nature of ideas and Hegel's historical conception of *Geist* are quite incompatible with one another, yet Schenker on occasion flits from one to the other as if they were interchangeable. I shall come back to this in chapter 5.

The conclusion I draw from all this is that discussion of putative influences on Schenker is frequently unproductive, partly because it is so often impossible to determine what they actually were, and partly because the important thing is not so much where Schenker found his ideas—many of which were in common currency—as the way he combined them to arrive at a distinctive or original conception. More productive, then, is the attempt to recapture the connotations of what Schenker wrote, as for example when his theoretical terminology resonates with contemporary aesthetic, political, or racial discourses: such dimensions of meaning would have been taken for granted by

Schenker's contemporaries, and there is nothing harder to recapture from the historical record than what is taken for granted. (I shall come back to this in the conclusion.) The interpretive endeavour of this book, then, is to construct a meaningful relationship in place of Peles's 'unbridgeable cultural chasm between our world and Schenker's': a reimagining that is as far as possible regulated by the historical record, but the prime objective of which must be to add depth to our understanding of what Schenker wrote. (To return to the example of Eugen Ehrlich, the parallel between 'living law' and Schenker's theory may tell us nothing about influence, but it opens up larger contexts—Jellinek's jurisprudence, Hegelian history—with which Schenker's writings resonate.) That is a position Philip Barford openly advocated thirty years ago (1975: 40): 'we are dealing mainly with analogies', he wrote, 'and although analogy is a bad argument, it can exercise a fertile influence upon our understanding of music theory'. It has also been stated more recently and circumspectly by Blasius (1996: xviii), for whom Schenker is 'but one agent within a larger epistemological economy'—and he adds, 'I do not feel it necessary to pursue such normative causal ideas as "influence" or "borrowing" or the like'.

There is however a final point I wish to make about Schenker and the philosophers, concerning not what Schenker knew about philosophy but what the philosophers knew about music. In 1916 Schenker confided to his diary that 'Hegel does not know that the truth of the arts lies solely in the fulfillment of their own laws . . . the inner laws [of music] are and remain mysteries solely of the genius and no other. Hence the entirely hopeless groping on the part of philosophers and aestheticians'.[23] Schenker's dissatisfaction is hardly surprising, for Hegel saw music as restricted to the representation of feeling; that in turn means that he saw it as an inferior mode of knowledge, 'associating it with a superficial, unreflective immediacy of apprehension that can never articulate the inner complexity of things' (Wicks 1993: 358). And in *Tonwille*, Schenker reflected on how unfortunate it was that Goethe did not understand music: 'who dares to doubt', he asks, 'that Goethe would have found only the proudest, most noble words to glorify the authentically German formal will and formal capacity, if only he had grasped its glory!?' (*T1* 215). Perhaps then, as he embarked on his life's work, one of Schenker's principal motivations (I shall mention two more in the course of this chapter) was to do for music what, because of their musical ignorance, the philosophers of the German idealist tradition had so conspicuously failed to do.[24]

[23] Federhofer 1985: 275 (entry of 18 May 1916); translated in Rytting 1996: 91.

[24] Pastille (1990: 43–4) suggests that Schenker's work might be seen as a fulfilment of Goethe's abandoned *Tonlehre*. Schenker complained in *Kontrapunkt* 1 about Schopenhauer's 'vague opinions' and 'lack of clarity' (*C1* 15–16), and about Nietzsche in a letter to Otto Vrieslander, 15 November 1917 (transcribed in Federhofer 1985: 290–1). For Kant's 'abysmal ignorance of music as an *art*' see Kivy 1993: 257.

Formalists against Formalism

I return now to the substantive argument concerning the *Geist* essay, and to Keiler's (1989: 286) reading of it as 'a vigorous attack on the formalism of Eduard Hanslick'. Korsyn comments in a footnote that 'there is much in "Geist" that Hanslick might have disagreed with, but to interpret it as a covert attack on Hanslick's formalism seems unfounded' (1993: 109n.). I would put the point more strongly than that. There are of course areas of disagreement between Schenker and Hanslick, such as Schenker's Leibnizian insistence towards the end of the *Geist* essay on the unchanging nature of musical content: his assertion that 'each and every content retains the power which it had originally, and it is up to us to perceive this vitality anew' (p. 330) might well be read as a specific critique of Hanslick's claim in *Vom Musikalisch-Schönen* that musical forms wear out, so that what was once beautiful may with the passage of time cease to be so.[25] (Even then, the practical outcome is the same: The challenge is to perceive music in its pristine state.) But it is my claim that there is such a close link between the basic conceptual framework of Hanslick's book and Schenker's essay that one may see Hanslick's approach as fundamental to Schenker's thinking, not only in 'Der Geist der musikalischen Technik' but far beyond.

Though it was originally published as long ago as 1854, *Vom Musikalisch-Schönen* went through a total of ten subsequent editions in which Hanslick revised and updated his text in order to reflect the latest thinking; at the beginning of chapter 6, for example, he inserted a reference to his friend Robert Zimmermann's two-volume *Allgemeine Aesthetik als Formwissenschaft*, published in 1865 (indeed later editions of *Vom Musikalisch-Schönen* were dedicated to Zimmermann). In this way, Hanslick's book remained a focus of debate over a long period: Keiler (1989: 293) mentions a controversy between Robert Hirschfeld and Friedrich von Hausegger (whom Keiler proposes as another source for Schenker's evolutionary approach to music)—a controversy prompted by the appearance in 1885 of the seventh edition of *Vom Musikalisch-Schönen*, of which Hausegger had written a critique. And the eighth edition, on which Geoffrey Payzant's translation is based, appeared in 1891. Not only was Hanslick still active as a critic in the 1890s, but also—for what it is worth—correspondence in the Jonas Collection indicates that Schenker had more extensive personal acquaintance with him than with Mach. Among this correspondence is another postcard, dating from early in 1894, in which Hanslick refers to Schenker's idea for a 'History of Melody' and says how much it interests him.[26] Hellmut

---

[25] Hanslick 1986/1854: 35.
[26] Postcard of 15 February 1894, transcribed in Federhofer 1985: 12.

Federhofer (1985: 12) speculates that this may be the larger work from which the *Geist* essay was supposedly taken, but whether or not that is correct, it makes sense that Hanslick would have been interested in the idea: in *Vom Musikalisch-Schönen* he had written that 'melody is the jumping-off point, the life, the original artistic manifestation of the realm of sound; all additional determinations, all inclusion of content, are tied to it', and that harmony is implicit in melody[27]—which is exactly the position that Schenker takes in the *Geist* essay. (Change 'melody' to '*Urlinie*', and it is the basic premise of Schenkerian theory.)

There is also a close affinity between Hanslick's and Schenker's views of the compositional process and the importance that they ascribe to it for the understanding of music, though here again the issue of common sources comes in. In *Vom Musikalisch-Schönen*, Hanslick writes:

> A musical idea simply turns up in the composer's imagination; he elaborates it. It takes shape progressively, like a crystal, until imperceptibly the form of the completed product stands before him in its main outlines, and there remains only to realize it artistically, checking, measuring, revising.[28]

If this formulation seems familiar, that is because Hanslick is consciously or unconsciously echoing a famous account of the compositional process: the letter—as it turns out, invented by Friedrich Rochlitz in the early nineteenth century, but that was not generally known at the time[29]—in which Mozart compared the music in his mind to 'a fine picture or a beautiful statue' that he could survey at a glance, with the committing of it to paper being done 'quickly enough, for everything is . . . already finished'. I shall come back to this quotation and the idea of creation inherent in it, but for now I want to draw attention to the change of imagery: Hanslick transforms pseudo-Mozart's 'statue' into a 'crystal', the result of which is to emphasise not so much the artist's imagination as the self-organisation of musical materials—and the idea that musical materials organise themselves in the composer's mind, even against the composer's wishes, is of course one of the most striking features of Schenker's early theorising, both in the *Geist* essay and elsewhere. It also raises obvious issues of intentionality and subjectivity, and these, too, are anticipated by Hanslick:

> We have established that the activity of the composer is a kind of constructing; as much, it is altogether objective. . . . The limitlessly expressive ideal material of the tones permits the subjectivity of his inner formative process to make its mark upon the products of his shaping. Since the indi-

---

[27] Hanslick 1986/1854: 69.

[28] Hanslick 1986/1854: 35.

[29] In his authoritative article on the subject, which includes the full quotation, Maynard Solomon (1980: 275) says that the letter's validity was first questioned in 1858 by Otto Jahn.

vidual musical elements already possess their own characteristic expressiveness, the predominant characteristics of the composer turn out to be such things as sentimentality, energy, serenity. . . . Once they have been absorbed out of the artistic process into the product, however, these characteristics are of interest as musical determinations, i.e., as the character of the composition, not of the composer.[30]

This corresponds precisely with what Schenker says in the *Geist* essay about the relationship between the subjective and the objective, and the way the composer's manipulation of these objective properties creates emotional effects. I said that, for Schenker, this is the basis for a practical criticism of music; it might also be seen as a rebuttal of Hegel's view of music as limited to the representation of feeling and hence an inferior mode of knowledge, in line with Schenker's 1916 diary entry.[31] But equally it is the basis of Hanslick's so-called formalism, itself arguably intended as a critique of Hegel,[32] and certainly one of the most ubiquitously misunderstood concepts in the literature of music. In a nutshell, Hanslick did not say that music does not, cannot, or should not convey feelings, moods, or emotions, but even in his lifetime he was read that way; this is why he wrote in his preface to the 1891 edition of *Vom Musikalisch-Schönen* that 'ardent opponents have accused me from time to time of mounting a full-scale polemic against everything that goes by the name of feeling, whereas every impartial and attentive reader can easily see that I protest only against the erroneous involvement of feeling in science'.[33] It is easy to understand Hanslick's perplexity: there should never have been any doubt as to what his basic thesis was—that the objective properties of music, rather than people's subjective responses to it, constitute the proper concern of musical aesthetics (Hanslick's 'science'). In this way, to borrow a phrase from Tony Blair's speechwriters, Hanslick directs enquiry away from the emotional and other effects of music, and towards the *causes* of those effects:

> The particular feature by which a melody has its power over us is not merely some kind of obscure miracle of which we can have no more than an inkling. It is rather the inevitable result of musical factors which are at work in the melody as a particular combination of those factors.[34]

Schenker's identical approach to emotional expression in music—that it must be understood in terms of the music's objective properties—appears not just in the *Geist* essay but more explicitly in the 1897 essay 'Un-

---

[30] Hanslick 1986/1854: 47.

[31] See note 23.

[32] In the penultimate paragraph of *Vom Musikalisch-Schönen*, Hanslick (1986/1854: 83) dissociates himself from 'Hegel's musical standpoint, which disregards the essentially formative and objective activity of the composer'.

[33] Hanslick 1986/1854: xxii.

[34] Hanslick 1986/1854: 33.

persönliche Musik' (Impersonal music).[35] He talks there of the purely musical origins of the emotional and descriptive effects in J. S. Bach's music ('question, answer, plea, importuning, persistence, moodiness, laughter, etc'), and adds, 'It was similar with Schubert, Mendelssohn and Chopin. . . . Their concepts and their notions were immediately transformed into moods, and their moods into music'.[36] Nothing could be more different, he continues, from today's programmatic composers, who 'all do as if they were uttering vastly important things, and proclaim their great personalities, note by note; yet everything is a vain delusion'. It is as if such composers—what he later called '"ideas" composers' (*FC* I 27)—try to force their subjectivity directly into their compositions, without first transmuting feeling into music. In this way, they bypass the objectivity that grounds genuinely musical effects.

But, as with Hanslick, this should not be misinterpreted as an argument against music's ability to convey poetic meaning. Schenker made this particularly clear a decade later when, in *Harmonielehre*, he discussed the famous horn entry at the point of recapitulation in the first movement of the *Eroica* Symphony: the horn is merely outlining 'a $^6_4$ chord of the kind almost regularly employed on the dominant', Schenker explains, and while the compositional realisation is such that 'this basic technical idea is almost wholly repressed and obscured by the prevailing sentiment', it is the technical idea 'that first made it possible to conceive and express the poetic element'.[37] Indeed, Schenker maintained in a discussion of the pianist Julius Röntgen, published in 1896, that 'in true tone-poets' (this time he cites Beethoven and Schumann) 'a musical event always has a higher poetic function in addition to its purely musical one' (*HSEK* 328). This is the principle that licenses the sometimes startlingly extravagant metaphors Schenker uses when talking about instrumental music, as for example when he says of a string figure in bar 6 of the third movement of Beethoven's Ninth Symphony that it is 'as if human arms were to reach longingly toward an object of such close proximity' (*BNS* 190): he spells it out in the first volume of *Meisterwerk,* saying of his analytical graphs that 'the devoted student is at liberty . . . to add other descriptive language if he wishes, *provided only that he correctly understands the subject matter*' (*MM1* 107, my emphases). And it is a principle to which Schenker adhered right up to *Der freie Satz:* all that changed—and, as in the case of Hanslick, encouraged a positivistic misreading—is the emphasis, for whereas on some occasions Schenker wishes to emphasise the potential of well-formed music to support poetic meaning, his purpose is increasingly often to deflect analytical attention back from the poetic to the purely musical. A good example of the latter is provided by *Der freie Satz:* 'Even though the

---

[35] *HSEK* 216–21, translated in Schenker 1988: 135–8.
[36] Schenker 1988: 135.
[37] Translation taken from *MW3* 32n.; see *H* 162–3.

story of Leonore provides opportunity for a music-drama', Schenker writes in relation to the third *Leonore* overture, 'the prime concern of the music must be, not her experience, but first and foremost that purely musical motion whose ultimate aim is the unfolding of one chord by means of the fundamental line and the bass arpeggiation through the fifth'.[38]

There is then a common nexus of ideas, with issues of subjectivity versus objectivity at its core, which Hanslick and Schenker had in common, and which provided the basis for an at least partly shared critique of the musical culture of their day.[39] I shall argue that Schenker's project, formulated in the 1890s but outlining the agenda for his life's work, was set up specifically in terms of this critique, but first I need to place Schenker (at this stage of his career best known as a music critic) within the context of contemporary critical practice in Vienna. One reason for the longevity of *Vom Musikalisch-Schönen* was that the central controversies of the midcentury were still alive near its end, and had even acquired new significance. In her study of Viennese music criticism during the years 1896–97, Sandra McColl comments that the 'new political Wagnerism on the rise among certain German nationalists born in the 1860s manifested itself largely as a grotesque caricature of the German national Wagnerism of the 1870s' (1996: 164); she cites the complaint of Richard Kralik (one of the Wagnerians in question, though born a little earlier) that the 'moderns . . . believe themselves to be making now the music of the future, but all they are making is the music of the past—of the forties and fifties' (220). In 1890s Vienna, then, the Wagnerian fault-line remained the central feature of the musical landscape, with Hanslick and the sometimes unwilling Brahms on one side, and on the other the not-so-unwilling Bruckner and the pan-German, increasingly anti-Semitic Wagnerians—McColl's 'political' Wagnerians—such as Camillo Horn and the pseudonymous 'Hagen' (whose real name is not known).

---

[38] *FC* I 137n. Other statements on this subject include *T2* 146 (an analysis of Mendelssohn's *Venetianisches Gondellied* op. 30, no. 6, in which Schenker outlines the scene depicted and comments that 'the master reifies all of that—water boatman, and song—in a single voice-leading progression'), *MM2* 2 (where Schenker comments of Chopin's 'Berceuse' that 'the neighbour-note formation . . . musically illustrates the rocking of a cradle'), and—as examples of the deflection from poetic to musical—*MM1* 5 (in referring to 'passions' [*Leidenschaften*], 'Bach will have wanted to say nothing more than that the creator of a fantasy must have taken pains to alternate motives, in order to produce tension and to transmit it to the listener. Nothing more') and *MM3* 70 ('Whatever the great masters may occasionally have imported into their music by way of extraneous ideas did not alter their musical thinking one iota, so purely did they think in musical terms'). There is also a more evenhanded formulation in the op. 101 *Erläuterungsausgabe* (Schenker 1972/1921: 58, translated in Goldman 1990: 115, Snarrenberg 1997: 103).

[39] I should however add that the relationship between Hanslick and Schenker is complicated by a curiously backhanded essay of 1895 which Schenker published in *Die Zeit* to mark Hanslick's seventieth birthday (*HSEK* 280–1). He summarises Hanslick's

It would be possible to make a case that in the mid-1890s Schenker occupied a relatively central position within this terrain, along with such critics as Hirschfeld and Theodor Helm. At this time Wagner regularly appears in the lists of geniuses for which Schenker always retained a weakness; in 'Die Musik von heute', published in 1894, a list of outstanding teachers (by which, Schenker says, he means educators, composers, critics, and philosophers) consists of 'Guido of Arezzo, J. S. Bach, Schumann and Wagner', while in February 1897 Schenker refers to 'misunderstood geniuses, like Handel, Mozart, Beethoven, and Wagner.'[40] Conversely, Schenker's admiration of Brahms was rather more muted in the mid-1890s than it became later in his life. Even in the obituary he published in *Die Zukunft*, where if anywhere one might expect eulogy, there are traces of the widely held view that Brahms's strength lay in his chamber music and not in the symphonies, and a distinct hint of criticism when Schenker writes, 'some will say: "He has also rejected modernity; for surely one should not be playing with old forms in a post-Beethoven symphony". And in a certain sense those who say this are correct'.[41] Karnes (2001: 234) also points out that Schenker's other obituary of Brahms, in the *Neue Revue*,[42] contains surprisingly sharp criticism of Brahms's tendency to withdraw from society—a tendency which, by comparison with the deaf Beethoven, Schenker calls 'excessive'.

As McColl says, however, what was principally unusual about Schenker's critical orientation was his open hostility to Bruckner, even as early as the 1893 review of *Psalm 150:* it is on the basis of this, as well as his support of Brahms, that McColl regards Schenker as representative of 'a "new conservatism" . . . in opposition to the extremes of political Wagnerism' (McColl 1996: 165). Terminology like 'conservatism' can be confusing in this context, however, owing to the curious relationship that obtained at this time between musical tastes on the one hand and social and political orientation on the other. What we might

---

official and academic honours, and then quotes a long passage (half the essay) from Helmholtz's *Die Lehre von den Tonempfindungen als physiologische Grundlage für die Theorie der Musik* (i.e. *On the Sensation of Tone*), in which Helmholtz speaks of music's expressive properties and agrees with Hanslick that music cannot specify the object of feeling without the aid of words: it is because of this contribution to the aesthetics of music, Schenker comments, that 'Hanslick's name will live on in the so-called aesthetics of music'. What makes the essay backhanded is Schenker's repeated references to 'the ice-flow of Hanslick's negation': it is as if, at this time, Schenker himself subscribed to the widespread misreading of Hanslick to which I referred. Another conceivable interpretation would see this as an early example of the denial of influence to which I also referred: so understood, Schenker's criticism of Hanslick would reveal the very influence that Schenker sought to disguise. However one reads it, this essay is 'rather strange' (Whittle 1993: 242).

[40] Schenker 1988: 134; McColl 1996: 113.

[41] Schenker 1991/1897: 2.

[42] *HSEK* 224–30.

see as social and political reaction, in the shape of an increasingly anti-Semitic pan-Germanism, was associated with the self-consciously progressive musical tradition that led from Wagner to Bruckner and the programmatic composers whom Hanslick and Schenker derided; by contrast liberalism, a declining force in the increasingly populist Vienna embodied by Karl Lueger (who became mayor in 1897), was always associated with musical conservatism. As the music theorist Rudolf Louis wrote in 1905, 'the artistic expression of the "Liberal" spirit was the academic epigonous classicism, that today appears to us so thoroughly done away with' (Notley 1993: 112).

Yet there is more to it than that. Given the manner in which Bruckner was appropriated by the pan-German anti-Semites (Notley 1997), it makes excellent sense to imagine Schenker increasingly aligning himself with the liberal tradition of which Brahms and Hanslick were conspicuous representatives—to the point that there were (unfounded) claims that both were Jewish.[43] And what composer in Vienna stood for 'academic epigonous classicism' if not Brahms, to whom Max Spiedel[44] had notoriously applied the term 'epigone' (a charge, incidentally, that Schenker directly refutes in the Brahms obituary published in *Die Zukunft*)? But here we can come back to the essay 'Unpersönliche Musik', published as it happens six days after Brahms's death,[45] where as we have seen Schenker compares Bach, Schubert, Mendelssohn, and Chopin—who transmuted their subjective feelings into musical objectivity—with the 'programme musicians' who force their subjectivity directly on the music, the 'New Germans' who 'only paint the words'.[46] For Schenker now develops his argument in a new and unexpected direction: against what he calls the 'classicists' who ape Beethoven's forms while lacking understanding of their 'ultimate secrets'.[47] Just who they might be is not spelled out—local suspects might include the Conservatory teachers Hermann Grädener and Robert Fuchs—but Schenker tells us how they compose:

> Most of our 'classicists' compose as follows: they lie in wait for their own fantasy; pursue—like birdcatchers—the necessary 'motives' and 'themes'; *force* the themes, when they have found some, into any old beautiful form;

---

[43] See e.g. Beller-McKenna 2005: chap. 6, Gay 1978: 275n.; the claim regarding Hanslick goes back to the postscript Wagner (1894: 104) added in 1869 to 'Das Judenthum in der Musik', which refers to 'his [Hanslick's]—albeit charmingly concealed—Judaic origin'. In what Notley (1993: 122) terms 'a rhetorical flight of fancy', Josef Stolzing referred to Hanslick, Brahms, and Kalbeck as all Jews. Notley (1999: 57–8) also refers to Georg von Schönerer's characterisation of the Vienna Tonkünstlerverein, which was set up in 1885 and was in effect a Brahms-Verein (and of which Schenker was a member), as a 'Cohnkünstlerverein'.

[44] And others, such as Hermann Levi in 1889 (Gay 1978: 247).

[45] 9 April 1897 (Ayotte 2004: 44).

[46] Schenker 1988: 135, 136.

[47] Schenker 1988: 137.

and glue and paste, according to old, well-tried and half-understood rules, until at last there is a beginning, a middle, and an end.

This process of cutting and pasting stands in conspicuous opposition to the pseudo-Mozart model of creativity, which (as will become clear) occupied a prominent place in Schenker's thinking, and the purpose of his article is to draw a clear distinction between the great composers of the past and the formulaic composers of the present day. His key claim is that 'most contemporary artists . . . are "formalists", no matter whether they are composers of programme music or classicists "in pursuit of themes"'.[48] Schenker clearly expects his readers to be puzzled at the description of programme composers as 'formalists', and attempts to justify his position by means of a rhetorical question he cannot stop himself from answering:

> For is a preconceived negation of purely musical laws—a preconceived transgression of the most primitive law which says that music must at all times clearly explain itself by musical means—is this not in fact, just as much of a 'formal scheme' as the preconceived, positive one of the classicists? Of course it is.

The premises of Schenker's argument are Hanslickian, but its effect is to refine the Hanslickian position by drawing a distinction between the really epigonous kind of classicism, the sort that results from cutting and pasting, and classicism in the pseudo-Mozart mould of Brahms, who—as Schenker wrote in his obituary for *Die Zukunft*, published just under a month later—'was not ashamed to imitate the old masters to the best of his ability—but always in new ways'.[49] It is a few lines after this that Schenker makes the remark to which he referred more than twenty years later, in *Der Tonwille:* 'No, the talent of the thirtieth century will still be smaller than the genius of the eighteenth century, one can be sure of that'.

While the purpose of 'Unpersönliche Musik' may be to draw distinctions within classicism and prepare for the rehabilitation of Brahms, at its core lies the relationship between music and preconceived, ultimately verbal, categories. And it is not only in relation to composition that midcentury debates about music and words still resonated in *fin-de-siècle* Vienna: they also related to musical listening and the discourses that surrounded it, and here there is a further context within which to place Schenker. From a present-day perspective, with shrinking and greying audiences and a pervasive sense of crisis within the classical tradition, it is easy to see the Viennese *fin de siècle* as a golden age of music. Yet not just Schenker but many critics of his day believed that music was in a state of decline, and saw the issue of listening as central to this. In his monumental doctoral thesis and a number of related pub-

---

[48] Schenker 1988: 138.
[49] Schenker 1991/1897: 3; the obituary is reprinted in *HSEK* 230–36.

lications, Leon Botstein has charted the development from the musical
literacy of the early nineteenth century, which was based on singing and
string playing (both of which require accurate pitch representation), to
the piano-based literacy of the period after 1848, for which it was necessary 'only to translate musical notation into numerical directions—
pitches into fingerings' (Botstein 1992b: 136). But there was a third
stage in this process, a new literacy based on listening rather than participation, and mediated by the written word. The result was that audiences came to know music not by playing it, not by reading it, but by
reading *about* it: as Botstein (139) puts it, 'one read about music the way
one read about developments in politics, cultural ideas, and science'.

   In some ways this was a positive development: it located serious
music firmly within the sphere of public debate in a way that is hardly
the case today and, as Karnes (2001) makes clear, the journalism to
which Schenker contributed in the 1890s was pursued at an often impressive level of intellectual sophistication. At the same time, this new
literacy clearly had a knock-on effect in terms of how people listened
to music. 'Listening no longer was a species of thinking musically', Botstein writes (1992b: 138): 'rather it became an act that helped verify
and vindicate a literary image'. That in turn led to the feeling that
whatever is meaningful in music should be capable of being represented in words: as Botstein puts it (144), 'the inexpressible became in-
tolerable. . . . [Music] became understandable insofar as it could be
translated explicitly'. Though Botstein traces this development back to
A. B. Marx in 1860s Berlin and Hermann Kretzschmar in 1880s Leipzig,
in Vienna the key date is 1893, when the Viennese Philharmonic Society first commissioned Hirschfeld to write programme books for each
of its concerts (something he continued doing until 1913). In format
these were not unlike Tovey's *Essays in Musical Analysis:* they consisted
of blow-by-blow accounts of the music, identifying themes or motives
and treating them like narrative or dramatic protagonists, so aiming to
develop a sense of coherence that might in some way substitute for the
process of score reading: as Botstein puts it (142), 'Hirschfeld sought to
develop in a sustained way his readership's sense of musical form and
to underscore the essential link between "understanding and emotion"'. But there was a Catch-22 here. The purpose of the programme
notes was to educate listeners, thereby remedying the superficiality of
contemporary listening habits against which so many contemporary
writers (including Schenker and for that matter Schoenberg) railed. But
at the same time the book-in-hand listening that it encouraged, with
the ears serving to verify and vindicate a literary image, only helped to
entrench the very superficiality it was designed to counter. It became,
to borrow Kraus's quip, the disease for which it claimed to be the cure.

   This provides a specific context within which to read Schenker's essays of the following year, 'Das Hören in der Musik' and 'Die Musik von
heute'—essays which are united by a common concern. 'Das Hören in

der Musik' critiques listeners who are satisfied with getting an initial impression of the music. Repeated listening, Schenker argues, is necessary if one is to achieve the kind of synoptic view of the whole that composers possess, a point 'high above the artwork . . . from which the spirit can clearly survey the artwork, all its paths and goals, the lingering and storming, all variety and limitation, measurements and relationships, by ear as if by eye' (*HSEK* 103); the resonance with the pseudo-Mozart concept of creation is obvious. (As I said, the emphasis on repetition is also present in the *Geist* essay, and Schenker's attack on impressionistic listening makes it hard indeed to entertain Korsyn's image of Schenker succumbing to Mach's influence and flirting with Viennese 'impressionism'). 'Die Musik von heute' is subtitled 'New variations on an old theme', and is essentially an update of Hanslick's position as expressed in *Vom Musikalisch-Schönen:* Schenker's starting point is the striking idea that 'If the relationship between art and the individual is to be a really happy one, one must not only be a lover of music, but be loved by it'[50]—an idea that, again as in the *Geist* essay, turns music into a subject. (A review from 1896 expresses the other side of the same thought: 'If only poor music could defend itself with its own strength against the rape and arbitrariness of composers!' [*HSEK* 336].) Yet most listeners 'are just chasing after the titillation of the ears and nerves', says Schenker, and he continues, 'Oh, no! Music needs and demands *active* enjoyment, enjoyment which is also mental activity when it appears to be mere enjoyment, and at the same time is genuine enjoyment which leads to mental activity'.[51] His next words, which are again based on the idea of music as a subject involved in dialogue with the listener, are even more directly related to the *Geist* essay, and I have already quoted them: 'And this need on the part of music is all the more intense and justified because music is denied for ever the kind of logic that is peculiar to the world of ideas'.

Here, then, Schenker's doubts concerning musical logic become linked to the negative critique of contemporary culture he develops from Hanslick. The basic problem is the same in composition and in the culture of listening and writing about music: it is wrongly assumed that music behaves like words, that musical content can be adequately represented by words, that music has a logic that can be translated into words. That is the case of contemporary composers, for whom 'the first creative force . . . is the intellect'; they 'try to "acclimatise", as it were, to nature what the intellect has given them by *artificially* pouring the brooding "warmth" of enthusiasm over what has been intellectually invented'.[52] But it is equally the case, Schenker continues, of 'a rather inferior and, calling a spade a spade, unmusical kind of music criticism

[50] Schenker 1988: 133.
[51] Schenker 1988: 133–4.
[52] Schenker 1988: 134.

which admittedly renders unto the public what is the public's due, but
does not render unto art what is due to art'. That remark may or may
not have been prompted by Hirschfeld's programme books, but at all
events it sets the pattern for Schenker's later, and increasingly vitriolic,
attacks on writers like 'Kretzschmar, Riemann, Grove, and the rest' (*CI*
xxv). And Schenker anticipates another (or rather several) of his lifelong obsessions when, in the same paragraph, he refers to this as just
one example of 'an unbelievably foolish and mindless method of musical education, which can only have arisen from the spirit of the
masses and of business': this is a rare example, for the 1890s, of the passionately pessimistic tone that we associate with Schenker's later writings, and the jeremiad reaches its climax with the claim 'Immorality
prevails, a *turpitudo* in musical life in general'.

It is hard to imagine Hanslick, not only a distinguished liberal but
also 'personally a charming and witty old gentleman',[53] being entirely
comfortable with the tone of this young lion's final comments. Nevertheless, Schenker's argument about the relationship of music and
words—whether expressed in programme music or in discourse about
music—is entirely Hanslickian in its premises. Hanslick anticipates
Schenker's attack on 'intellectual' composers, whether of the programmatic or classicist variety, when he speaks of the error of thinking 'that
composing is the translating of some kind of conceptual content into
tones', and adds that 'the tones themselves are the untranslateable, ultimate language'.[54] And when Hanslick writes that 'in music there is no
content as opposed to form, because music has no form other than the
content',[55] he anticipates Schenker's statement in the *Geist* essay that
'every content . . . has its own form. . . . What is called form is an abstraction' (p. 331), and it on this basis that Schenker says a few sentences earlier that 'it goes without saying that I am also an adversary of
the term "formalism"'. Keiler is right, then, in characterising Schenker
as an 'anti-formalist' (1989: 288), but only in a sense that makes
Hanslick an antiformalist too. And if it is the forced alignment with linguistic models that gives rise to formalistic ways of thinking about
music, then we can say that—no less than in the case of 'Unpersönliche
Musik'—the central concern of the *Geist* essay is the disparity of music
and words, or maybe it would be more accurate to say the mismatch
between music and how it has been theorised. Even in 1910, as
Schenker reminisced twenty years later in *Meisterwerk*, he was conscious of 'a total divide separating the art of listening to music from its
expression in words so great that any communication must for the

---

[53] Max Graf's possibly unreliable description (quoted in McColl 1996: 5). Graf
records that Hanslick offered him snuff, despite the fact that Graf had written articles attacking him; it is hard to imagine Schenker doing the same.
[54] Hanslick 1986/1854: 82.
[55] Hanslick 1986/1854: 80.

foreseeable future seem impossible' (*MM3* 8)—and that too is a view anticipated in the *Geist* essay, where Schenker says that 'practical music almost never concerns itself with those things which theory either ascribes to it or derives from it' (p. 322).

With all its complexities and contradictions, 'Der Geist der musikalischen Technik' represents a sustained if not quite successful attempt to rationalise Hanslick's critique of contemporary culture, to turn the exasperating assemblage of aphorisms that is *Vom Musikalisch-Schönen* into a systematic approach, and so help transform negative critique into positive action. To a striking degree, Hanslick and Schenker share a common conception of what a valid theory of musical understanding might be. Geoffrey Payzant speaks of Hanslick's 'conviction that an exact science of aesthetics was possible and would succeed rhapsodic treatments of the subject'—he puts this down to the influence of Herbart via Zimmermann[56]—and an illustration of this which I have already quoted is his claim that melodic effects are 'the inevitable result of musical factors which are at work in the melody as a particular combination of those factors'.[57] (Hanslick gives a similar claim a distinctly Schenkerian flavour when he says that a theme's expression is the result of these factors having been combined 'just as they were and not otherwise'.)[58] Again, there is a resonance between Hanslick's statement that 'all musical elements have mysterious bonds and affinities among themselves, determined by natural laws [which] reside, though not in a manner open to scientific investigation, instinctively in every cultivated ear'[59] and Schenker's promise in the *Geist* essay to 'explain the nature of harmonic and contrapuntal prescriptions almost solely in terms of their psychological origins and impulses' (p. 324). Schenker's 1895 essay, then, builds on Hanslick's agenda, seeking to provide the genuine, psychological explanations at which Hanslick repeatedly hinted only to swerve away into metaphor or circumlocution. Yet in *Geist* the promise remains unfulfilled; in the next section I shall attempt to trace the critical steps that led away from the position taken up in the *Geist* essay and (as we know, though Schenker could not) towards the later theory. At this stage, though, it is worth noting that, if the first of Schenker's prin-

---

[56] In Hanslick 1986/1854: xv. Given Herbart's influence in Austria, and the fact that Zimmerman (whom Johnston describes as 'a faithful interpreter of Herbart' [1972: 286]) taught Schenker's introductory course in philosophy at the University of Vienna, there has been remarkably little exploitation of the Herbart/Zimmermann tradition as a putative influence on Schenker. Even a casual reading of Lee Rothfarb's currently unpublished paper 'Nineteenth-Century Fortunes of Musical Formalism' brings to light a rich crop of apparent anticipations, among them the active nature of listening, the autonomous nature of musical beauty and necessity of analysis in understanding it, and the distinction between form and formalism; Zimmermann speaks of 'the fundamental forms that please or displease' and, most strikingly, of dissonance 'feigning consonance'.

[57] Hanslick 1986/1854: 33.

[58] Hanslick 1986/1854: 47.

[59] Hanslick 1986/1854: 33.

cipal motivations was to do for music what the idealist philosophers had failed to do, then the second may have been to plug the gaping holes in Hanslick's aesthetics of music, and so transform it—as I said— from a brilliant but negative critique to a plan of action.

What does Schenker mean when he speaks of 'psychological' origins and impulses? Korsyn (1993: 113–5) reads this, and the other references to psychology that permeate Schenker's works, in relation to the kind of experimental psychology that Mach pioneered. But that jars with Schenker's suspicion, at least as early as *Harmonielehre,* of scientific approaches to music,[60] and it is useful to bear in mind Alexander Rehding's (2003: 89) description of late nineteenth-century psychology as 'an ill-defined discipline' which 'occupied a comfortable middle position between the natural and the human sciences' (and was at times claimed by both). Another answer to this question, then, might turn on what Schenker's 'psychology' is most determinedly unlike: the Viennese tradition of fundamental bass theory nowadays associated primarily with Simon Sechter, but represented within Schenker's experience by Bruckner's Conservatory classes in harmony (first year) and counterpoint (second year), during which Schenker famously reports the composer to have said, 'Look, gentlemen, this is the rule. Of course, I don't compose that way' (*H* 177n.). 'What marvellous snarls of contradictions', Schenker continues, 'one believes in rules that should be laughed at'.[61]

In this book I do not enter in any sustained way upon the relationship between Schenker and the music-theoretical tradition of his time. But it might be summarised by saying that he drew on ideas shared with contemporary or slightly earlier theorists, mainly from Austria or southern Germany, such as Josef Schalk, Rudolf Louis and Ludwig Thuille (who coauthored a once influential *Harmonielehre*), or August Halm—drew indeed a good deal more than either Schenker or his followers would readily admit—but that he brought them together

---

[60] In *Harmonielehre* Schenker says that the acoustician may be able to describe the overtone series 'exactly and without flaw', but that he 'gets onto slippery ground . . . as soon as he tries to apply this knowledge to an understanding of art and the practice of the artist' (*H* 21; it is clear from 'Der Tonsystem' [note 81 below] that he is talking about Helmholtz, concerning whom he makes a related point in *Kontrapunkt* 1 [*CI* 29]). Later formulations are more sweeping: in *Meisterwerk* 2 Schenker claims that 'too much physics, acoustics, and mathematics have forever been dragged into music by outsiders' [*MM2* 45]). And in *Meisterwerk* 3 and *Der freie Satz* he states that his theory is an art, never a science (*MM3* 8, *FC* I xxiii), though Rothstein (2001: 210) reads these remarks as a dig at Guido Adler.

[61] It is hard to read passages like the following, from the *Geist* essay, as anything other than an evocation of Bruckner's classes: 'I . . . hope to bring what are called the "disciplines of harmony and counterpoint" into a welcome proximity to free composition, that is, to the actual life of music. . . . students would not, as is usually the case nowadays, have to spend years contemplating material that seems irrelevant and unproductive' (p. 324).

in an improbable synthesis of flexibility, power of abstraction, and gift for creative metaphor (a gift perhaps more characteristic of composers than theorists).[62] All these theorists, including Schenker, can be seen as reacting against the dogmatism of a theoretical tradition based on a limited number of rigidly applied principles, such as the insistence on deriving all chord progressions from fifth relationships: time and again, as Robert Wason shows (1985), Sechter and Bruckner forced themselves either into a position of denial when faced with music that did not conform to a largely anachronistic theoretical mould, or into sometimes ludicrously convoluted explanations of apparently straightforward progressions, usually involving substitutions of 'intermediate fundamentals'. (Wason [43, 84] refers to Sechter's 'dogmatic and uncritical extension of "principles" with no empirical checks', and to Bruckner as personifying 'the critical state in which music theory in general found itself at the end of the nineteenth century'.) Under such conditions, the appeal to psychology can be read as an appeal to reality, as is evident from Louis and Thuille's statement in their *Harmonielehre* that 'the point of departure for harmony as we see it is the truest and most exhaustive analysis possible of what a musician of our time actually hears in chords and their connections—uninfluenced by any theoretical prejudices'.[63]

But perhaps the best guide to what Schenker meant by 'psychology' is provided by Hanslick, who at one point in *Vom Musikalisch-Schönen* sets out something much closer than Mach's experimental psychology to the kind of approach Schenker actually adopted throughout his theoretical writings—including those sections of *Harmonielehre* which contain the word 'psychology' in their titles:[64]

> Investigation of the nature of each separate musical element and its connection with a specific impression (just of the facts of the matter, not of the ultimate principles) and finally the reduction of these detailed observations to general laws: that would be the philosophical foundation of music for which so many authors are yearning.[65]

This follows a few lines after Hanslick's reference to the power of a melody being not an obscure miracle but 'rather the inevitable result of

---

[62] Robert Morgan (1978: 73) describes Schenker's theory as 'a remarkable synthesis of some of the main currents of Western musical thought'. Compare Halm's judgement from 1920, specifically referring to Schenker's theory of *Stufen:* 'that there are chords which are more or less important, deliberate, and incidental (I mean harmonically, not artistically incidental), [and] likewise that there are apparent and real, inauthentic, and genuine modulations; certainly, this was known before Schenker. In spite of that, I believe that he illuminates harmonic events more effectively with his ideas' (translated in Wason 1985: 187n.). In fairness to Sechter, it should be pointed out that he has been seen as paving the way for Schenker's approaches to *Stufen* and prolongation (Bernstein 2002: 791).

[63] Translated in Wason 1985: 118.

[64] I.e., pt. II, division I, secs. I ('On the psychology of contents and of step progression') and II ('On the psychology of chromatic alteration').

[65] Hanslick 1986/1854: 34.

musical factors which are at work in the melody'—a formulation strongly suggestive of what Blasius (1996: 13) calls the 'contrapuntal laboratory' through which, in the first volume of *Kontrapunkt* (which Schenker had trailed in *Harmonielehre* under the title 'Psychology of counterpoint' [*H* xxvi]), Schenker systematically analyses subjective effects into their objective correlates. As Schenker puts it,

> the beginning artist learns that tones, organized in such and such a way, produce one particular effect and none other, whether he wishes it or not. One can predict this effect: it *must* follow! Thus tones cannot produce any desired effect just because of the wish of the individual. . . . This knowledge is to be gained only in contrapuntal theory. (*C1* 14)

There is also a strong resonance here with the *Geist* essay, where Schenker spoke of counterpoint as 'an utterly unique, historically conditioned, and continually evolving method of training', which 'develops the ability to select, from the infinite multitude of developments that it envisions, precisely the one that best suits the artist's disposition at a particular time' (p. 322): in this way the formulation in *Kontrapunkt* 1 represents a development of the argument about the relationship between the subjective and the objective which Schenker had made in 1895, and which had its origins in Hanslick. And the idea that theory should identify musical effects and relate them to their objective correlates is one that permeates many aspects of Schenker's work: it applies not only to strict counterpoint but also to free composition (the Ninth Symphony monograph proceeds largely by stating the effect at which Beethoven was aiming and then showing how the music was contrived to create precisely that effect), and—as will become clear later in this book—it lies equally at the heart of Schenker's thinking about performance.

If this is psychology, then it is a psychology that resists reduction to mechanical processes in the manner of Helmholtz's highly influential psychology of tone perception—as is indeed suggested when Hanslick writes that 'our musicians have not "constructed" music but have simply established and consolidated that which the prevailing, musically competent Spirit has, with rationality but not with necessity, unselfconsciously devised'.[66] (Even the 'not with necessity' might be seen as chiming with Schenker's early scepticism concerning musical logic.) All this then suggests a reading of 'Der Geist der musikalischen Technik' —a straight rather than deconstructive reading, so to speak—as an attempt to show precisely what its title suggests: how a true theory of music will reintegrate the 'spirit' and 'technique' that conventional thinking, what Schenker came to call false theory, has severed.

---

[66] Hanslick 1986/1854: 71.

Rehabilitating Musical Logic

The *Geist* essay is philosophical in tone: it does not turn from generalities to musical specifics, in the manner of Schenker's later theoretical writings. Despite this, and the possibility of its being a fragment from a larger work, it anticipates Schenker's life's work to a striking degree—not in the sense that the future theory is itself somehow adumbrated in it (Schenker studies has suffered badly from that kind of teleological interpretation), but in that it identifies the terrain within which the later theory will operate, reveals the problems to which the later theory will present itself as the solution. It attacks traditional thinking about music for being unrelated to practice, artificial, linguistically rather than musically driven; it even targets Rameau's harmonic theory in this context, thereby anticipating Schenker's infinitely more polemical treatment of the topic in the 1930 essay 'Rameau or Beethoven?' (in which he writes—in italics—that *'after Rameau . . . theory and practice go their own separate ways!'* [*MM3* 4]). It draws a firm distinction between the subjectivity of the composer and the objectivity of the music as a self-organising structure, suggesting that the focus of theory must be the means by which musical effects are created, with perceived effects being explained by reference to their objective correlates: this means that music theory is in some sense a psychological enterprise. It also implies that these psychological factors are reflected in the historical development of music, and should equally be reflected in pedagogy, to which it ascribes a key cultural role. All these are abiding features of Schenker's thinking as it developed through the successive stages of his work. The *Geist* essay even contains an almost uncanny premonition of *Neue musikalische Theorien und Phantasien*—uncanny because this was eleven years before the publication of *Harmonielehre* and nearly forty before *Der freie Satz*. It follows on a passage I have already quoted and can be brought out by the simple device of italicisation (p. 324):

> Because I will explain the nature of harmonic and contrapuntal prescriptions almost solely in terms of their psychological origins and impulses, I also hope to bring what are called the 'disciplines of *harmony* and *counterpoint*' into a welcome proximity to *free composition, that is, to the actual life of music.*

To say all this, however, still leaves outstanding the issue of Schenker's supposed antiorganicism, which would seem to entirely undercut the project the *Geist* essay might otherwise be seen as setting out: there is, so to speak, a black hole where the theory ought to be, a denial that such a theory is even possible—because without organicism, without causality, there is nothing for the theory to be a theory *of*. (The conclusion for *Kontrapunkt* 2 which Schenker drafted in 1917 under the title 'Von der musikalischen Kausalität, Rückblick und Epilog' states that 'under causality one has to imagine a drive, a necessity, that legitimises the tone akin to a living, logically thinking being': this 'logical motor', as Schenker went on to describe it, which lies at the very heart of Schenkerian theory, is precisely what the *Geist* essay disallows.)[67] I find it hard to accept Korsyn's image of a fashionably deconstructive Schenker who subsequently turned into a born-again organicist, but I am equally unconvinced by Keiler's attempt to explain away Schenker's antiorganicism as in some way the product of his opposition to Hanslick's so-called formalism. On my reading, the *Geist* essay is caught in an impasse. Having made his demonstration that musical logic can have nothing to do with the superficial, language-dominated categories of conventional thinking about music, Schenker is quite unable to see a way round his own arguments against the possibility of natural principles operating within the human province of art, and yet the whole Hanslick-Schenker agenda I have outlined turns on the possibility of defining musical logic as something more than an illusion. When he says that 'music is denied for ever the kind of logic that is peculiar to the world of ideas' it might, of course, follow that music has some other kind of logic, which is precisely Hanslick's position ('Music has sense and logic—but musical sense and logic').[68] It is however exactly at this point that, in Karnes's words (2001: 132), 'Hanslick declines to elaborate further', and in the *Geist* essay Schenker hardly does better himself: other than plainly inadequate references to repetition and melisma, one looks in vain for any indication that Schenker had more than the vaguest inkling of what 'musical sense and logic' might mean.

The inkling to which I am referring is of course Schenker's suggestion that music might be organic 'only inasmuch as the composer has *not intended* it', ceasing to be so the instant that the composer directs his imagination towards it. As a composer, Schenker no doubt had the experience of the notes sometimes seeming to write themselves, just as novelists speak of their characters taking over. But as a composer, Schenker was equally aware of the need to shape inspiration through conscious design: his basic critical objection to Bruckner, whom he characterized in the 1893 review of *Psalm 150* as 'a greatly inspired composer who does not have an adequate routine' (*HSEK* 41), is that he was incapable of this and that his music consequently lacked coherence. So Schenker's claim that conscious design is incompatible with organicism represents, in Rytting's words (1996: 107), a 'bizarre argument'. And it is exactly the bizarre quality that reveals the unwillingness of Schenker's antiorganicism. Indeed to call it antiorganicism is a misnomer: organicist vocabulary is ubiquitous in his reviews of the 1890s, and this shows that, as a practical critic, Schenker was convinced of music's organic nature and the aesthetic values that go along

---

[67] OC 51/1378.
[68] Hanslick 1986/1854: 30.

with it. (I have already quoted his statement in the *Geist* essay that we use the term 'organic' of 'works to which we can listen without upsetting our own abilities, capacities, and enjoyment'.) Schenker's problem is not then with music's organic quality as such, but in seeing how it can be translated into terms of theory. In this sense, the impasse of the *Geist* essay is a specifically theoretical one.

Schenker's solution to his problem, as Pastille explains in the article that kicked off the debate over 'Der Geist der musikalischen Technik', was almost painfully simple when it came, although it surely required him to set common sense to one side: he ceased to see the idea of music composing itself independently of the composer's conscious volition as an anomaly, and instead viewed it as the definitive attribute of the musical masterwork, the work of genius. (It is from this point that Schenker's theory becomes, properly speaking, a theory of musical genius.) There is an essay from 1896, just a year after 'Der Geist der musikalischen Technik', in which Schenker expresses the idea of the music composing itself, but with the crucial difference that he is not talking about 'art' music: 'Is not folksong', Schenker asks, 'the place where one, so to speak, hears the nature of music itself, where the order of the tones wished itself so and no other way without the reason of an individual commanding over it? Whoever invented the folksong . . . did not know in advance whether inspiration would come to him, it was there and everything came by itself and could not come in any other way' (*HSEK* 342). Even so, it is suggestive that Schenker adds: 'in the original geniuses alone does that event of nature return in the artistic creation that is also audible in folksong' (*HSEK* 345). But the best known expression of the idea, and the one Pastille cites, concerns Beethoven, and it comes from the discussion in *Harmonielehre* (1906) of the church modes, for Schenker a prime example of the false theory from which music has long suffered.

In a section headed 'The independence of great talent from the deficiencies of such theories', Schenker asks how Beethoven could have composed the 'Dankgesang' from his Quartet op. 132 in the Lydian mode when no such mode, in fact, exists, and gives his answer in one of his most memorable passages (*H* 60–1):

> A great talent or a man of genius, like a sleepwalker, often finds the right way, even when his instinct is thwarted by one thing or another or . . . by the full and conscious intention to follow the wrong direction. The superior force of truth—of Nature, as it were—is at work mysteriously behind his consciousness, guiding his pen, without caring in the least whether the happy artist himself wanted to do the right thing or not. If he had his way in following his conscious intentions, the result, alas! would often be a miserable composition. But, fortunately, that mysterious power arranges everything for the best. . . . [Beethoven] had no idea that behind his back there stood that higher force of Nature and led his pen, forcing his composition into F major while he himself was sure he was composing in the

Lydian mode, merely because that was his conscious will and intention. Is that not marvellous? And yet it is so.

The structure of this passage ([i] the artist intended to do wrong, yet [ii] everything was settled for the best: [iii] is that not wonderful?) is so close to the corresponding passage from the *Geist* essay (p. 329) as to suggest a conscious or unconscious rewriting. And if the example of Beethoven composing in the Lydian mode could still be seen as the exception that proves the rule, then by the time of volume 1 of *Kontrapunkt* (1910) the self-organisation of the tones—or as it might be expressed in more Hegelian language, music's self-realisation—has become the norm; genius consists in an understanding of this self-realisation, such that the master composers fully intended what they wrote without forcing their music into theoretical formulae, in the manner of the 'formalists'. Again I shall quote at length, to show how ideas abumbrated in the mid-1890s are developed fifteen years later:

> The artist learns to humble himself before the absolute character of tonal life. . . . He comes to know the effects that the tones must produce under one set of circumstances or another, and . . . he can only choose or not choose a given effect. . . . For the tones are always independent of the composer's mood, and are able to produce their effects only in keeping with the preconditions attendant on them in the individual case. . . . In the best of cases—and this applies precisely to geniuses, and only to them—intention (that is prediction of effect) and effect correspond perfectly; but in the great majority of cases the tones, acting entirely on their own and, so to speak, behind the back of the composer, produce an effect completely different from that intended. (*C1* 14–5)

Similar statements may be found in the op. 110 *Erläuterungsausgabe* (1914) and *Meisterwerk* 2 (1926);[69] indeed Schenker's later writings are littered with casual references to this idea, such as the reference in the first issue of *Tonwille* to the composer as 'a veritably passive tool of Urlinien' (*T1* 23).

To present this as a straightforward solution to Schenker's problem, as Pastille does, is however in important ways to oversimplify it. For one thing, it is a consequence of this solution that an impermeable line is drawn between the genius and the mere talent, with the former falling within and the latter outside the purview of Schenker's theory, and Pastille says this—but it might also be said that this is the source of the exclusive and circular quality that so many have found alienating in Schenker's thought (circular because if it is genius that defines the purview of the theory, then equally it is the theory that defines genius).

---

[69] For references and discussion see Snarrenberg 1997: 84–5. There is also an ironic reference in the fifth issue of *Tonwille* to the possibility of contemporary composers writing 'in such a way that the diatonic Urlinie appears of its own accord, behind their backs, as it were' (*T1* 212).

And the leap of faith—the denial of common sense—in the invocation of 'Nature' (or, as Schenker elsewhere has it, 'Music')[70] as a metaphysical agent helps to explain the extent to which, in Schenker's later years and after his death, the Schenkerian community took on the quality of a closed circle of believers; not everyone, like the White Queen, is willing to believe six impossible things before breakfast. Even Schenker may have had doubts about his solution. Whereas the sequence of quotations I have just presented might suggest that he simply changed his mind (at first he thought of music composing itself behind the composer's back, but later as fully intended by the genius), Robert Snarrenberg (1997: 85) demonstrates that Schenker continued to be ambivalent about how far the great composers were aware of the principles according to which they operated. Snarrenberg—who writes penetratingly about Schenker's use of the terms 'as if' and 'as it were' (*gleichsam*) to denote shifts in register—also locates a point of slippage in Schenker's hesitant invocation in *Harmonielehre* of 'Nature, as it were': after all, elsewhere in *Harmonielehre* Schenker claims with confidence that the overtone series constitutes 'Nature's only source for music to draw on' (*H* 20), while in later writings Nature is sometimes replaced by God. (In *Tonwille*, as I mentioned, Schenker cited Haydn's claim that God, not he, wrote *The Creation*, while in *Der freie Satz* Schenker linked the *Ursatz* to 'God and . . . the geniuses through whom he works' [*FC* I 160].) Besides, such grandiose assertions are hard to reconcile with Schenker's continuing insistence on the essentially psychological nature of his enterprise. Schenker's claims about the ultimate agency of music, then, do not just defy common sense: they are vague and contradictory, or perhaps we should see them as simply rhetorical and figurative. This last option, of course, leaves the epistemological issue unresolved.

Yet the invocation of God is helpful in this context, for it enables us to clarify the role in Schenker's solution to his problem of the idea embodied in the pseudo-Mozart letter: that the composition stands before the composer's mind, its temporal extension surveyable at a glance. In a study subtitled 'An Essay in Spurious Aesthetics', Peter Kivy argues that there is no need to look for a specifically musical source for Rochlitz's compelling image of musical creation, for a readily available philosophical source lay at hand: the venerable theological chestnut, which goes back to Boethius and Aquinas, 'how does God, who is eternal and unchanging, conceive of the course of history?' (Kivy 1993: 195) Kivy's claim is that the traditional answer to this question, in Boethius's formulation that 'just as you can see things in this your temporal present, so God sees all things in His eternal present' (196), has simply been transferred from divine to artistic creation. And while Kivy gives the impression that there were no immediate antecedents for Rochlitz's

---

[70] E.g. *H* 69.

image, the idea that music, though time-bound, gives access to the eternal may also be found in Jean Paul, while Goethe says in his description of the daemonic—a concept closely associated with creative genius—that 'it pulled time together and expanded space'.[71]

There were in this way multiple sources for the idea of perceiving an entire composition at a single glance that is built deep into Schenker's later theory, as for example when, in the 'Elucidations' I previously referred to, Schenker draws an absolute distinction between the geniuses who 'create from the background of tonal space' and the nongeniuses who 'compose entirely in terms of the succession of surface events' (*MM1* 113). ('Italian musicians', Schenker remarks in *Der freie Satz*, 'lost themselves in extemporaneous diminutions which remained nonorganic and unrelated to each other' [*FC* I 97].) Nevertheless, it was the pseudo-Mozart letter on which Schenker laid the greatest stress, prominently exhibiting it in *Der freie Satz* without raising the issue of its authenticity (*FC* I 129)—and it becomes clear from another of Schenker's late writings, an article published in the January 1931 issue of *Deutsche Zeitschrift* under the title 'Ein verschollener Brief von Mozart und das Geheimnis seines Schaffens' (A lost letter of Mozart and the secret of his creation), that this was not because Schenker was unaware of that issue. On the contrary, he claims that the rejection of the letter's authenticity mirrors the misunderstanding of Mozart in his own lifetime. He marshals quotations from Goethe to support its ideas on the one hand while on the other he stresses the link between its vision of compositional creation and his own theories: 'Mozart raises himself to a height beyond the worldly from which he sends us a solemn message from the realm of wonders of the background', Schenker says (1931: 669). And he continues: 'it is a joy to see how he was able to lend this wonder not only tones but also words: miraculous that he composed in this way, miraculous that he could speak of it!' In short, Schenker (669–70) concludes, the letter *must* be authentic because what it says is true:

> For too long the immaturity of musical insight has tried its hand in vain on the greatness of this letter of Mozart: now it is urgently recommended for inclusion to all biographers and editors of letters: its time has finally come! All doubts as to the authenticity of the letter must give way to the certainty that this divine message is neither forged nor revised, that it can stem from no other than Mozart himself!

We have seen how Hanslick paraphrased pseudo-Mozart in *Vom Musikalisch-Schönen*, and the idea of the composer surveying music at a glance features in the *Geist* essay, where Schenker writes, 'now it can

---

[71] See the references to Jean Paul's *Die unsichtbare Loge* (1793) and *Hesperus* (1795), and to the final part of Goethe's *Aus meinem Leben: Dichtung und Wahrheit* (published 1833 but written between 1821 and 1831), in Franke 2005: 39–40.

happen that the imagination of the composer (and also the imagination of an extraordinary listener) surveys the entire content, despite its consecutive nature, from a bird's-eye view, so to speak' (p. 328). Schenker had developed this idea of the bird's-eye view through the image of seeing a landscape in his 1894 essay 'Das Hören in der Musik', but the creative dimension is stated more explicitly in the essay on d'Albert from the same year, from which I have already quoted:

> In the literature of music there are works that came about in such a way that within the endless chaos of fantasy, the lightning flash of a thought suddenly struck down, at once illuminating and creating the entire work in the most dazzling light. Such works were conceived and received in one stroke, and the whole fate of their creation, life, growth and end already designated in their first seed.[72]

Such ideas were widespread in the 1890s, and indeed this conception of inspiration had been a commonplace of German aesthetic thought since the eighteenth century: as Karnes explains (2001: chap. 4), it was complemented by the idea of reflection, and the relationship between these is a recurrent concern of Schenker's writings from the 1890s (including, as we have seen, the essay on d'Albert and the review of Bruckner's *Psalm 150*). Like the idea of music composing itself, however, the image of 'the lightning flash of a thought' was not in itself the solution to Schenker's problem: the way out of the impasse lay in the association between these ideas and causality.

One of the striking features of Schenker's theoretical writing is his insistence on the application to aesthetics of a strict principle of causality, and this is worth setting briefly into context. There was in the second half of the nineteenth century a widespread reaction against the application to the human sciences of modes of explanation developed in the context of the physical sciences: Wilhelm Dilthey's philosophical hermeneutics (set out in his *Introduction to the Human Sciences*, first published in 1883 but elaborated over the following two decades) suggested that it was more appropriate in the human sciences to aim at understanding than at certainty, at elucidation rather than explanation. 'Elucidation' (*Erläuterung*) became one of Schenker's most characteristic terms (his first use of it seems to date from 1909 [Bent 2005: 88]), and Ian Bent has explored the parallels between Schenkerian analysis and the shuttling back and forth that typifies hermeneutical enquiry. But as Bent says (1994: 13), Schenker's use of hermeneutical principles is presentational: the analytical argument may oscillate between part and whole, converging on the final interpretation, but Schenker has decided on his interpretation before the hermeneutical process begins. He aims at certainty, rather than countenancing the possibility of alternative explanations, and at explanation in the sense

---

[72] *HSEK* 117, translated in Keiler 1989: 287.

of deriving effects from causes; hence the rhetorical question he asks in *Harmonielehre*, 'is it not true that a system must be strong enough to explain, without exception, all phenomena within its range?' (*H* 76). Despite his suspicion of scientific approaches to music, then, his epistemology is to this extent scientific rather than hermeneutical, which of course fits with his language of discovering, not creating or inventing, musical principles—and here there is an obvious contrast with Schoenberg, who in his *Harmonielehre* of 1911 wrote (with a perhaps fortuitous echo of the passage from Hanslick I quoted earlier) that music theory should be seen as a 'system of presentation—a system . . . whose clarity is simply clarity of presentation, a system that does not pretend to clarify the ultimate nature of the things presented'.[73] More on this in chapter 5.

It is Schenker's insistence on the strict matching of cause and effect, on demonstrating why things are—even must be—as they are and not otherwise, that is responsible for the impasse in the *Geist* essay: as we have seen, the root of his problem is that, despite contrary appearances, music 'lacks any principle of causation'. Korsyn (1988: 50), in his extended analysis of Schenker's concept of causation, quotes Schopenhauer's pithy statement of the problem of causality in music: 'the succession of sounds in a piece of music is determined objectively, not subjectively by me the listener; but who will say that the musical notes follow one another according to the law of cause and effect?' Or to put it another way, the problem is how, if you work from one note to the next, you can distinguish *post hoc* from *propter hoc* (without, that is, falling back into the narrowly prescribed formulae of Sechter's or Bruckner's theories). And this is where the idea of works being conceived in 'the lightning flash of a thought', in which time turns to space, comes in. Until around 1920, Schenker assumed, like everyone else, that musical causality must work through time, from earlier to later, as is vividly conveyed by a passage from *Kontrapunkt* 1: 'harmonies appear to be linked more intimately and with seemingly greater necessity the more drastically and obtrusively a tone of one harmony hooks into the flesh of the following one' (*C1* 291). Though this passage goes on to claim that 'Through these very necessities of a completely individual nature, music acquires "logic" no less than language or the other arts!', Schenker's conviction is unconvincing: no solution to the *post hoc/propter hoc* problem is in prospect. His solution—what I see as the fundamental insight of his theory and the key conceptual leap in its development—was to turn musical causality through ninety degrees, so to speak, so that cause-effect relations flow not from one note to the next but rather from the background to the foreground. In this way, a third dimension, a dimension of depth, is added to what Schenker himself referred to in *Kontrapunkt* 2 (*C2* 28) as 'causality in the horizontal

---

[73] Schoenberg 1978/1911: 11; I have discussed this at greater length in Cook 2002. The passage from Hanslick is at p. 61 above.

dimension' (by which he meant the linear) and 'causality in the vertical dimension' (the harmonic). As I shall argue in chapter 5, Schenker also saw this third dimension in terms of cause and effect, but he seems to have associated the word 'causality' with only the first two dimensions; the result is that it becomes less common in his writing. But it is useful to be able to refer to causality in the dimension of depth, and so I shall call it 'axial causality', borrowing the term from Schenker's later distinction between 'the axial cohesion that extends from background to foreground' and 'the lateral cohesion that functions horizontally at foreground level' (*MM3* 7).

Of course this terminology of background and foreground references Schenker's later theory, and commentators such as Pastille and Korsyn have charted the successive stages through which Schenker developed this idea of axial causality into its final form. The most explicit depiction of it does not appear until *Der freie Satz*, where Schenker writes: 'The phenomenon of form in the foreground can be described in an almost physical-mechanical sense as an energy transformation of the forces which flow from the background to the foreground through the structural levels' (*FC* I 162). But it is strongly suggested in a remark from the 'Vermischtes' (Miscellanea) section of *Tonwille* 5, where Schenker provides an informal commentary on one of the pieces analysed elsewhere in that issue, the fifth of Bach's Twelve Little Preludes—an analysis notable for the first of its two graphs, an early but well-developed example of the separation of the music into successive layers of elaboration. In the 'Vermischtes' commentary, Schenker briefly discusses each of the six layers in turn, and then concludes that 'the Urlinie, far beyond everything purely concerned with voice-leading . . . bears witness to tonality, becomes one with it, and constructs synthesis and form! . . . Only the feeling for the Urlinie . . . provided the logic for the prolongational transformations' (*T1* 213). The point is that the transformations take place between one level and the other: like prolongation itself, they work axially rather than laterally. And this axial conception is built into the format of the analytical commentary tried out for the first time in this 'Vermischtes' section, which became Schenker's standard mode of presentation from the last issue of *Tonwille* on—as illustrated in miniature by his *Kaiserhymne* analysis from that issue (more on this later), and in a more developed form by that of the Largo from Bach's third solo violin sonata in *Meisterwerk* 1. In all of these the commentary proceeds not bar by bar or section by section, as in the case of Schenker's previous analyses—not laterally, that is to say—but rather by successive layers starting from the background. It is organised on the basis of axial causality.

There are several important aspects of Schenker's later theory that arise out of the conjunction of the idea of axial causality with the 'lightning flash of a thought'. For one thing, the image of music existing in an 'eternal present', in which time is collapsed, makes it easier to imagine the rotation of musical causality to which I have referred. (There is an obvious comparison with the 'TWO-OR-MORE-DIMENSIONAL SPACE' that underlay Schoenberg's [1975: 220] conception of serialism.) The same image underwrites Schenker's claim of the privileged compositional viewpoint represented by his method of analysis, as when he refers in *Tonwille* to 'this graph, probably the most basic formulation of the creative fantasy, which in contrast to the Urlinie represents a sort of first elaboration', or claims in *Meisterwerk* 3 that his method reveals 'masterworks at the very moment of their conception' (*T1* 27, *MM3* 75). And this links with the conception of the genius as the new, and true, focus of a theory concerned—at last—with purely musical logic. But hardly less important is the final point: the invocation of a causality that is independent of the composer's conscious knowledge, however ambivalent Schenker may at times have been over this, enables the analyst to evade both the limited, pedagogical rules of the Sechter-Bruckner type and the objection, as Schenker puts it in *Der freie Satz*, 'But did the masters also know about all this?'.[74] It is in effect a license for analytical autonomy, a music-theoretical equivalent of Freud's delineation of the unconscious mind. It could also, of course, be seen as a decisive step in the depersonalisation of analysis, what Richard Taruskin (1995: 24) has called 'turning ideas into objects, and putting objects in place of people'—which, he adds, is 'the essential modernist fallacy'.

So where did Schenker find the idea of genius that plays so foundational a role his later theory? Some writers have made a connection between Schenker's description of the 'man of genius' as a 'sleepwalker' in the quotation from *Harmonielehre* and Jean Paul's statement that the genius is 'in more than one sense a sleepwalker' (Snarrenberg 1997: 85; Solie 1980: 155). Others have connected it with Schopenhauer's famous statement, which Schenker quotes in volume 2 of *Kontrapunkt*, that 'the composer reveals the innermost essence of the world and expresses the most profound wisdom in a language which his rational faculty does not understand' (*C2* 15; Schopenhauer goes on to draw an analogy with a 'magnetic somnambulist'). Equally one might cite Goethe's description of the artist 'as the tool of a higher world order, as a vessel found to be worthy of receiving divine influence', or closer to home Sechter's aphorism of 1852 that 'God is also the Creator of that which man has been able to produce, for everything comes from him. Oh artist, you have not bestowed your most beautiful ideas upon yourself, for they come from Him'.[75] But the idea of the genius as someone through whom a higher force speaks had been a commonplace of German-language culture since the eighteenth century and re-

[74] *FC* I xxii. The frequency with which this question appears in Schenker's work perhaps reveals a lack of confidence in the answer: see also *T1* 23 and 166, and *MM1* 10.

[75] Goethe as recorded in Johann Eckermann's *Gespräche mit Goethe in den letzten Jahren seines Lebens*, translated in Franke 2005: 73; Sechter translated in Wason 1985: 62.

mained so at the *fin de siècle* (Schoenberg, for instance, cites it in his *Harmonielehre* [1978/1911: 416]), which means that—as with the 'lightning flash of a thought'—simply to ask where Schenker found the idea is to ask the wrong question. One needs instead to ask what gave Schenker the idea of associating genius with causality.

And once the question is asked in this way, the answer is clear. Kant—for whom, as for other eighteenth-century writers, genius referred to a faculty rather than an individual—proposed the idea of genius functioning as Nature's agent precisely as a solution to the problem of how art, as an embodiment of human freedom, might at the same time reflect natural laws: '*Genius*', he wrote in his *Critique of Judgement*, 'is the talent . . . that gives the rule to art. . . . *Genius* is the innate mental predisposition (*ingenium*) *through which* nature gives the rule to art'.[76] At first sight, this might not seem to say much more than Schenker's 1896 statement about folksong, which I have already quoted, that 'In the original geniuses alone does that event of nature return in the artistic creation'. But what is missing there is the idea of causality as Kant had developed it. Kant, in short, is saying that Nature is the source of all artistic causality, which is how it comes about that even the composer of genius may have no conscious understanding of the principles governing artistic creation.[77] By 1921, Schenker knew this passage, for he quoted it, framed by extracts from Goethe and Lessing, in the preface of the op. 101 *Erläuterungsausgabe;* later in the same work, in the section on the fourth movement, he refers to the 'genius to whom is confided the connection between cause and effect in the life of tones'.[78] But the very fact that Kant's idea solves the problem of musical organicism so neatly makes it impossible to imagine that Schenker was acquainted with it in 1895: 'Otherwise', as Rytting says (1996: 117), 'it is difficult to imagine why Schenker would agonize over the issue when Kant had solved it in a way that Schenker would find so congenial for most of his career'. It is then conceivable that it was simply his discovery of this passage around the time of the op. 101 *Erläuterungsausgabe* that enabled Schenker ultimately to link the ideas of genius, the lightning flash of creation, and causality, and in this way square his theoretical circle. Equally it is possible that Schenker discovered the passage from Kant as early as 1896—hence the apparent echo

[76] Quoted from Kant's *Critique of Judgement*, trans. J. H. Bernard, 2nd ed. (London: Macmillan, 1914), p. 174, in Rytting 1986: 116. For the context of such thinking, including parallels from E. T. A. Hoffmann, Shaftesbury, and Goethe, see Watkins 2004: 195.

[77] Kant writes: 'the progenitor of a product for which he has his genius to thank, does not himself know how the ideas for it came to him, nor does it lie within his power to calculate them methodically or at will' (translated from *Kritik der Urteilskraft* in Franke 2005: 83).

[78] Schenker 1972/1921: 10, 68, translated in Goldman 1990: 135. Jonas's edition omits Schenker's next remark: 'Too bad that politicians, leaders of peoples, and directors of states do not also attend the school of genius!'

in his remarks on folksong—but that it took him over twenty years to fully work out its implications for musical causality.

At all events, Schenker's theory from the op. 101 *Erläuterungsausgabe* on represents the ultimate solution of the *Geist* essay's problem over organicism. Nevertheless it is clear that Schenker believed not only in musical organicism but also in the possibility of its theoretical explanation long before that. Is it then feasible to work backwards from 1921 so as to identify the point when Schenker came to believe in the possibility of theorising musical organicism? And where might we look for it? There is a sense in which the sustained thrust of Schenker's analytical work from the op. 101 *Erläuterungsausgabe* right up to *Der freie Satz* seems curiously unprepared for by the publications of the two preceding decades: while individual theoretical components developed in *Harmonielehre* or *Kontrapunkt* feed crucially into the later theory, there is not the same emphasis on structural organisation at the level of the individual composition, nor the same concern with combating conventional formal approaches that is found in the *Geist* essay and other writings of the 1890s. There is however a missing link in the unpublished— because unfinished—text *Über den Niedergang der Kompositionskunst,* which survives as a typescript in the Oster Collection: at one time it was thought to date from the period of the First World War (Kosovsky 1999: 8), but is now known to date back to as early as 1905, that is to say from the time when *Harmonielehre* (for which Schenker had intended it first as an afterword and then as a supplement) was in production (Drabkin 2005). As indicated by the title, the central topic of *Niedergang* is the musical decline Schenker traces from Berlioz to Liszt, Wagner, and Richard Strauss, and the narrative of which occupies the second half of the text. This narrative of decline remained a permanent element of Schenker's thinking (in the third sentence of *Der freie Satz* he pins the blame on 'the generation which lived during the third decade of the nineteenth century' [*FC* I xxi]), and its presentation in *Niedergang* turns on the contrast he draws with the music of Haydn, Mozart, and Beethoven, and more specifically with the principle of 'cyclic form' (Schenker's term for sonata form in *Niedergang* and other contemporary writings) as practised by these composers, the explanation of which takes up most of the first half—and the misunderstanding of which, Schenker claims, is 'principally responsible for the decline of the art of music in the nineteenth century' (*DAC* 43).

Schenker's central argument concerning cyclic form continues from where his attacks on the formalists of the 1890s left off (the link becomes most obvious when he refers to programmatic composers 'forcing a foreign logic on the work at the expense of musical logic' [*DAC* 72]).[79] His aim is to develop specific theoretical or analytical cri-

---

[79] More immediately, it might be seen as expanding secs. 130 and 132 of *Harmonielehre* (*H* 245, 249–50).

teria to distinguish formulaic models of sonata form from the real thing: form, says Schenker, 'can never be regarded as a schematic plan so long as it is possible to infuse with spirit a process that is basically more mechanical' (*DAC* 48). The resonance with 'Der Geist der musikalischen Technik'—and indeed with Hanslick—is self-evident, but there is also an anticipation of the later theory in the basic idea of explaining the obvious in terms of the nonobvious: the contrast between Mozart and Berlioz, for example, is drawn in terms of 'depth' versus 'surface', 'truth' versus 'appearance' (*DAC* 76). It would be tempting, too, to detect the glimmerings of Schenker's later hierarchical conception in the statement that, in the lesser masters of the nineteenth century (Schubert, Schumann, Chopin), 'there existed only a lyrical enthusiasm in the foreground of their selves, so to speak', or in Schenker's claim in the course of an extensive analysis of *Don Giovanni* that 'above all this irrationality hovers the spirit of unity in which the individual parts are resolved' (*DAC* 66, 89). At the heart of this terminological network, however, is the idea of 'synthesis' (at one point expressed as 'organic synthesis'). This is not a new term in Schenker's vocabulary: in 1901, for example, he wrote in a letter to Röntgen that music should embody 'above all, synthesis!—which must have spirit in every nook and cranny, and the less conspicuous [it is], the more beautiful; if obtrusive, then all the more contrived', while an article from 1896 speaks of synthesis as the balancing of detail and whole, and deplores its absence in modern music.[80] But it is hard to discern a clear theoretical impulse behind these essentially conventional expressions of critical approbation. The theoretical impulse is by contrast obvious in a passage like the following from *Niedergang:* 'in synthesis is contained the basic condition of art. . . . it makes *musical legislation* possible in the first place. Just as in the past, in the most learned form of fugue, musical laws were discovered, determined, and incontrovertibly demonstrated, so, too, the synthesis of the freer forms . . . leads to new musical laws' (*DAC* 52–3).

That statement sounds like a concise summary of the transition from *Kontrapunkt* to *Der freie Satz,* and the use of the term 'synthesis' (which Schenker glosses at its first mention in *Niedergang* as 'the connectedness of form' [*DAC* 52]) is in line with its ubiquitous use in his later writings. It is impossible to read *Niedergang* without sensing Schenker's conviction not only that music of the masterwork tradition is organic, but also that this organicism is capable of expression in theoretical terms. Yet it cannot be said that *Niedergang* actually achieves this. The central idea of 'synthesis' is nowhere clearly defined or explained: instead it is repeated obsessively, as if it were some kind of spell (from its first appearance the word appears ten times in eight sen-

---

[80] Letter of 13 April 1901 (NMI C 176–01), translated by Kevin Karnes, Schenker Correspondence Project website; 'Siegfried Wagner', in *HSEK* 181–5.

tences). In the *Geist* essay I spoke of there being a black hole where the theory should be: in *Niedergang* the outline of the theory is in place, but its core concept is a black box, or better it is a piece of dummy code that marks where a function should be. It promises but does not deliver on the fully operational concept of synthesis that Schenker later built on the principles of axial causality and prolongation. (There is a telling comparison with a paragraph from 'Noch ein Wort zur Urlinie' [Yet another word on the Urlinie], in the second issue of *Tonwille*, where Schenker uses the word 'synthesis' five times in as many lines, but here it has the theoretical support it previously lacked: 'the Urlinie leads directly to synthesis of the whole. It is synthesis' [*TI* 54].) If, as William Drabkin says (2005: 16), *Niedergang* 'comes unstuck in . . . the section on classical sonata form', then this was a problem that Schenker was not in a position to solve for many years, and it is hardly necessary to search further for an explanation of why he did not bring *Niedergang* to completion. While several ideas were transplanted from it into other publications (mainly *Tonwille*), and *Niedergang*'s narrative of decline forms an essential backdrop to the polemics against Wagner in the Ninth Symphony monograph, in some ways the real successor to—or final version of—*Niedergang* is *Der freie Satz*.

The first appearance of *Niedergang* in Schenker's correspondence is in the cover letter he enclosed with the manuscript of *Harmonielehre* when he sent it to the Stuttgart-based firm of Cotta, the eventual publishers: in this letter, dated 22 November 1905, he said that the manuscript was complete except for the 'afterword', on which he was still working, and that this was 'approximately the length of a printed gathering'—which equates to about seventeen and a half typewritten pages (Drabkin 2005: 6–7). In a letter dated 29 May 1906, however, Schenker talks about the afterword taking up 'between five and seven gatherings' and forming part of a second volume of *Harmonielehre:* as Drabkin explains, this corresponds closely to the length of the Oster Collection typescript. While work on *Niedergang* evidently continued well after this date—in a letter to Hertzka dated 8 January 1909 Schenker says that it 'is taking all my energy' (11)—it is then reasonable to suppose that the typescript dates from 1906 and that the subsequent work is represented by the handwritten annotations it contains. So should we place these first glimmerings of Schenker's ultimate theory of musical organicism in the years 1905–6? The narrative of decline in the *Niedergang* typescript is fluently written, but the section dealing with cyclic form is a mass of manuscript reworkings: as Drabkin puts it (16), 'the text begins to break down altogether'. It is tempting to imagine Schenker struggling as he wrote it out to develop for the first time some of the guiding ideas of the later theory. But according to Drabkin (16), 'none of these corrections or annotations . . . alters the sense of what Schenker is attempting to convey: at most they record changes of emphasis, the reordering of arguments, and references to writings and scores'. There is, then, the possibility that these ideas go back before 1905. But at this point the trail runs cold: the one other substantial piece of unpublished writing that may date from the period before *Harmonielehre*, also in the Oster Collection and referred to in Kosovsky's catalogue as 'Das Tonsystem', does not bear on issues of cyclic form, synthesis, or musical logic.[81] So we have to jump back to the published writings of the 1890s, and the point I wish now to establish is that when they are read in sequence, a distinct change of tone and vocabulary can be detected in them—a change that suggests a new confidence in the idea of musical logic and the possibility of theorising it.

One problem with studies of Schenker's writings from the 1890s is that there is a tendency to mix and match essays and criticisms of different dates, as if they were uniformly representative of 'early Schenker'; Keiler (1996: 181), for instance, launches into an elaborate argument concerning the different senses in which Schenker used the word 'organic' in order to explain the contradictions between the *Geist* essay and the *Die Zukunft* Brahms obituary, where a simpler explanation might be that Schenker changed his mind between 1895 and 1897. In a nutshell, as I said, organicist terminology is found throughout the essays of the 1890s, but it is only in the later part of the decade that Schenker seems to think of organicism as being both real (rather than illusory) and a property of the music itself. In the essay of 1892 on Brahms's *Fünf Gesänge für gemischten Chor a cappella,* op. 104, for example, Schenker speaks of the way Brahms 'colours the organicism of moods and thoughts . . . by logical means', but goes on to refer to 'the freedom with which the poetic idea created its own musical form, appropriate only to itself' (*HSEK* 18, 21): here it is the poetic idea which gives rise to musical form. In 1896, by contrast, Schenker says of Beethoven's Sonata op. 90 that the 'poetic event', with its own 'poetic reason', works 'music-organically', indeed as a 'musical cause': four years later,

---

[81] This document, which is untitled and carries no indication of date, exists in two forms: a handwritten text (OC 31/360–86), which contains many revisions, and a fifty-nine-page typewritten copy (OC 31/387–417). Both texts stop in the middle of a sentence—just as Schenker is starting to tell a story about Brahms—but in the first text this is at the end of a page, suggesting that the subsequent page or pages of the handwritten text had been lost by the time the copy was made. In essence 'Das Tonsystem' covers the same ground as the first subsection ('The natural tonal system [major]') of *Harmonielehre:* it covers the dual origins of music in nature and artifice, the separate derivation through inversion of the subdominant, the principle of abbreviation, the parallel between tonal and social relationships, and the limitations of acoustical approaches to music (here, unlike in *Harmonielehre,* Helmholtz is specifically named). It also includes a few elements from elsewhere in *Harmonielehre* (the idea that within certain limits—transgressed by Wagner—dissonance strengthens tonality, Nature using the artist as medium, Bruckner's distinction between the rules and how he composes). It does however suggest a reason for the artistic abbreviation of the overtone series that is not found in *Harmonielehre:* our mortal condition forces us to perceive in a limited manner what Nature unfolds over eternity, as a result of which 'nothing makes us more uneasy than not

then, Schenker sees the organic as inherent in the music. Again, whereas in the *Geist* essay Schenker had written that 'a contrived melody never has a determination so resolute that it can say, "Only that particular melody, and none other, may follow me"', in 1896—just a year later—he writes that the characteristic of the 'true artwork' is that the composer 'had to write precisely this and could not write it any other way' (*HSEK* 333). That might perhaps be interpreted as a comment about the creative process rather than the music itself, but this is clearly not the case of Schenker's description from the same year—which I have already quoted—of the folksong as the place 'where the order of the tones wished itself so and no other way . . . everything came by itself and could not come in any other way'. And in yet another essay of the same year Schenker writes that in a good composition 'the first strength of the beginning only completely exhausts itself at the end', continuing 'this particular, deeply internal drive of the thoughts—in a figurative sense one could grasp it with the Hegelian term as their self-movement [*Selbstbewegung*]—is named in the conventional sense with the playful word "form". . . . Thoughts without such a drive, that is without "form", can never retain their vitality' (*HSEK* 202–3). It may or may not be significant that the new confidence to which I have referred is here coupled not only with the idea of the psychological underpinning of form which Schenker would develop in *Niedergang* but also with a borrowing from Hegel.

It is however in terms of musical 'logic' that the development is clearest. As we have seen, Schenker specifically denies the existence of such logic in 'Die Musik von heute' (1894) and the *Geist* essay (1895); even when discussing the music of Bruckner, which conservative critics routinely condemned for its illogicality, Schenker seems to fight shy of the word, instead adopting circumlocutions like 'strange thought-grammar'.[82] By contrast, when in the *Die Zukunft* Brahms obituary of 1897 Schenker develops the reference in 'Die Musik von heute' to 'brooding warmth' into a riot of temperature terms (as well as introducing what would nowadays be considered a distinctly suspect image),[83] his purpose is precisely to distinguish between false and true logic in music:

---

knowing the origin' (typescript, p. 39), and it is to facilitate this that we reject overtones beyond the fifth. One could imagine this being a parallel document to *Harmonielehre*, addressed to a different audience, but on the basis of the handwriting, Drabkin (personal communication, 12 October 2005) favours an earlier date—which would fit with Jeanette's identification of it as one of Schenker's earliest theoretical formulations, on the basis of which Kosovsky (1999: 7–8) suggests that it belongs to the end of the nineteenth century.

[82] From Schenker's 1896 review of Bruckner's Eighth Symphony (*HSEK* 201).

[83] Schenker 1991/1897: 2. Hilde Spiel (1987: 79) refers to 'the leaning towards young and hairless adolescent females indulged in by some of the artists and writers at that time'; she quotes Adolf Loos's statement that 'one thirsted for immaturity', and adds that Loos 'was at one time accused in court of paedophilia and barely escaped conviction'.

In the same way that oratory and literature possess both dull statements which have been frozen stiff by the icy wind of abstraction (that is, which refer primarily to abstract concepts instead of concrete visual or aural experiences) and vibrant statements which radiate the vital warmth of life . . . music has both abstract statements and melodic statements. Of course, logic is intrinsic to both types of musical statements, or they would not be statements at all. But abstract musical statements rely entirely on cold logic while statements of the other type—melodies—pulse with a vital humor that may be likened to lifeblood. The melodies of all great masters contain the warmth of living breath; they sound as if they had issued from the lips of a beautiful child flowering into adulthood.

Whereas in his 1893 review of Bruckner's *Psalm 150* Schenker had referred to the 'cold' operation of reflection,[84] the implication of what he says in 1897 is that musical logic need not be cold: rather than being identified with reflection and hence opposed to inspiration, musical logic properly conceived integrates inspiration with reflection, spirit with technique—and this provides a rationale for the distinction Schenker drew in 'Unpersönliche Musik' (also from 1897), and developed in *Niedergang*, between the epigonous classicists—whose work lacks this integration—and those in the Brahmsian mould.

Nor is this the only positive reference to musical logic from 1897. There is a particularly telling reference in the review of a concert at the Hofoperntheater, where Schenker talks about how Smetana and Dvořák have succeeded in 'bringing their national music into a system'. And he adds:[85]

> The system is naturally that of German art, for this is best able to solve the principal problem of the logical development of a piece of music. . . . [Smetana] simply applied the German system to Bohemian music, and because he understood the German logic of music as it were in its necessity and sensibleness as no other, it was granted to him to present Bohemian music in a perfection which will not be surpassed. Since then Dvořák has also succeeded, always with the German system as a basis. . . . His chamber music in particular, with all its Bohemian roots, is blessed with such outstanding German virtues that it justly seems to us most highly attractive.

This is reminiscent of Guido Adler's comparison, which I quoted in the introduction, between the way nationally distinctive musical materials are worked up into classical structures on the one hand and on the other the Habsburg mission to 'join the particularities of the peoples into a higher unity'. But it goes further than that, and the point can be made through juxtaposition with a passage from a review of Haydn's

---

[84] *HSEK* 59, translated in Karnes 2001: 195.
[85] *Neue Revue* 8/2, *HSEK* 360–62 (quotation at 361); translation from McColl 1996: 176.

revived opera *Der Apotheker* that dates from two years earlier. Here
Schenker is making a broadly comparable point, but the vocabulary
and tone are both quite different:[86]

> It is no wonder that this Italian *opera buffa* smells strongly of the German,
> as it is teeming with phrase constructions and thought-constructions, in
> captivating rhythms and, here and there, modulations, all of which an Ital-
> ian of this same period hardly possessed at all, and which Haydn himself
> first discovered through his experience of his own German art.

The difference is that, by 1897, musical logic has moved to stage centre:
it is not only possible, not only warm, but also specifically German. And
while in 1895 Italian art can benefit from German technique (a parallel
with Lamborghini comes to mind), by 1897 Bohemian music achieves
perfection just to the extent that it is capable of being filtered through
German logic.

It may not be a coincidence that after this date one no longer finds
in Schenker's writings the unexpected open-mindedness to different
musical cultures that he demonstrated in the 1894 essay 'Das Hören in
der Musik'.[87] He writes there that 'he who lets himself be guided by the
principle of habituation [*Angewöhnung*] will soon reach the point where
he will be able also in Slavic, Bohemian, or Russian, Swedish, Danish,
[or] French music to savour that particular inner perfume that fills it'—
much in the manner, he adds, of a native listener (*HSEK* 103). But this
cannot be achieved without the repeated listening that brings about
habituation, he continues, and so he asks 'how many Germans believe
today that they have heard Smetana's music and refer to their having
opened their ears to it at this or that time? And yet, with how little
justification may they believe it!' In 1894, then, Schenker considers appreciation of Smetana's music to depend not (as in 1897) on the composer's adoption of German logic, but rather on listeners' preparedness
to open themselves up to the music's own characteristic qualities; he
even claims that without the repeated listening that brings about habituation, a music 'that was reared by foreign laws, by a foreign world
of views and feelings, a foreign nature, is met with intolerance and resistance, as if that music too did not also contain the beautiful blood of
music as a whole'. And another article from 1894, on folk music, makes
the pluralistic conception explicit: Nature, Schenker says, 'invents from
the same basic idea of music such countless kinds, differing to a degree
so as to be unrelated'.[88]

It seems that the new confidence in musical logic which Schenker
found in 1896–97 eliminated this willingness to valorise music in all
its variety, so giving rise to the exclusively Germanocentric musical

---

[86] *HSEK* 168, translated in Karnes 2001: 231.
[87] *Neue Revue* 5/2 (*HSEK* 96–103).
[88] 'Volksmusik in Wien' (*HSEK* 121).

worldview of which *Niedergang* forms the first sustained draft. The point may be made by means of a direct comparison. Sixteen years later, in the first volume of *Kontrapunkt*, Schenker exclaims: 'how can anyone dare to suggest that we look to musically inferior races and nations for allegedly new systems, when in fact they have no systems at all!' He adds that 'the babbling of a child, the first awkward sentences, certainly have a captivating charm, as do Arabic, Japanese, and Turkish songs': skilful artists have incorporated the latter in their music, he continues (citing Haydn, Beethoven, Schubert, and Brahms, as well as Dvořák, Grieg, and Rimsky-Korsakoff)—but their method was in each case 'not to loosen our system in order to incorporate a foreign one, but, on the contrary, to use our major and minor systems to express the foreign element' (*CI* 28). Not only is an explicit hierarchy of values in place, but also 'our' system has become the only possible one. And before long Dvořák, Grieg, and Rimsky-Korsakoff will be struck off the list.

Of course we cannot conflate Schenker's new confidence in musical logic from 1896–97 with the ultimate squaring of his theoretical circle in the early 1920s, and in the end it is not possible to be sure quite what theoretical ideas may have underlain that confidence. But it makes sense to see confidence, rather than a fully developed theory, as what was required to remove the blockage over organicism in music that was so evident in the *Geist* essay. And if the theory was in fact the last element of Schenker's project to fall into place, that only goes to show how it derived its basic motivation from a broader critique of contemporary musical—and not just musical—culture.

If there were critical developments in Schenker's thinking about musical logic during the later 1890s, then there are many other respects in which these years were a time of transition for him. The most obvious is the drastic curtailment of his critical output. Ayotte's (2004) listing of Schenker's articles includes thirty-one in 1896, fifteen in 1897, three in 1898, one in 1901, and then nothing until 1916. And this does not seem to have been because of a lack of demand: when in the middle of 1898 the *Neue Revue*, in which Schenker had published nearly a third of his 1890s articles, merged with *Die Wage*, the coeditor of the *Neue Revue*, Heinrich Osten, invited him to write for *Die Wage*, but Schenker declined (Karnes 2001: 60). As for composition, it is generally said that Schenker gave it up at the same time as criticism, but in fact this seems to have come a little later, though it is hard to be sure because of possible discrepancies between times of composition and of publication. It is true that Schenker's nowadays best known appearance on the compositional stage came as late as 1903, when the Berlin Philharmonic Orchestra premiered his *Syrische Tänze* in Schoenberg's orchestration, but as I said the original composition (for piano four hands) had been published in 1899;[89] it is telling that the scrapbook which Schenker maintained from 1902 to the end of his life, and which includes reviews of three performances of the Schenker/Schoenberg *Syrische Tänze*, contains reviews of just one other performance of Schenker's music in 1903, two in 1904, and one in 1905.[90] As for Schenker's other published scores, one (op. 1) appeared in 1892, four (opp. 2–5) in 1898, and one (op. 10) in 1899, while of his unpublished—and in some cases fragmentary—compositions, just six can be dated, three to 1897, and one each to 1893, 1898, and 1899.[91]

Nevertheless, Schenker remained at least to some extent active as a composer into the new century. A postcard of 1 April 1900 to his close friend the pianist Moriz Violin refers to a newly completed invention, which obviously links with the fact that his op. 5 (*Zweistimmige Inventionen*) was republished with additional material in 1901 (Federhofer 1985: 18). And it was in the same year that Schenker sent his compositions to Röntgen, with a letter (the one referring to 'synthesis') which gives no indication that Schenker did not see this as a continuing activity (191). Two years later, Ludwig Karpath refers to him as 'the Viennese composer Heinrich Schenker'—and this in an article not about Schenker's compositions but his 'discovery' of Haydn's folksong settings.[92] Indeed there is direct evidence that Schenker continued to harbour compositional aspirations as late as the end of 1905, when (as I have already mentioned) he tried to interest Cotta in publishing *Harmonielehre*, or as Schenker referred to it—taking the initial part for the ultimate whole—'Neue musikalische Theorien u. Phantasien von einem Künstler'. (It was only after Eugen d'Albert had interceded on Schenker's behalf that Cotta agreed to take on the book.) In his letter to Cotta, Schenker set out his reason for anonymous publication, which explains the 'by an artist' of the title:

---

[89] Erwin and Simms 1981: 25; a letter from Joseph Weinberger dated 5 January 1900 (OJ 15/12) refers to it as having just been published. In a letter to Jonas dated 21 December 1933, Schenker says that the *Syrische Tänze* were originally performed by Busoni and Schnabel, and that 'with [Moriz] Violin I played selections from them for old Hanslick, both in the Bösendorfer Salon and in many private houses'. He adds the curious remark that 'to some extent intimidated by the success', he 'abjured publication of further volumes' (OJ 5/18, transcribed and translated by John Rothgeb, Schenker Correspondence Project website).

[90] OC 2; this list does not include Schenker's arrangements of baroque music.

[91] Based on Ayotte's (2004: 5–39) listing, with the addition of dates for op. 1 (from Miller 1991: 179) and 'Mädchenlied, no. 1' (dated 1899 according to Lang and Kunselman 1994: 70).

[92] 'Discovery' in quotation marks because Karpath's article ('Eine Haydn-Fund?', *Signale für die musikalische Welt*, 23 December 1903, copy in OC 2/9–10) elicited a response from Rudolph Genée, who had already published some of Haydn's folksong settings in Berlin (OC 2/12). Schenker was involved because he was researching unfamiliar repertory for a piano trio including his friend Moriz Violin.

A critical edition of C. P. E. Bach, published by order of Universal Edition here, to which I have written a supplementary book, *A Contribution to Ornamentation*, has had such success with the press and the public that, in accordance with a long-standing human foible, hostile opinions have suddenly been expressed about my work as a composer, despite the successes of the performances, and despite the fact that firms such as Simrock, Breitkopf & Härtel, Weinberger, etc. have published my works. So as not to jeopardize my future work, I elected to assume anonymity for the time being.[93]

It is hard to see quite why Schenker's treatise on ornamentation might have provoked such a reaction when his earlier activities as a critic had not, however, and one wonders whether Schenker did not find in such supposed resistance to his developing success as a theorist a convenient explanation for his declining status as a composer. A 1904 review in the *Neues Wiener Journal* of a concert in which two of Schenker's unpublished choral works were performed introduces him as a respected theorist, going on to describe the compositions as 'visiting cards'.[94]

A different kind of observation might also be brought into play: it is hard to reconcile the nature of Schenker's compositions with his developing orientation as a theorist. The point can be made in terms of Schenker's most ambitious composition, the half-hour *Fantasie*, op. 2 (1898), which displays the composer Schenker's characteristic delight in virtuosity and rhetoric, building on neobaroque counterpoint and fugato to create sometimes overwhelming (and bombastic) climaxes, often also involving large-scale and perhaps rather mechanically handled rising sequences. If that sounds like a description of Liszt's B Minor

---

[93] Letter of 8 November 1905 (CA 1–2); the reference to d'Albert's intercession is in Cotta's letter to him dated 14 November (OJ 9/31). By 1908 Schenker had concluded that the anonymity was unsustainable (letter to Cotta of 5 June 1908, CA 79), and in the 2 December 1909 letter from which I have previously quoted (see note 17 above) Schenker told Cotta that he had come to regret publishing *Harmonielehre* anonymously, since it meant that his personal reputation did not benefit from the book's success; subsequent editions of *Harmonielehre* and volumes of *Musikalische Theorien und Phantasien* bore Schenker's name. (All letters transcribed and translated by Bent, Schenker Correspondence Project website.)

[94] Review dated 19 March 1904, in Schenker's scrapbook (OC2/14); the compositions were 'Agnes' and 'Im Rosenbusch die Liebe schleiff', from Schenker's *Drei Gesänge für Frauenstimmen a capella*, op. 8 (C12–3 in Ayotte 2004, undated). The reviews in the scrapbook are less helpful in understanding Schenker's abandoning of composition than one might hope (which is why I am consigning them to this note), for two reasons: first, the fact that the scrapbook begins only in 1902, and second, the extent to which the critics disagree with one another. Though there is general agreement in the reviews on pp. 11–3 of the scrapbook that the 'simplicity' and 'delicacy' of 'Agnes' made a better impression than the 'artificial modulations' of 'Im Rosenbusch', assessments vary from the highly favourable ('really fine and beautiful', 'noble invention and harmonisation', displaying Schenker's technique and 'rich artistic experience that harmoniously fuses old and new elements' and a 'surging, genuine enthusiasm for art that proves itself in different fields of musical cultivation') through the unenthusiastic (the works are of decent

Sonata, then the comparison is entirely appropriate. Moreover, a pianist and composer closely associated with the Lisztian tradition, Busoni—to whom the work is dedicated—played a major role in the evolution of the *Fantasie*. As Patrick Miller tells the story (1991: 184), Busoni proposed drastic formal revisions, to the extent of combining materials from what had been intended as two separate works (hence Busoni's question as quoted in Schenker's diary, 'what if . . . the legend and variations were united in one work, something like a fantasy?'), and in its published form the *Fantasie* embodies all Busoni's suggestions, including of course the title. This kind of reconfiguration was probably facilitated by the loose narrative organisation of the first movement (an introductory section 'A modo di leggenda' leads to Allegro passionato, Adagio, and Presto sections, again making the connection with the B Minor Sonata and its encompassing of multimovement form within a single movement). As for the second movement, oddly headed 'Preludio', it consists of a theme and seventeen variations, and in this way shares a common characteristic with virtually all of Schenker's other compositions, which are predominantly songs and highly sectional—often dance-based—piano pieces: they steer clear of issues of large-scale instrumental form, especially that built on development. In short, apart perhaps from some fragments for piano trio and string quartet,[95] there is no evidence of Schenker's engagement as a composer with the issues of 'cyclic form' which were occupying him as a theorist by the early 1900s, and one wonders whether it was not his realisation that as a composer he was essentially a miniaturist—conceivably underlined by his experiences over the *Fantasie*—that lay behind his comments in a diary entry of 4 October 1931: his compositions

---

quality, 'quite pretty . . . in the style of Robert Fuchs', mundane, lacking in colour, insignificant) to the devastating (they display a 'primitive' technique and do not even stimulate a negative assessment). The same kind of disagreements are found in relation to *Vorüber* op. 7 (OC 2/7–8) and the Schenker/Schoenberg *Syrische Tänze* (OC 2/5–7), of which one critic comments on their 'spirited swing' and 'erotic colour', while another says that they 'belong in the beer garden, not the Beethovensaal'—though a third critic tells us that the music was well received by the audience. And the publication of *Sechs Lieder* op. 3 is greeted with the harsh judgement that the songs would have been 'better left unwritten and unpublished' (OC 2/18). Even Röntgen, to whom Schenker had sent his compositions, seems to have been ambivalent, replying in a letter dated 22 April 1901 that 'In the inventions [Op. 5] you tread upon fairly twisted paths, and it is not always easy to follow you. In particular, the purely musical essence is not always readily apparent, even though the technical aspect is immediately interesting and impressive' (OJ 13/27 [2], translated by Kevin Karnes on the Schenker Correspondence Project website). All this probably boils down to what the music itself would indicate: that Schenker was a competent composer but in no sense a heavyweight. By contrast, reviewers highly praised his performances of keyboard music by C. P. E. Bach and Mozart ('superbly played by Heinrich Schenker', 'an understanding performer', OC 2/14, 2/18); as a choral conductor, however, he is declared 'impossible' (OC 2/11).

⁹⁵ C37–43 and C45–8 in Ayotte 2004.

were 'real "treasures"', he wrote, 'as unique in today's world as my theory', but then he added, 'it was always clear to me that I would become no master or much less surpass one'.[96] Seen this way, Schenker's theory would represent an exploration of precisely what he was not capable of as a composer. The psychology is by no means implausible.

In summary, there may have been a degree of approximation in Schenker's own later account of what happened, at least if one can trust the memory of his student Hans Wolf as recorded in the October 1937 edition of *Der Dreiklang:* 'I composed quite a lot when I was young,' Wolf reports him as saying during one of his lessons (1989/1937: 182), 'and my things were successful; but when I saw how Brahms was misunderstood, I suffered so much that I dropped everything and set about writing my theoretical works'.[97] But it certainly seems possible that Brahms's death in 1897 had some kind of catalytic effect on Schenker (Blasius observes that 'Brahms seems to occupy a strange and important position psychologically within Schenker's universe' [1996: 129]), and that it was from around this time that he felt he had a mission to fulfil as a theorist: that of course implies that he had by then come to believe that the problems of musical logic and causality were soluble, and that the genuine, psychological theory to which the *Geist* essay aspired was capable of being delivered.

At the same time, it might make at least as much sense to understand Schenker's definitive turn at this time towards Brahms as, in origin, less that than a turn *away* from Wagner, or from what the Wagnerian tradition had come to represent in the Vienna of the late 1890s. I have already referred to the posthumous centrality of Gustav Wagner in Viennese concert life of the 1890s, and his important role as late as 1897 in Schenker's musical universe. The extent of Schenker's enthusiasm for Wagner's multifarious activities is evident from an essay— really an overgrown review of Mahler's conducting of *Lohengrin*— published in the same year under the title 'Capellmeister-Regisseure' (Conductor-directors):[98]

> The figure of Richard Wagner is now beginning to fall apart into a thousand productive elements. . . . Each of his suggestions lives, as it were, a life of its own and is bearing fruit. . . . His powerful emotions . . . found in

[96] Federhofer 1985: 21, translated in Miller 1991: 178. Further light is thrown on Schenker's later attitude to his compositions by a letter from his pupil Angi Elias, which shows that she had been working with him on a graph of the first of his *Fünf Klavierstücke* op. 4 (letter of 11 July 1928, OJ 10/18).

[97] Translated in Miller 1991: 194. There is an echo of this in Schenker's letter of 29 April 1928 to von Cube: after describing his opportunity 'to experience Brahms late in life, to see him, to hear him speak, perform' as 'a joy about which I would have to write tears, if I were able to', Schenker continues that 'this pain concerning the dying art drove me to work feverishly (day and night)' (von Cube family collection, vC 14, transcribed and translated by Drabkin, Schenker Correspondence Project website).

[98] *HSEK* 236–40, translated in Schenker 1988: 138–41.

the masterpieces, without much prior cogitation, that is, on account of his spontaneous genius, things that were completely different from those the conductors of his time saw in them. . . . [This] was the beginning of a new philosophy of conductors.[99]

The tone here is as different as could be from Schenker's intemperate attacks on Wagner in the Ninth Symphony monograph (anticipated, as we now know, in *Niedergang*); the point can be made by a comparison between the monograph and the last of Schenker's early essays ('Beethoven-"retouche"', published in 1901),[100] which sets out the same basic critique of Wagner's reorchestrations of Beethoven, but presents them as an unfortunate lapse in an otherwise respected composer. (Curiously enough, it is once again Smetana who forms the starting point, the link being his and Beethoven's deafness.) In the 1995 article I previously mentioned, I suggested that the violence of Schenker's attacks in the Ninth Symphony monograph might have resulted from a kind of anxiety of influence: the reason, I speculated, was that Schenker—who as I have already mentioned was not in the habit of acknowledging music-theoretical debts—found some of his basic ideas in Wagner's writings. I was particularly talking about the idea of analytical reduction and its relevance for performance, but there are many other parallels between Wagner's and Schenker's thought, including not only the idea of Nature and unconscious creation (which Wagner, no doubt influenced by Schopenhauer, likened to sleeping or dreaming), but also the ideas of music representing a temporalisation of the atemporal, the fundamentally improvisatory nature of composition, its ineffability, and even the falsity of the modes. Keiler (1996: 184), too, has speculated along such lines, suggesting that 'it is not Wagner's music, apparently, but rather Wagner's theories about his music, and surely about other musical and aesthetic doctrines, that had this profound hold on Schenker, at least for a few years during this period'.[101]

What I now want to suggest is a parallel between Schenker's theoretical evolution, including his characterisation in 1897 of musical logic as specifically German, and the ideas embodied in Wagner's essay 'Was ist deutsch?' (What is German?), which had been published in 1878 (though written in 1865). This essay is a *locus classicus* for the binary opposition of German depth as against Latin superficiality, in turn associated with the essential as against the contingent: the German, writes Wagner, 'translates the foreign poem into German, in order to gain an inner knowledge of its content. In doing so he strips the foreign of its

---

[99] Schenker 1988: 139–40.

[100] *HSEK* 259–68.

[101] In an article derived from his thesis (which Keiler advised), Kevin Karnes (2002) has argued for the influence of Wagnerian concepts—whether or not directly assimilated—on Schenker's earliest analytical writing.

accidentals, its externals' (Osborne 1973: 48). That could itself easily be translated into a description of Schenkerian analysis, and in his later works Schenker consistently associates the German with 'depth' in the music-analytical sense, with composing from the background, and hence with genius. It is precisely this association that Bent invokes in relation to the op. 101 *Erläuterungsausgabe*, in which (as well as quoting Kant on the genius) Schenker introduced for the first time the principle of the *Urlinie*.[102] Bent (1991: 21) links this crucial theoretical development to 'the upsurge of consciousness of Germanity, of the allegedly special mode of German thought'.[103] (As Bent summarises it [17], 'the Frenchman thinks from the outside inwards, whereas the German thinks from the inside outwards'.) It is true that the word 'genius' appears only once in 'Was ist deutsch?', but it is in a telling context, for Wagner refers to 'the German spirit . . . which we call genius in the case of highly gifted individuals' (Osborne 1973: 49). Given Schenker's own association of spirit with causality,[104] and his use of causality and logic as virtual synonyms, we have then the following quintessentially Schenkerian cluster of ideas, each characterised as specifically German: depth, genius, spirit, and logic.

But as with the idea of genius, so Wagner's ideas of the German were very much in the public domain throughout the 1890s. What then might have placed the idea of the German at the centre of Schenker's thinking and given a special urgency to his project around 1897? I do not wish to anticipate the following chapters, but we need to bear in mind some of the nonmusical events of this time. It was on Good Friday 1897 (as it happens, ten days after Brahms's funeral)[105] that Emperor Franz Josef accepted the election as mayor of the charismatic and capable, but also anti-Semitic, Lueger (who had first topped the polls in 1895, when Franz Josef had refused to ratify the victory). It was in 1897 that Mahler was appointed to the musical directorship of the State Opera, precipitating a debate over his racial origins. It was in 1897 that the First Zionist Congress took place (in Basel, but it was the brainchild of the Viennese writer and activist Theodor Herzl). And the soundtrack for all this was provided by the pan-German Wagnerians, who had been becoming increasingly vociferous, fanatical, and explicitly anti-Semitic ever since 1890, when the decision of the Vienna Wagner-Verein not to become politically active had prompted the secession of its more militant members and the formation of a new Wagnerian

---

[102] At least in public: it appears in the revisions of the 'Freier Satz' chapter drafted for *Kontrapunkt* 2, dating from some time between 1917 and 1920 (Siegel 1999: 23–4).

[103] Here and elsewhere, quotations from Bent 1991 are taken from the unpublished English version Professor Bent kindly gave me.

[104] At least later on: 'To understand more fully the spirit latent in the historic development of our art, it is prudent to find precisely in the dissonant syncope a means of establishing a purely musical *causality*' (*CI* 291).

[105] Good Friday fell on 16 April; Brahms's funeral was on 6 April.

group 'dedicated as much to Schönerer's cause as to that of Wagner' (Notley 1999: 88). (I shall come back to Schönerer in chapter 3.) The Wagnerian tradition as a whole, then, was being increasingly appropriated for purposes of not just cultural but political and racial nationalism, just as Bruckner had been at a more local level, and this may help to explain not only Schenker's hostility to Bruckner but also the vitriolic tone exemplified by his reference to 'the utter impotence of contemporary composers' in the Brahms obituary published in *Die Zukunft*.

It is evident that there is no one factor that determined the formation of the Schenker project: rather we are dealing with an indefinite number of factors—aesthetic, conceptual, contextual—that came together at a certain time, in short with a unique and contingent configuration of motives and opportunities. But it makes sense to see it as largely an act of reappropriation, especially in view of the iconic value of 'Was ist deutsch?' (In 1889 the title of Wagner's essay had been borrowed for the first page of the first issue of the key Austrian anti-Semitic journal, the *Deutsches Volksblatt* [Notley 1993: 121].) As I shall argue in chapter 4, Schenker redefines the German in music: he wrenches it away from the Wagnerians and relocates it back in time to the Viennese classics, back to a legacy that is common to Jew and gentile. And there, perhaps, is the third and last of Schenker's principal motivations in the formation of his project.

2

The Reluctant Modernist

Curlicues and Catastrophe

For a fairly short essay, 'Der Geist der musikalischen Technik' was comprehensive in its scope of reference, touching on composition, performance, listening, writing, and teaching; if—as Schenker claimed in it—
'practical music almost never concerns itself with those things which
theory either ascribes to it or describes from it', then the sum total of
these things might be said to make up the scope of Schenker's theoretical project. As I have argued, the winding down by around the end of
the century of Schenker's professional activities as critic, composer,
and performer is more or less consistent with Hans Wolf's claim that
Schenker dropped everything to concentrate on his theoretical works,
at least when 'theory' is understood in this broad sense. One might then
think in terms of an initial phase of the Schenker project that runs up
to the First World War, with its core being made up by the first volumes
of the *Neue musikalische Theorien und Phantasien: Harmonielehre* (1906)
and the first volume of *Kontrapunkt* (1910), as well as the unpublished
Über den Niedergang der Kompositionskunst. There is also a second unfinished book: *Die Kunst des Vortrags,* recently published in a translated
version that creates at first sight an impression of coherence and completion the rather fragmentary materials brought together in it (mostly
written in 1911) do not really support.[1]

---

[1] *Die Kunst des Vortrags* is best read in conjunction with the extracts from Schenker's
annotated scores reproduced and discussed in Rothstein 1984.

There is however a second major area of activity during this period, which was not mentioned in the *Geist* essay: editing. This is perhaps a misleading term for what became a substantial project of textual criticism consisting of both scores and extensive commentaries, and overlapping into theory and analysis—but then the linkage between these areas of activity is precisely the point, and this extension of Schenker's activities is the logical outcome of the relocation of his primary focus from the music of his own time to that of the past (a change reflected also in such concerts as he continued to give up to 1911, which included performances of music by Handel, J. S. and C. P. E. Bach, and Mozart, sometimes in his own arrangements). It also makes excellent sense in terms of the Schenker project as a whole: editing, after all, bears in one way or another on all the musical activities discussed in the *Geist* essay (composition, performance, listening, writing, and teaching), and more than that, it plays the key role in the transmission into the present day and beyond of the music of the past. The more or less standardised format Schenker developed over these years, most fully illustrated in the so-called *Erläuterungausgabe* (commentary on musical content and sources, score, discussion of performance, discussion of secondary literature), reflects the fact that the editor has responsibility, in the most literal sense, for the survival of music.[2] In the period up to the beginning of the war, such work included a two-volume edition of C. P. E. Bach's keyboard works (1902), with *Ein Beitrag zur Ornamentik* (A contribution to the study of ornamentation, 1903) effectively forming an oversized introduction to the edition;[3] a published arrangement for piano four hands of Handel's first set of organ concertos (1904); a critical edition (really the first *Erläuterungsausgabe*) of J. S. Bach's 'Chromatic Fantasy and Fugue' (1910); the monograph on Beethoven's Ninth Symphony (1912), in effect an *Erläuterungsausgabe* without the edition; and the first two volumes of the *Erläuterungsausgaben* proper, Beethoven's op. 109 in 1913, and op. 110 in 1914. The third volume, op. 111, appeared in the following year.

In this chapter I take as my starting point *Ein Beitrag zur Ornamentik,* Schenker's first—or at least first surviving—work of monograph length, and one which might appropriately feature as an early document in the history of the period performance movement (along, incidentally, with the now forgotten *Instrumentations-Tabelle* which Schenker published in 1908 under the pseudonym 'Artur Niloff', and which gives technical details for a range of instruments going back as

---

[2] For a discussion of Schenker's odd relationship with this term—he used it in correspondence with Hertzka, yet it never appeared on the published editions—see Bent 2005, especially 106–7.

[3] Bent's (2005: 75) study of Schenker's correspondence with Universal Edition establishes that *Ornamentik* was originally intended as the introduction to the C. P. E. Bach edition (the decision to publish it separately was made in 1902), and that it was published in 1903 (not as normally stated 1904).

far as the eighteenth century; Schenker's views on historically informed performance sometimes seem surprisingly up-to-date when read today, and if Baron Alphons von Rothschild had agreed to to fund the 'Rothschild-Orchestra' Schenker once proposed to him [Federhofer 1985: 40], it is conceivable that we would think of Schenker as an early music pioneer as well as a theorist). Central to *Ornamentik*, as also to the associated edition, is what Schenker saw as the lack of appreciation of C. P. E. Bach's keyboard works, highly admired in their time by 'Haydn, Mozart, and Beethoven': Schenker asks, 'can merit become extinct, if it once existed as such? Can a work of art die, or be mummified, if it once lived so intensely? Or does the fault simply lie with us?' (*CSO* 15). As we have seen, Schenker had addressed precisely these questions in the *Geist* essay ('Each and every content retains the power which it had originally, and it is up to us to perceive this vitality anew'); the idea that music can die, he had said, is controverted by 'just a single case in which we are able to reinvigorate a lifeless content with active and youthful vitality' (p. 330). And this is to be achieved through a recognition of the music's timeless content, rather than through the kind of historical relativism Schenker recognised in the work of Hans von Bülow, who had previously edited these keyboard works, and whom Schenker (who thrived on controversy) treated as sparring partner in *Ornamentik* in the same manner that he treated Wagner, Riemann, Kretszchmar, and others in subsequent publications.

In the preface to his edition, Bülow had spoken of the need to avoid 'tastelessness, according to present standards' (*CSO* 22), and through filling out Bach's textures had aimed (again in his own words) at 'nothing more nor less than a translation from the keyboard language of the eighteenth century to that of the nineteenth—from the clavichordistic to the pianofortistic, if I may use such inelegant terms' (*CSO* 17). Schenker's pen positively drips irony as he counters this point of view (*CSO* 16):

> A bass that is entirely too meager, so few passages in thirds and octaves, so few noisy arpeggios and other kinds of passage work—surely, one must be correct in saying that even with the best will in the world such a thin and paltry sound cannot be considered sufficient in the present day—mark well, 'the present day'! And modestly—of course, very modestly—one places the blame, not on Bach himself, but on his favorite instrument, the meager clavichord. Yes, *it* is surely to blame!

Bülow, in short, puts forward 'an historical point of view that is tempered with feelings of goodwill and pity, etc.' (*CSO* 21). As he asserts the autonomy of musical content in the face of such compromising accommodations, Schenker marshals the full resources of his legal rhetoric (note the 'without prejudice' clause in the second half of the first sentence):

Of what serious importance is a somewhat thin texture, that is, if one were to admit that such thinness actually existed? In the presence of such genius, does one miss a few little notes, a few more chords, which at best merely accommodate the hand in the most mechanical sense? If the hand is given fuller chords and figurations to play, does it follow that for this reason alone the content is better? How does the musical idea, or indeed the succession of ideas, from which a piece derives its enduring value, benefit thereby? (*CSO* 19)

A duality is here emerging between the ideal, enduring content of the music on the one hand and on the other the mechanical means of its representation, so that at the heart of *Ornamentik* is an argument concerning the relationship between spirit and technique.[4] In essence, the charge against Bülow (and, as will become clear, the modern world he stands for) is that he does not know the difference between these: he understands Bach's embellishments as 'mere curlicues, purely instrumental effects, which lack both truth and emotion'—as means of compensating for the inadequacies of the clavichord (*CSO* 21). But understood properly, Schenker says, the embellishments are an integral part of the musical content: they are

a true part of the melody and a true contributor to its beauty. Like all melody, embellishments have life and expression. They are a manifestation of truth, artistic truth that transcends time and will endure to the end of time . . . if one takes care to prevent embellishments from degenerating to a purely mechanical component of finger dexterity.

And in the unfinished *Kunst des Vortrags,* dating from nearly ten years later but part of a more or less consistent development of ideas on performance that begins with *Ornamentik* and continues with the 'Chromatic Fantasy and Fugue' edition, Schenker reproduces the same thought (*AP* 71): 'passages and *fiorituras* are an integral part of older works and themselves share in the overall expressiveness'.

In this way, Schenker's Hanslickian insistence in the *Geist* essay that expressiveness is an objective property of the music reappears in *Ornamentik,* most explicitly in the claim that 'Bach sees in each embellishment a special and unique expressiveness, almost as if it were a living individual organism that could never be mistaken for another. . . . He regards every embellishment not merely as decoration but also as actual and self-contained expression' (*CSO* 51). In chapter 1, I made a link between Hanslick's claim that the power of a melody is not an obscure miracle but 'rather the inevitable result of musical factors which are at

---

[4] In *Tonwille,* Schenker makes a very similar argument concerning Mozart's music and the pianos of his day, this time with (A. B.) Marx as his target, and draws the same conclusion: 'If a given content is complete in itself from the standpoint of synthesis, without contradicting the instrument—and only internal considerations are crucial in this respect—what can change later through increase in sound, or the like, to the disadvantage of internal completeness?' (*TI* 67)

work in the melody', and what Blasius terms Schenker's 'contrapuntal laboratory' through which the individual musical and expressive quality of every element becomes known: as Schenker said in the first volume of *Kontrapunkt*, this is what makes it possible for the geniuses (but only the geniuses) to fully predict the effects of their music, resulting in an identity of intention and effect.[5] The development between *Geist* and *Kontrapunkt* 1 of this idea in the domain of composition is paralleled by a similar development in relation to performance. In the *Geist* essay, after speaking of the way counterpoint develops the composer's perception, Schenker went on to draw a parallel with 'the discipline of independent, mechanical finger-dexterity that every performing artist must acquire if he is to meet the technical and mechanical challenges of an artwork', and commented that 'under the best circumstances, the performing artist's inspiration can coincide felicitously with that of the composer' (p. 323).[6] Like the composer, then, the performer's business is the creation of the appropriate effects: early in *Die Kunst des Vortrags* (*AP* 5), Schenker is drawing a clear line between the musical effect and the means of its execution, while later he comments, 'Only if the performer is fully aware of the desired effect will he be able to convey it. This effect then serves to justify any means he might use to produce it' (78). And in the 'Chromatic Fantasy and Fugue' edition, Schenker expressed the same thought with uncharacteristic flippancy (but then, it is a reference to Michael Praetorius): 'even the nose may assist, as long as the proper meaning is conveyed' (*BCFF* 69).

In his study of the relationship between Schenker's musical thought and the legal thinking he encountered at the University of Vienna, Wayne Alpern (forthcoming) stresses the idea that freedom is secured by the operation of the law: in both Schenker's theory and Jellinek's jurisprudence, he argues, it is only within the framework of established laws that personal freedom is possible. These values permeate Schenker's writing about performance. As he sees it, performers have obligations, but they also have freedom in terms of the means by which these obligations are to be met, and the issue of freedom becomes one of the dimensions within which both *Ornamentik* and Schenker's later writings on performance play out the duality between spirit and technique. Virtuosos, Schenker complains, 'are merely slaves of engraver and hand position':[7] for them, execution has become an end in itself, with 'an academic cultivation of finger velocity' taking the place of 'inter-

---

[5] See pp. 61–2, 66 above.

[6] In an 1896 review published in *Die Zeit*, Schenker says precisely this of Johannes Messchaert, the baritone with whom he later toured and of whom (as a musician, if not as a person) he had the highest opinion: Messchaert, Schenker says, presents music not as 'rigid art finally congealed in word or tone' but rather 'in the liquid state of original feeling' (*HSEK* 324).

[7] From the editor's summary of the final section ('On the degeneracy of the virtuoso') of 'Vom Vortrag' (*OJ* 18/10), one of the constituent sources of *Die Kunst des Vortrags* (*AP* 84).

pretive methods', the result being that 'musical performance deterio-
rated into an artificial, systematized, narrow-minded, academic kind of
performance at high speed' (*CSO* 98). The central problem, as Schenker
explains it, is that for the virtuoso, technique does not arise out of musical content but is imposed on it in a spirit of uniformity, and so in the
'Chromatic Fantasy and Fugue' edition he condemns 'the school of
fingering whose adherents, because of ignorance or lack of understanding, prescribe a succession of fingers wholly determined by external criteria' (*BCFF* 69). In a passage from *Die Kunst des Vortrags*, Schenker draws
out the consequences of this critique:

> Every piece has its own special fingering, its own special dynamics. All
> practicing of studies misses the point, as fingering, dynamics, and position
> of hand in any particular piece are not applicable to any other. That is why
> the art of performance is unattainable for the many who, from incompe-
> tence, attempt to get by with an absolute model for fingering, dynamics,
> and hand position. (*AP* 77)

It is on this basis that, in *Ornamentik*, Schenker cries, 'away with mechanical, finished finger facility!'[8] This is a much less accommodating
position than the one he had taken in the *Geist* essay, but more damag-
ingly it also contradicts his insistence in both the 'Chromatic Fantasy
and Fugue' edition and *Die Kunst des Vortrags* on the performer's freedom to realise the musical effects in any way he or she sees fit. (For
what piece might 'its special fingering' include the nose?) And while the
attack on fingering systems and insistence on the uniquity of every musical context may represent a coherent exercise of logic, it is hard to see
how it could be transformed into a plausible pedagogical principle; perhaps it was in recognition of such basic flaws that Schenker never completed his *Kunst des Vortrags*, as he clearly intended at least up to 1925.[9]
    The attack in *Ornamentik* on Bülow and virtuosos in general is in
many ways an extension of the attacks in the essays of the 1890s on
formalists of all varieties: virtuosos impose their mechanical fingering
systems on music, without regard to its inner content, in the same way
that formalist critics and composers impose their verbal or verbally inspired formulae on it. And the original attack reappears: the 'classicists'
Schenker attacked in 'Unpersönliche Musik' are now 'pseudo-classi-
cists', who think of the sonata as 'a supposedly rigid form, fixed and un-
alterable as given,—in short, a formula' (*CSO* 33–4). Such 'counterfeit
form', a misrepresentation of the (real) 'Classical masters' when employed as a critical construct, becomes 'the more insidious' when embodied in compositions (*CSO* 35); 'preconceived ideas', Schenker con-

---

[8] *CSO* 99. Schenker maintained this position from now on: it resurfaces in the final
(1930) volume of *Meisterwerk* (*MM3* 76).

[9] He mentions it as 'forthcoming' in the first volume of *Meisterwerk* (*MM1* 37), as he
had previously done in the Ninth Symphony monograph (*BNS* 8).

cludes, are 'the death of all art' (*CSO* 36). In this way the original, in essence Hanslickian, critique is extended from compositional and critical formalism (the former now including music drama as well as pseudoclassical and programme music) to corresponding trends in performance, and through performance to broader social values. These values are already implicit in Schenker's use of terms like 'superficial' and 'mechanical', but become most evident when Schenker complains of the virtuosos' insistence on performing everything at high speed. 'Why should it be so difficult', Schenker asks in the course of a three-page footnote, 'especially for a man like Bülow . . . to rediscover the original slower tempo?' (*CSO* 98n.) At this point in *Ornamentik,* Schenker merely puts it down to 'a general decline', which is a redescription rather than an explanation, but a proper answer appears a few pages later, this time in the course of a two-page footnote: complaining about a detail of Bülow's articulation, Schenker comments (and here the ironic note returns), 'but in such an outwardly hectic life, one that encompassed so many different activities, where would Bülow have found even an atom of time to think about a small space in Bach's turns?' (*CSO* 102n.)

The polemical footnotes, threatening at times to overwhelm the main text, signal the return of the jeremiad-like tone I noted in 'Die Musik von heute': 'In Bach's music', Schenker writes, 'we find riches and the blessings that flow from them; in today's music we find poverty and wild but futile rebellion against the curse of poverty!' (*CSO* 29). But now the critique spills beyond music to encompass contemporary culture in general: it would be too much, says Schenker in a tone that anticipates Oswald Spengler, to expect understanding and enjoyment of Bach's ornaments 'on the part of our age, an age in such obvious decline—a decline that is of course strongly denied by those who make baseless claims for "progress"' (*CSO* 53). And as the attacks on 'our' age become more virulent, so the music of the (real) classics increasingly takes on a utopian quality. 'We perceive', Schenker writes, 'that any kind of schematic formula is foreign to their genius and that a natural spontaneity characterizes their creative activity' (*CSO* 34). Unlike the illusory freedom of modern musicians, 'the music of these geniuses is unconfined, and is but lightly chained to the eternal laws of nature. . . . The achievement of such freedom must surely remain their greatest, unsurpassable triumph' (*CSO* 34). And that brings us to the nub of Schenker's condemnation of Bülow's editing of Bach. Properly understood, that is to say in light of a grasp of the music's content, the performance of Bach's embellishments—and here Schenker is quoting from Bach's *Versuch über die wahre Art, das Clavier zu spielen* (Essay on the true art of playing keyboard instruments)—'requires a freedom of performance that rules out everything slavish and mechanical. Play from the soul, not like a trained bird!' (*CSO* 46) But Bülow makes it hard if not impossible for the performer to gain such an understanding, for his written-out ornamentations and added indications of 'expression' blur

and conceal the musical content: no longer a means of exercising freedom and promoting personal development, performance becomes a
matter of mechanically complying with written specifications. It is as if
the notation were to be mechanically translated into technique, without the intervention of what Bach calls the soul, and Schenker the
spirit. (I hope the echo of 'Der Geist der musikalischen Technik' is self-
evident.) And worse, Bülow does all this without acknowledging the
signs of his own intervention, so that performers may be playing Bülow
while thinking all the time that they are playing Bach. No wonder then
that Schenker refers to 'the harm caused by Bülow's disfigurement of
Bach's music—harm done not only to the master himself but also to
every pianist' (*CSO* 102n.).

One of the most striking characteristics of Schenker's writing—a
characteristic to which I shall refer repeatedly in this book—is the way
he slips, almost without transition, from discussion of the technical mi-
nutiae of music to the largest issues of culture or society: already in *Ornamentik* what begins as a discussion of editing turns into a discourse on
freedom and ends with a comprehensive condemnation of 'our age'.
By the time of *Kontrapunkt* 1 the intensity of rhetoric has increased by
an order of magnitude, even though the basic issue—the survival of the
classical tradition—remains the same. The notorious opening of Schenker's *Kontrapunkt* reads:

> We stand here before a Herculaneum and Pompeii of music! All musical
> culture is buried; the very tonal material—that foundation of music which
> artists, transcending the spare clue provided by the overtone series, cre-
> ated anew in all respects from within themselves—is demolished. The
> most marvellous and, one might say, 'created' of the arts, that art which,
> among all arts, caused the severest birth-pangs and thus was the last be-
> queathed to us—the youngest of the arts, *music*—is lost! (*CI* xvii)

Whereas the reference to the demolition of tonal materials represents an
attack on contemporary composers reminiscent of Riemann's attack on
Sachs, Hahn, and Vincent, the 'loss' is the result of what Schenker saw
as a catastrophic decline in performance standards. Soon he is asking

> what the *performers* play—is it really a symphony by Beethoven? . . .
> Where is it? Where is the authentic shape of the symphony as Beethoven
> himself conceived it? . . . Inferior instinct and (often) complete lack of se-
> cure knowledge on the part of today's performing musicians are the rea-
> sons that the masterworks—how bitter a truth!—have not been heard in
> our time in their authentic shape.

Schenker saw this as the result of a system of education based on false
theory: 'How thoroughly young people are misled in schools, conservatories, academies, and the like', he writes (*CI* xxiv), 'how many
crimes are committed there against music; how completely everything
is institutionalized in a way that leads from music rather than towards

it'. ('Volumes of protest, scorn, and anger', he adds, 'could and should be devoted to all of these matters'.) But the problem is not just one of education: it is also attributable to modern editors who bury the classics under a mass of identified editorial additions. ('What a dark force', Schenker adds: 'the teacher and editor in music!') And so Schenker concludes that 'our first task must be a real excavation before we can even begin work that will allow us to proceed (I do not say: "progress"!)'.

Composition, performance, listening, writing, teaching, editing: the Schenker project aimed at a comprehensive reform of musical culture. But again it is not just music that is at issue, for Schenker has not got far into his preface before he is complaining that 'we live in an era in which all values in human relationships are turned exactly upside down' (*CI* xix). In the remainder of this chapter, then, I shall set the idea of ornamentation—the central issue of Schenker's first foray into editing—into the broader context of contemporary Vienna by means of a series of cameos drawn from the visual arts: in this way I hope to suggest how Schenker's critique of music formed, and should be read as, part of a more general critique of *fin-de-siècle* culture.

Ornamentation and Critique in **Fin-de-Siècle** *Vienna*

It is usual to see Viennese modernism, particularly in the visual arts, as consisting of two largely overlapping waves. Both have to be understood in relation to the academic historicism of the post-1848 era (the *Gründerzeit*), as represented by the long-unfashionable painting of Hans Makart and the eclectic architecture of the Ringstrasse, the ring road around the old city that follows the line of the former walls: as Carl Schorske explains in his seminal book *Fin-de-Siècle Vienna: Politics and Culture* (1980: chap. 2), these were demolished in the 1860s in a self-conscious bid to transform Vienna into a modern European capital, and the Ringstrasse contains many conspicuous public buildings, each designed in a style reflecting its particular function. (Fig. 2.1, a photograph taken around 1888, shows the Parliament building, in the Greek style; the Rathaus or town hall, in the neo-Gothic style; the main University building, in Renaissance style, which opened in 1884, the very year Schenker enrolled; and the Burgtheater, in early baroque style.) It is hard not to think of this permanent backdrop to Viennese life when reading discussions of epigonism in musical life (at one point in *Ornamentik* [*CSO* 28] Schenker refers to 'us epigoni'). Even the generation who built the Ringstrasse entertained similar thoughts: 'Ours does not appear to be an age given to the creation of new styles in architecture', wrote Rudolf von Eitelberger, the first director of the Österreichisches Museum für Kunst und Industrie (itself on the Ringstrasse and now known as the Österreichisches Museum für Angewandte Kunst or MAK), and he added, 'the more attempts are made to invent a new style of building, the clearer it is that the vocation for such a creative ac-

Figure 2.1   Ringstrasse, ca. 1888. Used by permission of Austrian National Library Vienna, Picture Archive (sign. 111.800-C).

tivity is lacking'.[10] By the turn of the century, the most striking feature of the Ringstrasse, at least in artistically advanced circles, seems to have been its unreality. In 1898 Adolf Loos, of whom more shortly, compared it to the villages of canvas and pasteboard supposedly erected in Ukraine by Catherine the Great's favorite, Potemkin, in order to provide the backdrop for the empress's visit: 'Whenever I stroll along the Ring', Loos wrote, 'it always seems to me as if a modern Potemkin had wanted to carry out his orders here, as if he had wanted to persuade somebody that in coming to Vienna he had been transported into a city of nothing but aristocrats'.[11] And in 1900 Hermann Bahr—the same Bahr who contributed to the formation of Viennese 'impressionism'[12]—wrote:

> If you walk across the Ring, you have the impression of being in the midst of a real carnival. Everything masked, everything disguised. . . . Life has become too serious for that sort of thing. . . . Life has changed, costume has changed, our thoughts and feelings, our whole manner of living has changed, architecture must change also. (Vergo 1975: 90)

[10] Quoted in Vergo 1975: 88; more optimistically, however, Eitelberger continued, 'On the other hand, the more imaginatively, the more ingeniously one endeavours to unite given styles, the basic elements of already existing types of architecture, with the advances of modern technology, the more successful are the results'.

[11] Loos 1982/1921: 95.

[12] See chapter 1, p. 39; Schenker had personal dealings with Bahr when he wrote for *Die Zeit* (Karnes 2001: 61–4), and retained sufficient interest in him to clip and keep a substantial number of his newspaper articles, which are scattered throughout the Oster Collection.

He added, consciously or unconsciously echoing Loos, 'We . . . should be ashamed to live in the style of the princes and patricians of yesterday'.

The first phase of Viennese modernism—for which Bahr was the principal spokesperson—was the Secession, so called because its members seceded in 1897 from the established artists' association, the Künstlerhaus, in order to diversify their activities, particularly into the applied arts. The visual expressions of the Secession were confusingly variable, ranging from Viennese versions of the *art nouveau* and Arts and Crafts styles to premonitions of architectural brutalism: perhaps the main thing they have in common is a more or less determined avoidance of historicism, and particularly historical patterns of ornamentation. It is hard to encompass Schenker and the Secessionists in one thought, though oddly enough Busoni described Schenker's *Syrische Tänze* as 'secessionistic' (Erwin and Simms 1981: 25). But I can give my comments a musical spin in relation to the 1902 Beethoven exhibition, located in Josef Olbrich's 1898 Secession building (which, incidentally, had been paid for by the Wittgenstein family). Conceived around Max Klinger's heroic statue of the seated Beethoven (now at the Neues Gewandhaus in Leipzig), the exhibition space was designed by Josef Hoffmann in an asymmetrical, minimalist style, with walls that look brutalist in black-and-white reproductions (fig. 2.2) but—if Hans Hollein's 1985 reconstruction is to be trusted—were in fact a warm

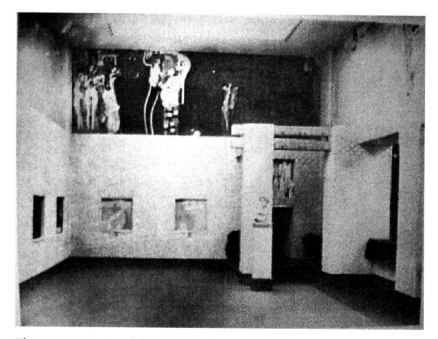

Figure 2.2 Interior of the 1902 Beethoven Exhibition. (*Source:* Vienna Secession website (www.secession.at/e.html).)

Figure 2.3 Klimt, 'This kiss for the whole world'. Used by permission of Österreischische Galerie Belvedere Vienna.

cream relieved by gold detailing. The minimalism of the design put maximum emphasis on the artefacts of the exhibition, the most famous of which are the series of friezes executed by Gustav Klimt. These have been subject to extensive commentary ranging from the allegorical to the psychoanalytical (examples include Schorske [1980], Bouillon [1987], and Shamsai [1997]), but sophisticated interpretation is not necessary for the points I wish to make. In fact, two details will suffice. Figure 2.3 shows 'This kiss for the whole world', the quotation from Schiller's 'Ode to Joy' explicitly referencing Beethoven's Ninth Symphony; whereas 'For Schiller and Beethoven, the kiss was political, the kiss of the brotherhood of man', Schorske (258) comments, 'for Klimt, the sentiment is not heroic but purely erotic'. Figure 2.4 is a flat and decorative figure, with abstract ornamentation employed for its own sake rather than to articulate the form, which Schorske (262) refers to as 'Music', though it is more often called 'Poetry'.

What did Schenker think of the Beethoven exhibition? I know of no reference to it in his writings, and it is more than likely that he didn't go to it; conservative critics made a point of staying away, and the Viennese music journals pointedly ignored it, apparently regarding it as an attempt to appropriate the prestige of a cultural icon for commercial purposes (few of the exhibits other than the Klinger statue and Klimt friezes had any relationship to Beethoven, and everything was for sale).[13] All the same, one could easily imagine the image at Figure

---

[13] For details and an analysis of the exhibition see Celenza 2004.

Figure 2.4 Klimt, 'Poetry' (or 'Music'). Used
by permission of Österreischische Galerie
Belvedere Vienna.

2.4 being in Schenker's mind when he wrote, in the preface to *Kontra-punkt* 1, about 'literalist' performers who play 'only on a single surface, so to speak—merely in a planimetric way—where they should play in several dimensions, as though in a stereometric way'.[14] The perhaps fortuitous resonance with the Beethoven exhibition is heightened when Schenker refers to 'the damage suffered by music through this artistic opportunism and ignorance', which leads him a little later to attack the '"dilettante"' who 'simply proclaims that art exists "for him"—for whom else?' (*CI* xviii). And this fits well with Schorske's (1980: 254) description of the whole exhibition as a prime 'example of collective narcissism . . . artists (Secessionists) celebrating an artist (Klinger) celebrating a hero of art (Beethoven)'. Then again, apart from a preview the day before the opening (at which Mahler conducted what had been planned as a full performance of the Ninth Symphony but ended up as an excerpt from the finale arranged for six trombones [Celenza

---

[14] *CI* xvii–xviii. In a letter to August Halm dated 3 April 1924, Schenker expressed the same idea in vocabulary that links it to his theory: Bruckner, he says, conceived music 'merely two-dimensionally. That space did not arise for him from a depth, where space links to space, belonging together, like bones, muscles, joints of my body' (DLA 69.930/12, translated by Rothfarb, Schenker Correspondence Project website).

2004: 209]), the exhibition took place in opulent silence, and it is hard to think of a more apt image for the situation of music as Schenker saw it: on the one hand an ostentatiously symbolic act of mythologising or deifying the composer that was heightened by the church-like layout of the exhibition space (a contemporary critic wrote 'This is a church of art, in which one enters into the edification and out of which one exits a believer');[15] on the other hand the silence of a world from which Beethoven's music itself has been lost ('is it really a symphony by Beethoven? . . . Where is it?'). My point in saying all this is not, of course, to provide flimsy evidence that Schenker did in fact attend the exhibition, a matter of no great consequence, but to recapture some of the possible connotations of Schenker's words at the time: attendance levels at the exhibition were high, and those who did not go could read about about it in the newspapers—including the *Neue freie Presse*, of which Schenker, like most of Vienna's educated classes, was a regular reader.

The conventional critique of the Secessionists is that, as Botstein (1997: 13) puts it, they did little more than 'exploit the decorative and sensual surface of art without getting at the ethical and epistemological essence of an older generation's corrupt taste': they critiqued the historicist ornament of the Ringstrasse generation, but merely substituted one style of ornamentation for another—or worse, one set of unrelated styles for another set of unrelated styles. The critique launched by the second-wave Viennese modernists (represented most conspicuously by Karl Kraus, Arnold Schoenberg, and Loos, who had himself seceded from the Secession) was more fundamental, in that what was at issue was not one or another type of ornamentation, but the idea of ornamentation itself. Peri Shamsai (1997: 312) expresses this in terms of cultural politics: the first-wave modernists, she says, appropriated established modes of representation by transferring them from the church or aristocracy to the figure of the artist (as in the layout of the Beethoven exhibition, or Klimt's stylised decoration referencing the ornate designs favoured by the aristocracy), whereas the second-wave modernists repudiated established modes of representation. It is in this context that the debate over ornamentation took on ideological and ethical as well as aesthetic significance.

The most telling document of this debate is Loos's well known essay 'Ornament und Verbrechen' (Ornament and crime), which was not published in German until 1929, but was largely based on ideas Loos had published in the late 1890s.[16] The essay is built round two ar-

[15] Ludwig Hevesi, along with Bahr one of the Secession's strongest supporters, translated in Shamsai 1997: 108 (where the ecclesiastical quality of the design is discussed in more detail).
[16] In particular 'The luxury vehicle', published in the *Neue freie Presse* (3 July 1898), where Loos (1982: 40) set out his evolutionary approach to ornamentation: 'The lower the cultural level of a people, the more extravagant it is with its ornament, its decoration. . . . To see decoration as a sign of superiority means to stand at the level of the In-

guments, of which the first is economic. Ornamentation represents wasted work, Loos argues, so that 'the lack of ornament means shorter working hours and consequently higher wages' (in Münz and Künstler 1966: 229). The very spuriousness of this argument (because, like Viennese modernism in general, it ignores industrial production methods) makes one wonder why Loos chose to make it at all—which might also be said of Schenker's occasional invocation of economic arguments in the favour of the masterworks.[17] The second argument is an evolutionary one, of the type familiar from the *Geist* essay or, of course, any number of other sources: ornamentation is characteristic of primitive peoples, Loos says, and the advance of civilisation goes hand in hand with a decline in ornament, so that tattooing—unexceptionable among the Papuans—becomes a sign of atavism or degeneracy in the modern world. ('There are prisons', he adds, 'in which eighty per cent of the prisoners are tattooed' [226]). And in a perhaps fortuitous rejoinder to Eitelberger's ambivalent comments on contemporary architectural creativity, Loos writes, 'don't you see that the greatness of our age lies in its inability to produce a new form of decoration? We have conquered ornament, we have won through to lack of ornamentation' (227). In short, he says, 'we have art, which has replaced ornament'—and then he adds, 'whoever goes to the Ninth Symphony and then sits down to design a wallpaper is either a rogue or a degenerate' (231). This is part of a network of references to the Ninth Symphony in 'Ornament und Verbrechen' which Jean-Paul Bouillon (1987: 101) reads as a deliberate dig at Klimt's frieze.

Historians of modernist architecture are not particularly known for their sense of humour, and the element of farce and send-up in 'Ornament und Verbrechen' is underrepresented in commentaries;[18] at least, it is hard to see how else to read Loos's ludicrous opening invocation of the ontogeny-recapitulates-phylogeny approach ('When man is born, his instincts are those of a new-born dog. . . . At the age of two he looks like a Papuan, at four like one of an ancient Germanic tribe, at six like Socrates, at eight like Voltaire' [in Münz and Künstler 1966: 226]). More importantly, these historians have tended uncritically to accept the evolutionary historiography of modernist architecture which Loos

---

dians. But we must overcome the Indian in us. . . . To seek beauty only in form and not in ornament is the goal towards which all humanity is striving'. For the complex publication history of 'Ornament und Verbrechen' see Tournikiotis 2002/1991: 23.

[17] A representative example is *BNS* 12–13: what industry 'can command figures of so many millions' as Beethoven, Schenker asks, and yet 'the most insignificant merchant . . . regards himself as a more economically necessary factor than Beethoven'. If only people would perform J. S. Bach's music properly, he adds, they would 'set money flowing to an extent undreamt of from such a source by today's society!'

[18] Exceptions include Vergo 1975: 172 and Masheck 2000: 171 (who argues that Loos's essay is sending up Alois Riegl).

himself did much to propound, and in particular the identification of
lack of ornamentation with progress. This in turn has resulted in a prej-
udiced reading of the heroes (there are few heroines) of the modernist
canon, which seeks to eliminate or simply fails to observe the ornamental elements in their work: hence for example Schorske's (1980:
339) reference to Loos 'abolishing all embellishment'. All this might
lead one to expect that Loos and Schenker, the arch modernist and the
arch antimodernist, would have no more points of contact than
Schenker and the Secessionists; after all, one of Schenker's complaints
in *Ornamentik* was precisely the contemporary 'denigration of embellishments', which he saw as a wrongheaded reaction against the 'mediocre composers' who 'began to overload their works with ornaments while misinterpreting their melodic function' (*CSO* 27). But the
matter is not that simple, and in the next section I shall argue for a
more nuanced understanding of the role ornamentation played in
both Schenker's and Loos's thought, as well as in Viennese modernism
more generally.

First, however, I want to briefly explore the academic rather than
artistic dimension of the ornamentation debate, since this throws up
further parallels with Schenker. The obvious comparison is with the
once highly influential writing of Aloïs Riegl, who was born in 1858
(ten years before Schenker) but whose early trajectory was in some
ways similar. Though born in Linz, he spent part of his childhood in
Galicia, and subsequently enrolled at the University of Vienna; there he
was taught by Hanslick's friend—and Schenker's teacher—Robert Zimmermann. From 1887 to 1898 he was curator of textiles at Eitelberger's
Museum für Kunst und Industrie, and thereafter he taught at the University—where he was the cofounder, with the slightly older Franz
Wickhoff, of the Vienna school of art history (Iversen 1993: 16; Johnston 1972: 152). Once again the starting point is the reaction against
Ringstrasse historicism. Riegl's insistence on the organic relationship
between art and its historical context, and on the impossibility of absolute values in art history, represents a theoretical rationale for the Secessionists' slogan, written over the entrance of Olbrich's Secession
building: 'Jeder Zeit ihre Kunst, jeder Kunst ihre Freiheit' (to each
epoch its art, to each art its freedom). Like Schenker's *Geist* essay—like
most of Schenker's work—Riegl's approach was based on a Hegelian
conception of history: it charts the evolution of an autonomous visual
'faculty', in the same sense that the *Geist* essay charts the evolution of
hearing. Most strikingly Hegelian is Riegl's famous—or infamous—
concept of the *Kunstwollen* (which is variously and awkwardly translated, but I shall say 'art drive').[19] This is an impersonal, historical force
that works through the individual artist, behind his consciousness,

---

[19] Following Sedlmayr 2000; see also Ostrow 2000 and Masheck (2000: 164), where
it is simply rendered *'what art wants to do'*.

without caring in the least whether the happy artist himself wanted to do the right thing or not: I borrow Schenker's words,[20] for Riegl's basic thought here is shared with Schenker (and for that matter with Loos, who saw the artist as 'a vehicle through which the cultural voice of each epoch could speak' [Shamsai 1997: 281]).

It is easy to draw more specific parallels between the *Kunstwollen* and Schenker's *Tonwille* (will of tones). I say this not simply because the words are similar, but because of the similarity between Schenker's idea of the tones forming themselves into patterns in the composer's imagination (or, in the language of *Harmonielehre*, striving to propagate themselves) and the decorative motifs that act as protagonists in Riegl's *Stilfragen, Grundlegungen zu einer Geschichte der Ornamentik* (Problems of style: Foundations for a history of ornament) of 1893, his most famous book and the one that introduced the concept of *Kunstwollen;* as Joaquin Lorda (2000: 113) says, 'Riegl narrates the successes of tendril ornament as if he were dealing with a Greek hero'. (Schenker himself spoke of music representing 'the motifs in ever changing situations in which their characters are revealed, just as human beings are represented in a drama' [*H* 12].) And the history Riegl traces is generated through what Henri Zerner calls 'the endless, tireless, compulsive reiteration of a very few fundamental motifs'.[21] It is, in short, a history derived from the formal analysis of material artefacts, and it is in this formalism that Zimmermann's influence is discernible. The chronology, coupled with the major impact of *Stilfragen*, could suggest that Riegl's book had a direct influence on Schenker's early writings: one might even speculate, probably wildly, that the projected *Geschichte der Melodie* would have attempted for music something like what Riegl attempted for the decorative arts. But once again there is no evidence of a direct link (the connection via Zimmermann is intriguing but probably irrelevant),[22] so it is much more sensible to see these as suggestive parallel developments of a common, basically Hegelian framework. The same applies to Riegl's search for 'higher, universal laws that all works of art uniformly obey without exception' (quoted in Iversen 1993: 5)—what Schenker would have called psychological laws—as well as to his espousal of 'the new art-historical view that knows how to penetrate beyond surface appearance' (quoted in Sedlmayr 2000: 15). And Riegl's bitter complaints about the 'cult of individual facts' in art-historical writing (quoted in Iversen 1993: 4) find an echo in Schenker's denigration, in the preface to his edition of C. P. E. Bach's keyboard music, of 'the letter-worship of antiquarian sticklers for literalness, whose adoration is sometimes extended to misprints'.

---

[20] From *H* 60 (see p. 65 above).

[21] In Riegl 1992/1893: xxii.

[22] Karnes (2001: 37n.) observes that issues of aesthetics are unlikely to have figured significantly in a required course for incoming law students.

But perhaps the clearest resonance emerges from Riegl's controversial relationship with the German architect and theorist Gottfried
Semper (who had died in 1879). Robert Morgan (2002: 258–9), who
notes some affinities between Schenker and Riegl, also observes the
parallel with Semper's concept of architecture and design developing
through the transformation of basic motifs *(Urmotive)*. However, the relationship of Semper and Riegl is like that between Hegel and Marx:
they have much in common just because they are diametrically opposed to one another. Riegl and Semper share the framework of evolutionary history, but their conception of the basic motifs is exactly the
opposite. Semper conceived them in terms of 'basic methods of making
and the material associated with them' (in Iversen 1993: 23), and this
is the context for Riegl's statement that

> in opposition to this mechanistic conception of the essence of works of art,
> I substituted in *Stilfragen*—for the first time, as far as I know—a teleologi-
> cal one, in which I see in the work of art the result of a specific and pur-
> poseful *Kunstwollen* that asserts itself in conflict with practical purpose, ma-
> terial, and technique. (71)

In other words, Riegl is opposing the materialist point of view, also associated with such contemporary architects as Otto Wagner and indeed
Loos,[23] that saw history as an unfolding of technique: instead he sees it
as the unfolding of the Hegelian spirit. (It would be no surprise to find
him referring, as Schenker did in *Kontrapunkt* 1, to 'the spirit latent in
the historical development of our art' [*CI* 291].) That does not mean
that issues of technique or material are not significant, but they are so
'only in affecting or qualifying an artistic impetus that is independently
under way' (Masheck 2000: 162).

And it is here that the resonances with Schenker's *Ornamentik* (and,
behind that, the *Geist* essay) reach their peak. As we have seen, one of
Schenker's fundamental arguments against Bülow is that Bach's embellishments must be understood musically, not in terms of the material properties of the clavichord (such as its alleged thinness of tone).
More generally, Schenker's attack on the virtuosos is an attack on the
conception of music in terms of technique rather than content: the
great composers of the past, Schenker says (now in *Die Kunst des Vortrags*),
composed 'according to the needs of synthesis, never merely according
to those of the hand',[24] and so technique—fingering, for instance—is

---

[23] For Wagner see Iversen 1993: 25; for Loos, see his 1898 essay 'Glass and Clay'
(Loos 1982: 35).

[24] *AP* 33. Schenker makes the same point elsewhere: in both 'Beethoven-"retouche"' and the Ninth Symphony monograph he argues that Beethoven's brass writing
is to be understood in terms of the musical idea and not the technical capacities of the instruments; in *Kontrapunkt* 1 'it would have been better if Bellermann had derived the
justification [of the *ligatura rupta*] from the tonal world itself rather than from the technique of the singer' (*CI* 340).

significant only in relation to an artistic impetus that is independently under way. Schenker makes the point still more explicitly in relation to practising: 'Certain difficulties', he writes, 'experienced by the composer himself, can only be borne and overcome through the *spirit* of the performer, not by practicing. . . . Virtuosos are defeated by such passages, and finger exercises are of no avail. Only the spirit can find the way' (*AP* 75). In this way there is a coherent—if coincidental—relationship between the ideas of spirit and technique adumbrated in Riegl's book and Schenker's article of two years later: in a sense, the central insight of the Schenker project is that technique only makes sense in relation to the historically developing mentality that Riegl called *Kunstwollen* and that Schenker, at this stage of career, called *Geist*—and, reciprocally, that it is only through the formal analysis of actual works of music that this mentality can be understood. One wonders if Riegl, too, might have characterised himself as a formalist against formalism.

Yet it is entirely characteristic of patterns in intellectual history that affinities in certain respects go along with divergence in others: that is because—as I suggested in relation to Hegel and Marx—the most significant affinities are in patterns of thinking, rather than in the specific conclusions to which they are directed. (Put simply, a stick has two ends.) I have already mentioned Riegl's disbelief in absolute values in art history, and indeed the motivating principle of the Vienna school of art history—which continued under Max Dvořák following Riegl's premature death in 1905—was that, because all art has to be understood in its own historical context, there can be no such thing as an absolute, universally valid hierarchy of value. Riegl wrote in a late essay that 'at the beginning of the twentieth century, most of us have come to the conclusion that there is no such absolute art-value, and that it is a pure fiction to consider ourselves wiser arbiters than were the contemporaries of misunderstood masters in the past' (Iversen 1993: 7). The practical consequence of this was that Riegl pioneered the study of such then disregarded periods as the late classical, early medieval, and baroque. His position was in fact not so different from that of Guido Adler, who moved from Prague to Hanslick's chair at the University of Vienna in 1898, holding it until 1927, and whose residual sense—shared by many Viennese contemporaries— that there existed timeless aesthetic norms was heavily mediated by historical understanding; as Margaret Notley (1999: 51) puts it, Adler's highly influential approach to the study of music history, based like Riegl's on the idea of style, 'recognized the different beauties of historically distant musics, regarding these compositions as something more than steps in the evolution toward classical style'. Like Robert Hirschfeld, Adler had taken his doctorate in prebaroque music, and while both had doubts about the direction of contemporary composition, they saw the canon of masterworks as extending at least as far as

Wagner.[25] All this suggests that the narrowing of Schenker's own personal canon in the years before 1905–6 (when the second sentence of *Niedergang* lists 'the proud procession of geniuses—Handel, Sebastian Bach, Emanuel Bach, Haydn, Mozart, Beethoven, Schubert, Schumann, Mendelssohn, Brahms')[26] placed him increasingly out of line with both the critical centre ground which he had to some extent shared with Hirschfeld and Helm in the 1890s and the new academic establishment, in this way contributing to the siege mentality that becomes increasingly evident in Schenker's writing during these years.

Modernists against Modernism

I spoke of the Ringstrasse being the backdrop of Viennese life since the 1870s, but if we are to take literally the idea of setting Schenker into his period context, then we should consider not just the city's public buildings but his daily environment: what did Schenker see every time he went out of his front door during the time when he was writing *Ornamentik?* From 1901 to 1921 Schenker—and from 1919 his wife Jeanette—lived in Reisnerstrasse (Chiang 1996: 44), and unlike many other buildings in this street, the one at which the Schenkers lived, no. 38, still survives. Reisnerstrasse is in the third district, the Landstrasse, which lies just outside the Ringstrasse; in general Landstrasse has slipped socially and is nowadays a largely working-class area—but Reisnerstrasse is in the best part of it, close to the Belvedere palaces and embassies, and just across Stadtpark from the old centre. (It is also just a block away from the Conservatory, now Universität für Musik und darstellende Kunst Wien, on Anton-von-Webern-Platz—but that is a coincidence, since the Conservatory moved there only in the 1990s.) No. 38 is a grand but comparatively sober example of Reisnerstrasse's scaled-down version of Ringstrasse eclecticism, with its rusticated pilasters and understated corbels (figs. 2.5–7). Nevertheless, there is a good deal of applied ornamentation: the moulded head above the main entrance is mirrored above the first-floor windows on the main facade, this time with festoons (note the alternating curved and straight pediments on this floor, with broken pediments above), and the motif is carried into the interior with the detailing of the main staircase. Neighbouring blocks embody similar features but often more exuberantly. At no. 24 the head over the door is complemented by garlands and full-length figures; over the road, disconcertingly lifelike putti strain to support a balcony, while an adjoining façade with more abstract applied ornamentation in a baroque style proves on inspection to incorporate

---

[25] The most comprehensive source for both Hirschfeld and Adler within the Viennese context is Botstein 1985.

[26] *DAC* 34.

Figures 2.5–7   Reisnerstrasse 38. Photographs by Georg Weckwerth.

Figures 2.8–10   Neighbouring buildings in Reisnerstrasse.

life-size figures lolling above the pediments over the second-story windows (figs. 2.8–10).

It may be a conceit to relate such images to Schenker's views on ornamentation, but they nevertheless represent the ubiquitous, taken-
for-granted (and hence never mentioned) context of the ornamentation debate in Vienna. Loos's complaint about the buildings of Vienna's
'Potemkin city'—that 'their ornamental details, their corbels, festoons,
cartouches, and denticulation, are nailed-on poured cement' (1982:
96)—applies as much to the domestic buildings of Reisnerstrasse and
any number of similar streets in the inner suburbs as it does to the public buildings of the Ringstrasse, and the same is true of Schoenberg's
comparison of harmony exercises 'dressed up with passing tones, changing tones, and other such ornaments' with architecture that 'sticks cheap
stucco over every smooth, straight surface, merely because its practi-
tioners cannot bear smooth surfaces and straight lines'.[27] Maybe then
it would not be going too far to detect a distant resonance with Schenk-

[27] Schoenberg 1978/1911: 202.

Figure 2.11   Adolf Loos's Michaelerplatz
house. Used by permission of Albertina, Vienna.

er's article 'Unpersönliche Musik', where he spoke of 'classicist' composers pursuing motives and themes, and then *forcing* them into any
old beautiful form'.[28] (The word 'form' applies to moulding plaster in
German as well as English.) At all events, to return to the mainstream
of architectural history, this kind of ubiquitous domestic vernacular
makes it easier to understand the huge controversy that was created by
Loos's Michaelerplatz house of 1909–11, actually a shop (the tailors
Goldman and Salatsch, until they went bankrupt in 1925) with apartments above (fig. 2.11). This apparently unexceptionable design brought
forth a stream of vitriol from the contemporary press: as the *Neue freie
Presse* thundered,

> Seldom has a work of architecture called forth such universal opposition,
> not even the 'cabbage dome' of the Secession. . . . The ground floor and
> mezzanine of proud marble . . . and above it all, a bare plaster wall, with-
> out the shadow of an ornament, pierced by tasteless window-openings, a
> desolate poverty above all this marble splendour. . . . How can anyone
> have thought it possible to harmonize this blatantly dissonant modernism
> with its timeless, historic surroundings? (quoted in Vergo 1975: 172)

Responses of this kind become more intelligible when considered
in light of a contemporary cartoon from another paper, *Der Morgen* (fig.
2.12). The figure in the foreground is the architect (Johann) Fischer

---

[28] Schenker 1988: 137.

Wien in der Karikatur.
XXXVI.
Das Loos-Haus auf dem Michaelerplatz.

Der selige Fischer v. Erlach: Schade, daß ich diesen
Stil nicht schon gekannt hab', dann hätt' ich den schönen Platz
nicht mit meiner dalketen Ornamentik verschandelt!"

Figure 2.12 Cartoon from *Der Morgen*.
(*Source:* Gravagnuolo 1982: 125.)

von Erlach—whom as it happens Loos greatly admired—and this makes the obvious point about the juxtaposition of eighteenth- and twentieth-century buildings, but what is striking is the way the Michaelerplatz house is represented. It looks like a product of 1960s brutalism. All the detailing of Loos's design is excised, and the unrelieved, staring windows bring to mind the only comment by Schenker about Loos of which I am aware, a diary entry from 1911:[29]

---

[29]Transcribed in Federhofer 1985: 286–7; Federhofer notes a further comment about the relationship between eye and eyebrow, evidently a reference to the derogatory de-

Figure 2.13   Building adjacent to
Michaelerplatz house.

The ornament usefully prepares for the opening in the wall: otherwise, if
the window were without ornament, the beholder would have only the
impression of a gap, brutally broken from the outside as if at the hands of
burglars. Through the ornament then, the beholder enjoys the opening in
the wall from the outside as the inhabitant himself now enjoys it from
within. The ornament thereby frees our idea of the window from the suspicion of being mere chance, malice, etc; against the architect Loos.

One might say that the difference between the cartoon and the real
building is a measure of the extent to which applied ornamentation
was a taken-for-granted element of the built environment, an almost
unconscious dimension of the way things looked.

But what are we to make of the *Neue freie Presse* report's reference
to the 'timeless, historic surroundings'? The writer is thinking less of
the adjacent building (fig. 2.13) than of the building directly across the
road: the Reichskanzleitrakt (fig. 2.14), the part of the Hofburg or im-

scription of the Michaelerplatz house credited to Franz Josef ('the house without eyebrows') and hence confirming it is the Michaelerplatz house that Schenker was thinking of.

Figure 2.14 Reichskanzleitrakt.

perial palace that contained the private living quarters of Franz Josef. The idea that this baroque confection, designed by Fischer von Erlach though not constructed until the late nineteenth century (Tournikiotis 2002/1991: 116), might be timeless is less an erratic aesthetic judgement than a reflection of Habsburg ideology. Art was one of the means by which imperial hegemony was naturalised: according to Shamsai (1997: 305), for whom the ideological function of art in *fin-de-siècle* Vienna is an essential dimension of the debates over modernism, 'by symbolically shifting the justification of the ruling class' authority from economics to culture, the privileged members of Austrian society replaced the historic foundations of social inequality with the essential difference between two natures'. And Peter Franklin (1997: 32), in his biography of Mahler, suggests that the Conservatory played a similar role:

> All the races that made up the ethnically diverse, 'multinational' Habsburg Empire were represented by Mahler's contemporaries at the Conservatory. The aim of their teachers was to make them all executants and officials of a traditional musical culture whose special value was defined by its universality and its transcendence of the popular, the ephemeral, the ethnic,

the worldly. The 'mastery' of the greatest works was taken to be synonymous with their structural articulation as models of a theoretical 'organic
unity'. In them, the boundary between what was artificial and what
seemed natural was intended to be . . . indistinguishable.

In this way it is not just ornamentation or its lack that carried an ideological resonance in the *fin-de-siècle* Viennese context (with my reference to 'the way things looked' locating the process of naturalisation):
the same can be said of many of the key terms of the debate around
music, including universality, transcendence, and organic unity, not to
mention the timeless aesthetic norms I previously referred to. I shall
come back to these matters in chapter 3.

To conclude the affair of the Michaelerplatz house, there was a
storm of protest when the scaffolding came down, and the civil authorities at first insisted on a new ornamental façade being 'nailed on',
to borrow Loos's words, but in the end a compromise was reached by
which symmetrically arranged window boxes were added as a substitute for the nonexistent architectural articulation of the windows. (The
early photograph in fig. 2.11 shows the window boxes, but they appear
not yet to have been planted up.) To our eyes, however, a much more
characteristic example of modernist minimalism than the Michaelerplatz house—and one which might better warrant Schenker's comment—is Loos's Steiner house of 1910, located in an eastern suburb of
the city. Or at least, this applies to the view from the garden (fig. 2.15):
as Nicolaus Pevsner says (1966: 21), this view is 'always illustrated
when the purpose is to establish him as a pioneer of the International
Modern of 1925–50'. ('The curious quadrant roof towards the street',
he adds, 'is discreetly left unseen' [fig. 2.16].)[30] But perhaps the most
remarkable feature of this house is the irregular arrangement of the
windows visible in the side view, which results from the disposition of
the rooms within (fig. 2.17): as Renata Kassal-Mikula explains, 'the elevation evolves from within so that the fenestration is dictated by the
disposition of the rooms' (in Waissenberger 1985: 202)—instead of, as
conventionally, the other way round. Years before he achieved it in
such a thoroughgoing manner, Loos described this as the touchstone of
the real architect: 'There are architects', he wrote, whose 'imaginations
create not spaces but sections of walls. That which is left over around
the walls then forms the rooms. . . . But the artist, the *architect,* first
senses the effect that he intends to realize and sees the rooms he wants
to create in his mind's eye' (Loos 1982/1921: 66). There are a number
of Schenkerian resonances here. One is the pseudo-Mozartian image of
the creative vision; another is the idea of creating effects that are not

---

[30] Planning regulations allowed only one story on the street; hence the dormer bun-
galow plus basement design. The house was subsequently altered to create a more conventional street frontage.

Figure 2.15 Loos's Steiner house, garden view. Used by permission of Austrian National Library Vienna, Picture Archive (sign. 105.493-C).

Figure 2.16 Loos's Steiner house, from street (before alterations). (*Source:* Borsi and Godoli 1986: 151.)

Figure 2.17 Loos's Steiner house, side view (before alterations). Used by permission of Austrian National Library Vienna, Picture Archive (sign. 105.494-C).

just subjective but objective, insofar as they are inherent in the physical properties of the artwork, as becomes clearer when Loos goes on to say that the architect 'senses the effect that he wishes to exert upon the spectator' (he cites fear, reverence, respect for power, gaiety, domesticity), and adds, 'these effects are produced by both the material and the form of the space'. But perhaps more intriguing is the resonance with the characterisation of German thought that Bent connects with Schenker's theoretical breakthrough at the time of the op. 101 *Erläuterungsausgabe:* 'the Frenchman thinks from the outside inwards, whereas the German thinks from the inside outwards'.[31]

I hope it is obvious that the purpose of drawing such parallels is not to argue for direct relationships of influence—which would be an absurd claim—but to suggest how patterns of theoretical thought are woven into the fabric of everyday experience, from which they acquire much of their meaning. I would now like to pursue the point deeper into the domestic interior, following Loos's maxim that a house should be 'discreet on the outside; its entire richness should be disclosed on the

[31] See p. 87 above.

Figure 2.18 Loos's Steiner house, interior. Used by permission of Albertina, Vienna.

inside'.[32] The Steiner house illustrates this in the striking difference between the almost forbidding public face presented by the exterior, with its blank walls and unseeing windows, and the intimacy and informality of its interior—an effect that results, for example, from the blackened, heavy beams (hardly the most familiar expression of Viennese modernism) and the variety of styles of furniture (fig. 2.18); despite the different economic status, the comfortable ambience is not so different from that of Schenker's study bedroom in his last (and no longer existing) flat, at Keilgasse 8, just round the corner from Reisnerstrasse (fig. 2.19). Loos's own flat, at Bösendorferstrasse 3 (fig. 2.20), is even more of a study in the vernacular, with fake beams and an inglenook fireplace that might reflect the influence of either Henry Richardson[33] or the English Arts and Crafts tradition; the furniture would be equally at home at Keilgasse 8, and is reminiscent of Paul Stefan's account of how Loos used to take his clients to street markets or junk shops, where it was possible at that time to buy Biedermeier furniture for next to nothing—unlike the Secessionist architects, who would 'indulge in costly experiments at the client's expense, redecorating entire apartments every two or three years in order to keep abreast of the latest fashion' (Vergo 1975: 165). Loos (1982: 125–7) satirised the way such architects

---

[32] Translated in Tournikiotis 2002/1991: 70 ('discrete' changed to 'discreet').
[33] Tournikiotis 2002/1991: 10; Loos lived in the United States from 1893 to 1896.

Figure 2.19 Schenker's study bedroom at Keilgasse 8. Used by permission of
Special Collections, University of California, Riverside Libraries, University of
California, Riverside, California.

Figure 2.20 Loos's flat (photograph from ca. 1909). Used by permission of
Austrian National Library Vienna, Picture Archive (sign. 14.491-B)

Figure 2.21 Biedermeier cupboard, Museum
für Angewandte Kunst, Vienna.

controlled their clients' lives, turning them into slaves of fashion, in his
'Story of a poor rich man', first published in 1900.

And Biedermeier furniture makes a good point of departure for a
closer consideration of Loos's use of ornamentation. Figure 2.21 shows
a cupboard with shelves from about 1830, the restrained interpretation
of classical detailing being most obvious in the simpified capitals of the
principal uprights (fig. 2.22). By comparison, a double cupboard designed by Loos in 1900 (fig. 2.23) creates a mildly orientalising effect
owing to its applied handles in the style of a Japanese *tansu*,[34] while the
sides and cupboard doors would probably have appeared brutally plain
to the artist of the *Der Morgen* cartoon. But it also embodies a number
of subtle classicising features, ranging from the fielded panels at the top

[34] A table with similar detailing is reproduced in Gravagnuolo 1982: 68–9, while a
tansu-like chest of drawers (also from about 1900) is illustrated in Tournikiotis 2002/
1991: 57.

Figure 2.22   Biedermeier cupboard, detail.

to the delicately tapered uprights (reflected in the mirror backing) that support the upper cupboard, with the junctions being articulated by a series of mouldings amounting in effect to capitals in a schematised classical order. And once you start looking for classical references in Loos's work, you begin to see them everywhere. It is, for instance, exactly the classical elements that the *Der Morgen* cartoon leaves out of the Michaelerplatz house, such as the columns of the central facade—columns that actually fulfil no structural function whatever—with their simplified but unambiguously classical capitals, or the cornice above them (figs. 2.24–25); one contemporary who *did* see these elements, incidentally, was Josef Hoffmann (the designer of the Beethoven exhibition), who wrote about the odd effect created by the 'antique columns and details of the fenestration, which did not altogether correspond to our own conceptions'.[35] Again, there are classical-style friezes on the street front of the Rufer house of 1922, at first sight as uncompromising as any of Loos's houses, and the most famous ex-

---

[35] This retrospective comment is quoted from Hoffmann's 'Selbtsbiographie', in Vergo 1975: 173.

Figure 2.23 Loos, cupboard. (*Source:* Gravagnuolo 1982: 71.)

ample of Loos's designing from the inside outwards; there are friezes inside the Strasser House (1919) and the earlier Bellack flat (1909/13), which Benedetto Gravagnuolo describes as 'a step backward . . . decoration of questionable taste . . . an anachronistic "tattoo"' (1982: 138). (He concludes by referring to the 'pathetically luxurious image of the room'.) Then there are Loos's projects for houses that were never built: between them the Konstandt, Bronner, and Stross houses (all from around 1920) feature columns, porticos, cornices with garlands, and even caryatids. The most extravagant example, however, is the one Loos himself referred to as 'the column liberated from its function' (Tournikiotis 2002/1991: 155): his unsuccessful competition entry of 1922 for the Chicago Tribune building (fig. 2.26). This is a design that looks today like the purest postmodernism, and one wonders whether, as with 'Ornament und Verbrechen', there may have been an element of send-up here (though send-up of what?). But it seems not: Loos

Figure 2.24–5 Loos's Michaelerplatz house, details. Photographs by
Panayotis Tournikiotis.

wrote of this design that 'The Big Greek Column will be built / If not in
Chicago [then] elsewhere / If not for the Chicago Tribune for someone
else / If not by me by some other architect'.[36]

This constant and explicit invocation of classical elements in Loos's
designs is matched by his writings: in 1898 he wrote that 'since the decline of the Western Roman Empire there has been no era that has
thought and felt more classically than ours' (Loos 1982/1921: 104); in
1910 that 'our culture builds itself from the knowledge of all the superior greatness of classical antiquity' (quoted in Shamsai 1997: 263); and
in 1924 that 'Classical ornament contributes discipline to the shaping
of the objects we use. It contributes order to our lives' (quoted in Münz
and Künstler 1966: 21). Yet there has been an equally constant unease
on the part of architectural historians about this aspect of the architect
who, above all others, is supposed in Schorske's words to have 'sought
to remove "style"—ornamentation or dressing of any sort—from archi-

[36] Quoted in Gravagnuolo 1982: 175.

Figure 2.26 Loos's design for the
Chicago Tribune building. Used by
permission of Albertina, Vienna.

tecture' (1980: 339); it is as if another ideology, this time that of architectural modernism, has stepped into the shoes of the ideology of Habsburg imperialism, with the consequence that Loos's designs have been seen by historians in very much the same way the *Der Morgen* cartoonist saw the Michaelerplatz house. (There is a striking musical parallel in Webern, whose elevation to a similar position of modernist sainthood resulted in the period features of his style, starting with the waltz-like lilt that runs beneath his rhythms, becoming invisible in his scores and inaudible in their performance.)

Some historians comment on Loos's classicism but find ways of explaining it away. Franco Borsi and Ezio Godoli (1986: 155), for example, refer to 'a timeless classicism that had been rebuilt from within', seeking in this way to eliminate the element of historical reference. (The invocation of 'timelessness' in this context, evoking the *Neue freie Presse* report on the Michaelerplatz house, is telling.) Panayotis Tournikiotis (2002/1991: 67, 24) seems to echo Borsi and Godoli when he speaks of Loos 'recognizing the timelessness of classicism' and realizing that 'he could make classical references without being bound by classical rules'—a position that sits awkwardly with the distinction he draws elsewhere between Loos's attack on 'ornamentation' and his approval of 'decoration considered as a set of rules . . . issuing from properly worked materials and from the "grammar" of classical language'. (If it is the rules that distinguish classical detail from superfluous ornamentation, then disconnected references reduce classical detail to ornamental cliché.) Referring to the Rufer house frieze, Ludwig Münz and Gustav Künstler (1966: 51) say that 'the decoration was not there for its own sake but to increase the effect of wall areas or to give a true conception of the shape of an external wall'. And Gravagnuolo (1982: 130), faced with the columns in the Michaelerplatz house, seeks to interpret the very concept of ornamentation out of existence:

> The columns of the arcade on the ground floor are not load-bearing but only pretend to hold up the mezzanine floor. . . . Why this apparent 'lie'? The most likely answer is that the arcade fulfills a much more important function than one of statics: it realizes architecture as representation of architecture, meaning as a staging of the urban spectacle.

But he seems unconvinced by his own explanation, for a page later he comes back to it:

> So the theoretical question of the inconsistency of the author of *Ornament and Crime* raises its head again. Is the column of the Looshaus an ornament? . . . the answer is in the negative. The column, here, is not a decorative form but a symbolic one. It is a symbol of the architecture of the metropolis and it is no accident that it will be reproposed for the 'Chicago Tribune'.

And when, later in his book, he reaches the Chicago Tribune building, Gravagnuolo (175) drives this argument to the desired conclusion: 'In as much as it is a conscious attempt to pour the history of the past into the future, the Column is, strictly speaking, a *modern* work'. Basically, it seems, Gravagnuolo is saying that if you can explain something symbolically then it is no longer purely ornamental—but since you can find a symbolical explanation for anything, the net effect is that the debate becomes meaningless. The more honest critics, then, are those who recognise the distance between Loos's modernism and the stereotypical associations of that word. Peter Vergo (1975: 177) speaks of the 'tension between radicalism and conservatism' in Loos's work; Münz and Künstler (32) accept that 'in many respects [Loos] was the most tradition-bound of modern architects'. And Pevsner, in his introduction to Münz and Künstler's book (21), writes that Loos's defence of classicism remains 'incomprehensible in so radical a thinker': he tries to explain it as a consequence of Loos's disappointment in his later life (but then classicism is found throughout Loos's work), and concludes hopelessly, 'so the interpretation attempted in this introduction must be faulty or the evidence must be incomplete. For the time being at any rate the enigma remains'.

It could be, of course, that the problem lies not in Loos but in the historiographical framework into which he is being inserted: what might be called the 'form follows function' paradigm associated, in particular, with the Bauhaus and Le Corbusier but frequently treated as the definitive model of architectural modernism in general. It is a paradigm that fits poorly with Viennese modernism. Loos's designs were as likely to conceal as to reveal function, as demonstrated by the columns of the Michaelerplatz house. And Loos was as suspicious of formalism as Schenker, as two quotations demonstrate:

> New forms? How dull! It is the new spirit that matters. Even out of old forms it will fashion what we new men need.[37]

> This room . . . brings us modern forms in the old spirit. . . . The correct thing would have been to make use of old forms in the new spirit.[38]

There is an affinity between Loos's use of old forms in the new spirit and the imitation of the classics 'but always in new ways' which Schenker commended in Brahms.[39] But the point is a more general one. Loos emphasises spirit, consciousness, attitude as opposed to its purely material expressions, just like Schenker and Riegl, those formalists against formalism; the relationship between spirit and technique, between the idea and its realisation, lies at the core of the ethical dimension of second-wave Viennese modernism. To put it that way is to invoke Schoenberg, and it is in relationship to Schoenberg that Loos has entered the histories of music: in his *Harmonielehre* of 1911, Schoenberg refers explicitly to Loos's denigration of tattooing and of 'decorators' (*Ornamentierer*).[40] And he continues with a story that reads like a direct pastiche of Loos—about how he designed a music stand, but the carpenter who was to make it explained how wasteful and inefficient the design was, and so 'I was thoroughly shamed. I had considered beautiful what was simply impractical'.[41] However, the Loos influence, so fully assimilated that it does not need explicit ascription, is most evi-

---

[37] Quoted in Smith 1986: 43.

[38] From an article published in *Die Zeit,* 18 December 1897 (Loos 1982: 93), referring to a room designed by Heinrich Lefler and others for an exhibition held at the Museum für Kunst und Industrie (now Museum für Angewandte Kunst) in late 1897.

[39] See p. 55 above.

[40] Schoenberg 1978/1911: 340, 270.

[41] Schoenberg 1978/1911: 270.

dent in the references (such as the one I have already quoted) to cheap stucco—the ethical dimension turning on the use of cheap materials that masquerade as expensive ones—and in statements like 'there is no style to carry one through, no ornament to give a lift; pomposity is out of the question, and fraud too. This is morality, an idea makes its appearance for what it is worth—no less, but no more either'.[42]

This ethical or moral modernism is an equally integral dimension of the Schenker project. Sometimes it becomes explicit, as when in (his) *Harmonielehre* Schenker writes, perhaps with particular reference to Schoenberg, that 'where the composer unmistakably reveals his intention to ruin the diatonic system, we have not only the right but, even more, the moral duty to resent the deceit against our art and to expose the lack of artistic instinct which manifests itself here even more drastically' (*H* 290; the comparison is with when this happens unintentionally, through sheer incompetence on the composer's part). But it is everywhere implicit in his attacks on the virtuosos with their mechanical conception of music, the editors who reduce the masterworks to a series of instructions for immediate execution, the false theorists who reduce the living forms of the past into mere formulas, the equally false composers who imitate these formulae: in each case, Schenker's concern is to valorise individual judgement and responsibility, to assert human values against the mechanical, and this is the source of the moralising and sometimes messianic tone which, if one does not understand it in context, can be one of the most alienating features of Schenker's writing. If we see this ethical dimension as central to Schenker's project, in the way it was for the second-wave Viennese modernists in general, then we shall better appreciate the concerns and attitudes of mind that link Schenker to the artists, writers, and musicians of his day, even though his brand of modernism was directed towards the narrowing historical repertory he perhaps had in mind when he referred to 'us epigoni'.

But then, as the example of Loos makes clear, modernism as an attitude of mind does not translate in any very direct way into aesthetic preferences, and certainly not in the direct manner supposed by those historians who have identified progress with the elimination of ornament; one might equally cite the example of Kraus, with his enthusiasm for Offenbach and Nestroy and his general nostalgia for the Vormärz (the period before the revolutions of 1848), not to mention the conservative political views he shared with Loos, Schoenberg, and of course Schenker. As Peter Gay (1978: 2) puts it, 'modernists hated modernity—they hated, in other words, the rule of the machine, the vulgarity of bourgeois society, the pretensions of parvenus, the waning of community'. There is in short as much modernism in Schenker's

---

[42] Schoenberg 1975: 369 (again dating from 1911).

conservatism as there is conservatism in Loos's, Schoenberg's, and Kraus's modernism. More on this in chapter 3.

Reinventing the Classics

Really, of course, Loos's 'new forms? How dull!' throws the baby out with the bathwater. It is not that second-wave Viennese modernists were unconcerned with forms and techniques: their point was rather that forms and techniques are meaningless except in the context of what Loos and Schenker called spirit, but we would be more likely to call ethical value. This means that a more adequate solution to Pevsner's enigma, and more generally to the problem of ornamentation in Viennese modernism, might be to take a qualitative rather than quantitative approach to it. The issue then is not how much ornamentation there is: it is what sort of ornamentation it is, what its ethical value is, whether it is good or bad. And this is exactly what C. P. E. Bach said in a quotation from his *Versuch* that Schenker included only a few pages into *Ornamentik:* 'good embellishments must be distinguished from bad' (*CSO* 18). But how? The short answer—C. P. E. Bach's answer, and at one level Schenker's answer—is through an adequate understanding of harmony and voice-leading, through sensitivity to context, through moderation. The longer answer, by contrast, involves the broader cultural significance of ornamentation which I have been trying to convey.

In her influential book *Reading in Detail: Aesthetics and the Feminine,* Naomi Schor (1987) seeks to understand the detail as a potentially countercultural force, tracing a range of resistances to 'what is perhaps most threatening about the detail: its tendency to subvert an internal hierarchic ordering of the work of art, which clearly subordinates the periphery to the center, the accessory to the principal, the foreground to the background' (Schor 1987: 20). As a major example of the policing of detail, she explores the aesthetics of the sublime, as represented by British writers from Edmund Burke (who was widely read in continental Europe) to Sir Joshua Reynolds: one-sentence summaries, which Schor (12) quotes, include William Hazlitt's 'the great style in painting consists in avoiding the details, and peculiarities of individual objects', and Reynolds's outline in the table of contents from *Discourses on Art* ('Genius—consists principally in the comprehension of *A WHOLE;* in taking in general idea only'). Like many eighteenth- and nineteenth-century writers, Reynolds's thinking revolves round the distinction between the genius who grasps the whole and the second-rate artist, the mere 'talent', who 'loses himself in the servile copying of nature in its infinite particularity' (12); that too is a conception echoed by Schenker's claim that the geniuses 'envision the form as a totality' whereas 'the non-geniuses . . . compose entirely in terms of the succession of surface events', or in his reference to the 'so-called heathens' who 'consider only the foreground of the work and lose themselves in its particulars'.[43] Detail, then, is characterised by Reynolds in prevailingly negative terms, as emerges very clearly in a passage from the Third Discourse (the emphases are Schor's [15]):

> All objects which are exhibited to our view by nature, upon close examination will be found to have their *blemishes* and *defects*. The most beautiful forms have something about them like *weakness, minuteness,* or *imperfection.* . . . [The painter] corrects nature by herself, her imperfect state by her more perfect. His eye being able to distinguish the *accidental deficiencies, excrescences,* and *deformities* of things, from their general figures, he makes out an abstract idea of their forms more perfect than any one original.

But here the parallel with Schenker begins to break down badly. One of Schenker's recurring complaints (at least up to *Meisterwerk*, perhaps less so in *Der freie Satz*) is against those who ride roughshod over details, from the listeners he criticised in the 1894 essay 'Das Hören in der Musik' for being satisfied with initial impressions to the virtuosos who—as he said in *Ornamentik*—'in a one-sided, academic cultivation of finger velocity . . . failed to develop the ability to "enliven" the tones appropriately and intelligently' (*CSO* 98). This is also the attack he makes in the Ninth Symphony monograph on 'Man-of-the-theater Wagner', who understood clarity 'only in terms of the hearing habits of a crowd of a thousand, of whom a more refined ear-culture is not to be expected' (*BNS* 68, 66). And in the essay 'Weg mit dem Phrasierungsbogen' (Abolish the phrasing slur), from the first (1925) volume of *Meisterwerk*, Schenker not only complains about the editor whose 'unmusical ear hasn't the foggiest notion of contrasts or details' (*MM1* 22), but also repeats the attack on modern musicians and characteristically generalises it to society at large:

> I believe that I am not mistaken when I say that musicians lost their power of judgement to recognize the subtlest interrelationships and, as a consequence, their ability to evaluate details in themselves as well as in relation to the synthesis. . . . I believe that I am also not mistaken in relating this unpleasant thought to the social and political ideology that understands unity only as uniformity. . . . Everywhere, in social and political life as in art, one thus finds the same laziness, the same fanatic compulsion to achieve unity along the path of uniformity, simply to avoid one's duty to the particular, a duty which the tireless achievers are themselves no longer up to. Uniformity has become the catchword. (*MM1* 30)

What is the difference then between Schenker's uniformity and Reynolds's sublimity? Through close readings of various passages from

---

[43] *FC* I 128 and *MM1* 113; Snarrenberg 1997: 154, quoting a passage in *Der freie Satz* (p. 5) that was not translated in *Free Composition*.

Reynolds (including the italicised terms in the quotation above), Schor develops a classic deconstructionist argument: as the teratologically charged vocabulary reveals, Reynolds is obsessed by the 'bad' detail, the detail that intrudes itself by insisting on its own autonomy, and in this way his ideologically loaded concept of sublimity unravels, with the detail functioning—as so often—as a deconstructive lever. This argument leads her on the one hand to an interpretation of the role of detail in Freud's theory of the unconscious, and on the other hand— and more relevantly to *my* argument—to Hegel's aesthetic theory and specifically his concept of sublation (*Aufhebung*, literally lifting something to a higher level).

I can illustrate the point by returning to Schenker's immediate environment and the applied ornamentation of Reisnerstrasse. There are examples aplenty here of what C. P. E. Bach called 'gewgaws which may deface the most perfect building', and one might wonder just what Schenker visualised when he quoted this phrase in *Ornamentik* (*CSO* 27). If such details are indeed 'gewgaws', if they are bad, then that is not necessarily because they are bad in themselves: it is because they are bad in context. As Schor (1987: 46) puts it, summarising the writer and photographer Francis Wey, 'the bad detail is a good detail that has gone bad by completely detaching itself from its support to become an end in itself, a detail for detail's sake'; the extraneous lolling figures of figure 2.10 are particularly obvious candidates. And the background for this thinking, as for much else in the study of material culture (Miller 1987: chap. 2) is Hegel's notion of objectivisation and sublation, the dialectical cycle by which the subject becomes aware of the other and assimilates it through a process of cognitive evolution. In effect, this amounts to a reconciliation between the interests of the detail and those of the whole. When looking at classical sculpture, Hegel says (and this is another passage quoted by Schor [1987: 27–8]):

> the eye cannot at first make out a mass of differences. . . . Nevertheless although these fine nuances are not noticed at a first glance, the general impression which they produce is not for this reason lost. . . . This breath of life, this soul of material forms, rests entirely on the fact that each part is completely there independently and in its own particular character, while . . . it remains in firm connection not only with its immediate neighbour but with the whole. Consequently the shape is perfectly animated at each point; even the minutest detail has its purpose; everything has its own particular character, its own difference, its own distinguishing mark, and yet it . . . counts and lives only in the whole.

Instead of seeking to eliminate or repress the detail as an acknowledged or unacknowledged threat to the whole, as does Reynolds, Hegel focuses on the degree to which the detail is assimilated within the whole while still retaining its own identity: the good detail is sublated, the bad detail is not.

Actually the most striking resonance in this passage from Hegel is not with Schenker, but with Schoenberg's claim in his *Harmonielehre* that 'of the acoustical emanations of the tone nothing is lost. . . . The more remote overtones are recorded by the subconscious, and when they ascend into the conscious they are analyzed and their relation to the total sound is determined'.[44] But Hegel's 'animated' corresponds exactly to Schenker's 'enlivened' in the criticism of virtuosos from *Ornamentik* I quoted earlier, and the idea of a dialectical relationship between part and whole pervades Schenker's writings. One example, which recalls the negative characterisation of the detail that Schor associates with Reynolds, comes from the essay on Bach's Partita no. 3 in the volume of *Meisterwerk*: critiquing a passage from Albert Schweitzer, Schenker writes that '"the detail" remains a conceptual embarrassment so long as it is not authenticated as a definite detail of a definite superordinate unified structure. The detail exists not for its own sake, but only in the context of a whole of which it is, precisely, a part' (*MM1* 50). Another, in which the dialectical aspect is particularly explicit, comes from the second *Meisterwerk* volume: in the opening paragraph of 'Von organischen der Sonatenform' (On organicism in sonata form), Schenker writes that

> the ultimate secrets of the particular must be penetrated if the general is to be comprehended correctly, since the particular is actually the bearer of the general. The task is difficult because, as it always turns out, the general easily seduces us into making things easy for ourselves and spares us any further trouble over the particular. By continually disregarding the particular, however, the understanding of the general is, so to speak, bereft of spirit. (*MM2* 23)

It is however in the analysis of specific details, the discrimination between one detail and another, that the conceptual framework of sublation comes most strongly into play (and if Schenker does not use Hegel's terminology, his use of the ostensively Kantian term 'synthesis' frequently overlaps with the idea of sublation). Summarising Hegel, Schor writes that 'as long as the clauses of a certain *aesthetic contract* are respected—avoidance of the contingent, maintenance of the guarantors of classical order (simplicity, regularity, symmetry)—the proliferation of details is authorized, even encouraged' (1987: 29), and this is the central message of Schenker's *Ornamentik:* Bach's embellishments are good, they are sublated, 'they are a manifestation of truth'.

It is a message which, in 1903, Schenker was unable to ground in theoretical terms: despite the cumulative weight of argumentation in *Ornamentik,* there is little more than an assertion of the essential nature of Bach's embellishment where a theoretical premise should be. (That is hardly surprising, given that he found himself in a similar situation

---

[44] Schoenberg 1978/1911: 21.

in the *Niedergang* typescript, which probably dates from three years later.)[45] The deficit becomes particularly obvious if one compares *Ornamentik* with Felix Salzer's essay of 1930, 'The Significance of the Ornaments in Carl Philipp Emanuel Bach's Keyboard Works', which reads almost like an attempt to do what in 1903 Schenker could not: it uses Schenkerian analysis, as Salzer then understood it, in order to demonstrate that 'Bach's ornaments . . . do not act like ornaments pasted on, as it were. . . . Rather, they actively participate in shaping the motives, and frequently even influence the voice leading' (Salzer 1986: 16). And Salzer (39) concludes, just as Schenker himself might, that 'we are in the presence of a masterly synthesis of voice leading, motivic structure, and ornamentation'. By contrast, what Schenker attacks is not ornament or detail as such, but anything that is nonsublated, that is not in a dialectical relationship with the whole—whether it consists of gratuitous embellishment in the performance of C. P. E. Bach's music, the work of mediocre composers who overload their work with ornaments, or for that matter the schematic, superficial forms adopted by composers under the influence of false theory.

Schoenberg would have agreed on that last point: in the period before the First World War he was as keen to eliminate schematic forms from his compositions (along with thematic statements, repetition, and so forth) as Schenker was to eliminate them from his theory. But while Schoenberg's negative comments on ornamentation in his *Harmonielehre* clearly echo Loos, there is what Shamsai (1997: 271) calls

> a fundamental difference between Schoenberg's and Loos's theorizing of ornamentation in their respective media. Loos believed that art and architecture progressively developed through the decreasing application of ornament, while Schoenberg asserted that the musical masterworks never contained a single ornamental note, which for him was synonymous with superfluity and decoration.

And she quotes from Schoenberg's unpublished essay of 1922, 'About ornaments, primitive rhythms, *etc.*, and bird song', where he writes 'It is certain that . . . in true works of art nothing is an ornament in the sense that one could leave it out' (Schoenberg 1975: 299). Dunsby (1977: 27) plausibly suggests that this essay—which specifically mentions C. P. E. Bach's *Versuch*—was stimulated by Schoenberg's reading of Schenker at this time, and the central assertion is in essence the same as Schenker's in *Ornamentik*: the ornaments are integral to the music, not optional extras that may be added or deleted at the performer's whim. (Schoenberg's essay is basically an attack on the interpretive freedom—freedom, that is, of the illusory sort—claimed by performers.) In *Harmonielehre*, Schoenberg gives the same idea a historical expression: he traces the development of passing notes from originally

---

[45] See p. 76 above.

unnotated ornamentations, and claims that 'certain ornaments are pre-
paring the future shape of music. . . . as someone finally dared to no-
tate the seventh chord, someone will also dare to fix these ornaments
[in notation]'.[46] In short, Schoenberg's position represents a state of
denial: for him 'the entire notion of ornament in music', as Shamsai
(272) puts it, 'was nothing more than a theoretical artifact, which
misconstrued the functional nature of the pitches in question'. For
Schoenberg, then, the conventional notion of ornamentation ('mere'
ornamentation) represents a purely evaluative category, without empirical content—which is just the argument Schenker had made about
organicism in the *Geist* essay (p. 328) when he was in denial about that
concept.

Of course Schoenberg's denial of ornamentation in the 1922 essay
is linked to the idea of 'true works of art': his argument would carry
more weight if there were criteria for distinguishing such works from
those (false) others in which (mere) ornament is to be found. But the
problem with the analytical approaches Schoenberg and his followers
such as Rudolph Réti developed was their undiscriminating nature: as
with Gravagnuolo's symbolical interpretations, motivic relationships
can always be found, and the status of a true work of art thereby demonstrated, so that the empirical component in the evaluation becomes
meaningless. Schoenberg's position accordingly suffers from the same
kind of circularity I complained of in Schenkerian theory, which defines
the masterwork in a certain way and then invokes the masterwork as
evidence for the theory. In Schenker's case, however, that does not pre-
clude evidence-based discrimination between musical details. In essence, the theory Schenker developed after the First World War can be
seen as a system of hierarchical entailments, such that what is non-
essential (merely ornamental) at one level may—or may not—become
essential at another level, and this is not a matter of whim but of the
operation of more or less well-defined transformational relationships.

This might also be linked to the discourse of freedom and constraint to which I have referred. In his earlier theory, Schenker attempts to maintain the element of freedom through the distinction between aesthetic effects and the means of their realisation, but as the
example of fingering and the nose shows, the distinction is in practice
unsustainable (for reasons evident to readers of Gilbert Ryle or Judith
Butler: 'effects' are in reality performative categories, defined through
their realisations). But this approach to freedom recedes as Schenker
develops his later theory from the premise of axial causality, because
freedom is now built into the relationships between structural levels:
just like the law, a given background precludes certain middleground
realisations, but in doing so opens up many legitimate possibilities—

---

[46] Schoenberg 1978/1911: 47, 320.

which is precisely the point of Alpern's, or rather Jellinek's, notion of 'intervening spaces'.[47] To borrow Schenker's terms from 'Weg mit dem Phrasierungsbogen', unity need not entail uniformity, but can encompass difference: as Schor says (1987: 31), 'music is the locus of the emergence of the tension always present throughout [Hegel's] *Aesthetics* between a drive toward unity, articulation, and wholeness and an equally strong countervailing drive towards fragmentation, disjunction, and particularization'. And it is appropriate that in building this idea of unity without uniformity into music theory, Schenker should have taken as his starting point the ornament, by definition the point of transition between obligation and freedom. Schenker's later theory, then, generalises the ornament: there is at each level a dialectical tension between part and whole, such that any given detail is not intrinsically good or bad, but good or bad by virtue of its relationship to that whole. It might in this way be said that Schenker rehabilitated musical detail.

It is not of course part of my claim that Schenker had any substantial conception of the theory of levels at the time he wrote *Ornamentik*—the comparison with Salzer's essay rams home the point that he did not—any more than I have claimed that Schenker built his theories on a specifically Hegelian conception of sublation: the point is rather that, as Tom Rockmore says (1993: 135), 'we are all post-Hegelians' and as such cannot escape the influence of his thought. (If that is so today, it was all the more so in *fin-de-siècle* Vienna.) My aim has rather been to suggest the extent to which Schenker's theory emerged through the development in a particular direction of ideas that were widespread at the time, and in the context of a debate on ornamentation that was seen as of fundamental importance across a range of cultural practices. But there is a further reason why I have thought it appropriate to bring the Hegelian concept of sublation into play. After describing the central issue of Hegel's aesthetic theory as 'insuring the delicate balance between the autonomy of the part and the unity of the whole', Schor comments: 'the choice of these words testifies to the profound complicity of the aesthetic and the political' (1987: 29). And she goes on to show how the concept of detail is an inherently political one, for instance quoting from Baudelaire's argument in *The Painter of Modern Life* that it is better to draw from memory than from life: an artist drawing from life, Baudelaire says (and again the italics are Schor's),

> will find himself at the mercy of a *riot of details* all clamouring for justice with *the fury of a mob* in love with absolute equality. All justice is trampled under foot; all harmony sacrificed and destroyed; many a trifle assumes vast proportions; many a triviality usurps the attention. The more our artist turns an impartial eye on detail, the greater is the state of *anarchy*. Whether he be long-sighted or short-sighted, *all hierarchy and all subordination vanishes*.

---

[47] See p. 42 above.

Such rhetoric is redolent of both Schenker and Schoenberg, who like all Viennese in the early twentieth century—but especially Viennese Jews—had been touched by the development of mass politics (the 'politics in a new key' which I shall discuss in the next chapter). A thread of violent political imagery runs through Schoenberg's *Harmonielehre*, as when he writes, 'The tonality must be placed in danger of losing its sovereignty [because] a ruler can only take pleasure in ruling live subjects; and live subjects will attack and plunder'.[48] And similar images occur in Schenker's work of the same title: 'the tonal system', he writes, 'could be seen as a sort of higher collective order, similar to a state, based on its own social contracts by which the individual tones are bound to abide' (*H* 84). Here there is a quite specifically Hegelian resonance (very possibly mediated by Jellinek), and I shall come back to this in the next chapter. But for now I want to focus on the characteristic Viennese trait which I said was prominent in Schenker's writing, and which the image of music as state exemplifies: a way of slipping almost instantaneously, as if by some conceptual wormhole, from consideration of tiny details to the largest issues of individual and society. The classic illustration of this trait is the story that, shortly before his death, Kraus was reproached for fussing over the punctuation of his satirical journal, *Die Fackel*, while the Japanese were bombarding Shanghai, and replied: 'I know it is all pointless when the house is on fire. But I must do this as long as it is possible for, if the people responsible had always taken care that all the commas were in the right place, Shanghai would not be burning' (Field 1967: 30). In the case of Schenker (who was an at least occasional reader of *Die Fackel*),[49] the nearest equivalent is in 'Weg mit dem Phrasierungsbogen', ostensibly an attack on the long 'phrasing slurs' favoured by turn-of-the-century editors of the classics. A few sentences after his complaint about today's musicians having lost the ability to evaluate details, Schenker makes exactly the same kind of transition:

> just as the masterworks, under the phrasing slur of the editors, glare at us in their uniformity, so all of music glares at us uniformly under the phrasing slur of the Enlightenment, whether or not the product of genius. . . . And yet I am convinced that the political and social phrasing-slur uniformity can deceive mankind only temporarily about its true, higher unity. Humanity will not remain a jarring sound in God's creation forever: Nature itself will force it once again to accept individual characteristics as the only true source of unity. (*MM1* 30)

[48] Schoenberg 1978/1911: 151.

[49] Schenker writes admiringly about *Die Fackel* in a diary entry of 7 December 1914, and dismissively in an entry dated 23 June 1927, in which he comments that it is the first issue he has bought in a long time (Federhofer 1985: 283–4, 285); Schenker's opinion of Kraus seems to have gone down during the war.

If not in quite so dramatic a form, such transitions are an almost ubiquitous feature of Schenker's writing—Scott Burnham (1992: 83), for example, refers to Schenker's 'strikingly Marxist interpretive move in relating Rameau's theory of inversion to the French Revolution'—and for the modern reader this is one of its most bizarre features. But it is also an essential feature. I have already said that one of this book's main claims is that Schenker's theory, at one level a way of thinking about music, is at another level a way of thinking about the relationship between individual and society—and what makes this possible is a Hegelian framework of thought, however loosely derived, that is always both aesthetic and political at the same time.

In this chapter, then, I have used the idea of ornamentation—the subject of Schenker's first book-length publication—to set the early stages of the Schenker project into the context of contemporary critique in the visual arts, ranging from the art-historical writing of Riegl to the work of the successive waves of Viennese modernist artists and designers. I focused in particular on Loos's incorporation of classical detail in order to illustrate the interpenetration and cross-fertilisation of what we see as 'modernist' and 'antimodernist' elements, and used this as a means of identifying some modernist and antimodernist elements in Schenker's work. But of course the idea of classicism works in a fundamentally different way when applied to the visual arts and to music. In architecture and design, classicism means the revival of an ancient tradition that was lost and rediscovered, whereas in music the 'classics' are the works of the late eighteenth and early nineteenth centuries in (principally) Austria and Germany—the continuous tradition within which Schoenberg did everything he could to locate himself as the successor to Beethoven and Brahms. But in the preface to the first volume of *Kontrapunkt,* Schenker presents the situation as more akin to that of the visual arts. Just in case the opening sentences aren't clear enough, he says it again later in the preface: 'music has basically been moribund for decades—despite Schumann, Mendelssohn, and Brahms—until it finally fell victim to the pervasive vandalism of our time' (*C1* xxv). And by 1922, when the second volume appeared, this has become

> If my theories (like all my other works) have been imprinted from the outset with the character of a rescue-effort (since the task at hand was to protect music from centuries of misconceptions by theory and historicism), the need for such endeavor has increased proportionately as the intervening World War has loosed all forces of destruction that have utterly eradicated musical art in the West. Today the task before us is more to transmit the essence of music to more distant eras, since we cannot expect it to be restored in the near future. (*C2* xii)

Read in the postwar context, the listing in 'Weg mit dem Phrasierungsbogen' ('There is no more Bach, no more Handel, no more Haydn or

Mozart or Beethoven: all trace of their spirit has been eradicated!'
[*MM1* 29–30]) sounds like a roll call of the dead.

In the *Geist* essay, and the other essays of the 1890s, Schenker at
times fearlessly diagnosed the failings of contemporary musical culture,
but the tone is forward-looking: that is why it makes sense to speak of
the Schenker project. By as early as 1910, however, well before the
First World War, a note of at times fantastical pessimism has settled on
Schenker's writing that it is hard to shrug off as mere rhetoric: the
Schenker project is now one of reconstruction, the attempt to reinvent
or—if that is too much to hope for—at least to codify a tradition that
has become foreign.[50] This is already implicit in Schenker's image of ex-
cavating the ruins of Herculaneum and Pompeii,[51] but the sense of foreignness is more fully conveyed by a remark I quoted in the introduction: during the discussion in *Der freie Satz* of keys (or, as he puts it,
'"keys"'), Schenker says that 'the masterwork remains inaccessible to
theory, and . . . its analyses resemble unsuccessful decipherings of papyrus rolls' (*FC* I 8–9). Perhaps it would be going too far to relate this
to Schenker's comparison in 'Die Musik von heute' between the 'older
composers' who 'spoke in the shape of music' and the 'New Germans'
who 'speak as if they were using a foreign language'[52] (itself, as I shall
argue in chapter 4, an appropriation of Wagner's critique of the Jews),
but the basic point is clear: we have to laboriously piece together the
music of the great German tradition, because it is no longer 'our' music
at all. What 'our' might mean in such a context is another issue that I
shall come back to.

For Robert Morgan (2002: 252), this is 'a theory conceived by
someone who, no longer part of the world theorized, is on the outside
looking in'. Through his extensive quotations from Broch and Musil—
and I shall return to this in chapter 5—Morgan suggests that there is a
sense in which Schenker's work, particularly his late work, represents
the construction of an autonomous world of the imagination: as early

---

[50] It is admittedly hard to reconcile the pessimism of 1910 and 1922 with the cheery
postcard Schenker sent to Hertzka on 14 January 1914 (WSLB 197, transcribed and
translated by Bent, Schenker Correspondence Project website), saying that 'the resur-
gence of the Classics to which I was the first to give impetus is now setting a whole host
of pens a-scribbling'. The discrepancy might prompt questions of how far Schenker's
published works represent his true feelings rather than an artfully constructed persona,
but then it might equally be argued that in this postcard he was spinning a sales pitch to
his publisher; like most people, Schenker presented himself differently to different people
under different circumstances.

[51] As made clear by a much later use of the same image: in the 'Vermischtes' section
of *Meisterwerk* 3 (1930) Schenker speaks of 'the worthy men of science who research the
remains of ancient culture', but goes on to ask 'who tells us about the spirit that must
surely have been expressed in thought, speech and writing in those long-ago days, and
that transcends those external objects, which when taken together are still unable to por-
tray true culture? Where is the spade that can dig through to the spirit?' (*MM3* 78)

[52] Schenker 1988: 135–6.

as 1910, Morgan argues (254), 'Schenker's "retreat into himself", the personal counterpart of his definition of music as a closed-off domain, was complete, and nowhere is his relation to modernism more evident than in this self-inflicted isolation'. (It is ironic that this resembles the critique Schenker made of Brahms in his *Neue Revue* obituary of 1897.)[53] To the extent that modernism involves the sense of drawing a line between past and present, of making a new beginning, one might then claim that there is something more radically modernist about Schenker's project than there is about Schoenberg's. That, at least, provides a perspective from which to interpret Schenker's contemptuous comparison between the shopkeeper-like 'modernity' of the composers of his day, and what Schenker calls 'our masters' eternal modernity'.[54] (It may or may not be relevant in this context that Schoenberg's father kept a shoe shop.)

After the Michaelerplatz house had been completed, Loos wrote, 'a modern artist—an enemy of mine—said to me: "You want to be a modern artist and you build a house that looks like an old Viennese house"'.[55] With Schenker it was the other way round: he would have liked to turn the clock back, but through his theory he reinvented the classics under the sign of modernism. He was an enthusiastic antimodernist, to be sure, but underneath that—and perhaps despite himself—he was a reluctant modernist.

[53] See p. 53 above.

[54] 'Let them only peddle their so-called "modernity" like shopkeepers; but, finally, they should leave undisturbed our masters' eternal modernity' (translated from the op. 111 *Erläuterungsausgabe* [p. 94n.] in Simms 1977: 114).

[55] Quoted in Borsi and Godoli 1986: 155.

3

The Conservative Tradition

Schenker's Politics

Schenker's writing—not just what he says but how he says it, even the words he uses—is deeply imbued by traditions of conservative thought that were widespread in the German-speaking countries at the turn of the twentieth century, whose origins stretch far back into the nineteenth century and whose point of culmination was National Socialism. But this is conservatism with a small *c*, political thought in the broader sense of cultural politics rather than the narrower sense of party politics: in the second section of this chapter I shall discuss these conservative ideologies and in particular the link between the idea of the 'natural' and music theory, while in the final section I shall explore some of the specific forms that cultural conservatism took in Vienna. But at the same time, cultural conservatism formed—to adopt one of the characteristic metaphors of the period—the soil within which political extremism developed, and a quite new tone develops in Schenker's writings around the time of the First World War. This is still not politics in the party-political sense, but in these writings Schenker has a great deal to say about topics such as democracy and the relationships between Germany and the victorious Entente powers, and it is these— as well as the scanty evidence of Schenker's political views in the narrowest sense—that I explore in this first section of the chapter.

As Kevin Karnes (2001: 179) says, 'there is very little trace of any explicit political ideology in any of Schenker's early writings':[1] there are

---

[1] 'Schenker' changed to 'Schenker's'.

occasional reflections of conservative rhetoric, such as when in 'Die Musik von heute' (1894) Schenker complains that the 'unbelievably foolish and mindless method of musical education . . . can only have arisen from the spirit of the masses and of business',[2] but the emphasis is firmly on the music. Much the same might be said of *Ornamentik* (1903), where the virtuoso is presented as a symbol of much that is wrong with the modern world—the cultivation of speed for its own sake, of the mechanical, of standardisation—but Schenker's argument remains a musical one, though informed by the broader critique of modernity. Even the notorious preface to volume 1 of *Kontrapunkt* (1910), where the diatribe against the modern world proliferates to the extent that Schenker has to draw it to an abrupt halt ('But now let us turn to the subject matter at hand' [*C1* xv]), is grounded firmly in the musical. If as I said Schenker is complaining by the third page that we live in a world whose values have been turned upside down, he soon pulls the argument back to the specifically musical point he wishes to make, which is that the dilettante, 'the average person' has been placed at the centre of musical culture: 'the genius', he writes, 'means more than the people who represent merely the soil from which he springs' (and there again we have the conservative metaphor that fed into the Nazi slogan 'blood and soil').[3] Indeed, a few pages later Schenker is fulminating against those who talk about vaguely defined cultural values when they should be talking about the music:

> Why lavish such care on discussion of the so-called *Zeitgeist*—often invoked, it has become a real nuisance and plague in our literature during the course of the last decades—when that other, more important, care that should be devoted to the works themselves is lacking? Why all this idle talk, when it is nothing but a cover-up for the incompetence of the author, whose specific musical knowledge obviously does not suffice to clarify the content of the compositions themselves? (*C1* xxiv)

But by the time of the much-delayed second volume of *Kontrapunkt* (1922), a fundamental shift has taken place. There are echoes of the preface to the first volume: 'the average person' reappears, still incapable of appreciating the works of genius, and when Schenker says that 'charlatans have already destroyed the pure tonal material' (*C2* xv) the reference to the initial sentence of the preface to the first volume is unmistakable ('the very tonal material . . . is demolished'). The basic balance, however, is completely different. The opening of the preface to the second volume provides a résumé of Schenker's work since the

---

[2] Schenker 1988: 134; see p. 58 above.

[3] *C1* 17. Schenker uses the same metaphor on other occasions, for instance in *Tonwille*, where he refers to 'genius and the propagating soil of humans' (*T1* 70), and later develops it in an unexpected direction: 'Just as a field needs manure, so, too, must today's ear . . . be supplied with fertilizer' (*T1* 119).

first ('exigencies of the present time', he says rather obscurely, compelled him to illustrate the laws presented in *Harmonielehre* and *Kontrapunkt* 1 through extended studies of individual works, in other
words the Ninth Symphony monograph and the *Erläuterungsausgaben*,
before resuming his theoretical work proper); the final two pages provide an overview of the new volume, and are preceded by another
rather obscure passage, to which I shall return, where Schenker draws
a comparison between music and the state, focusing on the respective
roles of nature and artifice. But the intervening pages—fully half of the
preface—are not about music at all. Or to be more precise, where
Schenker does touch on music, it is purely by way of illustrating a point
that is not in itself musical: he draws a parallel between political leaders and 'musical directors performing hack-works', and paints an astonishing vision of the German bourgeoisie and workers banding together to 'thunder the last movement of Beethoven's Fifth Symphony
to the West with the force thirty million strong until the people there,
deeply moved by the German genius, would gladly kiss any German
hand in gratitude' (*C2* xvi; Schenker is using 'the West' in the then
common sense of the Entente powers, in other words as a term in opposition to 'Germany'). Rather more lucid than this almost hallucinatory image of music as the ultimate weapon of mass seduction, however, is another passage in which Schenker concisely depicts the
situation of the German countries as he sees it:

> The World War resulted in a Germany which, though unvanquished in
> battle, has been betrayed by the democratic parties—the parties of the av-
> erage and the inferior, of half- and non-education, of the most flagrant in-
> dividuals ('each', as Brahms liked to say, 'a summit unto himself'—a sum-
> mit of humanity); the parties of incapacity for synthesis, of 'omnipotence'
> (that is: impotence), of the most irresponsible doctrinarism and the blood-
> thirstiest insatiability for experimentation, along with terrorism, genocide,
> forgery, the lie of 'the people', worship and aping of the West, and all that
> goes with it. This Germany has taken over from the hostile nations of the
> West their lie of 'liberty'. Thus the last stronghold of aristocracy has fallen,
> and culture is sold out to democracy, which, fundamentally and organi-
> cally, is hostile to it—for culture is selection, the most profound synthesis
> based on miraculous achievements of genius. (*C2* xiii)

There are resonances in Schenker's convoluted prose of the nonpolitical writings of the 1890s (the reference to 'individuals' could be from
the 1897 essay 'Unpersönliche Musik'), but these are no more than
fingerprints. Compared with the preface to the first volume of *Kontrapunkt*, the most telling difference is perhaps that whereas the earlier
preface rails shotgun-style against any and all manifestations of the
modern world, the later one has a clear target. Or rather it has a number of clear targets, for one of the striking aspects of the passage I have
just quoted is the way Schenker's anger is directed not just at 'the hos-

tile nations of the West' but at the enemy within, those Germans who
have aped the values of the West, the democrats who connived at the
surrender of the Central Powers when military victory might yet have
been won: this is the idea of the so-called *Dolchstoß* or 'stab in the back',
as propounded in 1919 by Arthur Moeller van den Bruck, of which
Fritz Stern (1961: 218) writes that

> No single idea played so powerful and so pernicious a role in postwar Ger-
> many as the notion that an undefeated army had voluntarily laid down its
> arms in the hope of a just peace. Because of it, Germans were able to feel
> that the Allies had tricked, not defeated, them—hence, that a moral wrong
> had been committed. From it evolved the invidious belief that the great
> army had been betrayed by civilian elements at home, by socialists, liber-
> als, and Jews.

In this way the antagonism Schenker portrays is not so much a simple
military one—the West versus Germany—but inheres in a more complex constellation of ideas: on the one hand democracy, liberty (a term
with specifically French connotations), terrorism, and the rest; on the
other aristocracy, genius, synthesis, the organic. It is like a rerun of
'Was ist deutsch?' with the musically loaded words (genius, synthesis,
organic) now translated to the political and military sphere, and with
the hint of neo-Darwinian theory ('culture is selection') adding to the
raciness of an already volatile mix.

In these respects the preface to *Kontrapunkt 2* is essentially a précis
of 'Von der Sendung des deutschen Genies' (The mission of German genius), the first article of the first issue of *Tonwille*, or to give the latter its
full title, *Der Tonwille: Flugblätter zum Zeugnis unwandelbarer Gesetze der
Tonkunst einer neuen Jugend dargebracht* (The will of tones: Pamphlets in
witness of the immutable laws of music, offered to a new generation of
youth). Conceived in the immediate run-up to the war, *Tonwille* was
originally planned as (in Ian Bent and William Drabkin's words) 'a gap-
filling series of wartime issues',[4] but as Schenker's ideas for the series
became more ambitious, the project was delayed, with publication
finally beginning in 1921. Bent and Drabkin say that '"The mission of
German Genius" set the agenda for the entire publication' (*T1* x), and
it certainly clarifies the larger purpose that lay behind *Tonwille*—in
Schenker's words, 'to show what constitutes German genius in music'
(*T1* 20), that is to say, through analytical demonstration to explain
what is German. (It is symbolic that, in the first issue of *Tonwille*, 'Von
der Sendung des deutschen Genies' [hereafter 'Von der Sendung'] is
immediately followed by 'Die Urlinie: Eine Vorbemerkung' [The Urlinie: A preliminary remark].) In a more literal sense, however, 'Von
der Sendung' can hardly be said to set out the agenda for *Tonwille* at all,

---

[4] *T1* vi; the 'gap' refers to the difficulties anticipated in completing the *Erläuterungsausgaben* under wartime conditions. Drabkin and Bent's prefaces to the two volumes of
the *Tonwille* translation are the principal source for the history of *Tonwille*.

for the essay contains barely a mention of music, other than the occasional inclusion in Schenker's regular lists of German geniuses of 'a Bach' or 'a Beethoven' alongside 'a Kant' or 'a Goethe', and a few final sentences where Schenker briefly outlines the scope of the series and explains that he is admitting Chopin 'to the Pantheon of German composers'. In that sense 'Von der Sendung' constitutes the culminating point in the changing balance I traced from the 1890s and *Ornamentik* to the prefaces of the two volumes of *Kontrapunkt*.

A prophetic tone and a network of biblical references are features of many of the articles in *Tonwille* (particularly the first five issues, after which the proportion of strictly musical content is significantly higher), but in 'Von der Sendung' a quality of ritual is built into the writing itself. Most obvious are the almost interminable listings, not only—as throughout Schenker's writings—of German geniuses ('Germany as the nation of Luther, Leibniz, Goethe, Schiller, Kant, of Bach, Haydn, Mozart, Beethoven, Brahms' [*T1* 17]) but also of Germany's enemies: Schenker refers at one point to

> the nations of the West . . . whose piracy, drug trafficking, commandeering of God's high seas, whose navalism, *Baralongerei*, slaughtering of women, children and old people inside and outside of concentration camps, the dissolute order of whose kings and aristocracy, whose Armagnacism, constant sorties to rob and plunder, squabbling over revolution, militarism, lust after *gloire*, Senegalese marriage relationships, Congolese atrocities, etc. etc.—in short, whose pronounced barbarism, nay cannibalism, they conceal from themselves and others only scantily behind high-flown language, verbal trickery, formality, and form itself (here is a random sample from the lying maw of that infamous civilisation: 'Sun King', 'great Revolution', 'revanche', 'disannexation', '*nobles traditions*', 'genius of the people', 'chivalry', 'eternal soldier of right', 'traditional justice', 'global conscience', 'battle against militarism', 'liberation of peoples', 'League of Nations' and so on, and so on). (*T1* 4–5)

Andrea Reiter (2003: 157) has analyzed a similar but even longer sentence from 'Von der Sendung' that contains 'no less that 15 relative clauses, interspersed with six infinitive phrases and four conditional clauses': she relates the prose style to eighteenth-century models but also to Thomas Mann, and comments, 'The highly stereotypical repetition of clauses and words together with the coinage of new words and the use of quotes and proverbs makes for the polemical *tour de force* of this passage'.

But the quality I would particularly emphasise in the passage above is that of ritual incantation, the effect perhaps akin to exorcism. And this ritual dimension extends into the very structure of the essay, at the core of which lie what might be termed a set of litanies, each consisting of a series of paragraphs presented in unnumbered list form (Ian Bent's translation renders these as tildes) and introduced by a catch phrase which the individual paragraphs illustrate. There is first a litany of betrayals, with the phrase 'betrayal was perpetrated' appearing four times in different variants, followed by annotated lists of traitors: capitalists, communists, antimonarchists, pacifists, journalists, intellectuals, Francophiles, aliens, the press, the Magyars, the Slavs, the Americans, and the 'neutral states . . . who were sly enough to turn their "sympathy for the West" into massive economic gain' (*Tl* 7). There follows a litany of false responses to the crisis, this time with different catch phrases but the same hypnotic effect: 'Germany will achieve nothing', 'it will achieve less', 'it will do no good', 'it will patently get us nowhere'. And the lists of false responses include shouldering guilt for war (here, as elsewhere,[5] Schenker refers to 'documents in the Russian secret archives' showing that the war was started by the Entente powers [*Tl* 9]), reconciliation ('Germany has never hated. On the contrary, as no nation before it, Germany has made available to the intellect of all people the powerful superiority of its language, more original as it is, infinitely surpassing all others in the richness of its vocabulary and expressive power—but has this spared Germany the hatred of those ungrateful nations?' [*Tl* 10]), and above all the embracing of democracy ('let the German democrat simply take a good look at democracy and do exactly what he sees Americans, Frenchmen, Englishmen, Italians, Poles, Czechs etc. doing. Let him break promises, violate treaties, infringe international law, steal private property, falsify maps, deface monuments, desecrate war-graves, lie, and commit murder as they do' [*Tl* 12]).

Then comes a litany of Germany's 'eternal enemies': the English ('the *Magna Carta* for himself, the noose round their necks for other nations. . . . England and true culture are as inimical as venality and probity. . . . Oh, what a miserable toad the Englishman is!' [*Tl* 12–4]),[6] the French ('who would just love—oh, how they would love!—to do away with the Germans once for all—yes, one actually hears such cannibalistic assertions!'), the Americans ('Groping through the vale of ignorance, driven on by greed, propelled forward by the profit-motive as if by a million hurtling Niagara Falls. . . . [America] has settled the war to the advantage of the dollar, having only ever entered it with that in mind' [*Tl* 15]), the Italians (here Schenker refers to 'the expropriation of the South Tyrol', ceded to Italy under the Treaty of St Germain), and the League of Nations (which follows 'the old thief's motto—wait till the booty is in the bag, then let order commence'); the German working class and especially the German Marxist ('a hypocrite . . . in search of a raise in wages' [*Tl* 17]) are also thrown in for good measure. Now

---

[5] See *Tonwille* 3 (*Tl* 136).

[6] I cannot resist quoting the particularly happy formulation Schenker finds for his opinion of English musicality in the 'Vermischtes' section of the first issue of *Tonwille* ('a *boa constrictor* cannot sing', *Tl* 45), or his claim in the third issue that 'The history of music cannot possibly accommodate the English' (*Tl* 45, 135).

comes a litany of injunctions, beginning 'Let the German people' and continuing through 'Let Germans', 'Let them', and finally 'let us': Germans should value German culture as something 'unattainable by the other nations', but above all,

> let Germans conclude that they are too good for democracy. . . . They must bend all their religious, intellectual, and moral resources to the task of communicating the concept of nation once and for all in all its fullness, so that it encompasses not only brawn . . . but also intellectuals, king, and aristocracy. (*T1* 17–8)

In view of this, Schenker says in a perhaps unexpected change of tone, Germans should not treat their enemies with 'hatred or contempt' but rather 'at any price seek to educate them toward humane and aristocratic ways' by 'holding up a mirror to them, so that they can see themselves as they really are' (*T1* 19). Finally Schenker declares that 'the present generation is destined to be a tragic clown among generations, and to perish in the shame and disgrace of insufficient cultivation'; for this reason 'the task of deliverance must await a new generation', whose task will be 'to gather together the immortal past with the immortal present in the manner of our Lessing or Herder, Goethe or Schiller'. (It is of course this 'new generation of youth' to whom *Tonwille* was offered.) And Schenker offers a concluding vision of this future: 'The past in its eternity will live anew as the present. What has passed away in the course of millions of years will nevertheless not have perished. The geniuses of all ages will become contemporaries of all generations, will become eternal contemporaries, and an eternal life for mankind will emerge, built at long last, as the true temple of the eternal one!' (*T1* 19–20)

I intended to comment but ended up with wholesale quotation: once you start you can't stop. That also seems to have been the experience of Martin Eybl (1995: chap. 1), who put his quotations from 'Von der Sendung' into footnotes only to have them swamp the main text (rather in the manner of Schenker's own footnotes in *Ornamentik*). This is a measure of the hypnotic power of Schenker's rhetoric—many commentators have wondered just how much Schenker's style of argument owed to his legal education—but it also poses a dilemma. Schenker's mobilisation of the new generation of youth had the intention, as he wrote, of 'nurturing an elite group' (*T1* 3). Conceivably reflecting in some way the Austrian Jewish youth movement of 1917–18 (Rechter 2001: chap. 3), this was obviously an exercise in fantasy politics by comparison with the *Hitler Jugend*—although one wonders who exactly *did* buy the first issue of *Tonwille*, of which, unless Universal Edition changed their plans, two thousand copies were printed:[7] Bent and

---

[7] See *T1* vi; a 1925 letter from Drei Masken Verlag (the Munich-based publishers of *Das Meisterwerk in der Musik*, effectively the continuation of *Tonwille* following Schenker's

Drabkin suggest that 'readers who lacked a basic grounding in music theory but nevertheless shared his artistic outlook would have viewed the analytical portions of *Der Tonwille* as the objective proof of his philosophy' (*T1* x), which is in some ways a chilling notion. But how are *we* to respond to a text that it hardly seems too strong to describe as designed to incite hatred, sometimes of a specifically racial nature ('Is it not the League of Nations that also, for example, placed the filthy French in such oafish control of Germany's Saarland, and permitted in the regions occupied by them the ignominy of its black troops—the advance party of its genitalitis, of the flesh of its flesh, of the cannibal spirit of its spirit'),[8] as well as circulating rumours that fall somewhere between the scurrilous and the hallucinatory (the 'stab in the back', the secret documents showing that the French and English started the war)? What about the question Schenker asks in the third (1922) issue of *Tonwille:* 'Did not the German workforce in German Austria recently prove itself utterly worthless by failing to kill a villainous English soldier who had assaulted a German official in English fashion because the wanton destruction was not going ahead fast enough for his liking?' (*T1* 28) There are passages in Schenker's writings of the 1920s that are objectionable by any reasonable standards, yet condemnation seems otiose given that Schenker died in his bed over seventy years ago—and would almost certainly have accompanied Jeanette to Theresienstadt had he lived longer.

Our principal and perhaps only responsibility, I would argue, is to understand—for to understand is not to condone, while to condemn without understanding is futile. Before coming back to the issues 'Von der Sendung' raises, then, let us confront the most grisly exhibits in the Schenkerian chamber of horrors. There is one passage in *Der freie Satz,* completed two years after Hitler came to power, which is so questionable that it was excluded from the excluded material in the English translation. (Gerald Warfield, the series editor of the short-lived Longman Music Series within which *Free Composition* appeared, explained in an 'acknowledgement' that Ernst Oster, the editor and translator, had reinstated some but not all of the material Oswald Jonas had deleted from the second German edition; all the deleted material, Warfield said, was now being included as Appendix 4 [*FC* I x]. But not the passage in question.) As translated by Carl Schachter (2001: 17n.)—the only

---

falling out with Universal Edition) suggests that at least the later issues of *Tonwille* had a print run of only eight hundred. Translating this into sales is complicated by the existence of considerable numbers of unsold issues, but the fact that Universal reprinted issues 1–2, 4–6, and 7–10 (as 'yearbooks') must be evidence of a viable market. (For details see *T2* x–xi.)

[8] *T1* 15–6; as Bent explains in the extensive annotations to his translation, Schenker's reference to 'black troops' probably means the Senegalese troops recruited for the war by France (*T1* 7n.).

mainstream American Schenkerian to have confronted these issues head-on—it reads as follows:

> The work of German musical genius lives its life in the wide tension-spans of its linear progressions. It is precisely the strength of the tensions and fulfillments that should be viewed as a blood test, as an attribute of the German race. In this sense, for example, the question of Beethoven's nationality is incontrovertibly decided: he is not 'only half a German', as some have wished—and still wish—to have it. No, the creator of such linear progressions must be a German even if foreign blood perhaps flowed in his veins! In this regard, the bringing to fulfillment of extended tension-spans is better proof than any evidence from racial science.

According to William Benjamin (1981: 157), Schenker's 'apparent racism was an emotional reflex which stood in contradiction to his personal belief system'. That sounds like special pleading. All the same, there is nothing in Schenker's statement to controvert Eybl's (1995: 25) judgment that Schenker's racism (as evident in his comments on the Senegalese troops)[9] was at least not grounded in racial theory of the National Socialist type: on the contrary, the remark that Beethoven 'must be a German even if foreign blood perhaps flowed in his veins' shows the extent to which, for Schenker, what is German is defined culturally and not biologically (it would of course be strange if Schenker had thought anything else). In fact, I assume that the idea of employing music theory as a new and more scientific test of racial purity is an example of Schenker's rather heavy, and sometimes dark, humour, along the lines of defeating the Entente powers by performing Beethoven's Fifth Symphony—or at any rate (because in this case Schenker helpfully says 'in a jovial mood') along the lines of the idea, also suggested in the preface to *Kontrapunkt 2*, of calling in 'a Jacques Offenbach, who would drive away today's delusions by putting all the false gods of the West and their German imitators, including Marx and comrades, onto the operetta stage for the purpose of general ridicule' (*C2* xvi). The problem, of course, is that even to joke about racial science, especially in something as permanent as a book, is to engage with it; once you have said that anything 'should be viewed as a blood test, as an attribute of the German race', it is too late. Plenty of politicians know that you can kill a career with the wrong joke.

More potentially serious, then, is evidence of Schenker's sympathies with the extreme right-wing regimes of the inter-war period. Ac-

---

[9] Including a particularly offensive, because throwaway, remark later in 'Von der Sendung': after saying that no 'Anglo-Saxon, French, or Italian mother could ever carry in her womb a Moses, a Christ [and so on, ending with Kant]', Schenker adds: 'Not even after intermarrrying black racial stock with *Gloire-esprit* could a French mother achieve this!' (*TI* 18). Here again Schenker's attitudes are reminiscent of Moeller, according to whom 'France had become an African nation, and "Strasbourg in French hands would be for German feelings like a white girl in colored hands"' (Stern 1961: 219).

cording to Hellmut Federhofer (1985: 356), Schenker was a supporter of Engelbert Dollfuss's Fatherland Front, which was seen—at least by Dollfuss's left-wing opponents—as an 'experiment in Austro-Fascism' (Field 1967: 215). And well before that, on 2 November 1922, Schenker wrote a letter to August Halm that included a lengthy diatribe against the democrats, concluding 'Consequently, I praise only the fascists! . . . . Germany needs fascists who will destroy the lie of "class", of those on-the-spot gluttons for whom we provide work and opportunity, and who as salary for this cushy life trample everything'.[10] There is also what Schachter (2001: 6) calls 'an appalling letter' of 14 May 1933, to Schenker's pupil Felix-Eberhard von Cube, in which Schenker praised Hitler and made a prediction history has not exactly borne out:[11]

> The historical achievement of Hitler, the extermination of Marxism, will be celebrated by posterity (including the French, the English, and all ex-ploiters of crimes against Germany) no less gratefully than the great deeds of the greatest Germans. If only a man were born to music, who would finally exterminate the musical Marxists: for this it would be necessary for the masses to become better acquainted with this inherently elusive art—but this is, and must remain, a contradiction in terms. 'Art' and the masses have never belonged together: so where would one ever find the quantity of musical 'brownshirts' necessary to chase away the musical Marxists? I have already provided the weapons; but the music, the true German music of the great [composers], is in no way understood by the masses who are supposed to bear the weapons.

In one sense this is just a development of the idea of a musical dicta-torship Schenker had whimsically (again in a jovial mood?) proposed in the fifth issue of *Tonwille:* a 'single, great Bach Society', Schenker wrote, should confer upon Bach

> the rank of something like an absolute artistic dictator, to speak in con-temporary terms, who calls the hard-pressed German music back to its senses. He alone is capable of bearing witness, with godly authority, to its own eternal laws; he alone, finally and for the first time clearly heard, would be capable of expelling all who, with commercial interests in place of musical ability, act out the part of Minister of Musical 'Reconstruction', expelling them back into the dark depths from which like a locust swarm they arose and surged destructively over the artistic fields. All hail the Bach Society! (*TI* 211–2)

But it is of course the specific references to Mussolini's fascists and Hitler's brownshirts that particularly jar in the 1922 and 1933 letters. In both cases, however, there are issues of timing to consider. The 1922 letter was written just two days after Mussolini assumed the prime

---

[10] DLA 69.930/11, translated by Lee Rothfarb, Schenker Correspondence Project website.
[11] Letter transcribed in Federhofer 1985: 329; translation from Drabkin 1985: 189.

ministership of Italy at the invitation of King Victor Emmanuel III: it was not until 1925 that Mussolini abolished opposition parties and transformed himself into a dictator. And whereas Hitler became chancellor on 30 January 1933, the Reichstag passed the enabling law that gave him dictatorial powers only on 23 March, some seven weeks before Schenker's letter. Schachter (2001: 6) comments that 'one can imagine his approving the strongly nationalistic and anti-democratic features of the Nazi regime, at least at first', and while the last clause might sound like wishful thinking on the part of an apologist, there is evidence (not quoted by Schachter) to back it up. On 13 July, Schenker's pupil Reinhard Oppel (who had also at first hoped that 'the Nazis would rid Germany of "cultural bolshevism"') wrote to him about his 'disenchantment with the new regime': on 23 July, Schenker noted in his diary, 'Letter to Oppel dictated: I confirm him in his scepticism' (Jackson 2001: 6).

As for Schenker's support for Dollfuss, this needs to be placed within the convoluted political situation of the Austrian civil war in 1934. The Mussolini-like regime Dollfuss established through a coup d'état in 1933 was as much an attempt to contain the Austrian Nazis as the socialists: Dollfuss banned the Nazis in June that year, but was assassinated in July 1934 in an abortive Nazi putsch (of which Hitler may or may not have had foreknowledge [Berkley 1988: 220]). And his regime was supported, at least in public, by many Jewish organisations and individuals, if only because (in Harriet Pass Friedenreich's words [1991: 195]) 'the most likely alternative to the corporate state in Austria after 1933 was not Socialism but National Socialism. . . . The enemy of their enemy Hitler had to be their friend'. But there is a more general point to be made here: present-day political categories, such as 'right-wing' and 'democratic', do not translate seamlessly to the realities of early twentieth-century Austria. Carl Schorske's basic thesis in *Fin-de-Siècle Vienna: Politics and Culture* is that the astonishing cultural creativity of this time should be understood as a form of displacement on the part of a liberal bourgeoisie excluded from political representation. This exclusion had been the consequence of Karl Lueger's strategy, in Schorske's words (1980: 136), of 'welding together a coalition of aristocracy and masses against the liberal middle classes' (with a generous helping of anti-Semitism as the catalyst), which culminated in the electoral victory of Lueger's Christian Socialists in 1895. As I mentioned in chapter 1, Franz Josef at first refused to ratify Lueger's election, but capitulated in 1897. On the one side, then, Lueger had engineered an alliance between aristocracy and masses; on the other, there was a de facto alliance between the emperor and the liberals (Freud smoked a cigar to celebrate Franz Josef's refusal to recognise the outcome of the 1895 elections),[12] and 'in such a context democracy and liberalism became contradictory terms' (138). This goes some way to

---

[12] As stated in a letter to Wilhelm Fliess (Berkley 1988: 104).

explain the nature and tone of Schenker's monarchical beliefs (a diary entry from 1918 notes that 'only an unscrupulous social democrat rogue could deny that especially the Habsburg monarchy has rendered the greatest services to the shards of people that today begin their self-determination in such a grotesque manner and with such a lack of gratitude'),[13] as well as those of such contemporaries as Schoenberg, who wrote long after the event—in 1939—of his 'belief in the necessity of the Habsburg empire' [Simms 1977: 123]). It also helps to explain the nature of their hostility to democracy and mass politics—a hostility that Schenker and Schoenberg shared with Kraus, Wittgenstein, and many others.[14] There was in fact a not unjustified sense among the Viennese Jews that Franz Josef was a bulwark against anti-Semitism, to the point that some of the more fanatical anti-Semites called him the 'Juden-kaiser' (Wistrich 1989: 179).

And this is just one example of how the idea of a continuum from left wing at one extreme to right wing at the other does not fit the realities of early twentieth-century politics in the German-speaking countries: the very name 'National Socialism', after all, illustrates the incorporation of what we would see as left-wing elements within an extreme right-wing ideology. Hugh Ridley makes this point in relation to the Weimar Republic, speaking of it as

> a system eroded equally from both left and right, in which the democratic/republican centre was hollowed away. . . . We are familiar with the image of the parliament of the Republic, the *Reichstag* itself, not as a semicircle (as in traditional models of parliamentary democracy, where the centre is closer to the two wings of politics, and where the extremes are furthest apart) but as a horseshoe, where the extremes are closest to each other and the rest of the perimeter (the centre) is out of touch with the extremes'.[15]

This phenomenon of 'hollowing out' is exactly what happened in Austria from the final years of the nineteenth century, and the history of apparently strange alliances in Austrian politics continued into the 1930s, with the combination of Social Democrats and anti-Semitic pan-Germanists who opposed Dollfuss. Accusations of support for the wrong side are therefore all too likely to be oversimplified as well as informed by hindsight. ('Much has become clear since 1945', writes Peter Gay

---

[13] Diary entry for 3 November 1918 (Federhofer 1985: 328).

[14] Theodor Herzl's 1893 account in the *Neue freie Presse* of a Socialist rally in Lille provides an insight into the fear of the masses, as well as perhaps the Francophobia, that is evident in these writers: 'Their murmuring swells, it becomes a dark and ominous flood in this still darkened hall. It runs through me like a physical premonition of their power. Indistinguishable from one another as individuals, together they are like a great beast beginning to stretch its limbs, still half conscious of its power. Many hundreds of hard heads and twice as many fists. . . . That is only one district in one city in France' (translated in Schorske 1980: 155).

[15] Ridley 1988: 23–4; 'parameter' changed to 'perimeter'.

[1978: 163], 'that was by no means clear in 1935, and seemed inconceivable in 1895'.)

It is also necessary to evaluate the at times hysterical tone of Schenker's writings during and after the First World War in relation to the specific circumstances of this period. When for example Schenker speaks in the preface to *Kontrapunkt* 2 of 'the blockade of the German stomach', this is not mere rhetoric but a reference to the widespread hunger caused by Allied blockades during 1916–17.[16] Salka Viertel, in conversation with Joan Allen Smith, recalled that in Vienna 'there was such a scarcity of food, and we were always so cold and hungry that, when we visited each other, one talked about nothing except where can one get some potatoes' [Smith 1986: 140]); in the winter of 1919 there was no fuel and people scavenged in the Vienna Woods (fig. 3.1). And then there was the great flu epidemic. The painter Egon Schiele died of the flu in 1918, while Max Dvořák—who, as I mentioned in chapter 2, became the dominating figure in the Vienna school of art history after Riegl's death—died in 1921 from the aftereffects of starvation. In the following year Schoenberg wrote to tell Kandinsky about the famine, adding that 'perhaps—for we Viennese seem to be a patient lot—perhaps the worst was after all the overturning of everything one has believed in',[17] but it wasn't over yet: Weimar-style hyperinflation reached a peak in 1924. (In *Meisterwerk* 3, Schenker refers to 'the random, fraudulent racking-up of prices on goods' during 'the unhappy period of inflation' [*MM3* 78].) The root cause was economic unsustainability resulting from the Treaty of St Germain (1919), which I described as reducing Vienna to an imperial city without an empire—and this perhaps makes it a little easier to understand the tone of Schenker's language when he writes that 'at Versailles and St. Germain . . . Western democracy . . . became synonymous with ultimate moral depravity. . . . Even savages and cannibals in their wild state are purer and more virtuous than the cannibal hordes of Versailles' (*T1* 7). Bent and Drabkin suggest that 'the flashpoint for *Der Tonwille* was the Versailles Treaty itself' (and the same has been said of *Mein Kampf*).[18] Many of the views Schenker developed in 'Von der Sendung' were, however, prefigured in 'Das deutsche Genie im Kampf und Sieg' (The German genius in war and victory), an eight-page article Schenker submitted to the *Frankfurter Zeitung* in September 1914, but which was rejected:[19]

---

[16] Schenker also refers to this in the third issue of *Tonwille:* 'the English have virtually reduced the Germans to starvation with their dishonorable blockade' (*T1* 135).

[17] Letter of 20 July 1922, in Schoenberg 1964: 70.

[18] Following and commenting on Michael Mann (1949), Eybl (1995: 15) notes the common origin of 'Von der Sendung' and *Mein Kampf* in the response to Versailles, but goes on to outline the obvious—and necessary—distinctions to be made between Schenker's and Hitler's world views. Bent and Drabkin's suggestion is in *T1* x.

[19] OJ 21/2; rejection letter at OJ 11/18 (see Lang and Kunselman 1994: 63). The article is subtitled 'Betrachtungen sub specie aeternitatis'.

Figure 3.1 Scavenging in the Vienna Woods, 1919. (*Source:* William Johnston, *The Austrian Mind: An Intellectual and Social History, 1848–1938*, © 1972, University of California Press.)

here, too, Schenker intones the lists of German geniuses ('a Bismarck or Goethe, a Kant or Seb. Bach'), asserts the links between the spirit of genius and 'Germany's inspired militarism', emphasises what 'Germans have given the world in art and science', and berates the English ('one calls the English conservative, when in reality they are bigoted').

I said that to understand was not to condone, and after all this we are still left with the aspect of Schenker's thought that Eybl (1995: chap. 1), for one, finds hardest to come to terms with: the authoritarian impulse that is expressed in the many hierarchies which make up Schenker's worldview (it is tempting but I think not very helpful to draw the obvious parallel with his music theory). This is not simply a matter of the hierarchy that places the German nation above the others, or the aristocrat above the masses, but a deeply embedded pattern of thought about the world in general, as becomes clear in a passage from the preface to *Kontrapunkt* 1, of which I previously quoted just the final clause:

> despite their mutual dependency—in terms of necessity of existence, they remain equal!—the man ranks above the woman, the producer is superior to the merchant or the laborer, the head prevails over the foot, the coachman is more than the wheel of the wagon he steers, the genius means more than the people who represent merely the soil from which he springs. (*C1* xix)

This is the natural hierarchy that democracy perverts: as Schenker picturesquely wrote to Halm in 1922, 'The horror of today is that the backside has decided no longer to want to be the backside, as though it depended on its defiance and no longer on whether nature installs brain nerves also into the backside'.[20] While there are any number of aspects of Schenker's system of values that are hard to accept today, it has to be said that neither the sexism nor the apparent disdain in which 'the average person' is held are particularly remarkable for the time. The same might be said of the rather Nietzschean belief in the capacity of the genius as leader, the dangers of which are only too obvious in hindsight: as Reiter (2003: 143) says, 'retrospectively, we realize Schenker's tragic political naivety. He seems to have had such confidence in the integrity of the leader-figure that he could not imagine a Hitler'. There is also the associated question of who, in so hierarchical a universe, is to make the decisions about who is a genius and who a mere talent or average person: there is an uncomfortable resonance between Schenker's announcement, in the final sentence of 'Von der Sendung', that 'the author now admits Chopin to the Pantheon of German composers' (*T1* 20) and Lueger's notorious quip, to which I shall later return, 'I decide who is a Jew' (Beller 1989: 195).

Then there is the problem of what Schenker does *not* say, particularly from the viewpoint of Viennese Jewry. It is curious that his diatribes are directed throughout at the Entente powers, even though Austria's war effort was directed principally at the Russians and it was the sense of fighting to revenge the decades of pogroms perpetrated by the Russians, particularly in Galicia, that encouraged many Viennese Jews to support the war effort with enthusiasm, feeling that it was—in Marsha Rozenblit's (2001: 40) words—'a Jewish war'. (Schenker, by contrast, called it 'an oil war' [*T1* 223]; some things do not change.) By coincidence Rozenblit (129) slips into the language of 'Von der Sendung' when she writes that, in the aftermath of the war, Jews understood that 'it would do them no good to go into permanent mourning for Habsburg Austria', and this brings home the complete absence in Schenker's essay of any consideration of how Viennese Jewry might best adapt to the collapse of the multinational empire and the resulting need to reconcile Jewish religion and ethnicity with the demands of the nation-state: even the specific predicament of Austria, as opposed to a Germany conceived primarily in terms of cultural politics, is absent. As what it purports to be, a political stocktaking after the war, 'Von der Sendung' is hard to take seriously.

And finally—despite these conspicuous omissions—there is the sheer length, in writing intended for publication, of Schenker's fulminations, with page following page without the least sense of development in intellectual or emotional response, or hence of conclusion or resolution except by virtue of sheer exhaustion; adding to this is the unremittingly violent quality of his vocabulary, the effect of which does not disappear in translation. These points can be made succinctly

---

[20] Letter of 25 September 1922 (DLA 69.930/10); translated by Rothfarb, Schenker Correspondence Project website.

through comparison with a passage Schoenberg inserted into the third edition of his *Harmonielehre*, which appeared in the same year as the first issue of *Tonwille:*

> Since we lost a war, there was little else for the others to do but win it: it was more to our credit that we lost it than it was to theirs that they won it. We were fully active. It is not that the war *was lost,* rather that *we lost it.* We set ourselves back a few notches; that is their war reparations. We do not need any; otherwise we should receive them, too. We are not only capable of continuing to exist without war reparations, as they think they cannot do, but they themselves consider our strength still great enough that we can even pay reparations. In light of that, who can claim that we are decadent![21]

In substance what Schoenberg is saying is close to what Schenker says in 'Von der Sendung', except that Schoenberg's idea of the 'fully active' loss of the war adds an extra twist to Schenker's 'betrayal'. (I shall come back to this in the conclusion.) Yet the tone and the scale could not be more different, as indeed were the steps they took in the aftermath of the war to further their musical aims. Schoenberg created the Society for Private Musical Performances (Verein für Musikalische Privataufführungen), a delimited site within which a new music that was at the same time a restoration of *Gemeinschaft* values could become a reality. (More on *Gemeinschaft* values shortly.) Schenker actually put forward a similar idea: in the double issue *Tonwille* 8/9 (1924) he proposed that 'the good, dear city of Vienna consider whether . . . it might wish to organize solemn festivals of the Viennese classics', with a resident orchestra and a brief for authentic performance (*T2* 122)—and maybe, if realised, this would have done more to halt the musical decline Schenker condemned than all the articles and books in which he condemned it. (Schenker's suggestion that this be modelled on Bayreuth might be seen as one of his many attempts to reappropriate for the classics the success of the 'New German' school in general and Wagner in particular.) But one has the impression that Schenker intended this as no more than a rhetorical gesture, like his calls for the restoration of the German masterwork tradition and the society to support it—unrealistically inflated but nonnegotiable demands which, predictably, had no discernable effect on the development of either music or society in Schenker's lifetime.

No doubt it would be possible to now launch into a further round of apologetic contextualisation. For instance, one might revert to the mismatch between the literary genres of Schenker's various writings and present-day music-theoretical expectations (though even contemporary readers, at least in England, could be puzzled by the juxtaposition of musical analysis and polemics: 'E.W' wrote in a review of the last volume of *Meisterwerk* that 'Herr Schenker's notebooks seem to

---

[21] Schoenberg 1978/1911: 425.

have got mixed').[22] Or one might relate Schenker's conception of a cultural elite—what Hertzka once referred to as 'a genius-aristocracy' [*T1* vii]—to the Beethovenian idea of an aristocracy of the spirit. (It was in a similar vein that, in 'Ornament und Verbrechen', Loos said that he was 'preaching to the aristocrats; I mean, to the people on the forefront of humanity who still fully appreciate the needs and stirrings of those beneath them' [Münz and Künstler 1966: 230].) But there is a point at which explaining turns into explaining away. As Botstein (2002: 239) says, Schenker's sentiments were 'extreme even in the context of the first decade after World War I', and there were many in Schenker's lifetime who found his attitudes hard to accept, both in themselves and in terms of their relationship (or lack of relationship) to the ostensive topic of his publications.

As early as the Ninth Symphony monograph, Schenker was defensive about his polemics (*BNS* 15): he refers to 'the objection that I might engage in polemic only for its own sake'—precisely the objection against which Halm sought to defend him in an article of 1917 which Schenker pasted into his scrapbook, and which refers to 'those who, like Schenker, did not practice polemics out of personal inclination, but let themselves be destined for such a duty by the crisis'.[23] (Perhaps it is no coincidence that Schenker had assured Halm, in a letter written the previous year, that 'I take the field against opponents only very unwillingly, and do it only when the opponent manifests a specifically tinged bacterium of the error or, in becoming aggressive themselves first . . . provokes my weaponry'.)[24] There is also a diary entry from 1920 in which Schenker records a conversation with an evidently critical Furtwängler: 'As usual', Schenker notes, 'I justify and defend my right to polemics, and . . . let myself be carried away so far as to say that I have the obligation to annihilate my opponents. "There you have it", F. says, "is it any wonder that they defend themselves?"'[25] (One wonders just how much Schenker learnt from his final-year course on dispute resolution; it would be only a slight exaggeration to say of Schenker, as Jacques Le Rider [1993: 255] says of Kraus, that 'his adversaries were not merely "wrong", they were liars and imposters, their errors tantamount to moral perversion'.) Again, Willi Kahl, reviewing issues 5 and 6 of *Tonwille* for *Die Musik* in 1925, started by describing the

[22] *Music and Letters* 12 (1931), 307 (there is a copy, together with a German translation, in Schenker's scrapbook, OC 2/84); German-language reviewers seem less puzzled by the generic mix. E[rnest] W[alker] also refers to Schenker's 'really appalling industriousness', observing that the graphic analyses of the *Eroica* cover 'about 40 square feet in total area' (306).

[23] Halm, 'Heinrich Schenker', *Freie Schulgemeinde*, 1 October 1917, p. 13 (OC 2/53).

[24] Draft letter of 29 December 1916 (OC 1/B9, version 1), transcribed and translated by Lee Rothfarb, Schenker Correspondence Project website.

[25] Diary entry for 16/24 April 1920, transcribed in Federhofer 1985: 112, translated by John Rothgeb in *BNS* xv.

exclusiveness of Schenker's musical aesthetics as 'bordering on mania', and condemned Schenker's *'furor Teutonicus* that borders on the grotesque'.[26] And Hertzka, whose support for Schenker extended as far as setting up the fictitious publisher's imprint *Tonwille-Flugblätterverlag* to issue *Tonwille* without damaging Universal Edition's other business interests, complained in 1922, with reference to the second issue, that 'our contract says expressly that [*Tonwille*] examines various topics in the field of music. In the fourteen pages of "Miscellanea", no topics whatsoever in the field of music are examined, but only topics in the field of politics and demagoguery'.[27] Improbably—and as a minor but telling demonstration of his sense of German rather than Austrian identity—Schenker had written in the previous year to the German elder statesman and from 1925 president of the Reich, Paul von Hindenburg, to complain about Universal Edition's 'internationalism', as expressed in their hiding behind the *Tonwille-Flugblätterverlag* imprint; he received a one-line acknowledgement.[28]

Among those outside Schenker's immediate circle, Schoenberg was sufficiently dismayed by Schenker's later writings to regret his earlier, more positive response to Schenker's work. In 1923 he wrote—but did not publish—a one-page article or memorandum entitled 'Those who complain about the decline', in which he referred to 'these Spenglers, Schenkers, and so forth' ('these loudmouths', he adds). He concluded:

> At least I never *praised* Spengler, but I am genuinely sorry for what I have said about Schenker. I so enjoy paying due tribute, or tempering criticism by dwelling on whatever there is to praise—but I almost believe that here I am in the wrong, and that this case calls for action with a firm hand, or even, perhaps, foot. (1975: 203–4)

Perhaps this response to the unacceptable face of Schenker is unremarkable in view of the opposed aesthetic positions of Schenker and Schoenberg; the same might be said of Adorno's reference to Schenker's 'loathsome political views',[29] while there is an Italian review of 1925 that refers to Schenker's 'unpleasant political observations' being 'a blot on his work'.[30] But there were people much closer to Schenker who equally deplored his views. Otto Vrieslander wrote—in the same year as Schoenberg's 'Those who complain about the decline'—that Schenker's 'political statements are not supported by all of his friends, especially as they take a very broad stance in the recent writings'; as early as 1919 Walter Dahms had questioned Schenker's right to make

---

[26] Kahl, 'Heinrich Schenker. *Der Tonwille:* Heft 5, 6', *Die Musik,* July 1925 (OC/67).

[27] Letter of 2 May 1922, translated in *TI* vii.

[28] Draft of letter from autumn 1921 (OC 24/14–5), translated by Drabkin in *TI* vii; Hindenburg's reply is at OC 24/18.

[29] Adorno 1992/1963: 281.

[30] A. E., 'Schenker Heinrich, Erläuterungsausgabe . . . ', *Rivista Musicale Italiana*, December 1925 (OC 2/68).

statements about the war when he had not experienced it at first hand.[31] Halm was even more outspoken, exclaiming in a letter to Schenker of 19 August 1922: 'For honesty's sake I must tell you that I have had enough of your attacks on England and its gang, and your glorification of the Germans'.[32] (It says something for both men that their relationship survived such remarks.) And then there is Jonas, perhaps the most committed of all Schenker's disciples, who wrote in an unpublished memorial lecture that when the war broke out Schenker 'confused German genius with the German nation in general, and this misjudgement led to digressions and outbursts in his musical writings that even the most convinced disciples could read past only with difficulty': in fact, according to Schachter—who had it from Jonas's stepdaughter Irene Schreier Scott—Jonas 'moved in the 1920s from Vienna to Berlin largely because he could not stand Schenker's politics, yet revered him so much as a musician and man that he did not want to get into disagreements with him'.[33] One can see why not. Even those who understood Schenker best, then, felt under no obligation to condone his political views, and no more need we.

The Logic of Nostalgia

For a modern reader, one of the most exasperating features of Schenker's writing on political issues, however broadly or narrowly defined, is his insistence that he is not talking about politics at all. On the first page of 'Von der Sendung', for example, Schenker claims that he does not 'for a moment wish to engage in politics as conventionally understood. He means only to investigate the special conditions required for the creation and acceptance of an artwork of genius' (*T1* 3); again, he writes in the fifth issue of *Tonwille* that some 'will perhaps accuse me of making a foray into politics. To them I say that is not a question of pol-

---

[31] Vrieslander, 'Heinrich Schenker und sein Werk', *Musikblätter des Anbruch*, February–March 1923, p. 78 (OC 2/63); Federhofer 1985: 90, citing a diary entry of 2 October 1919, itself a response to Dahms's letter to Schenker dated 26 September 1919.

[32] Federhofer 1985: 144, where the letter is transcribed in its entirety. Halm goes on to say that 'if one does not read a variety of newspapers, including foreign ones, all day long, then one knows far too little to have the basis for a judgement', which provokes an astonishing response from Schenker in his twelve-page reply dated 25 September: 'Even though totally without means, living from hand to mouth, during all the war years I had home subscriptions to no fewer than nine daily newspapers of all orientations (foreign and domestic) . . . . I suffered unspeakably, but did not let up in following the activities of the democrats, social democrats, nationalists, pacifists, internationalists in their newspapers, and in saving the most important records!' (DLA 69.930/10, translated by Rothfarb, Schenker Correspondence Project website).

[33] Jonas, 'In Memoriam Heinrich Schenker' (ca. 1967), quoted in Rothgeb 2001: 161n.; Schachter 2001: 12 (some further details may be found in Rothgeb 1990: 43). I conclude from all this that Alpern's (forthcoming) view that 'judged in historical context, Schenker's avid Germanity was not atypical or extreme' is perhaps too easily arrived at.

itics for me, rather it is only a question of culture, that obliges me . . . to defend it against scorn and misunderstanding' (*T1* 224). There is an obvious sense in which this is true. As I observed, Schenker says little in his polemics about Austria but much about Germany, and this is not because he was a pan-German in the political sense (that is, an advocate of political union with Germany) but because his nationalism was of a cultural rather than a political variety: the 'disjuncture . . . between the actual German political nation-state and the imagined cultural nation of generations of German patriots' (Applegate and Potter 2002: 16) was a fact of life for German-speaking countries not party to the unification of Germany in 1871. That, however, may sound like something of a lawyer's argument: how can Schenker fulminate for page upon page about the the iniquities of St Germain and Versailles, or the duplicity of the Entente powers who started the war, and then say that he is only interested in culture, not politics? There is an answer to this question, or at least there is a historical context within which it arises, but it will take longer to explain.

The cultural conservatism I described as deeply embedded in the German-speaking countries at the turn of the twentieth century had its immediate origins in the processes of modernisation that accelerated rapidly after 1871. As Edward Kravitt (2002: 76–7) explains, 'Germany's rapid industrialization created enormous social and economic upheavals. Magnates of heavy industry, bankers and stockbrokers formed cartels that honeycombed the country and stamped out competition. "Get-rich-quick" ventures created economic crises.' By far the most serious of these crises was the stock market crash of May 1873, known as 'Black Friday': the effects were particularly acute in Vienna, with fifty-eight of its seventy-two banks collapsing over the next five years (Berkley 1988: 11), and with many small investors losing their savings; predictably rumour had it from the start that this disaster was a 'Jewish betrayal' (McCagg 1989: 156). The consequence was a widespread popular reaction against capitalism and other expressions of modernity, in Kravitt's words bringing together 'small businessmen impoverished by great industry, skilled artisans displaced by machines, and peasants crippled by high mortgages' (77); he adds that the resulting 'conservative revolution, passionately anti-modernist and racist, persisted into World War I'. Despite (or possibly because of) the lesser degree of industrialisation in Austria, such attitudes were particularly strong there, and William McCagg sees the 1873 crash as the essential catalyst in both the collapse of Viennese liberalism and the rise of a new and more virulent anti-Semitism.

What Schorske (1980: chap. 3) calls 'politics in a new key' focused round the radical, pan-German right led by Georg von Schönerer (the inventor of the title 'Führer' and the greeting 'Heil') as well as, later, Lueger, and one of its most conspicuous expressions in 1880s and 1890s Vienna was the pan-German student fraternities (*Burschenschaften*) who,

as Berkley (1988: 74) puts it, 'would spend Saturday afternoon march-
ing up and down the University courtyard singing German national
songs; groups would then frequently break up to attack Slavs, Italians,
Hungarians and especially Jews'. (Fig. 3.2 shows an anti-Semitic brawl
that took place at the University in 1897.) It was the same increasingly
xenophobic pan-German students who became a feature of Viennese
musical life, sometimes disrupting concerts (Kravitt cites a demonstration at a Vienna Wagner-Verein concert given by Hugo Wolf), and—as
I said in chapter 1—effectively appropriating Wagner and Bruckner for
their cause. Given the fact that Hitler lived in Vienna from 1907 to
1913, there is every reason to trace a line of descent from the Viennese
politics of nostalgia to the Nazis' militant ideology of 'blood and soil',
and it is from this time on that (as Pamela Potter [1998: 176] puts it)

Figure 3.2   Anti-Semitic brawl at the University of Vienna, 1897.
(*Source:* Berkley 1988 (unnumbered plate after p. 126).)

'emotionally charged terms like *Volk, Gemeinschaft, Blut, Rasse,* and *organisch* defied definition or analysis. Rather they stirred feelings or longing for an ideal, unified German nation in an era of political and social fragmentation'.

Many writers on German thought during this period cite the terminology popularised by Ferdinand Tönnies in his book *Gemeinschaft und Gesellschaft,* published in 1887. These words are normally translated respectively as 'community' and 'society', but *Gesellschaft* is also the standard term for a commercial company, and this is a key to Tönnies's usage: *Gesellschaft* stands for a cluster of concepts including industrialisation, modernisation, capitalism, rationalism, internationalism, and anonymity, while *Gemeinschaft* stands for mutual support, cohesion, and organicism—the values of a nostalgically conceived, preindustrial society. These values underlay much of the work associated with legal studies at the University of Vienna: Johnston explains the legal theory of Eugen Ehrlich (whom I mentioned in chapter 1) in terms of 'the distinction between living law of Gemeinschaft and state-made law of Gesellschaft', and prefaces his discussion of the economic theory of Carl Menger (Anton's brother) by saying 'in what follows, the terms holism, organicism, feudalism, ascription, and particularism are used interchangeably to denote Gemeinschaft mentality. The terms individualism, nominalism, empiricism, industrialism, capitalism, and achievement-orientation designate Gesellschaft values' (Johnston 1972: 91, 78).

So it is not surprising that these values resonate strongly with Schenker's thought. And while Schenker does not seem to have employed the *Gemeinschaft/Gesellschaft* distinction in his own writings (unless one is to read this sense into his coinage of the term *Tongemeinschaft*),[34] he made extensive use of a cognate distinction: between *Kultur* and *Zivilisation,* terms now associated with Oswald Spengler's *Der Untergang des Abendlandes* (The decline of the West)—in which culture, understood as intrinsically aristocratic, ends at the beginning of the nineteenth century and is succeeded by the inferior form of civilisation, increasingly dominated by the masses—and Thomas Mann's *Betrachtungen eines Unpolitischen* (Reflections of a nonpolitical man).[35] A passage from the prologue of the latter shows how the *Kultur/Zivilization* distinction stacks up with other, related terms: 'The difference between intellect and politics', Mann writes, 'is the difference between cosmopolitan and international. The former concept comes from the cultural sphere and is German: the latter comes from the sphere of civilization and democracy and is something quite different'.[36] (Nationalism, then, is unambiguously encoded in Mann's statement a few pages later that 'Richard Wagner once declared that *civilization* disappears before *music*

---

[34] *MM2* 124 (see also Reiter 2003: 142–3).
[35] Reiter 2003: 148–9.
[36] Mann 1983/1918: 17.

like mist before the sun. He never dreamt that one day, for its part, music would disappear before civilization, before democracy, like mist before the sun'.)[37] Given that both Spengler's and Mann's books were published in 1918, and that Schenker read them,[38] it can be no coincidence that Schenker uses these terms in exactly the same sense in 'Von der Sendung', as when he says (referring to Germany) that 'the last stronghold of aristocracy has fallen, and culture is sold out to democracy', or refers to France as 'that infamous civilisation': *Kultur* and *Zivilisation* might then be said to carry the same connotations as *Gemeinschaft* and *Gesellschaft*, while adding a dimension of nationalist xenophobia. Schenker's clearest statement of the culture/civilisation distinction, however, comes in *Der freie Satz*, where he writes:

> Culture, tradition, the discipline of genius—these terms are all synonymous; they all have to do with the phenomenon of genius. Civilisation, however, relinquishes the support of the genius in every respect. When a generation begins to want a new culture, when it attacks tradition and the discipline of genius, it contradicts the true essence of culture. (*FC* I 159)

The point, however, is not so much one of specific terminology as of the pattern of thinking that lies behind it. Schenker does not, for example, use the *Kultur/Zivilisation* terminology in the *Meisterwerk* essay 'Weg mit dem Phrasierungsbogen', from which I quoted in chapter 2, but the binary pattern of his thought in a passage like the following maps directly onto it:

> For has there not been, for about the past two hundred years, a huge phrasing slur encircling the entire world, drawn by a few presumptious peoples of the so-called Enlightenment . . . around all the other peoples in contradiction to their individuality and also to the concept of a higher unity growing organically from contrasts? (*MM1* 30)

On the one side, *Zivilisation* is represented by 'the so-called Enlightenment' (what Schenker had described in 'Von der Sendung' as 'the genuinely shallow, quintessentially French "Enlightenment"' [*T1* 9]), which stands for the values of the West: democracy, capitalism, standardisation, and universalism, of which Schenker's 'huge phrasing slur encircling the entire world' is a striking image (maybe Schenker was thinking of the transatlantic telegraph cables, still being laid in the 1920s).[39] On the other side we have such keywords of *Kultur* as individuality,

[37] Mann 1983/1918: 23.

[38] Notes on Spengler in OC 12/287–91 and 828–42; references to *Betrachtungen eines Unpolitischen* in *Tonwille* (*T1* 168) and a diary entry dated 1 July 1925 (Federhofer 1985: 288). More precisely, it was the first volume of *Der Untergang des Abendlandes* that was published in 1918.

[39] See FTL Design's 'History of the Atlantic Cable & Undersea Communications' website, www.atlantic-cable.com/Cables/CableTimeLine/index1901.htm.

unity, the organic. And binary thinking of this nature predates not only Spengler's and Mann's *Kultur/Zivilisation* terminology but also Tönnies's *Gemeinschaft/Gesellschaft* terminology: both map effortlessly onto the series of opposed terms Ernst Hanisch extracts from Wagner's writings, listing them under the headings 'German' and 'Not German', and describing them as 'dichotomies typical of his age, which formed the ideological basis of the German *Sonderweg* and which were admirably suited for exploitation in 1914 and again in 1933' (Hanisch 1992/1986: 190–1).[40] It will be helpful to use a selection of Hanisch's terms as the basis for an annotated glossary of some of Schenker's core concepts.

One of Hanisch's dichotomies, to come back to the starting point of this discussion, is 'nonpolitical/political orientation'. This, then, is an older idea than Mann's book, which however did much to disseminate the idea of the nonpolitical, so that it is probably—again—not a coincidence that Schenker's explicit references to this dichotomy date from after 1918: in addition to those I quoted from issues 1 and 5 of *Tonwille* (1921 and 1923), he says in the preface to *Kontrapunkt 2* (1922) that it is 'no more political' to evaluate the nations of the West than it would be to evaluate the Roman Empire (*C2* xiii), and also notes in his diary on 12 February 1923 that he is opposed to democracy 'less in a political than a cultural sense'.[41] The thinking here, as set out by Mann, is that

> One is not a 'democratic', or, say, a 'conservative' politician. One *is* a politician or one is not. And if one is, then one is democratic. The political-intellectual attitude is the democratic one; belief in politics is belief in democracy, in the *contrat social*. For more than a century and a half, everything that has been understood in a more intellectual sense by politics goes back to *Jean-Jacques Rousseau:* and he is the father of democracy *because* he is the father of the political spirit itself, of political humanity.[42]

The conservative attitude, in other words, is not political: it stands above politics. It is then in this sense that Schenker is not talking politics when he sets out a conservative, antidemocratic, in short German position in his writings; he is just saying how things are, much as one might in evaluating the Roman Empire—and this explains the excessive certainty, the lack of any trace of self-critique, in what *we* see as Schenker's political writings. Indeed, Schenker spells this out quite explicitly in the fifth issue of *Tonwille:* 'So I do not do politics. I am simply conscious—

[40] One can always push these things further back: Hanisch's list in turn maps onto the 'cluster of terminological oppositions that structure organicist thought' which Korsyn (1993: 92) extracts from Schopenhauer's account of genius.

[41] Federhofer 1985: 95; this was prompted by a letter of three days earlier from Walter Dahms, suggesting that Schenker should clarify that for him '"democratic" is not a political but a cultural term'. In doing this, Dahms adds, Schenker will remove a potential weapon from his opponents.

[42] Mann 1983/1918: 16.

as few Germans are—of the cultural war, which is a nonpolitical, holy war' (*Tl* 549). It is also worth pointing out that precisely this way of thinking, when applied to music, gives rise to the idea of 'pure' music, understood as music that stands above the national characteristics that mark music as Bohemian, French, Italian, English, and so forth, and in this way paradoxically reveals itself as distinctively German: Schenker's slightly older contemporary Richard Wallaschek, who wrote music criticism for *Die Zeit*, expressed this particularly clearly in his *Ästhetik der Tonkunst* (1886) when he claimed that 'German music in fact has no national-characteristic element in its artistic works; it is pure beauty'.[43] (There is an echo here of the conservatory canon, defined by Peter Franklin in terms of 'its universality and its transcendence of the popular, the ephemeral, the ethnic, the worldly', which I mentioned in chapter 2.) German music, in short, stands in relation to other musics as the nonpolitical stands in relation to the political.

This provides the context for two more of Hanisch's dichotomies, which can be taken together: 'conservatism/revolution' and 'authority/democracy'. Defined as 'political', democracy is un-German, even unnatural, as Schenker implies when he says (in the preface to *Kontrapunkt* 2) that 'democracy stubbornly resists recognizing its own misconceptions and lies, its violations of nature and culture' (*C2* xiv). Schenker's thinking here falls squarely within a tradition that goes back through Mann's *Betrachtungen eines Unpolitischen* (democracy is 'in itself something un-German, anti-German')[44] to Wagner's 'Was ist deutsch?' ('Democracy in Germany is a purely translated thing' [Osborne 1973: 54]); it might also be traced back via a different route, through Jellinek—who as I said in chapter 1 denounced democracy as the tyranny of the majority (Alpern 1999: 1475)—to Hegel, who was wholly opposed to popular suffrage and regarded the constitutional monarchy as the only rational form of government (Singer 1983: 38–41). Schenker's invocation of Nature in this context also provides the clue to his views on revolution, views that might again easily be traced back to Hegel: as Schenker says in the second issue of *Tonwille*,

> To man it is forbidden to prove himself Nature's peer and, through an autonomous creative act, to set up something completely new and of equal rank in opposition to her law of consonance; man, after all, is a mysterious transformation of one of Nature's fundamental laws. But if the artist is content with newly inventing mere transformations, he obtains the reward of remaining newly safe and secure in them for ever. (*Tl* 51)

This is the position summarised by the motto Schenker adopted from 1921, 'Semper idem sed non in eodem modo' (Always the same, but

---

[43] Translated in McColl 1996: 221. A discussion of the 'German' in music, providing a larger context for Wallaschek's claim, may be found in Sponheuer 2002.

[44] Mann 1983/1918: 190.

not in the same way), which appears on the title pages of the *Tonwille* pamphlets and of *Der freie Satz*, as well as at the head of each part in *Kontrapunkt 2*. (The thought is reminiscent of Loos's 'old forms in the new spirit', which in chapter 2 I compared to Brahms's imitation of the classics 'but always in new ways'.)[45] Given that Schenker's reference to 'setting up something completely new . . . in opposition to [Nature's] law of consonance' is an obvious dig at Schoenberg and other destroyers of the pure tonal material of music, it is paradoxical that Schoenberg claimed exactly the same position—evolution, not revolution, as he frequently expressed it—for himself.

With two more of Hanisch's dichotomies, the closely related 'inwardness/superficiality' and 'depth of feeling/superficial distractedness', we come to Schenker's music-theoretical terminology. The image of music as some kind of opaque body, the surface of which conceals a content that lies behind it (inward) or below it (depth), is so ubiquitous in Schenker's theoretical writings, and so comprehensively thought into his analytical approach, that it would be pointless to illustrate it. I shall return to the specific trope of concealment in chapter 4; here I wish only to link the idea of 'inwardness' to the idea (which I mentioned in chapters 1 and 2) of the German thinking from the inside outwards. This was not a new idea: Hanslick, for example, speaks in *Vom Musikalisch-Schönen* of musical forms as 'not mere contours of a vacuum but mind giving shape to itself from within', a formulation with self-evident Hegelian origins,[46] while Robert Vischer wrote in 1873 that aesthetic understanding 'traces the object from the inside (the object's center) to the outside (the object's form)'.[47] The point is rather, as Bent suggested, how deeply this idea is embedded in Schenker's later thought, surfacing in the preface to *Kontrapunkt 2* (where Schenker refers to 'the power of growing outward from within' [*C2* xvii], though without making it clear whether or not he is talking about music); in *Tonwille 7* ('The tonal body has definite boundaries that arise from within, from its soul, and are not given to it from without' [*T2* 55]); and most spectacularly in *Der freie Satz*, where Schenker not only exclaims 'it should have been evident long ago that the same principle applies both to a musical organism and to the human body: it grows outward from within' but also quotes the 'ingenious words' of Hugo von Hofmannsthal:

[45] See p. 127 above.

[46] Hanslick 1986/1854: 30. Dahlhaus (1989/1978: 109–10) quotes this in the course of an argument for the Hegelian origins of Hanslick's book as a whole, claiming that 'Hanslick, the easily comprehensible writer, must be seen relative to Hegel, the difficult-to-understand philosopher, if one wishes to comprehend seriously what Hanslick actually meant, and wherein the problem he sought to solve consisted'; he adds that what is relevant here is not Hegel's own texts but rather 'the Hegelianism that had entered the common parlance of intellectuals' around 1850.

[47] Vischer, *Über das optische Formgefühl* [On the optical sense of form], quoted in Lee Rothfarb, 'Nineteenth-Century Fortunes of Musical Formalism' (unpublished paper).

'No part of the surface of a figure can be formed except from the innermost core outward' (*FC* I 6). If it is this process of growth that is embodied in the Schenkerian concept of prolongation, then what I call axial causality is the transformation of a long established metaphor of musical depth into a more or less rigorous theory.[48]

And if the working up of what were originally little more than evaluative categories into fully developed theory is something that belongs to the later phases of Schenker's career, then Hanisch has a further group of dichotomies that relate directly to Schenker's writings of the 1890s. 'Creativity and originality/imitation and exploitation' takes us to the heart of 'Unpersönliche Musik' (1897), with its critique of the 'classicists' who ape (imitate, exploit) the forms of the past; if, as Schenker complains there, 'the first creative force in most composers today is the intellect, and it is only what has been invented this way that they justify after the event',[49] then the emphasis Schenker places on the (genuine) creative process in a number of the essays from the 1890s represents a counterbalance. (Maybe it would be going too far to relate Schenker's emphasis on creation as against imitation to Józef Reiss's claim that in Galicia 'all forms of musical life were imitated'.)[50] That in turn brings into play another of Hanisch's dichotomies, 'morality/intellect': for Schenker, the 'false theory' of the formalists is immoral because—like Schoenberg's atonality—it is unnatural, externally imposed rather than growing outward from within, intellectual in the bad sense. Finally, 'idealism/materialism' links directly to the dichotomy between spirit and technique which gives the *Geist* essay (1895) its title, and which in chapter 2 I linked to the controversy between Riegl and Semper. But it also links with the opposition Schenker frequently invokes in *Tonwille* between the German *Geist* and French *esprit*, as for instance in the third issue: 'right on Germany's doorstep,' Schenker writes, 'sits the Lilliputian nation of the French, its soul still in diapers. . . . Its spirit is incapable of penetrating to the heart of truth. . . . This Lilliputian people calls it *esprit*. To the deep waters of the spirit it is nothing but—a puff of spray' (*T1* 134). Only a few lines later Schenker is saying that 'The Frenchman's truest talent . . . is now and always will be that of hating Germans and stealing their territory'.

It will already be obvious that these dichotomies constantly collapse into one another. And beyond them, there are many more specifically musical terms that become marked in terms of the basic di-

---

[48] Holly Watkins, who traces the idea of musical depth back through Hoffmann, Wackenroder, and Herder to late seventeenth-century Pietism, characterizes it in much the same way I characterized axial causality in chapter 1: she sees Hoffmann as 'adding a new dimension to music complementing its axis of horizontal or temporal unfolding', and relates this to the late eighteenth-century epistemic change identified by Foucault that 'makes analysis pivot on its axis' so as 'to relate the visible to the invisible, to its deeper cause, as it were' (2004: 181, 203).

[49] Schenker 1988: 134.

[50] See p. 11 above.

chotomies of *Gemeinschaft/Gesellschaft* or *Kultur/Zivilisation* (or, in its most reductive form, 'German/Not German'); this means they come to act as kind of code, without knowledge of which it may not be possible to grasp quite what is motivating Schenker's thought. In saying this I am effectively paraphrasing what Albrecht Riethmüller (2002: 299) has said from a position of much greater authority: 'In order for non-German readers to grasp the full impact of certain words and understand how they were used, it is often necessary to reconstruct their meaning in specific contexts'. And Riethmüller, who is not specifically talking about Schenker, cites the symphonic, musical logic (Schenker's 'causality'), thematic work, counterpoint, seriousness, depth, *Innerlichkeit*, pure music, and absolute music as terms with positive (German) connotations, commenting that they together 'form a plexus that suggests musical superiority, which in turn helps sustain the belief that music is "the most German art"' (297–8). By contrast, he adds, terms with negative, un-German connotations—and sometimes an anti-Semitic subtext—include 'slick, clever, lacking in ideas, sentimental, and full of kitsch'.

As Riethmüller's reference to 'the most German art' suggests, the concept of 'music' itself becomes marked in this context, and here I rely on Scott Burnham to make the point. Writing on the *Meisterwerk* 3 essay 'Rameau or Beethoven' (1930) and asking 'why is genius German, mediocrity French?' Burnham observes (1992: 84): 'By about 1800 music became a leading metaphor for spirit, the cultivation of music a metaphor for spirituality. As the primary focus of German profundity and universality, German music was the heart of a spiritual nation felt to be not only universal but distinctly ethnic at the same time'. (This already complex notion of a 'spiritual nation' of course became the more so after Germany became also a political state, but with different borders.) And Burnham concludes (85) that

> the attachment of these ideas to German nationalism is not just the result of post–World War I nationalist fervor, but is constitutive of German cultural history from at least the *Deutsche Klassik*, the age of Goethe and Schiller, Herder and Winckelmann. . . . The basic assumption of a spiritual homeland is in place long before any militaristic manifestations of nationalism.

But what is particularly telling in the present context is what Burnham says about Schenker's 'simplistic dichotomies of theory and musical art, mechanical chord structure and living voice leading, French mediocrity and German genius—they all work to the end of articulating a crisis to which his theory provides a synthesizing answer' (84). That is no doubt true. But it is not just true of Schenker. The logic of nostalgia meant that, to an extraordinary degree, the elements of conservative culture had become polarised: everything pointed either to *Gemeinschaft, Kultur*, German, or else to *Gesellschaft, Zivilisation*, not German. Everything, one might say, worked to the end of articulating a crisis.

There is however one further dichotomy which is of particular consequence for music theory (and the omission of which from Hanisch's list is surprising): nature/artifice. Of course the idea of the natural, of how things are, is closely linked to that of the nonpolitical (hence, as we have seen, democracy and revolution are both contrary to nature), and for Schenker one of the reasons that false theory is false is that it is artificial, imposed on rather than drawn out of nature (it is thought from the outside rather than the inside). In fact, in the *Geist* essay, the positive connotation of the natural as against the artificial becomes clearest at the point when Schenker argues that artifice has an essential role to play in creating the (illusory) effect of musical logic: 'I must ask', he says, 'that the term be divested of the derogatory connotation that adheres to it in common opinion' (p. 327). Schenker's awkward attempt at this point of the *Geist* essay to balance the competing roles of the natural and the artificial, the purely musical and the intellectual, anticipates the more accomplished juggling act he pulls off in *Harmonielehre* by means of the idea he terms 'abbreviation'. Like all music theorists working in this tradition, Schenker wants to demonstrate that music as we know it is not a purely artificial construction but grounded in the natural phenomenon of the harmonic series, while at the same time finding a way to avoid the out-of-tune seventh partial; he also needs to find a solution for the fact that, while the major triad (which he calls the 'chord of nature' [*FC* I 11]) can be derived from the first five partials, the minor triad has no direct model in the harmonic series. Schenker's elegantly simple solution to this conundrum cuts through the complexities of previous theorists' solutions. Just as we do not need to be told what Wallenstein had for lunch, says Schenker (the reference, which Schenker does not explain, is to Schiller's trilogy of that name), so the 'law of abbreviation' (*H* 13) requires us to abstract only what is essential from the harmonic series: the close-position major triad is an artistic abbreviation of the three-octave registral range encompassed by the first five partials, and in the same way the harmonic series is itself abbreviated, for purposes of art, through the elimination of all partials from the sixth onwards. (Though the sixth partial is in tune, Schenker has no need for it since he has an alternative derivation for the 5:6 minor third.) As for the minor triad, Schenker simply regards it as an artificial copy of the major triad. Having in this way extracted what he wants from the harmonic series, Schenker celebrates the 'wonderful, strange, and inexplicably mysterious fact' that the ear is attuned only to the first five partials (*H* 36), and moves on.

For the modern reader the problem is not understanding Schenker's argument but understanding its point. While there was of course a music-theoretical tradition of deriving music from the phenomena of acoustics, for Schenker and his contemporaries the solution must lie partly in the conservative ideology that coded natural as good and artificial as bad: this becomes most obvious when Schenker attacks

Schoenberg (though not by name) for attempting to demolish the very material of music through setting up 'something completely new and of equal rank in opposition to her law of consonance', so substituting artifice for nature. The ideological imperatives are equally evident in the contortions Schoenberg went through in order to justify his compositional procedures without relinquishing his claims on the natural. In the first place, as everybody knows, Schoenberg sought in his *Harmonielehre* to 'emancipate' the dissonance in the sense of denying that there was any categorical distinction between consonance and dissonance ('the distinction between them', he says, 'is only a matter of degree').[51] The curiously Hegelian passage I quoted in chapter 2 ('of the acoustical emanations of the tone nothing is lost') is in essence a denial of the principle of abbreviation: art, Schoenberg is saying, can and should take advantage of the full potential of the overtone series— which implies, though Schoenberg does not spell this out, that extended tonality is in fact not less but more natural than traditional tonality. Taken literally and developed systematically, this principle would erase any distinction between musical and acoustical theory, but that only goes to show that Schoenberg's purpose in advancing it is more polemical than theoretical.

In the second place, Schoenberg argues that music can be grounded in nature without being limited to specific expressions of it: 'Tonality is a formal possibility that emerges from the nature of the tonal material', he says, but it does not exhaust what is possible: the major-minor system 'is not the last word, the ultimate goal of music, but rather a provisional stopping place'.[52] Here Schoenberg is effectively making two not entirely compatible arguments at the same time. On the one hand he is accepting the evolutionary framework of much contemporary music-theoretical thinking, Schenker's included, but suggesting that extended tonality represents a higher stage of development than major-minor tonality, just as tonality represents a higher stage of development than the music of the Chinese or the gypsies.[53] On the other hand he is arguing that the rules with which music theory deals should be regarded as historically contingent and pragmatic, as 'a system that does not pretend to clarify the ultimate nature of the things presented'—but just before this statement, which I quoted in chapter 1, Schoenberg makes a clear bid to have his cake and eat it: there must exist 'natural laws' of music, he says, unconditionally valid for all times and places, only nobody knows what they are, 'and I believe they will not be discovered very soon'.[54] What we should not do, then, is confuse the pragmatic, historically limited rules we know with the natural laws we do not,

[51] Schoenberg 1978/1911: 21.
[52] Schoenberg 1978/1911: 27, 25.
[53] Schoenberg 1978/1911: 25.
[54] Schoenberg 1978/1911: 10.

which is where reactionary theorists and critics go wrong: 'what is most disastrous of all', Schoenberg says, is 'the belief that a *yardstick* has been found by which to measure artistic worth, even that of future works'.[55]

Schoenberg does not mention Schenker at this point, and of course there were many other theorists and critics of whom the same might be said, but all the same Schenker—the already established author of a publication of the same name published five years earlier (and the composer whose *Syrische Tänze* Schoenberg had orchestrated three years before that)—exercises a curious presence in Schoenberg's *Harmonielehre*. This becomes clear further on, when Schoenberg refers to 'Heinrich Schenker, a first-rate mind, a man of insight and imagination', and immediately adds 'I have not read his book; I have merely browsed in it', while later on the same page Schoenberg adds parenthetical qualifications of his remarks about Schenker: '(if I remember correctly)', '(I don't remember everything)'.[56] There is also a footnote where Schoenberg goes into quite unnecessary detail about his use of the term 'ascending' for root progressions: he recently obtained a copy of Schenker's *Harmonielehre*, he says, and thought he must have got the idea from there, since he originally 'read some of it' four years earlier, but on asking around his pupils he has been assured that he was using the term 'at least seven years ago'.[57] In this case, at least, Schoenberg seems to display an anxiety of influence that matches Schenker's, or maybe it was simply a sense of vulnerability as compared to the university- and (partly) conservatory-trained, as well as already extensively published, Dr Schenker.

As I argued in chapter 1, one of the foundations of Schenker's theoretical project was his refusal to compromise on the need for genuinely causal principles: if Schenker read the passage in Schoenberg's *Harmonielehre* where Schoenberg writes that 'whenever I theorize, it is less important whether these theories be right than whether they be useful as comparisons to clarify the object and to give the study perspective',[58] he must have thought it no better than Bruckner's 'Look, gentlemen, this is the rule. Of course, I don't compose that way'.[59] Yet there are some striking similarities between Schenker's and Schoenberg's thinking: it is as if they were both trying to patch together what they needed from the same pool of ideas, though sometimes the ideas point in the same direction and sometimes the opposite. Carl Dahlhaus has emphasised the mirror-image relationship between them: 'Traditional theory was rejected by both Schenker and Schoenberg', he says,

[55] Schoenberg 1978/1911: 8.
[56] Schoenberg 1978/1911: 318.
[57] Schoenberg 1978/1911: 119n. Schoenberg's library, now at the Arnold Schönberg Center in Vienna, includes not only Schenker's *Harmonielehre* but also *Ornamentik*, the Ninth Symphony monograph, and the first volume of *Kontrapunkt.*
[58] Schoenberg 1978/1911: 19.
[59] See chapter 1, p. 60.

but on opposite grounds: Schenker denied the concept of the "essential" dissonance and Schoenberg that of the "incidental". . . . Thus while Schoenberg demands that the consequence for the harmonic progression of even the most fleeting dissonance must be taken account of, Schenker postulates the exact opposite: that the dissonant nature of even the harshest vertical combinations must be disregarded in order to penetrate the musical surface and arrive at the horizontal progressions upon which coherence depends'. (1987: 135–6)

For Dahlhaus, as for Gianmario Borio (2001), Schenker and Schoenberg talk past one another: even when they seem to be referring to the same thing, there is no communication. I would rather make the same point I made in chapter 2 in connection with Riegl and Semper: to be diametrically opposed you must be working within a common framework. So Schoenberg's thought about nothing being lost from the acoustical emanations of tone is really the same thought as when Schenker speaks of what the artist has drawn from the harmonic series and 'how much of it, on the other hand, he has left, and probably will ever leave, unused' (*H* 21); it is just that they turn the thought in opposite directions. As for Schoenberg's claim that 'tonality is a formal possibility that emerges from the nature of the tonal material', this is in substance no different from Schenker's claim that 'Nature's help to music consisted of nothing but a hint, a counsel for ever mute, whose perception and interpretation were fraught with the gravest difficulties':[60] each wants to understand music as grounded in, but not limited to, the natural.

It is true that Schenker's formulation engenders the suspicion that there might be only one correct way of interpreting the hint, and so Suzannah Clark (1999: 86) writes that, for Schenker, 'the phenomenon could be misunderstood: the artist's misunderstanding of nature is to blame for church modes, pretonal music, and presumably non-Western music'. Yet Schenker is constantly emphasising how music cannot be derived directly from nature but must be mediated by the quite distinct principles of art: in *Harmonielehre*, for instance, he writes that 'the total content of a composition basically represents a real and continuous conflict between system and Nature', and in *Kontrapunkt 2* that 'the ultimate arbiter, beyond all such relationship with nature, is voice leading, which, in recognition of justifiable and higher needs of its own, often makes observation of the postulates of nature by no means desirable' (*H* 288, *C2* 127). To borrow the terminology of one contemporary discourse, he shows how culture can escape a slavish conformity

---

[60] *H* 20. There is perhaps an echo here of Hanslick's (1986/1854: 68) claim that 'nature is related to the arts as a motherly dispenser of the first and most important dowry', although when Hanslick goes on to speak of the materials furnished by nature he means this only in the sense of those from which instruments are constructed; he was sceptical regarding the natural origins of the tonal system, asking 'Has anyone ever heard a triad in nature?' (69).

to nature while at the same time adhering to underlying natural principles.[61] And what I referred to earlier as a rather obscure passage near the end of the *Kontrapunkt 2* preface shows Schenker extending the same thinking from art to governance. His starting point is the claim in *Harmonielehre* that the discovery of the overtone system 'has seduced modern theorists obstinately to insist in deriving everything (e.g., the fourth, the sixth, the seventh, the minor triad, etc.) from Nature' (*H* 44). As he now explains,

> No key at all could have been established, had not the way of pure Nature been abandoned, and the natural sequence of perfect fifths been adulterated with the admixture of the artificial, false, diminished interval between the VII and IV steps. There they sit for centuries, those faithful to utopian ideals, bourgeois and worker, snob by snob, and enthusiastically applaud masterworks that could be born only because they used the false fifth! Do they think that the synthesis of the state can be achieved without a false fifth, and do they expect of their product that it will appear more just and perfect than the state-syntheses of the past? They deceive themselves. Posterity will certainly applaud more heartily all those state-syntheses of the past, with their false fifths, than those allegedly natural, and yet so falsified, state-monstrosities of today. (*C2* xvii)

A passage like this, with its characteristically Schenkerian conflation of music theory and politics as well as its dialectical resonances, serves as a reminder of the wide range of different positions that were available within the ideology of cultural conservatism—differences which our lack of familiarity today with this entire framework of thinking can lead us to blur. Two comparisons will illustrate this. A much younger musician than Schenker, Paul Hindemith (born in 1895), developed the naturalistic approach in a direction that brought him closer to the ideology of National Socialism. In 1926 Hindemith wrote to Schenker: 'I am an enthusiastic and delighted reader of your books. . . . in them the foundations of musical creation are revealed, which . . . have always been and always will be valid'.[62] But Hindemith was much more extreme than Schenker in the way he derived music from Nature in his *Unterweisung im Tonsatz* of 1937, which he adapted—in certain respects toned down—as *The Craft of Musical Composition* (1945), from which the following quotations are taken. Like Schenker, or Schoen-

---

[61] As explained by Rehding (2000: 356, citing Alfred Vierkandt's 1896 book *Naturvölker und Kulturvölker*), 'human societal groupings could be divided into two kinds: natural people (*Naturvölker*) and civilized people (*Kulturvölker*). "Natural people" were subject to nature, while "civilized people" had subjected nature and formed a culture on its basis.' (The translation 'civilized' does not carry connotations of the later culture/civilization distinction.) Certain of Schenker's later remarks fit well into this framework, such as his references to 'Negro melodies, which have grown in the natural wild' or 'the distinction between real music and primitive nature-music' (*T2* 107, *MM3* 78).

[62] Letter of 25 October 1926, translated in Taylor-Jay (2004: 157n.), on which my discussion of both Hindemith and Pfitzner draws.

berg, Hindemith (1952: 15–6) speaks of 'the tonal raw material which Nature has made ready for musical use', but he goes on to say that its order 'is determined by a strict law, and is as immutable as the color series of the rainbow'. It follows that composition and theory 'can never disregard the conditions laid down by the facts of the existence of pure intervals'—the implication presumably being that Hindemith's own posttonal music is wholly natural, and in that sense tonal after all (45). This argument is highly relevant in the context of Nazi Germany in 1937, when Hindemith was desperately trying to secure a production of his opera *Mathis der Maler*, and Claudia Zenck sets Hindemith's language into this context: the system, she says, is presented as

> natural and lifted above time; the hierarchy is unchangeable. It forms the strong fortress (*die feste Burg*), the dam against the flood of products of an 'arbitrarily changing spirit' (*Geist*), which has led to 'confusion'. This is the mode of expression and argument of the art-politicians of the Third Reich.[63]

Then there is a clipping Schenker pasted into his scrapbook in 1926, perhaps with pride, which refers to 'the most eminent composer and the most eminent theorist of the present day, Hans Pfitzner and Heinrich Schenker';[64] following this prompt, one might pursue a more general comparison between Schenker and the composer who was his almost exact contemporary (born 1869). There is for one thing a partly comparable psychology of alterity: Pfitzner was born in Russia, and Michael Kater (2002: 178–9) suggests that 'although he was only two years old when his family moved to Frankfurt, Pfitzner's self-awareness as a "foreigner" probably was deep-seated and drove him to seek especially close bonds with the home of his forefathers'. (In the next chapter I shall explore parallel issues of identity in relation to the Galician-born Schenker.) Both Schenker and Pfitzner were stridently nationalistic (Pfitzner styled himself 'Hans Pfitzner the German'), but remained as far as possible aloof from party politics; it is telling, if trivial, that both found occasion to write to Hindenburg. Both shared a cultural pessimism that might in the earlier years be termed Schopenhauerian and later Spenglerian; Pfitzner felt that the golden age of music was now in decline, and like Schenker conducted a polemic against the Frankfurt-based critic Paul Bekker, seeing him as attempting to appropriate classical music for the modernist aesthetic. Pfitzner's attacks on the 'impotence' of modern composers reflected not only the terminology of Schenker's similar attacks from the 1890s on, but also the same complaints: that their music was intellectualised, artificial, mechanical (Kater

---

[63] Quoted in Taylor-Jay 2004: 158n.
[64] Excerpt from Alexander Berrsche, 'Beethoven. Ein Erziehungskapitel', *Die Kunstwart*, March 1927 (OC 2/71).

2000: 149). Pfitzner's conservatism was grounded in his belief that there existed timeless, natural laws, and he gave Schenker's idea of the 'power of growing outward from within' a new twist when he wrote that 'systems, rules, forms in music grow from music itself, just as with species of animals and plants in nature. . . . The rule against fifths has its own eternal correctness, as every real musician feels'.[65] 'Real' of course introduces the same kind of circular argument that I noted in chapter 1 in connection with Schenker's idea of the genius—and both Schenker and Pfitzner believed in the cultural centrality of the genius (Pfitzner even used the term *Meisterwerke* for his compositions). Both understood genius in terms of inspiration from above; Pfitzner called inspiration 'the breath of God',[66] and the drawing of him with two musician angels above which Karl Bauer made in 1918 (evidently a reference to Pfitzner's opera *Palestrina,* produced a year earlier) is perhaps as close a visual analogue for Schenker's 'Nature' dictating the 'Dankgesang' from Beethoven's op. 132 as we are likely to find.[67] And when Pfitzner says 'the melody of a Schubertian linden tree lives longer than the empires of Alexander and Napoleon',[68] his thought resonates strongly with Schenker's: in the Ninth Symphony monograph Schenker writes that 'empires can doubtless come and go', but musical laws remain 'immutable fron nation to nation, from race to race, from century to century', and in the second issue of *Tonwille* that 'Generation upon generation passes away, but the tonal line continues to live on as on the first day' (*BNS* 19, *T1* 54).

In the context of German cultural conservatism, however, many of these views border on the commonplace, so it is really the differences that count. I said that Schenker gave currency to the rumours, already widespread in 1919, that the Central Powers could have gone on fighting and that the reason for defeat was the 'stab in the back' by the democrats. (Since the usual version of this story also blamed the Jews, it might be said that Schenker was redirecting anti-Semitic propaganda.) And such references are not restricted to his overtly political writings: in 'The art of improvisation' (the agenda-setting, or at least the first, essay in *Meisterwerk* 1), for instance, there is an apparently innocuous reference to 'the stabs in the back which genius must suffer'.[69] But my description of this rumour as falling somewhere between the scurrilous and the hallucinatory looks exaggerated when set against some of Pfitzner's genuinely hallucinatory beliefs, such as that the Weimar Republic was 'an artificial creation of the international Jewish conspiracy—a Jewish republic' (Kater 2000: 148). Pfitzner made strenuous attempts

---

[65] Translated from Pfitzner, 'Futuristengefahr', in Taylor-Jay 2004: 50.

[66] Translated from Pfitzner, *Über musikalische Inspiration.* in Taylor-Jay 2004: 70.

[67] See p. 65 above. Bauer's drawing is reproduced in Taylor-Jay 2004: 37, fig. 2.1.

[68] Translated from Pfitzner, *Die neue Ästhetik der musikalischen Impotenz,* in Taylor-Jay 2004: 47–8.

[69] *MM1* 2; there are also casual references like *T1* 122.

to be recognised as the 'official' composer of the Third Reich (this was the context of *his* letter to Hindenburg [161]); he tried without success to cultivate personal relationships with Hitler, Goebbels, and Goering, but succeeded in establishing relationships with 'known murderous functionaries of the Third Reich', in particular Hans Frank (Kater 2002: 186). In 1947 he was brought before the courts for denazification, with the hearings being suspended more on the grounds of procedural incompetence than any positive demonstration of Pfitzner's innocence (Kater 2000: 177–80). It was at this time that Pfitzner set out his views on the war: it had been justified, Pfitzner wrote, because of the way the Entente powers had humiliated Germany in the First World War, and he still believed in

> Hitler's honesty and goodwill. He wanted to rejuvenate and liberate his fatherland and, beyond that, render a great service to *Europe* by driving out the Jews—if necessary, eliminate them by radical means. For in *World Jewry* he realized the singular danger for the fortunes of all peoples, and the one reason for all the malignancy in the world, in fact for just about everything. (180–1)

And by now, of course, the comparison with Schenker has broken down completely. Even if he had not died in 1935, the fact that Schenker was Jewish would have made it impossible for him to collaborate with the Nazis in the way Pfitzner did—but more to the point, there is no evidence that Schenker had any inclination to translate his verbal fantasies, however gruesome at times, into reality: that is the point I was making through the comparison with Schoenberg near the end of the previous section, and earlier through the comparison between *Tonwille* and the *Hitler Jugend*. Besides, 'what if' speculations really serve no purpose. If people are to be judged at all, then it must be on the basis of what they did, not what they might have done had things been different.

The Anachronistic City

The dichotomies I discussed in the previous section, and others aligned with them, riddle German-language music criticism at the *fin se siècle*. Table 3.1 lists the dichotomies mentioned so far, and adds some key terms drawn in part from Karen Painter's (1995) study of critical responses to Mahler during the period of his residence in Vienna (1897–1907). Several of these are already familiar from Schenker's writings of the 1890s and early 1900s. Active listening against overall impression is precisely the topic of his 1894 essay 'Das Hören in der Musik'; again, the contrast between the art of performance, properly understood, and virtuosity is a central concern from *Ornamentik* to the unfinished *Kunst des Vortrags*—and relates closely to Robert Hirschfeld's opposition of fantasy and mechanical precision (Botstein 1985: 900–901), so bring-

Table 3.1   Dichotomies in German-Language Music
Criticism at the *Fin de Siecle*

German	Not German
Community (*Gemeinschaft*)	Society (*Gesellschaft*)
Culture	Civilization
Non-political orientation	Political orientation
Conservatism	Revolution
Authority	Democracy
Inwardness	Superficiality
Depth of feeling	Superficial distractedness
Creativity and originality	Imitation and exploitation
Morality	Intellect
Idealism	Materialism
Nature	Artifice
Active listening	Overall impression
Art of performance	Virtuosity
Fantasy	Mechanical precision
Content	Timbre
Inner strength	Nervous twitching
Health	Neurasthenia
Bösendorfer	Steinway

ing in another of Schenker's own keywords. The dichotomy of content
(a further keyword) and timbre relates directly to the central claim of
Painter's article, which is that the virtuosic orchestration of Mahler's
music was heard by the more conservative critics as devaluing its inherently musical content, as appealing to the senses rather than to the
understanding: in 1907, for example, Hirschfeld compared Mahler's
Second Symphony to Debussy's 'obviously conscious dissecting and
unravelling of timbres, a splitting of tone and tracking of nerves, from
which we know only one thing: that it is almost unbearable' (Painter
1995: 237). Such responses were by no means limited to Vienna, as
Painter demonstrates by quoting from Walter Niemann, who was based
in Leipzig and wrote in *Die Musik seit Richard Wagner* (1913) that the
'whipping of our nervous system becomes the decisive feature of all
truly modern music. Music is transformed from the herald of human
spiritual life . . . into a physiological art of nerves, mood, and timbre,
externally defined' (238). Indeed, another passage from Niemann's
book offers a veritable lexicon of terms for the righthand side of table
3.1: impressionist music, he says (meaning 'impressionism' of the
French rather than Viennese variety, though either would be appropriate), is an expression of

> the weakness in heart and soul of our younger and youngest genera-
> tions—who increasingly Americanize, mercantilize, and industrialize all of

public life, with their pleasure in whipping of nerves, in sensation, and in glittering superficial appearance—and for the modern overvaluing of money, fame, material success, personality . . . and boundless sensuality. (246)

It was in the following year that Schenker first conceived what became his *Tonwille* pamphlets, 'offered to a new generation of youth'.

As Painter explains, such criticisms were by no means unprecedented: the dichotomy of content and timbre effectively replicates Nietzsche's claim of 1888 that in Wagner's music 'the color of the tone is decisive, *what* resounds is almost a matter of indifference', while two years earlier Nietzsche had called modern German music 'the greatest corrupter of the nerves' (Painter 1995: 239)—and more generally, of course, this kind of critique goes back to Hanslick's strictures, in *Vom Musikalisch-Schönen*, regarding what he called 'pathological' responses to music. (There is in this way a long tradition behind Schenker's complaint in 1921 that 'the ear has lost its capacity for larger structures [based] on the truly legitimate foundation of a healthy Urlinie and good voice leading'.)[70] But what is perhaps especially characteristic of the Viennese *fin de siècle* is the way these terms proliferate and ramify, forming DNA-like chains of association that reach into and polarise different aspects of society. A particularly clear example of this comes not from music criticism but from the literary historian Rudolph Lothar, who wrote in 1891 that

> nervous sensibility is characteristic of the last years of our century. I am inclined to call this trend 'feminism', for everything goes to show that women's will to power, their desire to compete with men, has meant that the female hypersensitivity of gaze, of leisure, of thought and of feeling, has been communicated to men and is taking over. (translated in Le Rider 1993: 107)

And Painter shows how the language of gender, whether expressed directly or through association, pervades the music criticism of the period. To cite just two examples from Hirschfeld, in 1900 he wrote in a review of Mahler's First Symphony (which he saw as a parody of the genre) of 'the disproportion between the ideas and their orchestral clothing', and explained that 'you apply lipstick—a few eighth-note rests—to the usual scherzo pattern, and immediately the pursed up scherzo motif seems like new'; nine years later, after Mahler's departure from Vienna, he wrote of the Third and Seventh Symphonies that the music seems more empty and hollow 'the more tightly we cling to the orchestral changing of clothes and bejewelling, I should like to say, to the cosmetic powers that give the meager motifs the appearance of meaning' (Painter 1995: 242, 243).

Though it dates from much later, and comes from a different liter-

---

[70] Translated from the op. 101 *Erläuterungsausgabe* in Morgan 2002: 251.

ary genre, Schenker is responsible for one of the most extravagant displays of such imagery: motives that are not grounded in the Urlinie, he wrote in the second volume of *Meisterwerk,* sound 'as though snatched out of thin air, unprepared, stuck together, like a splash of tinsel, like ear jewellery, nose rings, and so forth'.[71] (The nose rings sound like a throwback to the world of Loos's 'Ornament und Verbrechen'.) Though I shall not explore the topic at length, such imagery, encountered over a period of decades, might prompt a consideration of gendered language in Schenker's critical writings—particularly those of the 1890s, in which issues of gender seem to be closely associated with the terminology of cold and warmth which I commented on in chapter 1.[72] One of the sources in which Schenker's use of gendered vocabulary is most insistent is the *Die Zukunft* Brahms obituary (1897), where Schenker emphasises Brahms's masculine qualities so insistently that you begin to wonder quite what charge he is trying to counter: 'he never surrendered himself to any sentimentality that would have discredited his masculinity', Schenker tells us.[73] And a few sentences later he says that Brahms placed his art above close personal relationships—but, he adds, 'even in this regard he was thoroughly manly: he steered clear of all danger to his art, and never bemoaned his lonely state'.

So far, then, we have a rather stereotypical association of masculinity with independence, resistance to temptation, inner strength, on the basis of which we might confidently add 'Masculine/feminine' to table 3.1. But a paragraph earlier there is a more telling insistence on Brahms's masculinity:

> His character was full of manful self-control, and so he never abused his genius by bringing work to a close while still under the influence of his initial inspiration: for he knew that his rational judgement might later find a prematurely completed piece to be unsatisfactory in some respect.[74]

Here then reason—what in chapter 1 I referred to as reflection—is associated with 'manful self-control', implying the gendering of inspiration as female; that would also link with the dichotomy Schenker draws two paragraphs earlier between 'the icy wind of abstraction' and 'the warmth of living breath' (this is just before the reference to 'a beautiful child flowering into adulthood'), or a few lines later 'warm-blooded tones'. And indeed Schenker had spelt out this association of ideas quite explicitly in his 1893 article 'Anton Bruckner':

---

[71] MM2 18; Schenker is almost quoting from his letter of 3 April 1924 to Halm, in which he wrote that 'Where the whole is not figure, all figures sound merely pasted on like an instance of an ornament, like earrings, noserings' (DLA 69.930/12, translated by Rothfarb, Schenker Correspondence Project website).

[72] See pp. 78–9 above.

[73] Schenker 1991/1897: 3.

[74] Schenker 1991/1987: 2.

It is Bruckner's saddest shortcoming that his faculty of reflection can wed itself only with such difficulty—or even not at all—to his own feeling for beauty. With him, one hears the faculty of reflection carry out its difficult work coldly and alone. . . . And nowhere do the lovely rays of the so-called feminine principle, which lovingly, warmly, and devotedly protects and transfigures the whole, penetrate into the sober workshop of reflection.[75]

On the one hand then we have icy winds, reflection, sobriety, solitude (here is a further resonance with the Brahms obituary), the masculine; on the other rays of warmth, inspiration, devotion, plenitude, the 'so-called feminine principle'. But if, on the basis of their association with masculine and feminine, we now to add the rest of these terms to their respective columns in table 3.1,[76] the hitherto neat system of oppositions begins to go awry: 'reflection', for instance, ends up in the same column as 'fantasy', and 'inspiration' in the same column as 'intellect'. That, however, might be said to be Schenker's point, as highlighted by his metaphor of marriage ('his faculty of reflection can wed itself only with such difficulty . . . to his own feeling for beauty', in other words inspiration): if the interpretation I offered in chapter 1 is correct, then the basis of the positively valorised concept of 'musical logic' found in Schenker's writings from 1897 onward is precisely its synthesis of the previously opposed qualities of inspiration and reflection, spirit and technique. In this way Schenker's theory, built as it is on the principle of synthesis or sublation, might be seen as a means of escape from the endlessly replicated binary patterns of conservative thinking, even as they permeate his views on culture in general.

And this point can be generalised. After illustrating the Viennese critics' association of timbre and sensuality with the feminine, the artificial, and the decorative, Painter goes on to draw a comparison with Loos's campaign against the debilitating effect of female ornament, an integral part (though not one I discussed in chapter 2) of his critique against ornamentation in general—and here again one might invoke the idea of synthesis or sublation as a means of distinguishing between 'good' (left-hand) and 'bad' (right-hand) ornament, and more generally as a means of attempting a reconciliation between the columns of table 3.1. For instance, 'mechanical precision' might be said to be bad not in itself (as opposed to sloppy performance) but when it is pursued for its own sake rather than in the service of a musical conception, and the conservative critics' objection to Mahler's orchestration was precisely that it functioned autonomously rather than as a means of expressing content—in other words, that it was not subsumed within a

---

[75] 'Anton Bruckner', *HSEK* 57–61 (quotation at 59), translated in Karnes 2001: 159–60.

[76] As might be further suggested by Wistrich's reference (to which I shall return in chapter 4) to the 'warm, primitive solidarity exuded by *Gemeinschaft*'.

higher unity, not sublated. (In the same way, it is the autonomy of 'nervous twitching' that makes it intrusive.) And the relevance of the idea of sublation becomes still more obvious when Hirschfeld writes, in the same 1909 review I previously quoted, that Mahler cannot 'control large-scale form', so that 'the momentary effect . . . becomes an isolated goal in itself' (Painter 1995: 253). As I suggested in the previous chapter, the idea of sublation identifies precisely the terrain within which Schenkerian theory is designed to operate, not only mediating between the demands of momentary effect and large-scale form (in other words, providing the means to explain what Hirschfeld merely describes), but—to return for the last time to Painter's ostensive topic— even theorising the difference between 'good' and 'bad' orchestration: 'In the masterworks', Schenker wrote in *Der freie Satz*, 'orchestral colors are not mixed according to whim and at random; they are subject to the laws of the whole' (*FC* I 7). This is one of many elements of the Schenker project that remained incomplete at Schenker's death—perhaps one that was incapable of completion, like the theory of dynamics I mentioned in the Introduction. One wonders whether Schenker intended it as a rejoinder to what Schoenberg had written about tone colour in his *Harmonielehre*:

> we go right on boldly connecting the sounds with one another . . . simply by feeling; and it has never yet occurred to anyone to require here of a theory that it should determine laws by which one may do that sort of thing. Such just cannot be done at present. And, as is evident, we can also get along without such laws.[77]

It is easy to imagine Schenker snorting at that last remark.

I said near the end of chapter 2 that the Hegelian framework helps us to understand how Schenker's theory can be at the same time a theory of music and a theory of society, or more specifically of the relationship between individual and society. I shall soon come back to this, but first I want to explain the final dichotomy in table 3.1, which I have not mentioned and which without explanation must look out of place: 'Bösendorfer/Steinway'. Sandra McColl (1996: 60–1, 66) observes that, in *fin-de-siècle* Vienna, 'the true hero of every piano recital . . . was always Viennese, for the critics, intent on supporting the local industry, often made points such as these'—and then she quotes from reviews by Theodor Helm ('an outstanding Bösendorfer', 'the marvellous Bösendorfer', 'the magnificent Bösendorfer'), Max Kalbeck ('the marvellous Bösendorfer, which, as would a noble steed his rider, seemed to recognize its master [Busoni] immediately and willingly submitted to him'), and Albert Kauders ('the test of endurance, which on all occasions the magnificent Bösendorfer passed with flying colours, was so unusual and so tremendous that the triumph of the local piano industry must

---

[77] Schoenberg 1978/1911: 421.

justly be ranked beside the triumph of the artist'). But it wasn't simply a matter of supporting local industry: for several decades Viennese critics had been emphasising the special warmth, the articulacy, the voice-like quality that distinguished Bösendorfer pianos from others. Leon Botstein (1985: 500), whose fifteen-hundred-page thesis is a store-house of relevant material which I plunder in what follows, explains that 'the Viennese sought to retain a separate identity, a separate acoustic reputation for making sweet, flexible, warm-sounding instruments, which sang with a roundness of tone thought to be particularly suited to the repertoire of Viennese classics', and the distinctive Viennese action was one way this was achieved. What Botstein means by a 'separate' identity and reputation becomes clearer when, some pages later, he summarises the responses to a piano exhibition of 1867 as follows: 'What impressed all the Viennese critics was how Bösendorfer captured the light, integrated and "breathing" form of the Viennese piano, and camouflaged the sharp edges, in contrast to the "plump monstrous, cast-iron colossus" presented by the Americans' (545).

Insofar as one can extrapolate from *Die Kunst des Vortrags* and other sources, the qualities Schenker valued in piano performance equate closely to those Botstein characterises as Viennese. There are no recordings of Schenker's playing. A contemporary description by Hermann Roth refers to its objectivity, lack of vanity, strong conception of the whole, intellectual penetration, and artistic intuition,[78] but it is hard to translate such terms into specific performance characteristics: Roth's reference to 'objectivity', for instance, might suggest a restrained use of rubato, especially in the music of the Viennese classics—but then Schenker's most admired interpreter of Mozart was Carl Reinecke, whose performances of Mozart, some of which survive on Welte-Mignon piano rolls, are marked by an extraordinary flexibility of tempo.[79] William Rothstein has attempted to reconstruct Schenker's playing style on the altogether solider basis of the annotations in Schenker's own scores: 'It was characterized by great variety of touch and of shading', Rothstein writes (1984: 25), and 'by a surprising *lightness*, a lightness evident from his scores in the many *piano*s inserted

[78] Roth, 'Bekenntnis zu Heinrich Schenker', *Hamburger Nachrichten*, 17 September 1931 (OC 2/84).

[79] An example is the performance of the second movement of Mozart's Piano Concerto no. 26 in D Major, K. 537, recorded on Welte 237 (1905); my thanks to Daniel Leech-Wilkinson for drawing this to my attention. Schenker's views on Reinecke may be found in four different essays from *HSEK* ('Zur Mozartfeier' [no. 35], 'Carl Reinecke' [no. 82], 'Carl Reinecke, Die Beethoven'schen Clavier-Sonaten, Leipzig 1896' [no. 91], and 'Konzert Carl Reinecke' [no. 94]): he admired the ornamentation, brilliant passagework, and spirit of Reinecke's playing, which he considered closer than any other pianist's to how Mozart would himself have played his music. Eugen d'Albert, Anton Rubinstein, and Julius Röntgen emerge from the essays of the 1890s as Schenker's other favourite pianists; in *Die Kunst des Vortrags* he adds Busoni and Paderewski to the list of those who 'to a certain degree have achieved a unified whole' (*AP* 84).

within *fortes*, in the frequent accelerations . . . and in the careful group-
ing and shading of tones within figurations'). One might in any case
have anticipated this not only from Schenker's criticisms of 'the clumsy
plodding of relentlessly heavy playing' (*AP* 43), but also from the fact—
if it is a fact—that, before coming to Vienna, he had studied with Chopin's pupil Karol Mikuli.[80] Indeed a number of the features Mikuli ascribed to Chopin's playing and teaching made their way into *Die Kunst
des Vortrags*, perhaps the most striking being a legato quality comparable
to breathing or singing, as may be seen by comparing passages on legato from Mikuli's preface to his edition of Chopin's piano works (1879),
and from Schenker's unfinished text:

> under Chopin's hands the piano needed to envy neither the violin for its
> bow nor wind instruments for their living breath. The tones melted into
> one another, as wonderfully as in the most beautiful singing. (Mikuli,
> translated in Eigeldinger 1986/1970]: 275)

> Just as the violinist is enabled to connect several notes by a continuous bow
> stroke on one string, as the singer can connect several notes with one
> breath, similarly a quiet hand position is the only one that gives the possi-
> bility of playing several notes in succession so that they—melting into one
> another, as it were—form a chain of notes with the same effect as a legato
> group on the violin or in singing. (*AP* 21)[81]

And this is an idea Botstein (1985: 548) specifically associates with the
traditional Viennese sound ideal in contrast to the American: 'The older
ideal attempted to make the piano sing much like the human voice or
the violin', he says, whereas the Steinway grand 'accentuated the per-
cussive power, color, and volume of the piano'.

---

[80] The source for this is Oswald Jonas's entry on Schenker in *Die Musik in Geschichte
und Gegenwart*, which is less than clear: Jonas (1963: 11, col. 1670) says that Schenker
'received encouragement' (*Anregung*) in piano playing from Mikuli (the same phrase appears in the *Free Composition* biography of Schenker [*FC* I v], apparently based on the *MGG*
entry), which may or may not mean the same as 'he studied piano with Karol Mikuli'
(as stated in Snarrenberg's *New Grove* entry [2001: 22:478]; see also Drabkin 2002: 813).
Further testimony comes from Michael Mann, writing in 1949, according to whom
'Schenker toured eastern Europe as a "prodigy"-pianist, on which occasion he came into
personal contact with Carl Mikuli . . . for whom he was privileged to give a private performance' (Mann 1949: 9), but Mann does not state the source of this information, and
damages his credibility when, in the next sentence, he says Schenker was twenty-three
when he moved to Vienna. Rothstein (2001: 207) may well be correct in suggesting that
'Schenker was a pupil of Mikuli in the same sense that a few students at Juilliard were
pupils of Maria Callas: they sang—or in Schenker's case, played—for the master, and received a few pearls of wisdom in return'.

[81] Other parallels include variety of touch (Mikuli says of Chopin that 'He treated
the different types of touch very thoroughly, especially the full-toned legato' [Eigeldinger
1986/1970: 32], attitude towards studies (Chopin 'never tired of inculcating that the appropriate exercises are not merely mechanical but claim the intelligence and entire will
of the pupil' [Eigeldinger 1986/1970: 27], paralleling Schenker's views quoted in chapter 2 here), and use of the thumb (Mikuli says—in a passage from his preface not in-

Figure 3.3   Bösendorfersaal. Painting by Leo Delitz. Copyright
Wienmuseum.

In the latter part of his life at least, it seems that Schenker owned a
grand piano by Blüthner,[82] arguably the least Steinway-like of the major
German manufacturers. But there was more to the matter than the
pianos. The Bösendorfers the critics extolled were often heard in the
Bösendorfer-Saal (fig. 3.3), to which Schenker refers on a number of
occasions in his writings of the 1890s and indeed in which he performed in 1894 (Federhofer 1985: 18). Established in 1872 by Ludwig
Bösendorfer, the proprietor of the piano firm, and seating five hundred,

---

cluded by Eigeldinger—that 'Chopin unhesitatingly employed the thumb on the black
keys; he crossed it even under the fifth finger', while Schenker writes in his fingerings in
the 'Chromatic Fantasy and Fugue' *Erläuterungsausgabe* that 'the pedantic rules governing the use of the thumb are deliberately disregarded' [*BCFF* 68]); perhaps most significantly, Mikuli's pupil Raoul Koczalski left an account of the comprehensiveness of
Mikuli's own teaching, ranging from analysis to posture (Eigeldinger 1986/1970: 97),
that is strongly reminiscent of Schenker's own style of teaching. Antonio Cascelli (2003:
44–8) has made this last point in the context of a more general comparison between
Mikuli and Schenker.

[82] As stated by Federhofer (1985: 44n.), on the basis of a photograph of Schenker's
studio in the Keilgasse flat reproduced in Laufer 1981: 160 (original in OJ 72/19).

it was located in a converted riding school close to the Hofburg (hence, McColl [1996: 61n.] suggests, Kalbeck's equine imagery), and was generally agreed to have the best acoustic of any concert venue in Vienna. Moreover, it was not only for the warmth and intimacy of its acoustic that the Bösendorfer-Saal was known but also for its social intimacy: quoting Oscar Teuber, Botstein (1985: 725) writes that 'Boesendorfer sought to establish his hall as the "family space", the scene of intimate music-making. . . . Tickets were often hard to get, and the audience were always aware who was in attendance, bowing and greeting one another, much like a family'. In this way, Botstein says (652), Bösendorfer and his hall together symbolised the 'symbiosis between music and its audience' that the Viennese increasingly came to see as the distinguishing mark of their musical culture—but only as they mourned its passing.

In his later years, the famous surgeon, amateur musician, and friend of Brahms, Theodor Billroth (who died in 1894) saw the listeners of his own day as a mere vestige of the old culture of musical participation (Botstein 1992b: 143), and Schenker's 'Das Hören in der Musik', published in the same year as Billroth's death, might be read as an attempt to resuscitate the kind of attentive listening Billroth stood for; by the eve of the First World War, as Botstein says (1985: 810), audiences 'longed for an era only recently lost, when Brahms and Bruckner lived, when music was vital'. (Schoenberg was saying much the same as late as 1946.)[83] The Bösendorfer-Saal, then, became a tangible symbol of *Gemeinschaft*, a translation of Tönnies's idealised rural community into the terms of a modern metropolis: it was a site for the retrospective enactment of a communal identity that had perhaps never existed in the present tense, an embodiment of the myth of 'Alt-Wien' (527) on which Austria's modern heritage industry is built. (Schenker's 'solemn festivals of the Viennese classics' might then have been profitable too.) So when in 1913 the Bösendorfer-Saal, which Bösendorfer had only rented, was demolished to make way for an office building—ironically never built— this was inevitably seen in symbolic terms. Max Kalbeck described it as 'the farewell to old Vienna and the entrance of the new; the setting aside of the time honored in the name of the politics of the metropolis, the transformation of the artistic into the commercial' (822, 827).

But Bösendorfer's association with the *Gemeinschaft* ideal was more than symbolic. Like the modernists of the Wiener Werkstätte, he adhered to the values of craftsmanship rather than industrial production, writing in 1898—in what Botstein [1985: 752] calls 'an uncanny evo-

---

[83] 'In my youth, living in the proximity of Brahms, it was customary that a musician, when he heard a composition for the first time, observed its constructions, was able to follow the elaboration and derivation of its themes and its modulations. . . . there were even laymen who after one hearing could take a melody home in their memory. . . . That is what . . . amateurs like the renowned physician Billroth were able to do' (1975: 121). Schoenberg's implied positioning of himself in Brahms's circle seems a little crass.

cation of Marx's 1844 critique of capitalism'—that 'those factories that work with machines suppress the spiritual level of their workers by preventing the cultivation of the worker; they turn the worker into a mere bricklayer and day labourer, who legitimately and understandably has concern only for the raising of his wage and for strikes and socialism, but no longer for the piano, from which he becomes more and more alienated'. (The thought here is reminiscent of Schenker's complaint a quarter of a century later that 'the industrial machine robs the worker of his moral fibre' [*MM1* 104], not to mention his description of the German Marxist as 'a hypocrite . . . in search of a raise in wages'.)[84] This concern with craftsmanship extended to the materials used, for Bösendorfer opposed the tendency to replace as many wood components as possible with metal, arguing (in Botstein's words [533]) that 'wood was the key to the expressive and artistic sound of the piano; it was the natural link to the human impulse in music'. Here again there is—pardon the pun—a resonance with Schenker, who wrote in the fourth issue of *Tonwille* that 'the clavichord and harpsichord, because of the resonance of their all-wood construction, rendered polyphonic voice-leading transparently; such clarity is totally unattainable with the very different resonance of our instruments . . . [whose] sonorities lack light and air, they are literally stifled in their own fullness' (*T1* 165).

Bösendorfer was not in fact as inflexibly attached to the values of 'Alt-Wien' as his own pronouncements might suggest; in 1884 he patented a new, all-metal method of attaching tuning pins and brought in experts from the Technische Hochschule to confirm that it did not affect the tone (Botstein 1985: 601–2). But he was entirely hostile to the idea that scientific developments could create new artistic possibilities. Technical innovations could only be justified, he said, when they fulfilled a recognised artistic need (as in the case of the 'Imperial' grand with its extended bass register, inspired by Busoni [618]). Schenker thought the same: in a review dating from 1894, he claims that composers like Beethoven and Schumann went beyond what the pianos of their day were capable of, in that sense anticipating future technological developments—for which reason, he argued, one should always use the instrument best capable of realising the musical idea rather than insisting 'with historically coloured reverence' on the use of period instruments (*HSEK* 271). In a more general way, however, what is at issue is the belief expressed in Riegl's writings that the history of art is one of the unfolding of *Geist,* in relation to which developments in materials or techniques have a purely ancillary role—which in turn, as I said in chapter 2, parallels Schenker's attack on the virtuoso.

And at this point Bösendorfer's and Schenker's values become practically indistinguishable: just as the virtuosos with their mechanical technique reduced performance to a 'one-sided, academic cultivation of

---

[84] See p. 145 above.

finger velocity', so the much-vaunted scientific principles embodied in
Steinway pianos threatened to obliterate local practices, imposing a uniform tonal standard across the globe—as perfect a symbol of the capi-
talist internationalism, of *Gesellschaft* values, as Schenker's 'huge phrasing slur encircling the entire world'. It might seem perverse to pursue
such a comparison between Schenker and Bösendorfer, who was an
old-fashioned (that is to say preChristian Socialist) anti-Semite who
moved in very different social circles—though there is in fact a link of
sorts, for according to Federhofer (1985: 6) Bösendorfer paid half
Schenker's fees during his last year at the Conservatory, possibly in his
capacity as director of the *Gesellschaft für Musikfreunde* (whose archive
contains a letter from Schenker, asking Bösendorfer for a better piano to
practise on). Yet the comparison not only helps to situate Schenker's
values in their Viennese context but also illustrates yet again, and now
in a specifically conservative context, the trait I have repeatedly emphasised of slipping almost instantaneously from the smallest detail—
whether of editorial orthography or of piano timbre—to the largest issues of cultural identity and society. This trait transcends the distinction
(always a confusing one, as the example of Kraus shows) between Viennese modernism and conservatism, and draws attention to an aspect
of Viennese modernism that tends to be underemphasised in present-
day accounts of it.

Following Bahr, Le Rider (1993: 12) says that, in the last decades
of the nineteenth century, the Austrians sought to compensate for
Germany's military and economic success by 'turning inwards. . . .
[T]he Viennese would turn to "states of mind". Individuality and subjectivity were to be cultivated and explored at the expense of social
ideas and realistic styles'. But the image of a Viennese modernism par-
adigmatically focused around the psyche is the result of a historiography dominated by psychoanalysis, literature, and the visual arts at the
expense of the performing arts, and within the visual arts by painting
rather than architecture. It also fails to take properly on board the social ethics of Kraus, Loos, and the other second-wave modernists—or
indeed initiatives like Schoenberg's Society for Private Musical Performances of 1919–21, which is generally seen as representing a
withdrawal from the public sphere (Botstein refers to it as a forum
'through which to express superiority and distance'[1992c: 163]), but
which I have already suggested might just as well be seen as a nostalgic recreation of the *Gemeinschaft* ideal associated with the recently demolished Bösendorfer-Saal. Such acts of communal listening grounded
the 'essentially aristocratic vision' which Botstein (1985: 834) sees
music as embodying in *fin-de-siècle* Vienna: 'the command of the aesthetic experience', he writes, 'could elevate any individual, no matter
his station. Player and listener alike (if they absorbed and reflected the
spiritual idea of the musical experience) could become autonomous
individuals, free from the limitations of birth and wealth, each proud

and self-sufficient'. It is in the sense of this rather Kantian—and Beethovenian—vision that Bösendorfer, Schoenberg, and Schenker might all be said to have maintained, each in their own way, the aristocratic values of 'Alt-Wien'.

There are times when Schenker's nostalgia gets the better of him, as when in *Meisterwerk* 2 he says, 'We are very far away indeed from the happy state that existed when all musicians and listeners perceived tonal events with an instinct as lively as Bach's' (*MM2* 52)—a claim which of course entirely contradicts Schenker's usual insistence that genius has never been understood in its own time. But what I want to emphasise is the larger context such nostalgia provides for understanding the intimate association Schenker assumes to exist between music, the individual, and society. As regards the individual, I said in the introduction that the idea of music functioning as some kind of representation of the psyche was a commonplace of Romantic thought: there is then nothing very surprising in Schenker's asking 'must we not . . . recognize in the life of tones a life just like our own, dependent on reproductive urges and the laws of the soul . . . ?', or stating that 'In its linear progressions and other comparable tonal events, music mirrors the human soul in all its metamorphoses and moods'.[85] And Schenker continues, in the classic idiom of cultural conservatism: 'How different is today's idol, the machine! It simulates the organic, yet since its parts are directed toward only a partial goal, a partial achievement, its totality is only an aggregate which has nothing in common with the human soul'.

But it is with the relationship between music and society that I am primarily concerned here. Schenker's occasional casual references to 'the social relationships of tones' (*C2* xviii, from a discussion of the difference between two- and three-part counterpoint) might sound like nothing more than a metaphorical figure. But at other times Schenker spells out the relationship. For example, he implies that music can function as an ideal model of society when, in a passage I have already quoted, he writes at the end of the *Kontrapunkt* 2 preface:

> it is my fervent wish that mankind may ultimately be permitted to be guided through the euphony of art to the noble spirit of selection and synthesis, and to shape all institutions of his earthly existence, such as state, marriage, love, and friendship, into true works of art according to the laws of artistic synthesis.

[85] *TI* 217, *FC* I xxiii; the point about this being a commonplace is made by the (presumably coincidental) echo of Wackenroder's claim that 'in the mirror of tones the human heart gets to know itself' (translated in Watkins 2004: 190). Another representative formulation comes from *Tonwille* 8/9: 'Body, time, unfolding in space and time, goal setting, the pleasure of the journey, protraction of that pleasure, remembrance, repetition, contrast, expectation, striving, fulfilling, deception, and similar fundamental experiences of the human soul, to name only the most essential, are also repeated in music as a human art' (*T2* 115).

He does so again when in the fifth issue of *Tonwille* he tells the victorious allies that 'the love, family, and state that you yourselves have
made, all of this you will hear in the realm of our musical art . . . a
thousand times more clearly than you could ever see it' (*C2* xx, *T1* 223).
And I would like to propose three reasons—it might be more accurate
to say three predisposing contexts—for this association between music
and society. The first of these reasons I have by now sufficiently illustrated: a binary way of thinking that on the one hand shoehorns complex cultural values into one or the other side of a dichotomy, but that
in compensation encourages vertical connections, so to speak, between
dimensions of society that might seem unrelated within a less black-
and-white mode of conceptualisation. (The thought here, which I shall
develop in chapter 4, is that when dichotomies are aligned as in table
3.1, it becomes possible to substitute any term for another within the
same column, and that this underlies the trait of slipping from the
smallest details to the broadest issues.)

The second reason will take a lot longer to explain. I would like to
suggest that there is a specifically Viennese history of associating music
and social structure, and shall make the case by outlining three points
that could perhaps be developed into a continuous narrative. Allan
Janik (1987: 76) has written that 'in order to understand the origins of
some of the most salient intellectual attitudes and styles of the late
Habsburg era we may have to look further back into the city's cultural
history', and he goes on to describe the forced re-Catholicisation of Vienna in the seventeenth century: the highly ornamented building style
of the baroque period, he says, became associated not only with the
Counter-Reformation but also with Habsburg authority, and with the
luxurious, secular lifestyle that the rising bourgeoisie of the period
copied from the aristocracy (there is a resonance here with the way the
Viennese modernists borrowed modes of representation from the aristocracy).[86] This, Janik continues, was the context for the 'hilariously
devastating sermons' (77) in which, during the last four decades of the
century, Abraham a Sancta Clara turned theatrical rhetoric into an instrument of social critique—and it is this kind of public, ethically motivated critique that Janik sees as anticipating the tone and even to some
extent the content of the critique associated with second-wave modernists (and in particular the terms of the ornamentation debate I discussed in chapter 2). 'By considering Abraham', Janik concludes, 'we
begin to see how Viennese moral fervour could take such unusual
forms as, say, a theory of harmony with Schoenberg'—or a study of
C. P. E. Bach's ornamentation, or of editorial slurs, or the *Urlinie*.

The second stage in this join-the-dots history (and still part of my
second reason for the association between music and society) also takes
architecture as its starting point: by the early eighteenth century the

---

[86] See p. 102 above.

'dynastic' style—represented by Fischer von Erlach—had become a symbol of Habsburg authority, and Harry White sees in it a parallel to the music of the Habsburg chapels during the same period. 'No other centre of European culture', White writes,

> quite so intimately sustains the relationship between absolutism and the dogmatic authority of religious ideology; no other centre so strikingly absorbs from the south the whole apparatus of baroque music in the service of its own culture of rigid imperialism and certainly no other cultural matrix so tellingly discloses the extent to which music could be indentured to what Ivan Nagel describes as the 'baroque cosmos of power'.[87]

White's study focuses on what he calls the musical discourse of servitude, which he sees as 'conditioned on the one hand by a notably severe and intimate relationship to imperial or doctrinal propaganda and liberated on the other hand by the ascendancy of musical imagination over formal or ideological obligations': in particular he discusses the da capo aria and associated forms which 'encode that vital turn in musical affairs from corporate servility (however magnificent, however stupendous) to individual acts of musical imagination'. More specifically, he concentrates on the music of Johannes Fux (who was Hofkappelmeister to Charles VI from 1715): not even Fux, White writes, 'could hope to transcend the conditions under which he worked, especially because these conditions demanded that the individual musical imagination be rigorously subordinated to the exacting requirements of the Habsburg pursuit of moral and temporal power'. While the point I want to draw from this is that there was in early eighteenth-century Vienna an exceptionally high degree of social determination of musical expression (White refers to the 'fantastically regulated degree of public musical utterance'), it is also worth bearing in mind that Fux's *Gradus ad Parnassum*—which White sees as self-consciously embodying the concept of Habsburg style[88]—represents the strongest single music-theoretical input into the Schenker project. Despite numerous detailed cavils, Fux escapes the wholesale criticism that later writers attract in *Kontrapunkt:* in his introduction Schenker describes the *Gradus* as 'still the most excellent work on counterpoint' (*C1* 2), and he accepts its basic framework and prescriptions without question, as self-evidently the means by which the musical ear is to be developed.[89] As we saw in chapter 1, Schenker was making that assumption as early as the *Geist* essay.

---

[87] These quotations are taken from an unpublished paper given on 16 December 2002 at the Institut für Musikwissenchaft, Ludwig-Maximillians-Universität (Munich), to be incorporated in a monograph entitled 'The Musical Discourse of Servitude: Authority, Autonomy and the European Musical Imagination, 1700–1750'. My thanks to Professor White for letting me have a copy of this paper.

[88] Federhofer (1982: 69) thus references a key component of Habsburg ideology when he refers to 'the timeless character of the *Gradus*'.

[89] In *Der freie Satz*, Fux finds himself in the elevated company of J. S. Bach, C. P. E.

White's reference to music 'encoding' social values or structures of course takes us straight to Theodor Adorno, who constitutes the final point in my join-the-dots history. Adorno moved to Vienna in early 1925, after hearing excerpts from Berg's *Wozzeck;* he studied composition with Berg, as everyone knows (and also piano with Steuermann, which not everyone knows). However, as Richard Leppert says, 'Adorno did not find Vienna to his liking',[90] and he stayed for only about six months, though returning on several occasions over the following two years. But that seems to have been long enough for him to become thoroughly impregnated with the Viennese nostalgia for Vormärz values. Vienna emerges from his writings as a kind of Lothlórien, where the lingering influence of the aristocracy long kept capitalism and bourgeois values at bay, and Adorno saw this as crucial to the development of the Viennese classical style in music:

> What that great music was anticipating, as reconcilement, it had read on the walls of that anachronistic city where feudal forms and bourgeois freedom of thought, unquestioned Catholicism and philanthropic enlightenment got on well together for so long a time. Without the promise emanating from Vienna, deceptive as it might be, the most high-flying musical art of Europe would scarcely have been possible.[91]

And this provides the context for Adorno's approach to the relationship between music and society. Central to it is his distinction between the 'alienated masterpieces' (to borrow the title of his study of the *Missa Solemnis*) of Beethoven's late period on the one hand and, on the other, the works of his middle period, in which there was fleetingly a correspondence between the interests of the individual and those of society. Rose Subotnik (1976: 248) explains the way Adorno saw musical and social analysis as linked:

> just as Hegel (born the same year as Beethoven) appeared to resolve, through his concept of the State, the contradictions between individual and general will which disturbed Kant's notion of freedom, so, too, Beethoven, in the second-period style, apparently found the musical means to reconcile the contradiction between subjective freedom and objective form, that is, to synthesize subjective and objective principles in the sort of wholeness or totality on which freedom depended for survival. . . . What distinguishes such movements, in short, is their apparent ability to derive the principle of formal organization not from any outside source but from

---

Bach, and Schenker himself as part of the 'only feasible sequence' of music instruction: 'in strict counterpoint (according to Fux-Schenker), in thorough-bass (according to J. S. and C. P. E. Bach), and in free composition (Schenker)' (*FC* I xxi–ii).

[90] Adorno 2002: 4.
[91] Adorno 1976/1962: 162.

within themselves, and thus to establish as a reality the musical analogue of the free individual, the 'musical subject', which has mastered external constraint and determined its own destiny.

When Adorno talks in such terms about the relationship between music and society, he is talking quite specifically about an accommodation he sees as taking place in Vormärz Vienna and perhaps nowhere else: he is offering not so much a theory of musical meaning as a theory of musical meaning *in Vienna,* and he is doing so in terms that resonate with a number of Schenker's own concerns (subjectivity and objectivity, synthesis, growing outward from within, the free individual, destiny). Indeed, in a radio talk he gave in the last year of his life (1969), Adorno returned to these issues and specifically mentioned Schenker in relation to them: 'in Beethoven', he said, 'the forms . . . could be said to re-emerge from out of the specific process of the composition. It is actually tonality itself which . . . is both theme as well as outcome, and in this sense the Schenkerian concept of the Fundamental Line to some extent correctly applies here'.[92] However, he continues,

> Beethoven's genius consists precisely in the fact that this process does not remain on a general level, but, on the contrary—and in a manner which corresponds exactly to the great tradition of German philosophy (the philosophy of Hegel above all)—it plunges itself from the most generalized and unspecific into the most extreme concretion in order thus to lead back to the binding forces of the Universal once more. . . . and it is precisely here, because of this peculiar change of emphasis, that Schenker has not gone the whole way.

Adorno wouldn't be Adorno if it was possible to be entirely sure of his meaning, but this passage may confirm Max Paddison's (1993: 170) assessment that Adorno's understanding of Schenker 'seems to have been somewhat limited'. Adorno appears to be saying that Schenker's approach emphasises the generalised, the abstract, at the expense of the particular, the detail—whereas I have been arguing that it is much better seen as an attempt to translate into musical terms the Hegelian notion of sublation, understood as the reconciling (Adorno's word) of the interests of part and whole. Adorno claimed not only that there was a 'special relationship between the systems of Beethoven and Hegel'[93] but also—as I mentioned in the introduction—that 'Beethoven's music is Hegelian philosophy', so it would be reasonable to see the concept of sublation as implicit in his discussion of the relationship between individual and totality in middle-period Beethoven. But he spelt it out in the 1969 radio talk:

---

[92] Adorno 2002: 167.
[93] Adorno 1998: 13, 14.

> The whole—if I may be permitted to express it in Hegelian terms—is itself
> the relation between the whole and its individual moments, within which
> these latter obtain throughout their independent value. . . . If one really
> takes the whole as one's point of departure then also simultaneously im-
> plied here is the obligation to grasp the logic of the individual mo-
> ments. . . . And correspondingly, if one takes the constituent elements as
> the point of departure one's task is to understand how these elements in
> themselves, and frequently in contradiction to one another, and then
> through this contradiction, also simultaneously generate the whole.[94]

I don't think Schenker would have disagreed with the substance of this;
indeed it is not so different from what he had written himself in 'Von
organischen der Sonatenform'.[95] But he would surely have thought it
far too vague and hermeneutical—in Schenker's vocabulary a negative
term associated with writers like Kretzschmar. For Schenker, the point
of theory was to transform such valid but woolly insights into specifically and demonstrably musical terms.

If it seemed perverse to pursue a comparison between Schenker
and Bösendorfer, it must seem all the more so to compare Schenker
with Adorno. Yet there is more to such a comparison than the relatively
superficial parallels I have mentioned so far, or the striking echoes of
Gemeinschaft ideology that resonate through Adorno's writings, including the hierarchy of musical listeners he presents in *Einleitung in die
Musiksoziologie*— a kind of latter-day version of Schenker's 'Das Hören
in der Musik'—or his views on jazz and chamber music. (Richard Leppert writes that 'for Adorno chamber music . . . was a site of momentary refuge, a place of promise, imagination, and perhaps memory,
where another kind of individuality might be thought, seen, and indeed heard . . . a space for a lost sociability . . . an enactment of musical respect and friendship':[96] it is hard to read this without thinking of
the Bösendorfer-Saal, itself for twelve years a memory by the time
Adorno first arrived in Vienna.) One might summarise the relationship
between Schenker and Adorno by saying that where their views aren't
identical they are diametrically opposed, which is to say—again—that
the framework of thought is the same even when the polarity is reversed: Schenker is to Adorno as Hegel is to Marx (and that, incidentally, might explain the 'strikingly Marxist interpretive move' Burnham
identified in Schenker's linkage of Rameau's theory to the French Revolution,[97] as well as the 'uncanny evocation' of Marx that Botstein identified in Bösendorfer). And as far as the relationship between music
and society is concerned, I would suggest that the common framework

---

[94] Adorno 2002: 174.

[95] See p. 132 above.

[96] In Adorno 2002: 522, basically summarizing chap. 6 of Adorno's *Einleitung in die
Musiksoziologie;* one thing he omits is Adorno's (1976/1962: 88) claim that 'chamber music
in the emphatic sense of the term has been confined to the German-Austrian region'.

[97] See p. 137 above.

of thought is the one Subotnik referred to: Hegel's concept of the State, that is to say the just, organic form of government which he saw as best represented in the contemporary (early nineteenth-century) Prussian monarchy.

As Peter Singer puts it, 'in Hegel's rational State the interests of the individual and the collective are in harmony'; there is a reciprocal relationship between them, just as 'I need my left arm and my left arm needs me. The organic community will no more disregard the interests of its members than I would disregard an injury to my left arm' (Singer 1983: 43, 35). It is in this relationship, and the freedom to choose and take responsibility for one's actions that it entails, that the organic state is 'rational', and in this respect Hegel sees it as quite different from French ideas of creating a new, rational state from first principles ('The leaders of the French Revolution understood reason in a purely abstract and universal sense which would not tolerate the natural disposition of the community. . . . The result was the Terror' [35–6]).[98] Here we see not only the framework within which Adorno is approaching Beethoven's middle-period music but also a source for much of the *Gemeinschaft* ideology I have discussed, including the view of monarchy as the natural form of government and the suspicion of abstract intellectualisation, not to mention the Francophobia. It is not surprising that—as I hinted in chapter 1—there are in addition strong resonances with the legal theorists associated with the University of Vienna, in particular Georg Jellinek. Hegel's idea that 'we must search for what is rational in the existing world and allow that rational element to have its fullest expression' (36), as against the revolutionary aim of building from scratch on abstract principles, is consistent with Ehrlich's idea of 'living law', which I have already mentioned (as well as with Schenker 'semper idem, sed non in eodem modo'). But it is also one of Jellinek's basic premises: as Wayne Alpern puts it (1999: 1469), 'law could never be created by the fiat of mere legislation, but only discovered through scientific analysis of its historical evolution'. And just as Hegel saw the Prussian monarchy as the ideal form of government, so for Jellinek it was the medieval Teutonic state. Like Hegel, Jellinek saw democracy as 'elevating the subjective will of the private individual over the objective will of the state' (1472)—an association of democracy and a negatively viewed subjectivity which is just as characteristic of Schenker's polemics[99]—but equally he viewed the Roman state as excessively authoritarian, destroying individual

---

[98] Stephen Rumph (1995: 61) has interpreted Hoffmann's essay on Beethoven's Fifth Symphony in terms of the organic state, linking this to Hoffmann's position as a Prussian civil servant: he documents the values of wholeness that underlie the idea of the organic state, and argues that 'This concern with organic totality and unity finds an aesthetic correlate in Hoffmann's well-known analysis of the symphony's thematic unity'.

[99] As in the *Kontrapunkt* 2 reference quoted above (p. 142) to 'the democratic parties—the parties of . . . the most flagrant individuals'.

freedom through excessive codification and standardisation. Here, as Alpern points out (1498), there is a particularly close parallel with Schenker.[100]

However what is more important in this context is that Jellinek's central concern was precisely the reconciliation of the interests of individual and state, and the role of the law in achieving this: 'To recognize the true boundaries between the individual and the community', he wrote in 1895, 'is the highest problem that thoughtful consideration of human society has to solve' (Alpern 1999: 1470). It is on this basis that Alpern proceeds to develop his own interpretation of what he calls 'Schenker's musical jurisprudence', and the influence, presumably mediated by Jellinek, of Hegel's concept of the State constitutes my third— and much delayed—reason for the association of music and society in Schenker's writings. The crucial point is the one I made at the end of chapter 2: the framework of Hegel's thought, and more specifically his fundamental notion of sublation, is simultaneously political and aesthetic. The relationship between individual and state is the same as the relationship between the musical detail and the whole, and this is the homology on which Adorno's interpretation of middle-period Beethoven is based.

Given the widespread association between music and society I have documented, it isn't surprising that other music theorists of the time also employed social and political metaphors based on the idea of the tone as an individual. To take just one example,[101] in his *Harmonielehre* Schoenberg writes that 'the tone lives and seeks to propagate itself'—a thoroughly Schenkerian idea—and works out this image in explicitly political terms: 'the fundamental tone', Schoenberg says at one point, 'has a certain sovereignty over the structures emanating from it just because the most important components of these structures are, so to speak, its satraps, its advocates, since they derive from its splendor: Napoleon, who installs his relatives and friends on the European thrones'.[102] And in chapter 2 I quoted from another such passage, which I now give in full:

> The tonality must be placed in danger of losing its sovereignty; the appetites for independence and the tendencies towards mutiny must be given opportunity to activate themselves; one must grant them their victories, not begrudging an occasional expansion of territory. For a ruler can only take pleasure in ruling live subjects; and live subjects will attack and plunder.[103]

---

[100] The parallel between Jellinek and Schenker is developed at greater length in Alpern's forthcoming thesis.

[101] Another, outside Vienna, would be Halm, who specifically compares music with the State; see Rehding 2001: 150–3.

[102] Schoenberg 1978/1911: 313, 128.

[103] Schoenberg 1978/1911: 151.

Schoenberg's imagery is, as usual, vivid and thought-provoking; he even makes use of the term 'sublation' (*Aufhebung*) in order to characterise what is usually translated as 'suspended tonality' (*aufgehobene Tonalität*)[104]—although, curiously, this means that he is using it in contradistinction to the tension between sovereign and rebel, centre and periphery, that characterises tonality in general. (As Schoenberg puts it, 'the one musical art form that does not have such a central power, opera, is merely a proof of the other possibility: suspended tonality'.)[105] Schenker's *Harmonielehre*, by contrast, adopts the general framework of sublation precisely to characterise the tension inherent in music in general, and in so doing develops the parallel between music and society in a more thoroughgoing manner. Schenker's starting point is the same as Schoenberg's: he speaks of 'the egotism of the tones, each of which . . . insisted on . . . its right to procreate its own descendant generations'. This Darwinian world must however be accommodated to the requirements of the community, and Schenker now casts the composer in the role of what Alpern (1999: 1484) terms the jurist: 'The artist now was faced with an immensely difficult task. He had to reconcile in one system all those urges inherent in the individual tones . . . as well as their mutual relationship. . . . The common interest of the community that was to arise from the mutual relations of these tones demanded sacrifices, especially with regard to the descendant generations' (*H* 30). A few pages further on he develops this idea, referring to 'the sacrifices which each tone had to make if a community of tones was to be established usefully and continued stably' (*H* 40). And later he glosses this in the specifically political terms I cited in chapter 2: 'the tonal system . . . could be seen as a higher collective order, similar to a state, based on its own social contracts by which the individual tones are bound to abide' (*H* 84).[106]

Writing before the war, then, in 1906, Schenker sees the tones as protagonists in a musical state. Robert Snarrenberg specifically associates this with the Hegelian State when he writes (1997: 69): 'The tone is an individual with rights and obligations, governed by law, moved by freedom, motivated to act, acting both rationally and rightly'. To put it another way, the 'community of tones' is exactly what its name ought to lead us to expect: a direct expression of *Gemeinschaft* values, symbolising or enacting the balance between whole and part that Adorno saw

---

[104] I owe this observation to Julie Brown.

[105] Schoenberg 1978/1911: 370.

[106] Schenker spells out this parallel at greater length in the unpublished text 'Das Tonsystem' (see chap. 1, n. 81 above): 'Just as it is fine (*schön*) if there is a balance between the demands which the individual makes of the state, and conversely those that the state makes of the individual, so it is fine if a similar balance obtains between the rich development of individual generations of overtones on the one hand, and the total idea of tonality on the other' (36).

as represented in middle-period Beethoven—or, to put it in more explicitly Hegelian terms (and picking up Snarrenberg's reference), the freedom that results from the happy coincidence of the will of the individual and the institutions of the State. In the aftermath of the war, however, Schenker seems to have seen the relationship of music and society in an even more direct way, and to make the point perhaps all I need to do is repeat the ending of the preface to the second volume of *Kontrapunkt*, this time suggesting that we read it not as a rhetorical flourish but quite literally, as a statement of what music might offer at a time of social and political collapse:

> It is my fervent wish that mankind may ultimately be permitted to be guided through the euphony of art to the noble spirit of selection and synthesis, and to shape all institutions of his earthly existence, such as state, marriage, love, and friendship, into true works of art according to the laws of artistic synthesis.

But the point can be made more concretely with reference to the analysis in the final issue of *Tonwille* (1924) of what Schenker calls Haydn's *Österreichische Volkshymne*—the so-called *Kaiserhymne* which gave its tune to the modern German national anthem (and on which Haydn based a set of variations in the second movement of his Quartet op. 76, no. 3). Although this is basically a technical analysis, Schenker makes the political connection quite explicit: 'The Austrian national hymn', he begins his article, 'which confesses to political synthesis in a deep and sincere manner, is paid homage by Haydn with an incomparable artistic synthesis' (*T2* 135). And at the end of the main part of the article (which concludes with some ancillary comments on the sketches), Schenker writes of the climactic g^2 with which the final phrase begins, and of the measured descent it initiates, that 'one may transform the proud words of the Emperor, *justitia regnorum fundamentum* [justice is the foundation of monarchy], into the equally proud words of the artist, *justitia artis fundamentum* [justice is the foundation of art]'. Here the idea of justice precisely reflects the jurisprudential Schenker of the Hegel-Jellinek tradition: justice is meted out to the tones through balancing their competing demands, in precisely the way a monarch must—and in particular the ruler of a supranational state such as the (by 1924 defunct) Habsburg empire. It is the same justice that defines political and artistic synthesis, a term that for Schenker was inseparable from 'the aristocracy of genius' (*T1* 54). In his commentary on the *Kaiserhymne* analysis, however, Joseph Lubben (1995: 44) goes even further in spelling out what is at stake: the elements of the music, he says, are 'interdependent and mutually supportive, cooperating in achieving g^2 and investing it with a manifold musical importance'. This is musical *Gemeinschaft*.[107]

---

[107] Lubben (1995: 82–3) goes on to argue that Schenker's musical justice in fact has 'almost nothing to do' with 'monarchic hierarchy', and explains the disparity between

In short, the principles of music are the same principles by which harmonious interpersonal relationships and a just state may be secured. To understand music, as composer, analyst, or active listener—as genius, mere talent, or even average person—is to have internalised the essential principles according to which society should be framed and life lived. No wonder then that Schenker invoked Hegel so prominently at the beginning of chapter 1 of *Der freie Satz:*

> The origin of every life, whether of nation, clan, or individual, becomes its destiny. Hegel defines destiny as 'the manifestation of the inborn, original predisposition of each individual'.
>
> The inner law of origin accompanies all development, and is ultimately part of the present.
>
> Origin, development and present I call background, middleground, and foreground: their union expresses the oneness of an individual, self-contained life. (*FC* I 3)

There is however more to be squeezed out of this quotation, which Michael Cherlin (1988: 121) describes as 'explicitly Hegelian, and explicitly dialectical', and in the conclusion I shall come back to it.

So did Schenker see the *Kaiserhymne* as not just a symbol of the Austria that was past but also, properly decoded, the blueprint for a new political synthesis within which German genius would once again flourish? Does this mean that we should reverse the direction of Adorno's homology and devise interpretations of Schenker's analyses that translate the relationships of tones into social or political relationships, that read them as models for an ideal, or at any rate a better, society? (Even the nostalgia-smitten Adorno recognised that Vormärz Vienna was not as perfect as Beethoven's music: 'To the extent that Beethoven's second-period work attains an actual synthesis', Subotnik writes [1976: 250], 'it is Utopian, ahead of its time, and more nearly whole than contemporaneous society'.) In his thesis Alpern attempts something along these lines, commenting on two of Schenker's Mozart analyses in a manner that brings out the implied references to legal or social structures, but one has the sense that he is saying no more than Schenker has already said, merely substituting terms like 'level of jurisdiction' and 'local authority' for the standard analytical terminology. That, however, is just the point. It is the same point as with the relationship between music and emotion, the objective and the subjective. As I explained in chapter 1, neither Hanslick nor Schenker sought to deny the emotional qualities of music: what they said is that music can be explained only in objective terms, but that when we explain it

---

the two halves of Schenker's equation in terms of the difference between 'an idealism of eternal values . . . and a pragmatism centered on quotidian processes'. I would argue that the parallel is in fact much more direct than this suggests, provided that monarchy is viewed within the Hegel-Jellinek framework to which Schenker subscribed.

in objective terms we are always talking about its subjective qualities at the same time. In the same way, there is no need to translate Schenker's analyses into social or political terms, because they are always already about society and politics. Music, to paraphrase Hanslick, is about community—but musical community; it embodies the principles of a just society, but in musical form. It is not a question of translating the analyses but of understanding them—which, for Schenker, meant understanding the principles of musical, personal, and social justice they embody. And it is in that broadest of all possible senses, rather than in terms of his tediously xenophobic diatribes, that I regard politics as central to Schenker's conception of music.

4

The Politics of Assimilation

Schenker's Project and Jewish Tradition

There has been an element of denial in this book so far. I have made occasional, casual references to Schenker's situation as a Jew from the eastern empire, an *Ostjude,* in a city where a newly virulent form of anti-Semitism was developing. But I have avoided developing these references, in order to now develop the whole topic in a coherent manner. And that means that whereas the preceding chapters have followed a basically chronological succession—centring on the 1890s, the first decade of the twentieth century, the First World War and its aftermath, in each case with a key text to ground the argument—I now offer a further pass over this material, considering first some possible links between Schenker's project and aspects of traditional Jewish thinking, and then the relationship between German cultural conservatism and anti-Semitism, together with the options this created for Viennese Jews. Finally I revisit some of these issues in the context of Schenker's relationship to two of the most significant figures of his intellectual universe.

As I said in the introduction, Schenker came from an area of what is now western Ukraine, close to the borders of Poland (of which it formed part between the two world wars); until 1919, however, it was part of Galicia, a province on the eastern fringes of the Austro-Hungarian empire—close to tsarist Russia—which was given a measure of administrative autonomy in 1869, the year after Schenker's birth. 'Compared to western Europe or even Bohemia in the nineteenth century', writes William McCagg (1989: 116), 'Galicia was a roadless, cold, foothills region leading nowhere': it was predominantly agricultural, with a majority population of Ruthenians (Ukrainians) of whom, in 1910, 92 percent worked on the land (182), and with minority populations of Poles (a largely impoverished gentry class) and Jews. Outside such centres as Lvov, which was home to some thirty thousand Jews (113), most of the Jewish population lived in the small, predominantly Jewish towns known as shtetls. Schenker was born in Wisniowczyk, about 130 kilometres southeast of Lvov and, at least in 1939, 'a minuscule town . . . comprised of a Post Office, four stores and unbelievable swarms of flies' (Kimel 2006); with a population of 1,759 according to the 1869 census (Federhofer 1985: 1), it was big enough to support a synagogue but hardly big enough to qualify as a shtetl. But the nearby small town of Podhajce (now spelt Podgaytsy or Pidhaytsi), where Schenker's father practised as a doctor, would have been typical, with just over four thousand Jews out of a total population of just under six thousand in 1880;[1] a pre-1918 postcard of the central square (fig. 4.1) shows the seventeenth-century Great Synagogue (the shell of which still stands). Writing after the destruction of the Jewish community in the Second World War, a former inhabitant, Baruch Milch, described it as 'a town full of Jewish life where there was a class of Jewish intelligencia, of Rabbis, of leading businessmen, of excellent craftsmen, scientists and men of repute and ordinary happy Jewish families,'[2] while the editor of the memorial volume *Sefer Podhajce,* (and musicologist) Me'ir Shim'on Geshuri, stresses its religious traditions: Podhajce, he writes,

> excelled in well-rooted, vivacious Judaism with a tradition of hundreds of years, and an alert and lively Jewish community that was concerned for the existence of the nation and its future. In addition to this, the city excelled in its scribes, scholars, wise men and illustrious rabbis who were known also outside the bounds of the city and the country.[3]

The term 'shtetl' has acquired rosy but possibly unjustified connotations through, in particular, the writings of Joseph Roth, who himself emigrated from Galicia to Vienna and nostalgically portrayed the shtetl as an ideal community, 'momentarily spared the march of modernity and progress with its falsification of familial ties and erosion of the warm, primitive solidarity exuded by the *Gemeinschaft*' (Wistrich 1989: 657); the same nostalgic image emerges from many of the contribu-

---

[1] This information is available in the two main historical sources on Podhajce: Dabrowska et al. 1980 and the memorial volume Geshuri 1972. The latter includes a necrology, in which the name 'Schenker' does not appear, and photographs of prewar Podhajce.

[2] Milch, 'Podhajce—After the Destruction', in Geshuri 1972: English sec., p. 12.

[3] 'An Eternal Light', in Geshuri 1972: 7.

Figure 4.1 Postcard of Podhajce; on the right, the Great Synagogue. From Edward Victor's 'Synagogues on postcards and stamps' website (http://www .edwardvictor.com/Podhajce.htm).

tions to *Sefer Pohajce*. Steven Beller (1989: 110) offers a historian's characterisation of the shtetl and its relationship to the surrounding countryside: 'though the shtetl was set in the countryside', he says, 'its rôle was exactly that of a shtetl, *Städtchen*, a little city. Compared to the big city it might appear rural, but for the Jews who lived in it the shtetl was a civitas dei, an outpost of (Jewish) civilisation in the savage hinterland of the Polish and Ruthenian peasants'. While this Jewish population was largely impoverished (McCagg refers to them as 'caught in the vicious circle of Orthodoxy, destitution, and lack of education' [1989: 183]), it also provided virtually the whole of the Galician middle class (117), and as such was vulnerable to resentment on the part of a rural population inclined to see the Jews as exploiting their own labour (183). Galicia then had its own history of anti-Semitism—as indeed did Podhajce[4]—and, throughout the last decades of the nineteenth and first decades of the twentieth century, a history of Jewish emigration.

Coming himself from a professional though impoverished family background, Schenker exemplifies the established route from shtetl to metropolis via education, being sent as early as possible—or rather ear-

---

[4] In his 'History of the City of Podhajce', Geshuri (1972: 42, 44) records that in 1891 there was an outbreak of intense anti-Semitism in the Polish newspapers following the leasing of land in Podhajce to two assimilated Jews, and describes Podhajce as an early centre of Jewish nationalism (in the 1870s) and Zionism (in the 1880s).

lier than possible, through the falsification of his birth date I mentioned in the introduction—to the German Gymnasium in Lvov, the main Galician centre of education for enlightened Jews. (Marsha Rozenblit notes that in 1875 only 730 Galician Jews sent their sons to secondary school, but of those, 32 percent attended the Lvov Gymnasium [2001: 29].) Schenker completed his schooling at the Gymnasium in Brzeżany, about 30 kilometres north of Podhajce, before winning his government scholarship to study law at the University of Vienna. He arrived there in 1884, at the age of sixteen as against the normal matriculation age of eighteen (presumably as a further result of the falsification of his date of birth);[5] this was a well trodden path, as demonstrated by the fact that, during the years when Schenker was studying at the University, the student body was 33 percent Jewish, with about a quarter of them originating from Galicia (Beller 1989: 34; Wistrich 1989: 60). There are also two further respects in which Schenker's early career path was not untypical: first, he studied law, most probably at his parents' insistence, when it is clear from the letter to Max Kalbeck I cited in the introduction that it bored him and that it was already music to which he wanted to commit himself;[6] and second, he progressed from law to music criticism. Of the music critics active in Vienna during the 1890s, Hanslick, Kalbeck, Kralik, Schoenaich, Wallaschek, and von Woerz all began by studying law (McColl 1996: 24–9).

Although in principle the 1867 Constitution had given equal rights to Jews, it was in practice impossible for those who had not converted to reach the higher career levels in academia, law, or the civil service (Kobler 1967: 28; Wistrich 1989: 148), and so provincial Jews who came to Vienna frequently became Christians, sometimes changing their names and thus over the course of a generation or two assimilating to the extent of discarding their Jewish identity. But unlike Schoenberg, who converted in 1898 (unusually, to Lutheranism), Schenker never converted: he is better understood in terms of the kind of assimilation advocated a generation earlier by Adolf Jellinek, the chief rabbi of Vienna and father of Georg, for whom (in Robert Wistrich's words [1989: 139], but quoting Jellinek)

> Assimilation . . . did not in the least imply the abandonment of Jewish religious teachings, historic festivals, or traditional ceremonies, nor the renunciation of the glories of the Jewish past and its hopes for the future;

---

[5] A footnote in Karnes (2001: 36–7n.) indicates that Schenker could not have gained admission at this age had the University been aware of his real age (in Harry Zohn's view this would have only been possible for a 'Wunderkind'); the University records transcribed by Chiang (1996: 48–50) give his age on matriculation as seventeen, and consistently make him either one or two years older than he really was.

[6] Karnes (2001: 38) draws a parallel with Herzl, whose parents supported his ambition to become a writer but insisted that he study law in order to have a marketable qualification.

rather it meant that 'the Jews should not differentiate themselves from their non-Jewish fellow citizens in speech, clothing, manners, social behaviour'; that they must adopt the interests and welfare of the states to which they belong as 'true, loyal, and selfless sons of the fatherland'.

The extent of personal commitment to Jewish culture and religion naturally varied widely among assimilated Viennese Jews, in many cases consisting of little more than observance of the key elements of tradition ('circumcision and Bar-Mitzvah for the boys, Rosh Hashana, fasting on Yom Kippur, Passover, and, of course, the religious services connected with marriage and funerals' [Thieberger 1988: 175]); even that may give a misleading impression, for George Berkley (1988: 53) refers to 'the frequency with which Jewish homes displayed Christmas trees in December and dispensed Easter eggs in April'. All the same, there is a tension here between what one might call inner and outer identity, for being a Jew in *fin-de-siècle* Vienna was never a purely private matter. Jews were required to identify themselves as such in census returns and (if above a certain income level) contribute to the central organisation of Reform Judaism, the Kultusgemeinde (Thieberger 1988: 174).

Fissures in identity were ubiquitous in the circumstances in which Schenker found himself. In Vienna he was not a Christian, but equally— as a university-educated musician and writer—he was far removed from the predominantly working-class majority of Galician Jewish immigrants, who tended to retain their own cultural identity for at least the first generation, rarely converting or marrying outside their own community (Wistrich 1989: 54). And 'removed' in this context means not only socially and culturally but also physically, since the Jewish working classes were concentrated in the second district of the city, Leopoldstadt, where Schoenberg was born, or the twentieth, Brigittenau; by contrast, Landstrasse—where Schenker lived from 1893 to the end of his life[7]—was a middle-class and predominantly non-Jewish area. (In 1910, the Jewish population of Landstrasse was 6 percent, as against 34 percent in Leopoldstadt [Oxaal 1988: 30].) There were fissures of a kind in Schenker's childhood circumstances, too: in a manuscript booklet written in 1918 for Schenker's fiftieth birthday and presumably based on what Schenker had told him, Moriz Violin recorded that Schenker's father 'fled, day and night . . . to the beloved library, to his professional journals, in order to keep abreast constantly of all the new discoveries and progress made within the medical sciences'.[8] In-

[7] See chapter 2; a full listing of where Schenker lived as a student, and thereafter from 1891 to 1935, may be found in Chiang 1996: 43–4. (He lived at Traungasse 1 and Richardgasse [now Jaurésgasse] 11 before moving in 1901 to Reisnergasse 38, and from 1920 to his death at Keilgasse 8, all in the Landstrasse.)

[8] Moriz Violin, 'Zu Dr Heinrich Schenkers 50. Geburtstage', found between pp. 53 and 54 of Schenker's scrapbook (OC 2); quotation transcribed and translated in Karnes 2001: 35–6.

tellectually, that is to say, he distanced himself from his immediate, physical circumstances, instead identifying himself with a national or international, but virtual, community—which is, of course, precisely what his evidently precocious son did in the domain of music. In this way, as Botstein (2002: 243) puts it, 'Schenker's family was twice removed from the majoritarian Polish environment, first as Jews and second as advocates of German culture'.

And that conforms to the larger pattern by which the educated Jews of the eastern empire identified themselves with German culture, constructing their own identity through membership of a largely imagined German-speaking community, which is also to say through differentiation from local Christian or indeed Jewish culture. (As Pekacz explains [2002: 40], 'Leading members of the Galician rabbinate opposed any and every sort of cultural assimilation among the Jews, especially enlightened schooling', such as the German education Schenker received at the Lvov and Brzeżany gymnasia.) The fame of the German classics, Beller writes (1989: 150–1), 'extended from the most assimilated in Vienna to the shtetls of Galicia', so that 'for many Jews the encounter with Friedrich Schiller was more real than their encounter with actual Germans', and the same might be said of Goethe, to whose texts Schenker repeatedly turned as a song composer. In this way, Beller says (147), 'in places where Jews were, so was German culture, even if there were hardly any Germans'—which again underscores the extent to which the community of which educated eastern Jews saw themselves as part was an imagined one, dislocated from the circumstances of immediate existence. And this sense of being part of a virtual community remained even when they emigrated to Vienna: Beller observes that for Jews like Kraus 'there was a feeling that they were defending the values of Vienna's German civilisation against the Viennese' (186), and Schenker—who as I mentioned wrote in 1931 'I am the *only* living musician'[9]—evidently felt the same. The imaginary, if not fantastical, construction of this Germany is conveyed by an extraordinary compound adjective Schenker coins in the third issue of *Tonwille,* shortly after his complaint about the workforce failing to kill an English soldier:[10] 'Lessing-Herder-Goethe-Schiller-Jean Paul-Bach-Haydn-Mozart-Beethoven-Kant-Moltke-Hindenburg-German' (*Tl* 128). And the cultural rather than political nature of this construction is underlined by an entry Schenker made in his diary in 1925, at the height of the Weimar Republic, in which he referred to Germany rather than Austria as 'my home country by choice'.[11] (By that time Galicia had become part of a quite separate political entity, Poland.)

I referred in chapter 3 to Carl Schorske's influential thesis that Vi-

[9] See p. 11 above.
[10] See p. 147 above.
[11] Diary entry of 30 September 1925 (Federhofer 1985: 317).

ennese modernism, or more generally the explosion of creative and intellectual activity in the Viennese *fin de siècle*, is to be explained as a form
of displacement resulting from the exclusion of the liberal bourgeoisie
from processes of political representation. There has long been controversy concerning the extent to which this bourgeoisie was Jewish, and
in consequence the extent to which the nature of Viennese modernism
may have been determined by the juggling of identities I have described: George Steiner, for example, strongly argued for the predominantly Jewish nature of Viennese modernism, whereas Peter Gay (1978:
21) countered that 'it is sheer anti-Semitic tendentiousness, or philo-
semitic parochialism, to canvass the great phenomenon of Modernism
from the vantage point of the Jewish question'. Beller's 1989 study
was, among other things, an attempt to resolve this issue through marshalling demographic data; on the basis of this he concludes that 'the
non-Jewish liberal bourgeoisie, which Schorske assumes, to all intents
and purposes did not exist', and his whole book drives towards its final
sentence: 'The awkward but inescapable conclusion seems to be that it
was indeed its Jews which made Vienna what it was in the realm of
modern culture' (Beller 1989: 243, 244).[12] This opens the way to an attempt to understand aspects of Viennese modernism in terms of Jewish
cultural or religious traditions, and for Beller 'what we see in Vienna in
the first decades of this century, in the radical ethical individualism of
Kraus or Wittgenstein, owed the great weight of its influence to a radically transformed Judaism, all the more powerful for being a hidden,
perhaps unconscious factor' (236). Without necessarily taking up a position on the general debate regarding the Jewish contribution to cultural activity in *fin-de-siècle* Vienna, is it then possible to trace significant
traits that derive from Jewish tradition in Schenker's thinking?

As Beller's reference to Kraus and Wittgenstein suggests, one of the
most plausible links with Jewish tradition concerns the ethical dimension of what in chapter 2 I referred to as second-wave Viennese modernism (and Beller might well have added Loos's or Schoenberg's
names to his list). Beller (1989: 228) quotes a statement by Kraus in a
1934 issue of *Die Fackel* that he 'thankfully recognizes in the spiritual
scorn which he possesses in liberal measure, in the veneration for des-
ecrated life and defiled language, the natural force of an incorruptible
Judaism'. (The reference to 'defiled language' creates an instant resonance with Schenker, who was in the 1920s a member of the Deutsche
Sprachverein, a society devoted to preserving the purity of the German
language [Drabkin 1985: 188].) As for Wittgenstein, Beller cites his famous statement that 'ethics and aesthetics are one and the same' (again
he could just as well have used statements by Loos or Schoenberg), and
relates it to what he calls 'Jewish stoicism', a term he borrows from

---

[12] Needless to say, not everyone accepts this 'inescapable' conclusion: for an attack
on it see Barnouw 1999.

Claudio Magris and by which he means 'the belief in an indestructible individual ethos which cannot be affected by an external and relative system of values'.[13] But things like this are perhaps better illustrated than explained, and Beller cites two representatives of this tradition, both from an earlier generation. One is Rabbi Boruch, of whom his great-grandson Manès Sperber wrote:

> He spent his whole life 'learning', studying the holy scriptures and their commentaries . . . in the very early morning he would run out of the house to take his cold bath. He ran because he had no time to waste. When the doctor advised the old man to moderate his zeal, he explained to him: 'I cannot afford to lose one minute, for only now am I *really* beginning to understand. Only now is it becoming clear to me what the only true reality is'.

Beller comments of this that 'It was the search for the *real* truth which took him away from the banalities of the world around him; he despised the pretentiousness of wealth and social status' (117). (Here the idea of belonging to a virtual world distinct from immediate circumstances merges into that of reality versus appearances.) The other is Lazar Auspitz, the grandfather of the famous sociologist Theodor Gomperz, of whom Gomperz wrote:

> His whole being was grand: the strength of his will, his independent-mindedness, the autonomous nature of his judgement. He approached as near as possible the ideal of the cynics and stoics of 'freedom from delusion'. He hated all prejudice, all conventionality, all vanity (in a letter he called this 'the false wish to impress'). His mind was only concerned with what was true, which he pursued with a heavy, often curt seriousness, and with an impatient disdain for the devotees of any type of deluding superficiality. (119)

It might be tempting to think that, despite the generation gap, such quotations provide some kind of glimpse into the psychology of the second-wave Viennese modernists, and of Schenker, whose work could certainly be said to be characterised by 'heavy, often curt seriousness', and the sheer volume of whose published and unpublished writings and sketches testifies to the same kind of single-mindedness Rabbi Boruch displayed. (The sense that there is only one, true reality chimes with what in the next chapter I refer to as the 'monism' of Schenker's later thought.) But Beller's substantial claim is that Jewish stoicism survived the transition from the religious culture of the shtetl to the predominantly secular culture of the metropolis, with the emphasis on individual autonomy and ethical responsibility simply being translated from one context to the other (118–9). So he cites the maxim 'music should not decorate, it should be true' (121), and comments that 'this

---

[13] Beller 1989: 121, 114; the Wittgenstein quotation is from the *Tractatus* (para. 6.421).

slogan of the Schoenberg circle simply used the criteria of an ethical stoic in a field where it had no place traditionally, in aesthetics'; he suggests that Schoenberg's explicit invocation of musical logic (most obviously in his serialism) represents an 'invasion of the world of aesthetics by the ethical impulse of truth', and comments that 'it does not seem improbable that this stemmed from attitudes whose origins lay in his Jewish background' (234). In this way the whole debate about ornamentation which I discussed in chapter 2 might be seen as resulting from the application to art of traditional Jewish thinking, a connection underlined in Schenker's case by his suspicion of the idolatrous tendencies of the Christian religion as compared to that of the Jews, who—according to a diary entry for 1916, triggered by a reading of Oskar Schmitz's essay 'Die Judenfrage'—have 'expressed the religious idea most purely'.[14]

And this provides a fertile context within which to understand many of the fundamental traits of Schenker's own thought: his unshakable belief in absolute truth and the existence of unchanging laws, as well as his desire to ground aesthetic values in them; the weight he places on the ethical dimension of music ('We receive not only profound pleasure from a masterwork, but we also derive benefits in the form of a strengthening of our lives, an uplifting, and a vital exercise of the spirit—and thus achieve a heightening of our moral worth in general' [*FC* I 6]); his emphasis, in contrast with the Catholic tradition of Vienna, on the necessity of individual engagement with authoritative texts and his distrust of all mediators (here he made the connection between religion and music himself, writing of the masses who 'prefer to go—yes, we see it every day—with the priest instead of Christ, with the rabbi instead of Moses, with Bülow instead of Beethoven' [*CI* xxiii]);[15] and of course, going back to Lazar Auspitz, the disdain for 'any type of deluding superficiality'—a term Schenker translates from the language of religion to that of music theory. In 1933 Schenker managed to cram all these ideas, together with two of his most revered composers, into a single sentence when he wrote that 'Brahms's rejection of mere appearance results from his deep involvement with the reality that lies behind appearance: strict counterpoint, the eternal truth of composition, which Beethoven termed "the eternal religion"'.[16]

The principle that aesthetic ideas function as a surrogate for religion helps to explain much that is otherwise perplexing about the tone of Schenker's polemics, not to mention the prophetic dimension I men-

---

[14] Diary entry for 19 June 1916 (Federhofer 1985: 315).

[15] Adorno (1992/1963: 206) made the same connection, though not in relation to Schenker: 'In the aversion of Mahler and Schoenberg to hierarchic mediations of whatever kind we may discern traces of a secularized Jewish theology'.

[16] From Schenker's commentary on Brahms's 'Oktaven u. Quinten u.A' (Mast 1980: 151).

tioned in chapter 3. Schenker was quite explicit about it: in a letter to Oswald Jonas from December of the same year, he writes that

> it would be better to present the Germanic people with my monotheistic music-teaching as the Old Testament was presented to the whole world: after 2,000 years the successors to the Germanic people may disavow Schenker as they disavow Rabbi Jesus, but all along the teaching has made its effect and achieved propagation in the world.[17]

And another of the excluded exclusions from *Free Composition* asks: 'Shall I therefore proclaim my monotheistic doctrine of art from a Mount Sinai and thereby seek to win confessors of it?'[18] Nor was it only himself whom Schenker cast in the Mosaic mould: 'As if he had descended from a musical Sinai where he had received the laws of synthesis from God's hand', Schenker writes in the *Tonwille* essay on the A minor Sonata K. 310, 'Mozart passed these laws on to humanity as signs of wonders. But they did not comprehend him' (*T1* 64). The resonance with Schoenberg's *Moses und Aron* hardly needs underlining.

Some of Schenker's contemporaries specifically acknowledged the influence of Jewish tradition on their thought. I have already mentioned Kraus, who 'attributed his reverence for language to his Jewishness' (Beller 1989: 231), while in 1949 Wittgenstein wrote—admittedly in the specific context of religion—that 'my thoughts are one hundred per cent Hebraic' (Chatterjee 1992: 150). But a particularly interesting comparison might be made with Freud, whose grandfather was a Hasidic rabbi in Galicia (Wistrich 1989: 540). My argument throughout this book has been that Schenker's theory was not simply a theory, in the standard modern sense of that term, but part of the broader programme for action I call the Schenker project. (Schenker himself used stronger language: the sentence following the reference to 'Rabbi Jesus' in the December 1933 letter to Jonas reads 'Above all, the "Mission"!') And Wistrich (571) makes a similar point regarding Freud when he describes psychoanalysis as

> not just a theory but a *movement* with a quasi-political and quasi-religious character that sought to save the world for an enlightened ideal. . . . In practice, the undisputed leader at the centre wanted corroborators rather than collaborators, a devoted band of apostles who would help establish his immortality and eventually carry his teachings to the wider society.

Wistrich also explains that Freud 'transmitted to his disciples a latent sense of chosenness, pride, and Jewish self-consciousness which encouraged them to believe in a psychoanalytic mission of universal redemption'—and it was only from 1907, when Carl Jung and Ludwig

[17] OJ 5/18 (21 December 1933), transcribed and translated by John Rothgeb, Schenker Correspondence Project website.
[18] Translated in Snarrenberg 1992: 113. For the excluded exclusions see p. 147 above.

Binswagner joined the group, that it included any non-Jews (571, 566). There is an obvious comparison with the way Schenkerian theory was disseminated through a small but devoted band of disciples who saw his theory as a kind of esoteric knowledge that demanded absolute personal commitment: in a memorial article Viktor Zuckerkandl, himself one of Schenker's students, wrote how 'under the leadership of our teacher, we could consider ourselves the scouts of a new way of thinking on music and art', adding that their campaign against the falsification of art 'was almost a religious war'.[19] And with the rise of the National Socialists, Schenkerian theory was equally open to being characterised as a 'Jewish science' (not only Schenker but also Jonas, Salzer, and indeed Zuckerkandl were listed in Theophil Stengel and Herbert Gerigk's *Lexikon der Juden in der Musik*).[20] Indeed, some of the problems that developed as Schenkerian theory become assimilated into the academic establishment after 1945, which I touch on in chapter 5, might be seen as resulting from a quasi-religious loyalty that was readily (and perhaps justifiably) interpreted as an academically disreputable dogmatism.

If Schenker self-consciously took up a position of opposition to conventional music theory and (at least after he had given up hope of obtaining a post at the conservatory) the institutions that supported it, perhaps even consciously cultivating a reputation for iconoclasm, then this put him into a position comparable to that of Freud, according to whom to 'profess belief in this new theory called for a certain degree of readiness to accept a position of solitary opposition with which no one is more familiar than a Jew'.[21] And the Jewish dimension resurfaced when, following Jung's admission to his circle, Freud wrote to Karl Abraham that he should be 'tolerant and do not forget that it is really easier for you than it is for Jung to follow my ideals, for . . . you are closer to my intellectual constitution because of racial kinship' (quoted in Wistrich 1989: 566). In reply, Abraham referred to 'this intellectual kinship', adding 'After all, our Talmudic way of thinking cannot disappear just like that'. He then enlarged on this last point: 'Some days ago a small paragraph in *Jokes* [i.e. Freud's book *Der Witz und seiner Beziehung zum Unbewussten*] strangely attracted me. When I looked at it more closely, I found that, in the technique of opposition and in its whole structure, it was completely Talmudic' (567). The technique of opposition to which Abraham refers is comparable to the kind of dis-

---

[19] Zuckerkandl, 'Bekenntnis zu einem Lehrer', *Anbruch*, May 1935, p. 124 (OC/91).

[20] Berry 2004: 435, according to whom five of Schenker's other students were also listed (in either the original 1940 publication or the 1941 supplement), as well as Oster. Drabkin (1985: 189) notes that Schenker was marked 'H' for 'Halbjude'—possibly, Drabkin suggests, because the views expressed in writings such as 'Von der Sendung des deutschen Genies' met with Nazi approval.

[21] Quoted from Freud's esssay 'The Resistances to Psycho-Analysis', in Wistrich 1989: 564.

putation, or polemic, with sometimes long-dead authorities that Schenker engages in, for example in *Kontrapunkt* (where, in Ian Bent's words [2002: 593], he 'not only took over long passages from Fux's text, but also introduced a bibliographical depth that was quite novel to the pedagogy of his time by conducting reviews of the literature, quoting Albrechtsberger, Cherubini, and Bellerman in turn, and adopting their music examples to meet his purposes'). The result is the building up of layers of commentary along the lines of Beller's (1989: 86) characterisation of 'the "Talmudic" method, with its emphasis on the multi-level interpretation of a small text': that might even suggest an affinity with Schenker's analytical method, however fortuitous the resonance of Beller's 'level' may be. Perhaps then Schenker's otherwise puzzling reference to himself, in a diary entry of 18 May 1916 (Federhofer 1985: 314), as 'the Ibn Ezra of music' refers to the kind of exegetical commentary for which the eleventh-century Spanish writer was famous; more adventurously—or recklessly—it could be related to Ibn Ezra's contribution to the dissemination among Christians of traditional Judaic learning.[22]

Leon Bostein (2002: 246) states it quite unambiguously: Schenker's 'insights were made possible in part by habits of mind trained in Judaism'. He argues in support of this that 'Schenker was far more traditionally active as a Jew than Schoenberg', who—as Botstein (1992c: 173) has written elsewhere—'combined a nearly traditional Jewish habit of close reading of texts and an attachment to inner meaning with a sharp sense of the limits of language'. The habit of close reading to which Botstein refers is predicated in the traditional religious context on two major assumptions. The first is that, as the Word of God, a religious text is inherently significant: this is the basis of all Jewish practices of hermeneutics, including the esoteric numerological practices of the Kabala (practices of which there is a stronger trace in Schoenberg's thinking than in Schenker's).[23] When near the beginning of the Ninth Symphony monograph Schenker writes in a prophetic, single-sentence paragraph 'In the beginning was content' (*BNS* 4), it might then not be entirely far-fetched to see the reference to the Gospel of John as not only an expression of Schenker's longstanding suspicion of words about music[24] but also marking the transference of a Jewish practice of

---

[22] 'He became a propagator among the Jews of Christian Europe, who were unacquainted with Arabic, of the science of Judaism, a science which had been founded long before with that language as its literary medium' (Gottheil and Bacher 1904: 522).

[23] The common-sense fun Schoenberg (1978/1911: 318) made at Schenker's expense regarding Schenker's celebration of the number 5 ('The number five is of course, in itself, no less mysterious than all other numbers, nor is it any more mysterious') turns a little sour when set against Schoenberg's own numerological tendencies, for which see Ringer 1990: chap. 10.

[24] It was in connection with the invitation to lecture on the Ninth Symphony, which Schenker turned down but which ultimately gave rise to his monograph, that Schenker

close reading from the Word to the musical text. The second major assumption is that, however authoritative the written text may be, it nevertheless stands in need of oral interpretation—and it is precisely this kind of interpretation Schenker provides in relation to the musical masterworks, those biblical texts of musical culture, in this way seeking to rectify—as Robert Snarrenberg puts it (1997: 144)—'a serious breakdown in the process of cultural transmission'.[25]

In an article the aim of which is to interpret Wittgenstein's writings as 'a distillation and extension of Jewish tradition, both rabbinical and mystical', Ranjit Chatterjee (1992: 143, 147) argues that the traditional distinction between the literal meaning of a text (*peshat*) and its interpreted or figurative meaning (*derash*) is fundamental to Wittgenstein's philosophy of language. He quotes from the second volume of Spengler's *Der Untergang des Abendlandes*, published in 1923, which refers to the idea of 'a secret revelation, or a secret meaning of the Scriptures, preserved not by being written down, but in the memory of adepts and propagated orally': the interpreted meaning lies beneath the literal, superficial meaning, and is accessible only to those who have the knowledge necessary to understand it. In support of his argument, Chatterjee (159) cites various remarks of Wittgenstein's that revolve around concealment, of which one ('If you have a room which you do not want certain people to get into . . . the honorable thing to do is to put a lock on the door which will be noticed only by those who can open it') is reminiscent of an oddly gratuitous quotation from Hugo von Hofmannsthal that Schenker included in *Der freie Satz:* 'One must conceal the depths. Where? On the surface' [*FC* I 6]). That in turn might be linked with the epigram with which August Halm set the tone for his 1913 book on Bruckner's symphonies, 'If you wish to understand the invisible, look carefully at the visible', which Lee Rothfarb

wrote of the 'total divide separating the art of listening to music from its expression in words so great that any communication must for the foreseeable future seem impossible' (pp. 58–9 above). Incidentally, Schenker's later assertion, in *Kontrapunkt 2*, that 'In the beginning is consonance!' (*C2* 216) must presumably represent a revision of the earlier claim, more precisely locating the true source of musical content: Schenker's frequent self-references—and this in an age long before the personal computer—give the impression that he knew his earlier writings by heart.

[25] The tension between the idea of an authoritative and inherently meaningful text and the need to interpret it bears on a similar tension I earlier identified in Schenker's thinking (Cook 1991), but was unable to rationalise convincingly: on the one hand every detail of a composer's manuscript has its own intrinsic meaning, is an integral element of the text (which construes the text as, in Nelson Goodman's terms, autographic, i.e. incapable of reduction to a replicable symbolic expression), while on the other hand, as editor, Schenker is perfectly ready to regularise what the composer wrote, so accommodating it to symbolic representation on the basis of his theoretical understanding (an allographic model). The first approach leads to the facsimile edition (of which Schenker's 1921 edition of Beethoven's Sonata op. 27, no. 2 is an early example), the second to the kind of critical edition represented by Schenker's other editorial output.

(1996: 65) reads as an adaptation of an adage from the Zohar: 'Only through that which is disclosed can man reach that which is undisclosed'. This nexus of ideas highlights the role that the trope of concealment plays in both Jewish and music-theoretical traditions—a role that becomes particularly prominent in Schenker's case when he writes (again in *Der freie Satz*) that 'the fundamental structure amounts to a sort of secret, hidden and unsuspected, a secret which, incidentally, provides music with a natural kind of preservation from destruction by the masses' (*FC* I 9). That last comment might be read as having a particular Jewish resonance to which I shall shortly return.

As I said of the correlative idea of superficiality in chapter 3, however, it is not so much a matter of listing the extraordinarily—one wants to say obsessively—frequent references to secrets, the hidden, the concealed throughout Schenker's writings, at least from the first decade of the century on:[26] the point is rather, as I hinted a few pages back, the way the idea is built into the fabric of his analytical method. 'Simplicity', says Schenker, 'does not lie on the surface' (*FC* I xxiii), and neither does truth, and thus musical analysis—like psychoanalysis (Gay 1978: 46)—is predicated on suspicion of the obvious, the plausible. This links neatly with what Adin Steinsaltz describes as the most striking aspect of Talmudic reasoning: the 'inability to accept simple and apparently satisfactory proof, and the continued search for incontrovertible evidence'.[27] Just as a religious adept sees through the world of appearances to a reality that underlies it, then, just as Freud saw through the 'discordant phenomena' (Wistrich 1989: 538) of the conscious mind to the underlying content of the unconscious, so the Schenkerian analyst penetrates through the dissonances and other 'illusory effects in the foreground' (*FC* I 11) to the truth that lies behind them: as Schenker proclaims in the first issue of *Tonwille*, 'the Urlinie provides truth in the world of tones' (*T1* 21). A few lines earlier, Schenker has written that 'While motives and melodies bustle about before our ears in repetitions that are easily perceptible, the Urlinie begets repetitions of a concealed, most sublime sort in its primal womb': particularly in the middle-period writings, it sometimes seems as if Schenker cannot mention the derivation of surface events from underlying layers without adding such words as 'concealed', 'secret', or 'mysterious'. (So perhaps, for him, the Hofmannsthal quotation was not so gratuitous, appearing as it does during a discussion of the principle of growth outward from within—the subject of Schenker's other Hofmannsthal quotation, which I cited in chapter 3.) Nor does Schenker ever seem to tire of emphasising the misleading nature of appearances, for instance how an apparent

---

[26] For examples and discussion see Snarrenberg 1992 and Bent 2005: 125–32.

[27] Quoted (from Steinsaltz, *The Essential Talmud*) by Alpern (forthcoming); Alpern lays a great deal of emphasis on affinities between Schenker's thought and practices of Jewish religious exegesis specifically associated with Galicia.

consonance may stand in for an underlying dissonance (itself, of course, standing in for a genuinely foundational consonance).[28] Whether in religion, psychoanalysis, or musical analysis, then, truth takes the form of revelation, being accessible—like Wittgenstein's lock or Chatterjee's *derash*—only to the adept: 'A wonder remains a wonder and can be experienced only by those blessed with special perception' (*FC* I 27). And in each case it is the role of the mediator—in the first the priest, in the latter two the analyst—to interpret what is concealed and so make it accessible to others (a position which, in Schenker's case, sits awkwardly with the distrust of mediation to which I referred).

There is also a further image through which both Freud and Schenker expressed the distinction between surfaces and depths. In 1899, Freud told Wilhelm Fleiss how, underneath one of his patients' fantasies, he had found 'a scene from his primal period (before twenty-two months) . . . a scene that is everything at the same time, sexual, innocuous, natural etc. I still scarcely dare really to believe it all. It is as if Schliemann had once again dug up Troy, hitherto thought legendary' (Gay 1978: 45). This is the same archaeological metaphor Schenker invoked at the end of the preface to *Kontrapunkt* 1 when, having bemoaned the decline and fall of musical culture, he wrote that 'In view of these circumstances, our first task must be a real excavation before we can even begin work that will allow us to proceed'.[29] Like Freud's use of the image, Schenker's entails digging through the surface to recover what lies beneath, removing the layers of accretion or misrepresentation that have built up over the years. But a further stage is implied when Schenker speaks in 'Capellmeister-Regisseure' of the 'restoration of the masterpieces' through adequate interpretation,[30] or when as editor he speaks of 'reconstructing' the music of the past (his edition of the complete Beethoven piano sonatas, which came out around 1923, was entitled *Klaviersonaten, nach den Autographen und Erstdrucken rekonstruiert von Heinrich Schenker.*) And here a further precedent in nineteenth-century Viennese Jewish tradition comes to mind: Salomon Sulzer, the famous cantor who did more than anybody to establish the musical practices of Reform Jewry, and who wrote in the preface to the first volume of his *Schir Zion* (1845), 'I considered it my duty to pay as much regard as possible to tunes handed down to us from antiquity and to free their ancient, venerable essence from subsequent arbitrary and distasteful embellishments. I want to restore them to their original purity' (Mandell 1967: 225). It is worth noting in this context that on 20 January 1900, ten years after Sulzer's death, a memorial concert was held under the auspices of the *Gesellschaft für Sammlung und Conservirung von Kunst und historischen Denkmälern des Judenthums:* in the pro-

---

[28] See e.g. *CI* 186, *MM2* 52.
[29] *CI* 25; see p. 97 above.
[30] Schenker 1988: 141.

gramme sheet Schenker is listed as the accompanist for the third and fourth items—a rare example of his public association with Judaism.[31]

Yet having said all this, there are some glaring problems with the whole approach to the contextualisation of Schenker's thought that I have been outlining so far in this chapter. A basic problem is that it is prone to rely on pocket characterisations of Jewish traits that can come uncomfortably close to essentialism, or that are simply too loose to support any kind of rigorous thought. As an example, Alexander Ringer writes: 'Unity, oneness, and indivisibility have been the perennial hallmarks of Jewish thought. . . . The Jewish longing for unity was at the root of . . . the analytical thought of Heinrich Schenker, who in May 1933 made note of a curious "parallel: in the cosmos the single cause is God—in music the only cause is the Ursatz!"'[32] The trouble with this argument is obvious: 'unity, oneness, and indivisibility' are such broad categories as to take in any number of other religious or philosophical traditions (a further issue, to which I shall return in chapter 5, is how far this is in any case the kind of unity Schenker was concerned with). And in the same way, it is far too easy to provide alternative sources for practically all of the putatively Jewish traits I have described. J. P. Stern (1979: 45), for instance, observes that Nietzsche and Karl Marx, no less than Freud (and, we might add, Schenker), built their thinking round 'a briefly statable leading idea . . . by means of which the secret of all that men do is to be explained', adding that 'Each of these leading ideas . . . is said to be the hidden secret in the depths of men's souls', and as such 'unavailable to man's "ordinary", that is motivated and therefore unenlightened, consciousness'. Again with reference to Freud, Peter Loewenberg (1992: 136–8) proposes the influence of the classical stoics as an alternative to Beller's Jewish stoicism, while Beller (1989: 86) himself points out some other possible sources for the 'Talmudic' quality of Freud's interpretive approach. Similarly, the Roman law in which Schenker trained at the University of Vienna is an alternative example of a core text that is subject to layers of successive interpretation, while the idea of stripping away layers of accretion to recover texts in their original form is fundamental to the dominant discipline of nineteenth-century humanism, philology—the discipline that provided the most direct model for the development of musicology. And any number of ascetic religions embody the idea of penetrating through appearances to a deeper, hidden reality, including the Indian religions on which Schopenhauer drew; indeed, Schopenhauer himself came close to viewing music this way when he wrote, 'if we glance at purely instrumental music, a symphony of Beethoven presents us with the

---

[31] The programme sheet is reproduced in Botstein 2003: 17 (this article, from an exhibition catalogue, is otherwise basically a German version of the second half of Botstein 2002).

[32] Ringer 1990: 20; the diary entry is for 17–21 May 1933 (Federhofer 1985: 320).

greatest confusion which yet has the most perfect order at its foundation'.[33] Such language can also be found much closer to home, in Viennese music theory of the generation before Schenker: Sechter writes in his 1853–54 book *Die Grundsätze der musikalischen Komposition* that those who wish to build music theory on the chromatic scale 'do not want to retain the inner essence, but merely the outward appearance'.[34] And as we saw in chapter 3, not only is the critique of superficiality embedded in the general discourse of German cultural conservatism, but in music criticism it goes back to before Hoffmann, who at one point speaks of the hidden, 'secret meanings' that may be revealed to 'the serious, deeply penetrating observer'.[35] Nor do Jewish traditions have a monopoly on single-mindedness, absolute truth, or the idea of the individual's ethical responsibility. The list could go on.

These are, of course, the same kinds of problem that I discussed in chapter 1 with reference to the possible philosophical influences on Schenker, but there is one important difference. The basic principles of German idealist philosophy were ubiquitous in educated German-speaking circles, and therefore what is at issue is how far Schenker was drawing on one particular source as against another, or whether the influence was at a sufficiently general level that such distinctions are meaningless: that he worked within the general orbit of the German idealist tradition is not in question. However, the extent and nature of his familiarity with Jewish tradition is less easy to assess. This problem is not unique to Schenker. Questioning claims that Kraus's writing exhibits Talmudic qualities, Beller cites Sigismund Mayer's statement, in a book published in 1918, that (in Beller's paraphrase) 'none of the Jewish children understood Hebrew, and there were complaints to this effect at the time' (1989: 85). Beller concludes from this that 'claims that most of the Jewish élite displayed forms of the Jewish tradition can fairly safely be said to be pure rhetoric with no basis of fact'; even if they did observe Bar-Mitzvah, he comments acidly, they probably saw it as just an occasion for presents.[36] In the same way, while Ringer (1990: 178) insists that Schoenberg was always 'an unreformed Jew at heart', implying that his conversion was merely 'nominal', there is a danger of uncritically accepting Schoenberg's later, retrospective construction of his Jewish identity: as Moshe Lazar (1994: 37–9) says, 'We know hardly anything substantial as relates to Schoenberg's parents

---

[33] Quoted from Schopenhauer, *Die Welt als Wille und Vorstellung* (The world as will and representation) by Barbara Whittle (1993: 279), in the course of a detailed comparison between Schopenhauer's and Schenker's music-theoretical ideas.

[34] Translated in Wason 1985: 34; it was the same advocates of the chromatic system whom Riemann stigmatised as 'Social Democrats' (see p. 8 above).

[35] Watkins 2004: 196 (Hoffmann's remark relates to the engravings of Jacques Callot, not to music); see pp. 165–6 above.

[36] Beller 1989: 84, citing Felix Braun.

and their "Jewishness". We do not know whether any traditional holidays (Passover, Yom Kippur) were even partially observed' (37–9). In the case of Schoenberg, at least, there is little basis for distinguishing rhetoric from fact.

It might be argued that the situation in the case of the second-generation Schoenberg was fundamentally different from that of Schenker, who was not only himself an immigrant, but an immigrant from Galicia: after ridiculing claims of Talmudic influence on Kraus, Beller (1989: 85) concedes that in the case of figures like Sperber and Roth, both of whom came from Galician shtetls, 'it is not so easy to reject the idea of some sort of direct Jewish influence', even if it cannot be proved. And in the case of Freud, whose family originated in a Galician shtetl (and whose grandfather, as I mentioned, was a rabbi), we know that he studied Jewish scriptures with his father, while in his thesis Wayne Alpern makes a similar argument about Jellinek in order to substantiate the link between Schenker's thought—legal as well as music-theoretical—and Jewish religious tradition. What then of Schenker himself? We know that his parents were both Jewish and married by the Jewish rite,[37] and that his wife, Jeanette, was Jewish; we know that he was buried in the Jewish cemetery (the interment certificate from the Kultusgemeinde is in the Jonas Collection)[38]—but that only tells us what we already know, that he was Jewish, since all Viennese Jews who had not converted were buried there. All the same, there are some documentary sources to put a little more flesh on the bones. A diary entry for the first day of Passover in 1907 (30 March) reads 'evening with mother at uncle's place. Aunt Lschak for Feast of Passover. Old memories . . . !' Schenker did not however observe Jewish holidays when scheduling his teaching: in 1913–14 he taught throughout the periods of Passover and Hanukkah, as well as regularly on Saturdays, and it is striking that some of the students he taught on Saturdays were themselves Jewish. (By contrast he did not teach on Sundays, on Good Friday, or over Christmas.)[39] And while none of this bears directly on the extent of Schenker's Jewish learning, the apparent absence of documentation indicating personal study of Jewish scriptures is probably significant, considering how little either he or Jeanette seem to have thrown away. Alpern argues that 'the depth of his knowledge is evident even from the numerous Biblical citations in his writing', for instance citing Schenker's mention of Ibn Ezra as evidence of 'a profound understanding of Jewish theology', but there is an obvious flaw in this as an argument for the specifically Jewish quality of Schenker's thought:

[37] Letter to Violin of 29 December 1927 (Federhofer 1985: 3).

[38] OJ 35/6.

[39] I am indebted to Ian Bent for the 30 March 1907 diary quotation and the information from Schenker's lesson books, as well as for the idea of using them to check Schenker's observance of holidays.

Schenker's writings incorporate as many references to specifically Christian traditions as to specifically Jewish ones.

In short, any attempt to determine the extent to which Schenker's thinking drew on Jewish tradition can be no more than speculative, though we can say with confidence that important aspects of his thought—wherever he may have drawn them from—resonate strongly with that tradition. We are however on firmer ground when we try to relate his identity as a immigrant Jew to the conditions and perceptions of *fin-de-siècle* Vienna, which I shall suggest are crucial to an understanding of the basic motivation of the Schenker project.

The Logic of Alterity

According to the Holocaust scholar Daniel Goldhagen (1997), to ask when anti-Semitism developed—whether in nineteenth-century Germany and Austria, or anywhere else—is to ask the wrong question. Goldhagen sees anti-Semitism as a structural feature of the European worldview since the Middle Ages. Seen this way, anti-Semitism is a constant: what varies is the nature and extent of its translation into action, so that the right question is why the expression of anti-Semitism changed in the way it did in nineteenth-century Germany and Austria, resulting in what Edward Kravitt (2002) calls the 'new' anti-Semitism —which finally became the eliminationist anti-Semitism of the Third Reich.

At all events, and as in the case of the broader currents of cultural conservatism I discussed in chapter 3, it probably isn't necessary to trace the 'new' anti-Semitism back before the 1870s, in particular the stock market crash of 1873 and the coining in 1879 of the word 'anti-Semitism' by Wilhelm Marr (in his pamphlet *Der Sieg des Judenthums über das Germanenthum* [The victory of Judaism over Germanism]). In Austria, a further major ingredient was the level of Jewish immigration from the eastern empire, particularly following the extensive Russian pogroms of 1881: these seriously destabilised the Jewish population of Galicia, just over the border. (Major emigration from Podhajce began in the 1880s, just when Schenker himself left, with the first Podhajce organisation in America being founded in 1895.)[40] Further impetus was provided by the Galician pogroms of 1898, when the Ruthenian peasants rose up against the Jewish middlemen whom they saw as exploiting them, and by the First World War, when rival armies repeatedly swept across Galicia, with the shtetls bearing the brunt of the onslaught and pogroms following in their wake (McCagg 1989: 203)—so that

---

[40] See Dabrowska et al. 1980, Geshuri 1972: 88, and 'History of Congregation Masas Benjamin Anshe Podhajce' (in the Podhajce section [compiled by Jean Rosenbaum] of the JewishGen ShetLinks website, www.shtetlinks.jewishgen.org/podhajce/Podhajce%20in%20New%20York.htm, accesssed June 2006).

when in *Der freie Satz* Schenker wrote about the 'brutal ranting and rav-
ing' at 'bullfights, cockfights, massacres, pogroms' (*FC* I 159), there was
nothing abstract about that final reference. Geshuri records that the
Jewish population of Podhajce 'for the most part escaped westward';[41]
the majority of Galician Jewish emigrants went to America (of the
320,000 Jews who arrived there between 1891 and 1914, 85 percent
were Galician [McCagg 1989: 183]), but even if absolute numbers emigrating to Vienna were smaller, the effect in a city of two million was
much greater, with the Jewish population rising from 73,000 in 1880
to 175,000 in 1910 (Rozenblit 1984: 17). As a result, the figure of the
unassimilated eastern Jew—Orthodox, sometimes uneducated, and retaining distinctive dress, accent, and culture—became increasingly
common in the streets of Vienna: as McCagg puts it (148), by 1900 'Vienna Jewry had become a class society, deeply fissured by the differences between rich and poor, renegades and faithful, Orthodox and reformed. The Galicians were then an unassimilated "bottom class"'. But
it is Joseph Roth who most vividly spells out what this meant: 'The
more Western the origin of a Jew', he told a friend,

> the more Jews there are for him to look down on. The Frankfurt Jew de-
> spises the Berlin Jew, the Berlin Jew despises the Viennese Jew, the Vien-
> nese Jew despises the Warsaw Jew. Then there are still the Jews from way
> back in Galicia, upon whom they all look down, and that's where I come
> from, the lowest of all Jews.[42]

It is because of this that David Rechter (2001: 10) describes the idea of
'Austrian Jewry' as 'something of a chimera': there was in reality no
such single entity.

It is however the business of anti-Semitism to construct the perception of such an entity, and the 'new' anti-Semitism involved a crucial change in the nature (or, following Goldhagen, expression) of anti-
Semitism itself. Here, even more than in the rest of this book, I am
shoehorning a vast and complex topic into a few sentences, but the
basic distinction between cultural and racial (or biological) anti-Semitism is obvious enough. If to be anti-Semitic is to believe that there is a
Jewish problem, then to be a cultural anti-Semite means to believe that
the solution is conversion and assimilation. This was a widespread view
among nineteenth-century liberals, for whom 'the "good" Jew was the
Jew who had become as German as possible, civilized because not Jewish any more' (Beller 1989: 123). It is also the position Wagner took in

---

[41] Geshuri 1972: 44.

[42] Quoted in Wistrich 1989: 657. McCagg (1989: 217) offers a complementary per-
spective on the stratification of prewar Viennese Jewry: 'upper-class Habsburg Jewry was
"Austrian" with a vengeance, meaning that it spoke German; that it identified with the
Germans; that genealogically it was made up of the offspring of German-speaking Bo-
hemian-Land Jews; and that just as German Jewry did, it looked down its noses at the
Yiddish-speaking Jewry of the east and would not even marry them'.

his highly influential 'Das Judenthum in der Musik' (Judaism in music) of 1850, a key statement of anti-Semitism in general, which ends by saying, 'To become one of us, the Jew has first to renounce Judaism'; now changing to the vocative, Wagner adds, 'Without a backward glance, take part in this work of redemption through self-denial, for then we are one and indivisible' (Osborne 1973: 39). Admittedly, like most highly influential texts, 'Das Judenthum in der Musik' affords multiple interpretations through its self-contradictions (earlier in the essay [30], Wagner has said that even the converted, assimilated Jew 'stands alien and alienated in the midst of a society he does not understand'), and the whole topic is a controversial one, but it seems clear that Wagner's anti-Semitism is in essence cultural. In his Mailamm speech of 1935, Schoenberg (1975: 503) said, with tongue in cheek, that 'Wagner, perhaps not sure of his own pure Aryan blood, gave Jewry a chance: "Out of the ghetto!" he proclaimed, and asked Jews to become true humans, which included the promise of having the same rights on German mental culture, the promise of being considered like true citizens'. (Hence the 'we' of Wagner's final sentence.)

But 'if Wagner were relatively mild', Schoenberg continues, 'if Wagner considered only the mental and moral accomplishments of Jews, his followers stated the racial differences'. The 'racial science' to which Schenker perhaps unfortunately referred in *Der freie Satz*[43] was more an effect than a cause of racial anti-Semitism, the basic principle of which is encapsulated in Schönerer's maxim 'It matters not what the Jew believes: filthiness inheres in his race' (Lazar 1994: 14). For Schönerer, race was a matter of biology rather than culture, and the consequences of this view were spelt out very clearly in 1897, in an article published in the *Deutsche Zeitung* (despite its name a Viennese newspaper) about Mahler's appointment to the Court Opera, which was represented in some quarters as 'part of a conspiracy of Jews to dominate Germans':

> Someone seems to have become conscious that the appointment of a *Jew* would be most unpopular, that it would arouse sensation and justified opposition. It seems to have occurred even to Mahler himself, because three weeks ago, and thus at a time when in any case he already knew of his imminent appointment, *he had himself baptized* (!) Of course, that does not change the facts at all, that at this stage in one of the few non-Jewified artistic institutions in Vienna from now on a Jew will be in a position to call the tune. The consequences will be inevitable: the Viennese public will not be held to blame for the proper response to this violation of its patent wishes.[44]

[43] See p. 148 above.

[44] *Deutsche Zeitung*, 11 April 1897, translated in McColl 1996: 102; Mahler's conversion had in fact taken place nearly six weeks earlier, on 23 February (Kravitt 2002: 75n.). The *Deutsche Zeitung* was both anti-Semitic and pan-Germanist; Painter (1995: 244n.) calls it 'almost a mouthpiece for the mayor Karl Lueger'.

This 'new' anti-Semitism undercut the basic premise of assimilation. Theodor Herzl expressed what was at issue in the same year,
1897, writing that the Jews had 'attached themselves to the German
nation with all their hearts . . . too closely, it would seem. Then all of
a sudden they found themselves shaken off. All of a sudden, they were
told they were parasites. . . . One jerk only, and they were no longer
Germans but Jews' (quoted in Wistrich 1989: 133). But the point is
perhaps made most expressively by Beller (1989: 162, 164), according
to whom

> Jews had thought they were joining a movement of cultural and social
> revolution to create a Germany united in the new culture. Now they were
> confronted with a movement which believed in the *Gemeinschaft* of the
> blood alone. . . . They had assimilated to a great and glorious culture but
> the society for that culture did not exist. (162, 164)

And that of course is the context for the development of Zionism, originally an anti-Semitic proposal by Marr to send the whole of world
Jewry to Palestine (Lazar 1994: 17–8), but taken up at first by the Jewish student associations at the University of Vienna (Wistrich 1989:
chap. 11) and after 1894 by Herzl, who as a journalist in Paris had wit-
nessed the notorious Dreyfus trial and returned to Vienna convinced
that the strategy of assimilation was no longer a viable option. Vienna
remained the centre of the Zionist movement until Herzl's early death
in 1904, a year after the rejection at the Sixth Zionist Conference of the
so-called 'Uganda option', by which a temporary Jewish homeland,
named 'New Palestine', would have been established in that country
(Lazar 1994: 35).

If Viennese Jewry was already split between rich and poor, Orthodox and reformed, metropolitan and provincial, Bohemian and Galician, it now became split between the Zionists and the many who continued—tragically, in some cases up to the outbreak of the Second
World War—to believe in the possibility of assimilation. One reason
why many assimilated Jews failed to recognise the seriousness of their
predicament is that they saw anti-Semitism as directed not at themselves but at the sometimes conspicuously unassimilated *Ostjuden:* not
only did this lead them to underestimate the threat to their own position, it also led to a kind of Jewish anti-Semitism. Conversely, Orthodox Jews saw the assimilated Jews as a greater threat than the anti-
Semites: an article in the Orthodox newspaper *Der Israelit* claimed in
1894 that the anti-Semites

> are not as great a misfortune for us as our own covenant-betraying Jewish
> brethren. . . . The existence of reform Judaism in itself is a greater calamity
> for our holy Jewish cause than all the truths and lies taken together which
> anti-Semites serve up in their small local newspapers with their tiny circles
> of readers. (Lazar 1994: 18–9)

The Zionists even welcomed anti-Semitism as furthering their cause, as expressed in Herzl's pithy maxim 'the worse the better'[45] (a position Schoenberg [1975: 503] expanded, in his Mailamm speech, into 'as always when Jewry was endangered by assimilation, Providence for once constrained us by her powerful hand to fulfil our duties as God's elected people, and made the new-starting racial anti-Semitism her instrument'). This in turn horrified the Reform Jews of the Kultusgemeinde, who 'feared that the Zionists were reversing the gains of decades of struggle for emancipation and integration of Austrian Jews into the monarchy as full-fledged citizens' (Weitzmann 1988: 141).

More lethal in its effects than this fracturing of Jewish identity, however, was something suggested by Beller's reference to 'the *Gemeinschaft* of the blood alone': the mapping of the now racially (or biologically) defined category of Jew onto the system of linked oppositions I discussed in chapter 3, associated with *Gemeinschaft* and *Gesellschaft*, *Kultur* and *Zivilisation*, German and not German. Ernst Hanisch (1992/ 1986: 191) follows his list of dichotomies, which I borrowed as the basis for my discussion, with the statement that 'all these negative, non-German qualities came together in one figure of hate: the Jew', and the point is simplicity itself: you just write 'Not Jew' at the bottom of the left column in table 3.1 (under the heading 'German'), and 'Jew' at the bottom of the right column, under the heading 'Not German'. In referring to this as the logic of nostalgia—or now a logic of alterity— I mean to imply that there is a kind of substitutional calculus such that any right-hand term may be rewritten as 'Jew', while conversely the input 'Jew' will activate any other term in the right column, establishing a relationship of opposition with any term in the left column. And the same, of course, applies to 'German', only with the columns reversed. In this way, the racially defined categories of 'German/Not German' and 'Jew/Not Jew' become available as master tropes, activating and equally being activated by the entire range of cultural, 'nonpolitical', and 'natural' values basic to German conservatism (which makes it possible for texts to articulate unmistakable anti-Semitic messages without even mentioning race). One very easy way to make the point is to compare Karen Painter's and K. M. Knittel's respective articles on Viennese critical responses to Mahler, published back-to-back in the same issue (spring 1995) of *Nineteenth-Century Music*. In Painter's article, on which I drew in chapter 3 for the application of the conservative dichotomies to music criticism, race appears as just one of a number of semantic dimensions, along with gender, the decorative, and so forth. In Knittel's article, very much the same dichotomies are at work, only now they are organised around race as the controlling dimension.[46]

---

[45] Quoted in Wistrich 1989: 189.

[46] Kravitt (2002: 83–4) criticises Knittel on the grounds that she interprets as racially

But the most extreme illustration of this kind of binary thinking is provided by Otto Weininger, the classic exemplar of the self-hating Jew whose suicide in 1903, at the house where Beethoven had died, made him a *cause célèbre* in Jewish modernist circles: Schoenberg refers in the preface of his *Harmonielehre* to 'Weininger and all others who have thought earnestly',[47] while Wistrich adds Kraus, Wittgenstein, Broch, Musil, and Trakl to the list of Weininger's admirers (1989: 532). The point can be made through a single quotation from Weininger's *Geschlecht und Charakter* (Sex and character), published in the year of his suicide:

> The decision must be made between Judaism and Christianity, between business and culture, between male and female, between the race and the individual, between unworthiness and worth, between the earthly and higher life, between negation and the God-like. Mankind has the choice to make. There are only two poles, and there is no middle way.

Wistrich (526–7), who quotes this, comments: 'Weininger's antitheses with their critique of decadence, their polarization of culture and civilisation, Geist and Geld, soul and intellect, genius and talent, virility and femininity, Christianity and Judaism, reflect the commonplaces of a post-Nietzschean dilettantism in Central Europe'. And he adds a few pages later (534) that for Weininger '"the Jew" conceptually embodied the negativity of the cosmos, rather than Jewry as an ethnic or religious minority'. (One is reminded of Pfitzner's—or Hitler's—blaming the Jews 'for all the malignancy in the world, in fact for just about everything'.)[48] Judaism, in other words, is now a human characteristic that is most fully expressed in racial Jews, but is inherent in human character—and it is this that enables Weininger to claim that 'even Richard Wagner, the deepest anti-Semite, cannot be absolved from having a tinge of Jewishness'. (Weininger is advancing a theory that anti-Semitism results from the mixture of Jewish and non-Jewish characteristics.) That, given Schoenberg's admiration for Weininger, may provide the context for his tongue-in-cheek remark about Wagner's perhaps not being sure of his own pure Aryan blood.[49]

Ritchie Robertson, who discusses these passages from *Geschlecht und Charakter*, comments that 'Weininger here directs attention away from the substantive character attributed to "Jewishness" and towards

---

marked what were in many cases standard critical terms. In specific cases (Kravitt cites Graf's reference to Mahler's 'nervousness') this may well lead to misreadings. But the ease with which such terms can be—and were—aligned with race demonstrates Knittel's larger point.

[47] Schoenberg 1978/1911: 2.

[48] See p. 175 above.

[49] But not necessarily: there was a widely circulated, though false, belief that Wagner was part Jewish (see Magee 2001: 358–61).

the mechanisms of anti-Semitism and Jewish self-hatred' (1992: 83). But what this means is that the concept of the Jew becomes increasingly bereft of empirical substance; it becomes, as Robertson puts it (87), 'an identity without content', a malleable discursive construction capable of being used in a political context to forge the most unlikely alliances between individuals or groups whose only common feature is the logical value 'Not Jew'. That is exactly the point of Lueger's maxim 'I decide who is a Jew' (repeated almost exactly by Goering in connection with Erhard Milch), which I mentioned in chapter 3 and linked to Schenker's admission, in 'Von der Sendung des deutschen Genies', of Chopin to 'the Pantheon of German composers'. And here we can bring a further element into play. The Jew as discursive construction is defined, in the absence of any other means of definition, through alterity, through being 'Not German'. It is in this context that the Jew becomes increasingly defined as Asian, as illustrated for example by Rudolf Louis's characterisation of Mahler's musical language: 'he speaks a musical German, but with the accent, inflection and, above all, the gestures of the East, of the ever-so-eastern Asiatic Jews'.[50] But in such contexts 'Asian' itself functions as a mark of alterity rather than a geographical specification, as encapsulated in the definitive representation of this constellation of ideas, the mythical being and portmanteau Other depicted on the poster of the Nazi's 1938 'Degenerate Music' exhibition: a Jewish negro wearing the star of David.[51]

I shall return to the logic of alterity later in this chapter, but first I want to relate the general circumstances I have been describing to Schenker's own life. At first sight, one might think that Schenker's exhaustive assimilation into German culture, as well as the cultural nationalism that increasingly characterised his writing after the turn of the century, would render his Jewish identity passive or dormant, and therefore of no great importance for an understanding of his project. Other Viennese Jews record that they had almost forgotten they were Jews until some traumatic event awakened that knowledge, like Herzl, who said that until as a student he read Eugen Dühring's book *Die Judenfrage als Rassen-, Sitten- und Kulturfrage*, 'I really no longer knew that I was a Jew. Dühring's book had an effect on me as if I had received a blow on the head' (Wistrich 1989: 247). But in the case of Schenker, we know of no such traumatic event, even though he arrived at the University of Vienna just as the student body was becoming a hotbed of anti-Semitism. On the contrary, the views on Judaism and his own

[50] Quoted in Kravitt 2002: 89. This particular trope seems to have begun as an assimilated Jewish characterisation of the *Ostjuden*, in Karl-Emil Franzos's exotic Jewish tales published in 1876 as *Aus Halb-Asien: Kulturbilder aus Galizien, der Bukovina, Südrussland und Rumänien*, and ended as a form of Jewish self-characterisation (Wistrich 1989: 53, Gay 1978: 143), as illustrated by the example of Schoenberg mentioned later.

[51] For some anticipations of this conflation of the Jewish and black stereotypes see Lazar 1994: 21.

identity as a Jew that he recorded in his diary remained more or less consistent throughout his life.

Perhaps the clearest statement of that identity is a diary entry for 29 October 1930, where Schenker writes: 'I have not let myself be baptised, and have, when asked, proclaimed that I am Jewish with pride and love, indeed, with the greatest conviction. . . . But to run into the street and shout out my profession would only make me look ridiculous' (Federhofer 1985: 318). He says in the same diary entry that Furtwängler knows he is Jewish (and so does Hammer, of whom more shortly), but what is more revealing is an entry for 17–21 May 1933—a few days after the letter praising Hitler to which I referred in chapter 3, and the same entry that draws a parallel between God and the Ursatz[52]—in which Schenker records that he has told Jonas, who 'is shaken by my profession to Judaism' (320). The reason this is revealing is that Jonas was himself Jewish: it seems then that, unlike Freud, Schenker was not in the habit of sharing his 'racial kinship' with his disciples. (A new dimension enters into Schenker's letters to Jonas from now on: in December of the same year he says that 'up to now I have maintained the repute of a blonde Germanic type and have therefore long since been *persona gratissima* among all Catholic, antisemitic and such news media', and adds, 'thus I invite those in the know to join me in operating under cover. . . . I hope you understand me correctly.')[53] Nor was Schenker's coyness about his Jewish identity limited to the 1930s. A decade earlier, around 1923–25, there were criticisms— on the part of 'baptized Jews', Schenker says—that he was dishonestly concealing his Jewish identity: [54] at least, according to Schenker's diary, that is what he told Viktor Hammer on 30 September 1925. But what Schenker did not tell Hammer, he adds, are the reasons for this: 'that my profession to Germany as my adopted homeland by no means organically requires a profession to Judaism—only the Jew who lives in Germany but belittles the German in favour of the international has to account for the contradiction that he perpetrates', and that 'it is my duty to execute my work, but not to first run the risk that an intrinsi-

---

[52] See above, pp. 149, 214.

[53] Letter of 21 December 1933 (OJ 5/18), transcribed and translated by Rothgeb, Schenker Correspondence Project website.

[54] The remark about 'baptised Jews' is in a letter of 6 May 1923 to Otto Vrieslander, whose two-part article 'Heinrich Schenker und sein Werk', *Musikblätter des Anbruch* 5/2 (February 1923), 41–4, and 5/3 (March 1923), 72–9, appears to have sparked off the criticisms; evidence concerning this rather obscure episode may be found in Federhofer 1985: 316–8. Federhofer speculates that the criticisms originated in the circle around Universal Edition, with which (as explained in the introduction) Schenker was at this time in dispute, which would fit with a remark Schenker made in a letter to Halm dated 3 April 1924, following an account of his publishing tribulations: 'How the hearts of the Jews Hertzka, Kalmus and brother, etc., do wallow!' (DLA 69.930/12, translated by Rothfarb, Schenker Correspondence Project website).

cally superfluous admission may perhaps throw the work into question' (317).

There is also a much earlier instance of the same coyness, in a series of letters between Schenker and Busoni concerning Schenker's *Syrische Tänze,* which as I mentioned Busoni arranged for Schoenberg to orchestrate for a modern music concert series in Berlin (Erwin and Simms 1981: 25). Schenker had sent Busoni a copy of his *Syrische Tänze* (in their original form for piano four hands), and in February 1900 Busoni wrote back, referring to 'the *Syrian* (why this concealment?) *Dances* that I often play'.[55] And in a letter from September 1903 concerned with the orchestration, Busoni reverted to the topic, writing 'just a suggestion: don't you want to call the child by its real name and title your dance suite simply "Jewish dance songs"? The impression would only be bettered'.[56] Ringer (1990: 9) comments of this that 'for all we know [Busoni] had fallen prey to the common misconception of the augmented second, beloved of eastern European cantors and folk singers, as the identifying interval of everything "Jewish" in music, although one as familiar as Busoni was with parts of eastern Europe where Turkish musical influences still persisted must have known better'. Actually Busoni *did* know better. The style of the *Syrische Tänze* is unmistakably that of dance music from the Eastern European Jewish tradition: the first two dances, in particular, are full of the rhythmic types, melodic figures, and patterns of accentuation characteristic of the Moldavian hora alongside other, more classical elements.[57] According to Charlotte Erwin and Bryan Simms (25), 'Schenker had originally intended to call them "Dances or Suite on Jewish Folksongs" (*Tänze oder Suite nach jüdischen Volksweisen*), but he altered the title for fear it would limit their appeal in conservative Vienna'. A manuscript copy in the Jonas Collection, however, gives an early version of the work a title that might in *fin-de-siècle* Vienna have been considered even more compromising, with strong Galician connotations: 'Hasidic Dances' (*Tänze der Chassidim*).[58] Though one wonders who could actually have been taken in, the title under which Schenker's musical reminiscences were published nicely fudges the issue, in effect projecting the music's Jewish qualities onto a remoter and at that time less controversial Other, and in this way helping to deflect any association with the composer's own identity; the artwork, with its lexicon of all-purpose orientalising images, adds to the effect (fig. 4.2).[59] Given the extent to which

---

[55] Letter of 11 February 1900, transcribed in Federhofer 1985: 82.

[56] Translated in Erwin and Simms 1981: 26.

[57] My thanks to Abigail Wood for her expert advice on this.

[58] OJ 23/16. The entry on Podhajce in Dabrowska et al. 1980 confirms that its Jewish population was predominantly Hasidic; indeed Alpern (forthcoming) describes it as lying at 'the epicenter of Hasidism'.

[59] The dedicatee is Baron Alphons Mayer von Rothschild, who (as I mentioned in

Figure 4.2   Schenker, *Syrische Tänze*, cover.

Viennese anti-Semitism was changing in nature at this time, it may not be inappropriate to draw a parallel with Chatterjee's (1992: 158) observation, admittedly referring to the 1920s, that 'by an overt expression of interest in such core Jewish texts [as the Talmud], Wittgenstein would risk raising eyebrows in times of maximal anti-Semitism and blowing the concealing cover that he apparently wished to maintain'. It can certainly be said that, for many Jews, the trope of concealment— so central to Schenker's theory of music—had a long history in the circumstances of everyday life: 'for centuries', writes Gay (1978: 199), 'Jews had learned to be inconspicuous'.

Perhaps then there is not so much to be read into Schenker's enactment in his own life of the tropes of concealment characteristic of his

the introduction) was Schenker's pupil in the 1890s and contributed to the publication costs of *Neue musikalische Theorien und Phantasien;* this may have added to the sensitivity of the title, given that the Rothschilds were widely seen as epitomising Jewish capitalism (and were mentioned as such in 'Das Judenthum in der Musik' [Osborne 1973: 24]).

theoretical writings; perhaps the experiences evoked in the pages of Schenker's diary are simply the normal experiences of assimilated Viennese Jews at the *fin de siècle*. Wistrich (1989: 51) writes that 'nothing was more guaranteed to arouse their ire than the sight of a bearded, caftan Jew in the streets of Vienna with his "Yiddish singsong intonation", reminding them of their not so distant past in the pre-emancipation ghettos', and this is an experience that left its trace in Schenker's diary: in May 1916, at a time when the war had particularly swelled the number of Hasidic Jews in Vienna, Schenker recorded that, at the Café Vindobona, 'Lie-Liechen [Jeanette] had occasion to see a specimen of the eastern Jewry that, despite considerable assets, arouses antipathy'.[60] (Fig. 4.3 shows two *Ostjuden* on the Mathildenplatz, photographed at just about this time.) But ire is not what is reflected in Schenker's diary entries about the *Ostjuden*. An entry for 29 September 1915, headed 'Galician Jews', begins by saying that 'one accuses them of . . . assimilating only with difficulty' (Federhofer 1985: 312), which is exactly the complaint that motivated the Jewish anti-Semitism to which I referred. However, Schenker's diary entry takes a quite different tack. 'I maintain', he continues, that

> the question of race here plays the least isolating role; instead it is my opinion that solely their boundless poverty comes into consideration as the cause. Whoever, like them, lives from hand to mouth, under the most difficult circumstances, hated, despised, and excluded, persecuted, often burdened with a large family, unrecognized in their strengths (for example their education), does not find the disposition to assimilate in his shattered organism. They are like soldiers on the field: burdened with fear for survival and in constant battle. . . . That Jews otherwise find it easy to acquire better manners one may see in those who have become wealthy.

If these more assimilated Jews retain in their diction some traces of their racial origins, he adds, then that is no more than might be said of Polish, Czech, or Slavonic immigrants. For Schenker then it is social circumstances rather than the specifics of race or religion that inhibit Jewish assimilation: 'Give Jews equal rights and let them share the leadership of the state', he wrote in the 1916 diary entry prompted by Schmitz's 'Die Judenfrage', and 'immediately all religious differences vanish'.

It was presumably under the impact of the Dreyfus Affair that Schenker wrote in his diary for 1899 that Europe fails to acknowledge the Jews' right to existence because they lack their own land (Federhofer 1985: 311). That was of course Herzl's starting point. And much later, after the war, Schenker makes the same point in a diary entry recording a discussion with Jeanette: the Jews maintain their identity through their strong sense of family, he writes, but for spiritual progress

---

[60] 13 May 1916, transcribed in Federhofer 1985: 313.

Figure 4.3 *Ostjuden* on the Mathildenplatz. Used by permission of Austrian National Library Vienna, Picture Archive (sign. PCH 17.954-B).

a homeland would be needed.[61] Schenker's scepticism concerning Zionism, as reflected for instance in a diary entry of 4 February 1917 (316), may then have been as much pragmatic as principled: if a Jewish homeland was not achievable, then assimilation remained the only option, and the diary entry following the discussion with Jeanette continues that, in the absence of a homeland of his own, 'the Jew must, in order to be active spiritually, adopt a homeland and be active in a culture that he chooses'. And that takes us back to what Schenker did not tell Hammer, 'that my profession to Germany as my adopted homeland by no means organically requires a profession to Judaism'. In this way, Schenker's choice—his word—to construct his identity as an assimilated German Jew resulted in a narrow path between maintaining that identity and a concealment easily construed as denial. One might add that, during his lifetime, that path became even narrower, to the extent that, by the end of his life, it no longer really existed.

To say that Schenker's experience was unexceptional, then, is not to belittle it. Writing specifically of the Galician immigrants who settled

[61] Diary entry for 1 November 1925 (Federhofer 1985: 318).

in Leopoldstadt or Brigittenau during and after the First World War, Joseph Roth observed: 'it is frightfully difficult to be an *Ostjude;* and there is no harder fate than that of the alien Eastern European Jews in Vienna. For the Christian Socials they're Jews; for the German nationalists they are Semites. For the Social Democrats they are unproductive elements' (translated in Wistrich 1987: 111). Schenker, of course, was not one of the unassimilated *Ostjuden* Roth was referring to. But then, neither was he one of the upper-class Jews who (in McCagg's phrase)[62] looked down their noses at the *Ostjuden,* nor again was he a convert. He was simply one of the many middle-class Jews of Vienna who acknowledged their faith if asked, as Schenker put it, and quietly went about their business. And it was precisely for such Jews that the new anti-Semitism created a strictly logical aporia. Assimilation, whether of the Jellinek type or the full-blown version of the converts who changed their names and so buried their identity, was becoming less and less a viable option. Zionism offered an internally consistent alternative and a concrete plan of action, but was unlikely to be attractive to those who saw themselves as first and foremost Germans. As a Galician immigrant and citizen of the imaginary Germany of not only Goethe and Schiller but also Mozart and Beethoven, Schenker had constructed his identity in terms of the tradition of cultural conservatism I discussed in chapter 3: indeed Hermann Roth virtually said as much when in 1931 he wrote of Schenker that 'being a musician and a passionate, conservative "Germanness" forcefully come together for the native of Galicia'.[63] But Schenker had done this at exactly the time when that the German conservative tradition was being transformed in such a way as to render the terms 'German' and 'Jew' polar opposites: that is what I meant by a strictly logical aporia. He had assimilated to a great and glorious culture, to repeat Beller's words, just as the society for that culture was disappearing.

Schenker and Others

In this book I have been attempting to define Schenker in relation to some of those in relation to whom he defined himself, or in relation to exponents of patterns of thought within which he also thought or against which he reacted: Hanslick, Bösendorfer, Loos, Riegl, and even Adorno, among others. In this section I focus on such patterns of similarity and alterity in relation to two of Schenker's most significant others: Wagner, the anti-Semite in relation to whom I shall argue that Schenker forged much of his thinking through opposition or appropriation; and Schoenberg, with whom Schenker had a desultory and gener-

---

[62] See note 42 above.

[63] Roth, 'Bekenntnis zu Heinrich Schenker', *Hamburger Nachrichten,* 17 September 1931 (OC 2/84).

ally unsatisfactory relationship,[64] but who offers present-day interpreters an obvious point of comparison in terms of the possible responses to the Jewish predicament in *fin-de-siècle* Vienna.

It is common knowledge that Schenker at first admired Wagner but before long became violently critical of his music and its effect on musical culture in general: as early as *Niedergang,* Schenker wrote—and his tone is significant for my argument—that 'a higher moral duty compels me not to shirk from setting out my arguments against his colossal presence' (*DAC* 98). In chapter 1, I drew a number of parallels between Wagner's and Schenker's thinking, in particular proposing a link between Wagner's essay 'Was ist deutsch?' and the constellation of ideas associated with Schenker's squaring of his theoretical circle (depth, genius, spirit, and logic). The fact that, in chapter 3, I drew on Hanisch's list of dichotomies in Wagner's thought for my outline of the tradition of cultural conservatism within which I situated Schenker is further indication of the affinity of their thinking, as more generally is the view held by both Wagner and Schenker that the corruption of taste had resulted in a disastrous decline of musical culture (as illustrated for Wagner by the provincial Kapellmeisters, and for Schenker by the virtuosos). Up to now, however, I have been tiptoeing round the blindingly obvious fact that Schenker was Jewish and Wagner was the author of 'Das Judenthum in der Musik', of which Schoenberg (1975: 503) wrote in his Mailamm lecture that in his youth 'you could not be a true Wagnerian without being a follower of his anti-Semitic essay', and that is the aspect I now at last address.

It was not just a matter of the contemporary relevance of an essay already several decades old. In 1883, the year before Schenker left Galicia, the festival organised by the German students of Vienna to commemorate Wagner's death was turned into a political demonstration, the 'pro-Prussian and antisemitic overtones' of which represented 'an outright challenge to the very existence of the multinational state' (Pollak 1987: 62): the echoes must still have been reverberating when Schenker reached Vienna, and marked a definitive move away from the cultural rather than political Wagnerism epitomised by the Akademischer Wagner-Verein, of which Guido Adler (himself a Bohemian

---

[64] The fault seems to have been more Schenker's than Schoenberg's, judging by an exchange of letters in which Schoenberg unsuccessfully tried to persuade Schenker to support his Vereinigung schaffender Tonkünstler (Erwin and Simms 1981). It is hard to know what to make of Schenker's reference, in his letter to Halm dated 25 September 1922, to 'Schoenberg—whom I saw often and who virtually loved me' (DLA 69.930/10, translated by Rothfarb, Schenker Correspondence Project website), but it seems that despite his comments in 'Those who complain about the decline' (p. 157 above), Schoenberg always retained an admiration for Schenker's writings: in a letter of 1938 to Hugo Leichtentritt, Schoenberg listed those writers on music whose work had interested him, beginning with 'all Heinrich Schenker's writings' (Schoenberg 1964: 207). The feeling seems not to have been reciprocated.

Jew) had been a founding member in the early 1870s. On the one hand, as I have already said, the association of Wagner and anti-Semitic pan-Germanism continued to strengthen through the 1880s and 1890s, as represented in the sphere of music criticism by Richard van Kralik and especially Hagen, and in the broader cultural sphere by figures such as the race theorist and friend (from 1908 son-in-law) of Cosima Wagner, Houston Chamberlain, who lived in Vienna from 1889 to 1909. On the other hand, anti-Semitism itself became more and more prominent, as evidenced by—in brief—the twelfth point added by Schönerer to his 'Linz' programme (1885), the United Christian manifesto calling for the exclusion of Jews from official posts (1889), the founding of the Verein zur Abwehr des Antisemitismus (1891), Schneider's asking the Lower Austrian Diet 'why shouldn't this people . . . be exterminated?' (1894), Lueger's election victory (1895), the student fraternities explicitly declaring themselves anti-Semitic (1896), and in 1897 the First Zionist Congress together with Franz Josef's reluctant acceptance of Lueger as mayor; the last of these was particularly traumatic because it exposed the hollowness of many Viennese Jews' belief—celebrated by Freud's cigar—that the emperor, '"their" emperor' (Henisch 1967: 370), could protect them against anti-Semitism. And then there were the Galician pogroms of 1898. In this context, the present-day debate about whether Wagner's anti-Semitism was merely cultural or also racial is really beside the point. The point is that it was received and propagated as racial in *fin-de-siècle* Vienna.

I suggested in chapter 1 that Schenker's definitive turn to Brahms at around the time of the Brahms's death might equally be understood as a definitive turning away from Wagner and his 'New German' followers, and what I wish now to propose is that the issue of race played a central role in this. It is Wagner, of course, who had linked issues of race and music aesthetics in the first place, most explicitly in the lengthy postscript he added for the 1869 republication of 'Das Judenthum in der Musik'. There Wagner interpreted *Vom Musikalisch-Schönen* as a tract aimed—in the period translation of William Ashton Ellis—at 'establishing modern Jewish music [by which Wagner means Mendelssohn] as the sterling "beautiful"' (1894: 105): the result, he claimed, was that 'the musical Jew-Beauty took its seat in the heart of a full-blooded German system of Æsthetics. . . . The musical Jew-Beauty was now uplifted to a thorough dogma' (113). It is against this background that I wish to read aspects of Schenker's project as responses to, or refutations of, the racial stereotypes of which 'Das Judenthum in der Musik' (in Dieter Borchmeyer's words [1992/1986: 171]) 'exhausts the whole xenophobic arsenal'.

I begin with an aside that must have touched a raw nerve with both Schenker and Schoenberg: 'Contact with our culture', Wagner wrote, 'has not, even after two thousand years, weaned the Jew away from the peculiarities of Semitic pronunciation' (Osborne 1973: 28). In

1934, the year after he reconverted to Judaism, Schoenberg reminisced on the circumstances of his childhood: 'Marked at school by strange appearance, strange pronunciation', he said, 'one stood out!'[65] It might be tempting to see this as a piece of retrospective self-orientalisation on Schoenberg's part—more on this later—but that would be wrong: Schoenberg was still working to improve the quality of his German accent as late as the 1920s (Brown 1994: 56). The same might perhaps not be expected of Schenker, whose 1915 diary entry headed 'Galician Jews' says that 'with discomfort one notices mannerisms and gestures that they retain even once they have stepped into better circles'.[66] There is something slightly odd about Schenker's 'one' and 'they' given that he was a Galician Jew himself, and this perhaps masks an element of autobiography. Schenker's student registration forms at the University of Vienna included a statement of his first language: in the seventh, eighth, and last of these forms his first language is given as German, but in the rest as Polish (Chiang 1996: 48–50). What 'Polish' means in this context is uncertain, but Austrian bureaucrats were in the habit of recording Yiddish-speaking Jews as Polish-speaking, since Yiddish was not recognised as a national language (Rozenblit 2001: 29). And there is some evidence that even in the later part of his life Schenker—like many Galicians—spoke German with a Yiddish accent.[67] This may go some way towards explaining the 'discomfort' Schenker's diary records, the more so when contrasted with the other side of his assimilation, his extraordinary mastery of the tradition of German music—a mastery which, in a classic immigrant pattern, rendered him more German than the Germans, and certainly more German than the Viennese. (I shall soon come back to this.) And that in turn could provide an explanation of the particular targeting of 'Von der Sendung des deutschen Genies' on which I commented in chapter 3: not so much against the victorious powers as against the enemy within, those Germans—or Austrians—whose Germanness was found wanting.

---

[65] Translated in Lazar 1994: 41. In his essay 'Wien', written in 1960 and incorporated into *Quasi una fantasia*, Adorno (1992/1963: 208) comments curiously on Schoenberg's alterity, saying he 'was surrounded by the aura of the alien, the stranger who does not quite belong or fit into Western civilisation. . . . When I saw him for the first time, I was amazed by his gypsy-like appearance. . . . Schoenberg's foreignness reminds one of the role played by the Spaniards in Cubism'.

[66] Diary entry of 29 September 1915 (Federhofer 1985: 312).

[67] Oral information from Hedi Siegel, based on recorded comments by Greta Kraus relating to the early 1930s, and on a small mistake in Schenker's unpublished 'Von der Stimmführung des Generalbasses', which he dictated to Jeanette around 1917. Schenker refers in this to the thoroughbass manual by J. S. Bach transcribed by Spitta in an appendix to his Bach biography, which includes a set of examples under the title 'Mehrere Erleuchterung zu geben sind folgende Exempel ausgesetzet worden'. In Schenker's text, however, this appears as 'Erleichterungen', which is how it would have sounded if Schenker spoke with a Yiddish accent. My thanks to Professor Siegel for sharing this with me.

When he speaks of 'Semitic pronunciation', Wagner is making a more general point: 'The Jew speaks the language of the country in which he has lived from generation to generation, but he always speaks it as a foreigner', and that makes it impossible for him 'ever to speak colloquially, authoritatively or from the depths of his being' (Osborne 1973: 27). Wagner then applies this to music (just as Louis did when characterising Mahler as speaking 'a musical German, but with the accent, inflection, and above all, the gestures of the East'). He takes the idea of alterity even further when he compares Jewish musicians with 'parrots who repeat human speech', adding that they are 'just as lacking in feeling and real expression as these foolish birds'.[68] (It is tempting to read Schenker's approving quotation of C. P. E. Bach's 'play from the soul, not like a trained bird!', which I quoted in chapter 2, as prompted by Wagner's remark.) And it follows that 'in this language, this art, the Jew can only imitate'; even as talented a musician as Mendelssohn, Wagner adds, 'was forced quite openly to snatch at every formal detail which characterized the individuality of whichever forerunner he had chosen to copy' (28, 35).

This accusation seems to have particularly rankled with Schoenberg (1975: 503), who said in his Mailamm speeech:

> we soon had to learn from men like Houston Chamberlain that there is a racial difference between Jews and German—that not only is the Aryan race a very superior race destined to rule the world, that not only is the Jewish race an inferior race and one to be detested, but, we had also to realize, the Jewish race possessed no creative capacity.

Schenker may have been equally offended by Wagner's attitude to Mendelssohn (whom Schenker regarded as among 'the greatest of the great composers' [*BCFF* 61] and constantly coupled with Brahms in *Niedergang*), but his response is different: he takes Wagner's argument on board but turns it round so that it ends up pointing in the opposite direction. Schenker's emphasis on the 'improvisatory' nature of German composition—on the way the German composer speaks music as a first language, unlike modern musicians who are more like schoolchildren speaking Latin[69]—might be seen as a simple extension of Wagner's thought. But in the 1897 essay 'Unpersönliche Musik', Schenker gives Wagner's argument a distinctive twist. Referring specifically to 'the composers from the school of Berlioz and Liszt', Schenker writes:

[68] Osborne 1973: 31.

[69] Draft letter to Emil Hertzka, dated 5 May 1914 (WSLB 211); both the draft and the final letter are transcribed and translated by Bent, Schenker Correspondence Project website. A related remark in *Kontrapunkt* 1 ('performances often sound as though a Japanese or Chinese were to pick up a text by Goethe without sufficient knowledge of the German language' [*CI* 18]) may once again carry an implied Wagnerian reference: in 'Das Judenthum in der Musik' Wagner compares Jewish music to 'hearing a poem by Goethe translated into that Jewish jargon we know as Yiddish' (Osborne 1973: 33).

just as one can draw conclusions from the colour and inflection of spoken words about the inner agitation of a speaker, whether it is genuine or artifical, violent or weak, and whether or not it tallies with his innermost essence, one can surely deduce from a composer's musical diction whether he is truly agitated. And it has to be said that they all speak as if they were using a foreign language. They lack immediacy and, in order to write, must constantly picture to themselves how they ought to appear inwardly if they had reason to be excited this way or that.[70]

And now he adds a sentence I quoted in chapter 1: 'the older composers spoke in the shape of the music; the "New Germans" only paint the words'. For Schenker, then, it is the 'New Germans', the Wagnerians, the anti-Semites who prattle meaninglessly in a language they do not understand: the qualities Wagner figures as German inhere instead in the tradition of absolute music that Wagner had dismissed as 'musical Jew-Beauty'. In this way Schenker adopts the framework of Wagner's discourse, and in particular its oppositional character (that is how the Entente powers can eventually replace the 'New Germans' as Schenker's vilified other), but he reverses its direction.[71]

The relationship between Schenker and Wagner becomes the more telling as we draw closer to the issues of logic and causality, surfaces and depths that lie at the heart of Schenker's theory. We might start with the association with Judaism and superficiality implicit in Wagner's reference to Mendelssohn snatching at details. This is expanded in 'Über das Dirigieren' (On conducting), where Wagner describes Mendelssohn rehearsing Beethoven's Eighth Symphony: 'he would pick out a detail here and there—almost at random', Wagner says (1970: 303), while 'for the rest, this so incomparably buoyant symphony flowed down a vastly tame and chatty course'. In *Der freie Satz,* by contrast, it is the 'so-called heathens' who lose themselves in the particu-

---

[70] Schenker 1988: 135–6. In *Die Kunst des Vortrags*, Schenker makes exactly the same point about performers: 'Most virtuosos who go onstage prove themselves artistically not up to the works they are performing; they speak the tonal language like a badly learned foreign tongue. In order to survive in the battle at competition, they grasp at unallowed means of false effect that they want to pass off as marks of their own individuality' (*AP* 84).

[71] There is in this way a long history behind Benjamin's (1981: 169) apparently casual reference to contemporary musicians who 'approach music from the outside, as if they had memorized the lines of a play in a language which they could not speak'. There is also a further, perhaps trivial, example of Schenker adopting Wagner's discursive framework but reversing its direction in the *Geist* essay, where he is speaking of music's vocal origins: 'Only later', Schenker says, 'did it summon up the courage to sail out from the shores of language into the free, open sea of more distant musical intervals' (p. 321). The apparent reference is to Wagner's essay *The Artwork of the Future,* in which Wagner casts Beethoven as a mariner, setting out from the old world of instrumental music to discover the new world: 'Staunchly he threw his anchor out; and this anchor was *the Word*' (Wagner 1892: 126). Schenker runs with Wagner's image but inverts it: for Wagner the old world is instrumental music and the new one vocal, whereas in Schenker's version it is exactly the other way round.

lars of the foreground,[72] while—as Schenker continues—'confessors of a true divinity are those who worship the background'; his question 'Shall I therefore proclaim my monotheistic doctrine of art from a Mount Sinai and thereby seek to win confessors of it?' which I have already quoted, follows two sentences later. Again, then, Schenker points Wagner's anti-Semitic slur in the opposite direction. But it goes much further than this. For Wagner, the Jew

> listens only superficially to our music and its life-giving inner organism. By this cursory listening he only discerns superficial similarities to the one thing he can understand, that which is peculiar to his own nature. So, to him the accidental externals of our musical and artistic life must seem to be their essence. (Osborne 1973: 33)

In thus confusing accidentals with essentials, the Jew displays characteristics that are exactly the opposite of those of the German, as set out fifteen years later in 'Was ist deutsch?' There, Wagner writes that the German eagerly studies foreign texts (Wagner is talking specifically about poetry, but the point is a general one), and this is 'no mere idle gaping at the foreign, merely for the sake of it: his intention is to understand it in a German fashion. . . . In doing so he strips the foreign of its accidentals' (Osborne 1973: 48). In this way he gains an understanding the foreigner lacks: 'it was predestined for the German spirit to assimilate the foreign . . . in the utmost purity and objectivity of intuition' (44).

There is in Schenker the occasional direct echo of Wagner's argument, as in a 1929 diary entry commenting—of Brahms—that it took German genius to fully express the national qualities of Hungarian music (Federhofer 1985: 255). More fully, however, Schenker adopts Wagner's strategy of defining the self in opposition to a vilified other, but reverses the polarity. If it is the 'New Germans' who mistake accidentals for essentials, then it is Schenker who demonstrates the distinction between the essential and the accidental, so providing a properly theorised definition of such woolly Wagnerian concepts as 'life-giving inner organism'. It is in this way that, as I suggested, Schenker can be seen as providing his own answer to the question 'What is German?', which Wagner ultimately came to admit that he had failed to answer[73]—and the continuing topicality of which extended even beyond Schenker's lifetime, given its centrality for the musicologists of the Third Reich (Potter 1998: chap. 7). One might also say that here, instead of defending the values of German culture against the Viennese (as Beller put it), Schenker was quite specifically

---

[72] See pp. 129–30 above.

[73] In 1878 Wagner added a postscript to the original essay saying that he 'no longer considers himself qualified to answer the question "What is German?"' (Rather 1990: 194–5).

defending it against the Germans. Indeed it would be possible to claim that—in a supreme irony—it was the destiny through his writings of Schenker, the Jew, to secure Germany's musical past just as another Jew, Schoenberg, saw it as his destiny through his compositions to secure Germany's musical future: hence the similarity between the triumphalist rhetoric of Schoenberg's famous claim, through serialism, to have ensured the supremacy of German music for another century (Rufer 1962/1959: 45), and Schenker's claim—which I quoted in the introduction—that 'it is none other than Vienna that will, through my theory, for a second time assume the leadership in music, a leadership that no nation on earth will ever again be able to destroy'.[74]

The curious thing is that this reversal of Wagner's anti-Semitic polemic seems to be already latent in Wagner's own writing. As we have seen, Wagner claims in 'Was ist deutsch?' that, by stripping it of its inessentials, the German gains an understanding of non-German culture that foreigners themselves lack: 'he makes the foreign work yield a picture of its purely human aspects', Wagner says, adding that '*Parsifal* and *Tristan* were shaped anew by Germans: and whilst the originals have become mere curiosities . . . in their German counterparts we recognize poetic works of imperishable value' (Osborne 1973: 48). Yet only a few paragraphs earlier he applied precisely the same logic to the Jews: 'It everywhere appears to be the duty of the Jew to show the nations of modern Europe where there may be a profit they have overlooked, or not made use of' (47). This formulation only needs translation from the language of commerce to that of culture in order to yield Wittgenstein's claim that 'It is typical for a Jewish mind to understand someone else's work better than he understands it himself' (quoted in Chatterjee 1992: 153). And perhaps Wagner, who despite his public anti-Semitism insisted on Hermann Levi conducting *Parsifal*, was conscious of this. Like Schenker, who spoke of them as 'the persecuted, the robbed, shoulder to shoulder!'—indeed like many others—Wagner repeatedly drew parallels between the Germans and the Jews;[75] Borch-

---

[74] *MM3* 9; see p. 11 above. Schenker continues, with a certain bathos, 'and towards which all designs of political hegemony will crumble to dust, even those of the French nation which, without an ounce of originality in body or spirit, and utterly devoid of breadth or depth of being, constantly harried the other peoples of Europe in body and spirit, and now even threatens them with their demise'. The reason why the French are brought in at this point is that this passage is from 'Rameau or Beethoven? Creeping Paralysis or Spiritual Potency in Music?' a less than evenhanded assessment of Rameau's place in music theory; what is interesting, or depressing, is the way Schenker's charges— that the French are uncreative and shallow—simply recycle Wagner's stereotypes.

[75] The Schenker quotation is from a diary entry for 16 October 1926, prompted by a letter complaining of German anti-Semitism from Schenker's brother-in-law Victor Schiff (Federhofer 1985: 319); see also diary entries for 26 October 1915 and 18 December 1929 (Federhofer 1985: 319, 315). An example of the 'others' is Jakob Wassermann's image of the two mirrors: 'No non-Jew could possibly imagine the heart-rending position in which the German Jew finds himself. With his twin loves and his struggles on two

meyer refers to 'a feeling of envy which had its roots in the conviction that Jewishness is the "only possible counterpart" to Germanness in world history' (1992/1986: 180). But it goes further than this. In the postscript to the 1869 republication of 'Das Judenthum in der Musik', Wagner envisages the possibility of 'intelligent and high-minded Jews' acting as the redeemers of German music: 'Much may be permitted and overlooked in the broad-minded Jew by his more enlightened congeners,' he says, 'since they have made up their minds to live not only *with* us, but *in* us', and the reason for his exposé of the Jewish mentality is that only such openness will enable 'this element . . . to be assimilated with us in such a way that, in common with us, it shall ripen toward a higher evolution of our nobler human qualities' (Wagner 1894: 120–1). The element of self-justification in this may be tortuous, but the basically Hegelian argument is clear: the sublation of the Jewish element will lead to a higher self-realisation of the German. Put bluntly, the continuation of German music is in the hands of the Jews, who 'have preserved a feeling for genuineness which the Germans have entirely lost'.[76]

There is then a very telling context behind what Schenker told Jonas just after the remark, in his letter of 21 December 1933, about operating under cover:[77] 'the product of the German music-geniuses', he says, is 'destined to become a *new message to the world from the Jews for the coming eternities*' (the emphasis is Schenker's).[78] He says it again a few months later: 'why should the Jews not . . . learn music from the other peoples and propagate it through the ages, since the other peoples have probably abandoned it for good? That way the Jew would join to his religious monotheism the belief in one musical *Ursache!*'[79] (The idea that the Jews learnt music from others in the first place further strengthens the Wagnerian connection.) And from here there are two routes to a point of conclusion that must now be obvious. Julie Brown (1994: 59) cites the postscript to 'Das Judenthum in

---

fronts he has been pushed to the very abyss of despair. The German and the Jew: I once had a metaphorical dream, but I am not sure it is easily understood. I placed two mirrors so that they faced each other, and I had the feeling that the two human images contained and preserved in those two mirrors were about to tear each other up' (translated in Ringer 1990: 3).

[76] Quoted from Cosima Wagner's diary (22 November 1881) in Borchmeyer 1992: 180.

[77] See p. 224 above.

[78] The idea that, even when assimilated, the Jews would continue to be a 'light among nations' was common among Jewish thinkers of the Enlightenment: see Beller 1989: 140. Kraus wrote that the Jews were 'fated to dissolve entirely into their surrounding cultures, and nevertheless still to remain a ferment', because they were forced to confront issues of their identity in a way others were not, while in *Der Weg ins freie* Schnitzler has one of the characters voice a similar view (217).

[79] Letter to Jonas dated 2 August 1934 (OJ 5/18, 49, translated by Rothgeb, Schenker Correspondence Project website).

der Musik' in order to suggest that Schoenberg consciously or unconsciously saw his mission as the one set out by Wagner, and I am suggesting the same of Schenker. That is the direct route, but there is also a route that is longer and more scenic, or at least speculative, the implication of which is that the logics of alterity with which I have been concerned in this chapter were not specifically Jewish but endemic in the multinational empire. Wagner's idea of the Jew living 'not only *with* us, but *in* us' is reminiscent of Weininger's concept of the Jew as an abstract, or even metaphysical, entity; indeed Wagner directly anticipated this in a letter to Nietzsche, describing Jewishness, as well as Germanness, as 'a purely metaphysical concept'.[80] As I said, this is what leads Weininger to extend Wagner's idea of the role of the Jew in German music by applying it to Wagner himself: not only did Wagner have the 'tinge of Jewishness' in his character that made him anti-Semitic, but (in Julie Brown's words [forthcoming]), 'For Weininger, someone who was "only a German" could never express the essence of *Deutschtum* in the way Wagner did'.

And that in turn is reminiscent of the strange, or unfortunate, remark of Schenker in the original edition of *Der freie Satz,* which I quoted in chapter 3: 'the creator of such linear progressions must be a German even if foreign blood perhaps flowed in his veins!' If the explanation I offered there, that Schenker is making a joke, is not convincing, then perhaps another might be that the strangeness of the remark is a symptom of a thought Schenker represses rather than articulates: that Ludwig *van* Beethoven could perhaps have been the German genius he was *because* foreign blood flowed in his veins.[81] That, after all, would link up with other representatives of German musical genius the foreignness of whose blood is more self-evident. One of course is Chopin, whom Schenker admitted in 'Von der Sendung' to the 'Pantheon of German composers', and whose music is cited in *Der freie Satz* more frequently than that of any other composer except the (not quite German) Beethoven, and more frequently in *Harmonielehre* than any except Bach and Beethoven (Bent 1986: 137): the circularity of the argument that defines great music as German and concludes from this that German music is great becomes particularly conspicuous when Schenker writes in *Meisterwerk* 1 that 'for the profundity with which Nature has endowed him, Chopin belongs more to Germany than to Poland' (*MM1* 81). It is tempting in view of the 'outsider' psychology I outlined in the introduction to imagine the thought on the tip of Schenker's tongue: Chopin, like Schenker, is more German than the Germans just because of his Polish origins.

Of course there may also be more straightforward reasons for the special role Schenker assigns to Chopin. One, if true, is what I men-

---

[80] Letter of 23 October 1872, quoted in Borchmeyer 1992/1986: 180.

[81] Beethoven's grandfather came from what is now Belgium, moving to Bonn in 1733.

tioned in chapter 3: Schenker's supposed childhood exposure, through Mikuli, not only to Chopin's music and pianistic tradition but also to his conception of musicianship, of what it means to be a musician. Another, and more secure, is the fact that Chopin's works had been published in the late 1870s by Breitkopf & Härtel, which (as Jim Samson explains [1994: 6]) was 'tantamount to a sort of adoption. . . . he became a sort of honorary member of the German tradition'. But it's not just Chopin. Though not formally admitted to the pantheon, Smetana is also singled out in 'Von der Sendung': during one of the litanies I referred to in chapter 3, Schenker writes that

> betrayal was constantly being perpetrated in their own backyard . . . by some Slavic nations belonging to Austria who, to this very day, fail to realize that on the scales of true genius one solitary figure, Chopin, and perhaps also just the one string quartet, *From My Life*, by Smetana, are worth more than all that the nations of the West have produced; nations which, seduced by feeble-minded, wrong-headed leaders, surrendered themselves to those barbarians in totally undeserved servitude [etc. etc.]. (*TI* 6–7)

As Bent (1986: 136) has pointed out, this can be linked back to an article on Smetana which Schenker published in 1893, in which he hailed *From My Life* as a 'shattering piece of autobiography which bears the stamp of Beethoven'.[82] He also makes some other suggestive remarks: 'In his originality', writes Schenker, 'I discern clearly a certain substratum of stylistic receptivity; and yet there is no resemblance to the outward style of any other composer: it is only sheer artistic insight. . . . it was always Beethoven, Schubert, or Schumann who came to mind, and yet I was acutely conscious of the difference of outward style' (*HSEK* 53). We could unpack this by saying that on the surface ('outward style') Smetana's music is not in the least German, but underneath (the 'substratum') it is pure German. Of course, that is not quite what Schenker said in 1893: he said it was 'sheer artistic insight' (a formulation reminiscent of Wallaschek's characterisation of German music as 'pure beauty').[83] But it is exactly what Schenker said in the 1897 review of music by Smetana and Dvořák, which I emphasised in chapter 1 because of Schenker's positive use in it of the idea of musical 'logic': these composers, Schenker said, were able to 'present Bohemian music in a perfection which will not be surpassed' because they used 'the German system as a basis'. For Schenker, it seems, it is through the juxtaposition of German and Bohemian music that the essential features of German music—what is German about it—emerge. The German is defined through the logic of alterity.

---

[82] *HSEK* 52 (the article is from *Die Zukunft* 4 [1893], 37–40, reprinted in *HSEK* 48–54). Translations are taken from Bent 1986: 136.

[83] See p. 164 above.

Smetana, then, earns his mention in 'Von der Sendung' as the non-German who helps to define the German, or at any rate who seems to have played a special role in the development of Schenker's theoretical thought. But even that does not represent the extent of Schenker's engagement with Smetana. In his thesis, Kevin Karnes has drawn attention to Schenker's first (and last) *feuilleton*, which appeared in 1894 under a title that referenced Smetana's quartet.[84] In it Schenker reports on what appears to have been a major research effort, and one that obviously resonates with Schenker's own provincial origins: a biographical study of Smetana, focused around

> the mysterious reason why Smetana, with all his inner perfection and the great ease with which he went to work, did not also develop more strongly the self-assurance and maturity required to break open the bounds of his provincial homeland, and to achieve during his lifetime the world-wide fame that crowns his grave today.[85]

In 1893, we learn, Schenker had travelled to Bohemia in order to talk with Smetana's widow and daughter. He also tried, without success, to meet Smetana's former student Marie Breyl and to see the composer's diaries, letters, and critical essays: 'only when we come to understand the whole, rich corpus of his letters, and the diary that he kept throughout his life', writes Schenker, will we 'become truly enlightened about the master's innate and acquired artistic experiences'.[86] In short, Schenker was hoping in 1893 to penetrate to the core of Smetana's creativity through biographical study, but did not achieve his goal: 'When I left his daughter's house', he writes, 'I had to think back once more to the riddle posed by the destiny of Smetana's life. The solution was not to be found, even with those who stood so close to him in life'.[87]

Viewed in this light, the concept of musical logic as a kind of inner narrative of musical creation which I presented in chapter 1, and which Schenker adumbrates in 1897 with specific reference to Smetana, might be seen as a different and more fruitful route to the same goal Schenker sought in his 1893 *feuilleton*. It is also worth adding that the issue of Bohemian music was highly topical at this time, in part because of the language ordinances presented to the *Reichsrat* in April 1897, which proposed that Czech should become the official language of government in Bohemia and Moravia, alongside German, thereby favouring the Czechs (who were as a matter of course bilingual) at the expense of the German minorities (who were not); the resulting controversy resulted in the resignation, in November, of the prime minis-

---

[84] 'Aus dem Leben Smetana's (Ein Besuch bei Fr. Smetana's Witwe)', *Neues Wiener Tagblatt* 28/245 (6 September 1894); reprinted in *HSEK* 109–14.

[85] Translated (from *HSEK* 109–10) in Karnes 2001: 228, from which I have taken additional information on Schenker's *feuilleton*.

[86] Translated (from *HSEK* 112) in Karnes 2001: 228.

[87] Translated (from *HSEK* 114) in Karnes 2001: 229.

ter. Even before that, however, the inclusion of a high proportion of works by Smetana and Dvořák in both the concert and opera seasons had provoked protests from critics like Hagen, who complained that 'the Czechs rise ever more boldly to the top in our native land, in the city of our fathers, take over German soil', while following the promulgation of the ordinances Hans Puchstein wrote with specific reference to the production of Smetana's *Dalibor* (and prodigal use of italics) that 'of course we *should not undervalue that which is foreign because it is not German, but our theatres must be forbidden to perform any foreign work as long as a German work which is just as good remains unknown by our public, and the German journalist who does not co-operate with all his strength in fulfilling this postulate makes himself guilty of a serious offense against his nation*'.[88] Under conditions of such xenophobia, and confronted with arguments that overlapped with those of the anti-Semites, Schenker's demonstration of the German basis of the Bohemian composers' music would have served both to promulgate a more generous conception of the German than the narrowly nationalistic or racial one, and to underline the indispensable contribution of the outsider to German culture. (That, after all, is what Schenker's quip—if it was a quip—about the *Urlinie* as racial science amounts to, only expressed in the language of the 1930s.)

I shall not discuss the last of the significant others in Schenker's musical canon—Domenico Scarlatti—in this kind of detail. He is not mentioned in 'Von der Sendung' (where the Italians in general fare little better then the French, English, and Americans), but appears in other Schenker publications from *Ornamentik* to *Der freie Satz*, where Schenker writes: 'In only a single instance—that of Domenico Scarlatti—the Italian spirit revealed a superb capability for absolute diminution' (*FC* I 94). But despite that, Schenker continues, and despite his friendship with Handel, 'he had neither successors in his native country nor any real recognition of his unique worth'. These remarks summarise what Schenker had written in *Meisterwerk* 1, where he had again stressed Scarlatti's 'noble friendship' with Handel and emphasised how 'Scarlatti suffered the customary fate of genius: he was for ever estranged from his fellow-countrymen. Italy was part of him, yet not the converse: he was no part of Italy'.[89] Or to put it in the language of Schenker's comment on Chopin, Scarlatti belongs more to Germany than to Italy. And later in the same volume of *Meisterwerk*, in the first sentence of the article on Chopin's Etude op. 10 no. 6, Schenker couples

---

[88] *Ostdeutsche Rundschau*, 17 November 1896, and *Deutsches Volksblatt*, 6 October 1897; translated in McColl 1996: 89, 96, on which my account of the controversy over the language ordinances draws.

[89] *MM1* 67–8. There is a minor but telling contradiction here: the lack of Italian recognition of Scarlatti shows that he was 'no part of Italy', whereas the nonrecognition of German geniuses (their 'customary fate') does not show that they are no part of Germany.

Scarlatti's name with Chopin's: 'As was the case in Italy with Scarlatti, so too in Poland Chopin stands isolated—a musical genius. And, like Scarlatti, he too was forever estranged from his home people, albeit he came from the people, felt their spirit within him and expressed that spirit with fervour' (*MM1* 81). And that of course provides the link with Schenker the immigrant from the mud puddle of Galicia, where all forms of musical life were imitated, cut off from his native land after the empire was dismembered: the excessively yet imperfectly assimilated *Ostjude* who has a unique contribution to make to the understanding of German music, and maybe even to its survival. At this point, then, the scenic route joins up with the direct one—and the resonance of Schenker's personal project with the one mapped out by Wagner is amplified by a diary entry from 1910, in which Schenker writes that, just because they have no home, the Jews are 'in the world-historical sense the compulsory instructors of all humanity'.[90] It also brings us back to Robert Morgan's image of Schenker, which I quoted at the end of chapter 2, as 'someone who, no longer part of the world theorized, is on the outside looking in', or as Morgan elsewhere puts it, a 'consummate cultural "Grenzjude" [frontier Jew]: alienated from his musical culture yet convinced he can save it' (2002: 265). I shall take up these matters once more in chapter 5.

First, however, I want to pursue—this time much more briefly—the comparison with Schoenberg implied by the parallel between my argument about Wagner and Schenker on the one hand and, on the other, Julie Brown's argument (in her article 'Schoenberg's Early Wagnerisms') about Wagner and Schoenberg. In short, Brown reads Schoenberg's conversion to Lutheranism and concurrent change of compositional direction as an act of double self-sacrifice in response to Wagner's call on 'intelligent and high-minded Jews' to 'become one of us': a sacrifice of both Schoenberg's Judaism and the Brahmsian tonality that had up to this point characterised his music. Although Brown does not trace it through to the period when Schoenberg abandoned the aspiration to assimilate, the theme of sacrifice continues to resonate through Schoenberg's later career. The moment of truth when Schoenberg realised the assimilationist option was no longer viable is usually said to have come in 1921, when he was asked for his certificate of baptism while on holiday in Mattsee, near Salzburg—though at other times Schoenberg said that he 'became aware of the shipwreck of assimilationist aspirations' while in the Austrian army in 1917, or again in 1919.[91] Whatever the truth of this, Schoenberg's statements of an explicitly Zionist position begin in 1924, when (in his 'Position on Zion-

---

[90] Diary entry, 13 April 1910 (Federhofer 1985: 311).

[91] Translated in Lazar 1994: 110 (letter to Peter Gradenwitz, 20 July 1934), 106 (letter to Webern, 4 August 1933: Schoenberg says it is fourteen years since he first realised this). For the Mattsee incident see e.g. Reich 1971/1968: 124.

ism') he argued that only military victory could secure a Jewish state in Palestine against its enemies (Lazar 1994: 54), and in *Der biblische Weg* (The biblical way, 1926) he presented his belief in the necessity of an exodus of European Jewry in the form of a psychodrama. From 1933 there is an escalation in the register of Schoenberg's Zionist proclamations. He wrote in a letter of 13 June 1933, 'It is necessary to give up all Western acquisitions; we are Asians and nothing essential binds us to the West. . . . We must return to our origins';[92] this is another example of the self-orientalisation I referred to earlier, using an anti-Semitic label to construct an identity marked by alterity. A few weeks later, on 4 August, Schoenberg wrote to Webern to tell him of his recent reconversion to Judaism ('I have finally cut myself off for good—even though with difficulty, and a good deal of vacillation—from all that tied me to the Occident'), adding that he plans 'a long tour of America, which could perhaps turn into a world tour, to persuade people to help the Jews in Germany': he explains that he considers this 'more important than my art, and am determined . . . to do nothing in the future but work for the Jewish national cause'.[93] And on another occasion during the same year he states it explicitly: 'I offer the sacrifice of my art for the sake of Jewry'.[94]

William Benjamin (1981: 159) writes that 'Schenker approached humanity from the standpoint of the Hebrew prophetic tradition in a way which links him to the mature Schoenberg'. But it is as if common features appear in mirror image. Schoenberg takes Wagner's call to heart, both religiously and musically: for Brown (1994: 57), he 'departed from the Brahmsian path of absolute music and turned to "New German" ideals', and in that as well as his conversion lies his sacrifice. The unconverted Schenker, by contrast, turns Wagner's critique back on the 'New Germans', not only increasingly transferring his allegiances to Brahms but also—arguably—sacrificing his developing career as composer, performer, and critic; this throws a new light on Schenker's supposed statement to Hans Wolf which I quoted in chapter 1 ('I composed quite a lot when I was young, and my things were successful; but when I saw how Brahms was misunderstood, I suffered so much that I dropped everything and set about writing my theoretical works').[95] Again, in a letter to Hertzka, Schenker writes of his 'pleasure in making sacrifices for a sacred cause'[96]—he is talking specifically of the Ninth Symphony monograph and op. 109 *Erläuterungsausgabe*—while a diary entry for 20 December 1931 says how, despite every conceivable

---

[92] Letter of 13 June 1933 to Dr Jakob Klatzkin, translated in Lazar 1994: 105.
[93] Letter of 4 August to Webern (see n. 91 above).
[94] Translated in Lazar 1994: 118n.
[95] See p. 85 above.
[96] Letter of 19 February 1914 (WSLB 200), transcribed and translated by Bent, Schenker Correspondence Project website, in which Schenker goes on to say that all sacrifices have their limit, and asks Hertzka to attempt to raise official funding for his work.

sacrifice, his mission has condemned him to worry and fear over his livelihood (Federhofer 1985: 44). But as I said, he never had a moment of truth in which he rediscovered his Jewish identity, presumably because he never forgot it in the first place; he does not seem to have had second thoughts about Zionism, and the nearest Schenkerian equivalent to Schoenberg's Zionist activism would perhaps be his rather fantastical attempt to mobilise 'a new generation of youth' through the *Tonwille* pamphlets—or his decidedly fantastical nomination of himself, in the second (1922) issue of *Tonwille,* as 'the educator of future generations of French musicians', a task he says he will undertake 'not in the French manner, but by the German way of truth'.[97] Actually Schoenberg's activism also belonged more to the realm of fantasy, or as Lazar (1994: 107) terms it, daydreaming, than reality: his plans to advance the cause of international Jewry sometimes read like something out of *Der biblische Weg,* for example when in 1946 Schoenberg imagines himself as the 'President of the Gov[ernment] in Exile of the Jewish Nation', recognised as such 'by all great powers and by most of the smaller nations', on board a ship donated to the cause by President Truman. Lazar (108) comments tellingly: 'Nowhere in Schoenberg's writings do we encounter any of the names of Jewish leaders who were involved in the political or military struggle of the time, be it Weizmann, Jabotinsky, or Ben Gurion'.

Yet there is, after all, a sense in which the idea of emigration might perhaps be applied to Schenker: what could be called 'inner emigration', were it not for the negative connotations that term has acquired as a result of Nazi collaborators using it to excuse their actions. (Joseph Lubben refers to Schenker's 'personal political exile' [1995: 85].) Just as, for the Jews of Galicia, the Germany of Schiller and Beethoven had come to represent an imaginary 'promised land of freedom' (Beller 1989: 164), not so much Germany as 'Germany'—just as, for Wagner, 'the true German Reich is a kingdom not of this world. It is not an earthly Zion' (Rather 1990: 216)—so there was an imaginary equivalent to political Zionism. And strangely, it was Herzl who articulated it most clearly, though only to his diary: 'No one thought of looking for this promised land where it is, and yet it lies so nearby. There it is: inside ourselves! . . . The promised land is wherever we carry it!'

---

[97] *TI* 45. As it happens, both Schoenberg and Schenker imagined themselves in ministerial positions after the First World War: Schoenberg (contributing in 1919 to a set of 'Guidelines for a Ministry of Art', the rest of which was authored by Loos) proposes educational reforms, the decommercialisation of concerts, and a major overhaul of copyright legislation, while Schenker (who actually imagines himself as 'Secretary of State for the Arts in German Austria') calls upon the musicians of Vienna not to emigrate to the West, on the grounds that 'those so-called cosmopolitan cities are nothing more than provincial towns by comparison to our Vienna, which has radiated out such shafts of purest genius as will not fade for millions of years' (Schoenberg 1975: 369–73, *TI* 47–8).

(Schorske 1980: 164). It is not impossible that Schenker read this, since Herzl's diaries were published in 1922, but that is not my point: rather I put forward this poetic image of hope beyond hope as an aid to our understanding of the final, and in some ways most disheartening, phase of the Schenker project.

5

Beyond Assimilation

Schenker's Rosenhaus

According to William Johnston (1972: 131), 'Aestheticism healed what politics abraded, uniting Jew and gentile, cabby and lord, beggar and emperor in common veneration for the arts'. He is talking about the open-air festivals that took place at the Prater (a legacy from the days of Beethoven that went on almost up to the 1914–18 war). 'Those who wonder why Vienna did not explode under racial and bureaucratic tension', he adds, 'should ponder this spectacle of all classes joining to celebrate ties that bound them'. Such festivals were then the outdoor version of those more intimate enactments of *Gemeinschaft* that I described in chapter 3 as taking place in the nostalgic space of the Bösendorfer-Saal, where—to repeat Leon Botstein's words—'player and listener alike . . . could become autonomous individuals, free from the limitations of birth and wealth'; the same might be said of such contemporary Viennese concert associations as the Wiener Konzertverein and the Vereinigung Schaffender Tonkünstler.[1] And among the barriers of birth which music could help to bridge was, of course, race. In fact the vision of chamber music as a social practice through which racial markedness

---

[1] Notley (1999: 59–63) documents the way these groups 'aspired to create a less distant, more interactive relationship with audiences', and cites the Erstes Wiener Volksquartett für Classische Musik (founded by August Duesberg), which invited audiences to vote on their concert programmes, aiming thereby to create an 'almost personal communication' between musicians and audience.

could be bracketed, if only for a little while, was replicated throughout Germany, to the extent that—as Philip Bohlman puts it (1991: 259)—'the history of chamber music in some German cities transpired largely within the Jewish community from the mid–nineteenth century until the 1930s'. Bohlman links this not only to the social dimension of chamber music as the symbolic and actual interaction of autonomous individuals but also to the aesthetics of absolute music: 'the absence of specific meaning within the text allowed meaning to accrue only upon performance', he says, 'thus empowering any group—for example, an ethnic community—to shape what it will from absolute music'.

In saying this, Bohlman is thinking along the same lines as the contemporary Viennese critic David Josef Bach, according to whom absolute music—unlike programme music—can speak to all classes because of its 'soulful' rather than 'intellectual' nature (Berkley 1988: 50), and this is a perhaps underemphasised aspect of the absolute versus programme music debate. But what Bohlman is describing (and goes on to relate to the role of chamber music in present-day Israel) is an example of a more general and widely recognised phenomenon. Steven Beller writes that 'if the Jew was still to cast off his Jewishness in an antisemitic social environment the assimilation would now have to take place on ground that was socially, nationally and ethnically neutral', with art and natural science being the prime examples (1989: 212, 214); he continues, 'when Karl Kraus sought a sanctuary from racial prejudice, it was to the world of *Geist* that he turned. In attempting to escape the problem of being Jewish, Jewish individuals retreated into the same world as their ancestors had inhabited, that of the intellect'. Just as Schenker's father had done in Galicia, so Schenker did this in Vienna, and in the last decade of his life it is tempting to suggest of him, as Peter Gay (1978: 33) does of Freud, that he 'lived far less in Austrian Vienna than in his own mind'. Though he does not specifically connect it to the Jewish context, Robert Morgan (2002: 273) makes a similar point by means of a quotation from Adorno (at that time living, like Schoenberg, in Los Angeles): 'For someone who no longer has a homeland, writing becomes a place to live'. And Morgan continues:

> Schenker, trapped in cultural and historical exile, created such a 'place to live': an alternative, self-contained Utopia, safely sequestered from outside events, where the 'great works' of the Western tradition, despite all inconsistencies and complexities, could be shown to coexist in a perfectly ordered system, with all their components joined in mutual cooperation, working with clockwork precision. Constructing such a system was not only an immanently modernist gesture, it was an immanently human and understandable one.

But the Jewish context adds a further dimension to this gesture. Marsha Rozenblit (2001: 156) speaks of the debate about Jewish identity that was prompted by the demise of the multinational empire: 'An endless stream of articles in the liberal and orthodox press', she writes, 'reflected the turmoil and conflict that accompanied the Jewish quest to reconstruct an identity that would fit changed political realities'. And it was precisely at this time that Jews of both Zionist and non-Zionist persuasions made the attempt to reconceive Jewish identity in terms of a political autonomy modelled more or less closely on that of the nation-state. David Rechter (2001: 12) comments that this 'experiment in Jewish autonomy' collapsed rapidly as the new nation-states came into operation, and so—in Rozenblit's words (156, 160)—the Jews of these nation-states effectively abandoned the attempt to forge a new identity, simply maintaining 'their old identity even if it did not fit the situation in the new nation-state'; in short, they 'retreated to the comfort of Jewish ethnic identity'. On the reading I offered in chapter 3, Schenker's contemporaneous essay 'Von der Sendung des deutschen Genies', generally seen as evidence of Schenker's political involvement, rather marks his disengagement from serious consideration of the politics of the real world: as an exercise in the politics of fantasy, with its constant emphasis on Germany and apparent unconcern with the practical situation of Austrian Jewry, it reflects a personal identity constructed through cultural assimilation. (Perhaps the clearest statement of this comes in the fifth issue of *Tonwille*, where Schenker writes: 'just as all of your imperialisms, your money-bags, foundations, trusts, businesses, armies, presidents, statesmen, and all your fathers and children are nothing before a short, tiny prelude by Sebastian Bach, so shall you be nothing before him who first heard and communicated this prelude, all of you, every one of you shall be nothing before me, a German speck of dust!' [*T1* 223].) If the comfortably ordered system of Schenker's theory as formulated in his final writings in this way represents a music-theoretical equivalent of Rozenblit's retreat from an impossibly chaotic world, then in its autonomy it might be seen as the translation of another Jewish dream, in its own way a promised land.

Other than a modest recrudescence of his journalistic activity from around the mid-1920s, with articles for a relatively broad readership in such journals as *Der Kunstwart*,[2] Schenker's principal output following the final issue of *Tonwille* (1924) is quickly summarised: the three volumes of *Das Meisterwerk in der Musik* (1925, 1926, and 1930); the analytical portfolio *Fünf Urlinie-Tafeln* (published in 1932 by Universal Edition and in the following year, as *Five Analyses in Sketchform*, by the David Mannes Music School, but now generally known by the title of the Dover Publications reprint, *Five Graphic Music Analyses*); the annotated edition of Brahms's *Oktaven u. Quinten u.A.*, produced for the composer's anniversary in 1933; and of course *Der freie Satz*, which was pub-

---

[2] The Munich-based journal *Der Kunstwart* became *Deutsche Zeitschrift* in 1931; it was in the latter that Schenker published his article of the same year on the pseudo-Mozart letter.

lished posthumously. But this picture is rather misleading, because *Der freie Satz* had been occupying Schenker since as early as 1917, when as I mentioned a very preliminary version of it was drafted in the form of a chapter for *Kontrapunkt 2*, under the title 'Freier Satz' (Siegel 1999); by 1920, Schenker was envisaging it as a third volume of *Kontrapunkt* (hence the notation 'II³' by which he sometimes referred to it, meaning the third volume of the second part of *Neue musikalische Theorien und Phantasien*). By 1925, it had become what it is now, the third and final part of *Neue musikalische Theorien und Phantasien*, with the title '*Der freie Satz*' first appearing a year later (*TI* 21n.), but even then it was subject to repeated redrafting and reorganisation, as testified by the enormous quantity of related material in the Oster Collection.[3] The manuscript was dictated to Jeanette—which may in part explain what Ernst Oster calls its 'poetic, sometimes almost rhapsodic quality' (*FC* I xii)—and according to his pupil Felix-Eberhard von Cube, Schenker 'took the manuscript everywhere with him, and never let it out of his sight' (Tepping 1983: 91). Schenker's diary records the difficult conditions under which he worked towards the end as his health gave way, and as I mentioned he finished correcting the proofs less than three weeks before his death on 14 January 1935. In his funeral address, Anthony van Hoboken wrote how the completion of *Der freie Satz* 'consumed his remaining strength. With it, the gigantic struggle of his life was completed'.[4] But it is not just the eighteen-year genesis and the timing of its completion that fulfils the mythological requirements for the work long seen by Schenkerians as the summit of its author's achievement: it is also an unevenness—particularly in the last stages of the book, where you have the impression that Schenker is racing against time—that has allowed plenty of scope for interpretation and appropriation on the part of subsequent scholars. (There is a parallel with such other highly influential works as Saussure's *Cours de linguistique générale* and Wittgenstein's *Philosophical Investigations*.)

First-generation Schenkerians, precisely because they saw *Der freie Satz* as the summit of Schenker's life's work, invested a great deal of effort into demonstrating not only its internal consistency but also the logical, if not inevitable, manner in which Schenker's earlier work led to it. Oswald Jonas saw *Der freie Satz* as 'the definitive form, indeed the codification of all Schenker's concepts' (*FC* I xvi); it was then only logical for him to claim that Schenker 'established his terminology (first the term "*Urlinie*") before he himself was able to arrive at a completely clear formulation of the concept'.[5] Yet this latter formulation carries with it the quite misleading implication that the later concept was al-

---

[3] Files 20–3, 35–8, 51, 74, 76, 79. The basic source for the early history of *Der freie Satz* is Siegel 1999.

[4] Loose typewritten sheet between OC 2/90 and 91.

[5] Jonas 1982/1934: xv.

ready latent in the original use of the term, just waiting to be discovered. These demonstrations sometimes crept into the editing of Schenker's writings, which as a result acquired something of the Talmudic depth I referred to in chapter 4: in the case of *Free Composition* (the English translation, or maybe one should say version, of *Der freie Satz*) it is necessary to disentangle the work of Schenker—and Jeanette, of whom Schenker wrote in a codicil to his will 'my work was her work as well'[6]—from that of Jonas (who revised Schenker's text for the second German-language edition, eliminating certain passages and adding some footnotes of his own together with a preface), Oster (who edited and translated Jonas's text,[7] again making some deletions and adding footnotes and a preface of his own), and John Rothgeb (who following Oster's death in 1977 translated most but not quite all of the deleted passages, relegating them to the notorious appendix 4, checked Oster's translation, and added further footnotes), not to mention the series editor (Gerard Warfield, who added a note explaining the above, though not quite accurately), and Allen Forte, who added an introduction to complement Schenker's own introduction.

As for the teleological dimension, this may be illustrated by the annotations added by Jonas to *Harmonielehre* (and retained in the 1985 English translation), which seek out anticipations of ideas elaborated in *Der freie Satz*, or even correct what Schenker wrote in light of his later theory. ('We have left the illustrations used by Schenker throughout the work as nearly as possible in their original form', Jonas writes in his introduction; 'We have added, however, an Appendix to this Introduction in which a number of illustrations are presented in the form which, according to all probability, Schenker would have given them at a later stage; and we have added the necessary explanations for this hypothetical development' [*H* viii].) Other, silent changes included the reordering of sentences and sometimes whole paragraphs, and significant deletions from Schenker's text. As William Drabkin (1973–74) was the first to point out, this kind of editorial bowdlerising—Drabkin was talking specifically about Jonas's version of the *Erläuterungsausgaben* of Beethoven's last sonatas but the point is a general one—amounted to a thoroughly unhistorical approach to Schenker's work, because it did not seek to interpret Schenker's earlier writings in their own terms and in light of contemporary circumstances: instead it postulated a normative version of 'Schenkerian analysis' (as in the title of Allen Forte and Steven Gilbert's *Introduction to Schenkerian Analysis*, based mainly on *Free Composition* and *Five Graphic Music Analyses*), which was assumed to

---

[6] It is this codicil, dated 25 May 1934, that directed that *Der freie Satz* should be dedicated to Jeanette (OJ 35/6).

[7] Oster's translation actually had its origins in a 'rough draft' Allen Forte had prepared but had not been able to place with a publisher; Forte handed it over to Oster in 1962 (Babbitt et al. 1977: 341).

be represented with greater or lesser accuracy and completeness in Schenker's different writings.[8] I put this in the past tense because there is now an established tradition (represented for instance by Joseph Lubben and Robert Snarrenberg) of viewing Schenker's writings in a historically informed manner, and so valuing for their own particular strengths and weaknesses the different musical insights represented by the different phases of Schenker's theorising. While what I have to say about *Der freie Satz* falls within this tradition, I begin—again prompted by Morgan—by viewing Schenker's last book as a literary work, and against the background of other literary works.

Morgan (2002: 267–70) situates Schenker in the context of the Austrian novelists of the period after the First World War, like Hermann Broch and Robert Musil, whose works reflect the fragmentation of established value systems and of a sense of individual identity; as he puts it (269), 'Schenker resembles Musil in his conviction that the new world arising from the rubble of the past has been deprived of its essential connections: it is all surface, fragments, lies. And both men react with corresponding despair to the surrounding chaos'. Morgan contrasts this with the late Schenker, who 'finds escape, but only into a private realm, its order hidden beneath the surface, accessible but to a privileged few'. This might in turn prompt direct comparison with other German-language novels of the period—Hermann Hesse's *Das Glasperlenspiel* (The glass bead game) of 1943 would be an obvious candidate—but the retreat into what Carl Schorske calls 'the garden' was an established trope of earlier Austrian literature. Schorske (1980: 281–95) chooses as his principal example Adalbert Stifter's novel *Der Nachsommer* (The Indian summer) of 1857—as the date might suggest, a nostalgic evocation of the time before 1848, just as writers after 1918 attempted to evoke the prewar years. It takes the form of a *Bildungsroman* in which the protagonist, Heinrich Drendorf, seeks refuge from a storm and so stumbles upon the Rosenhaus: a country estate owned by Freiherr von Risach, who becomes Heinrich's 'mentor and surrogate father' (289), to the description of which most of the novel is devoted. The Rosenhaus is, as Schorske says (288), 'the central symbol of Stifter's

---

[8] Because it is so self-evident by present-day standards that Drabkin's position is right, and that the Jonas/Oster position represents a basic failure of scholarly practice, it is worth quoting Edward Laufer's arguments (1981: 163) against the reinstatement of (most of) the deleted passage from *Der freie Satz*: 'Regrettably', he writes, 'in a well-intentioned but misguided act of scholarly rectitude, all of Ernst Oster's excisions from Schenker's text were restored, in an appendix. Any curious person could always consult the German edition. Oster's deletions were carefully considered and within his right as an editor. In all cases they involved irrelevant, speculative material, sometimes of a metaphysical nature: interesting, to be sure, but having nothing to do with the musical discourse and only obfuscating the artistic and philosophical positions. And, one might add, they provide grist for the malevolent'. Laufer's argument that people can always read the original seems perverse: why then translate it at all?

social ideal, a Paradise Regained'; it is a lexicon of *Gemeinschaft* values presented in the context of nostalgia for the Vormärz, full of resonances with Schenker's work. It epitomises the Beethovenian aristocracy of the spirit for which Schenker (like Schoenberg) yearned, its artful horticulture operating just as music does in Schenker's world, by harnessing the forces of nature to 'create a setting of beauty for the flowering of the human spirit' (289). Risach even devotes himself to reconstructing and restoring the masterpieces of the past, in the form not of music but of old art objects and furniture, 'removing the overlay of later ages . . . to purify the works that could edify the spirit' and so 'keeping the past alive' (291). As Schorske comments, Risach is in this way 'not a creator but a curator', and so the Rosenhaus has 'the character of a museum': it represents 'an essentially static harmony of elements from which man, by his labor, eliminates the dissonance' (292, 291, 309).

Schenker was an avid reader of Stifter—there are notes on Stifter in both the Oster and Jonas collections[9]—and, though it would be absurd to push the comparison too far, it is possible to read *Der freie Satz* as a music-theoretical analogue to Stifter's novel. Schenker's last book has a kind of narrative organisation that none of his others have, an organisation that subordinates empirical reality to abstract idea. Rather than structuring it, as he easily might have, in the form of a narrative quest from foreground to background—in other words, as a kind of music-analytical detective story—Schenker takes the reverse course: *Der freie Satz* is organised as a journey from the background to the foreground, from the abstract to the concrete. Its three parts deal successively with the background, the middleground, and the foreground, in the manner of the late *Tonwille* and *Meisterwerk* analyses to which I referred in chapter 1 (and in this chapter I am picking up on the music-theoretical narrative I there traced up to the 1920s). Although the detailed organisation within each part varies, there is a common plan that moves from the general to the particular (so that in part II, for instance, chapter 1, 'The middleground in general', is followed by chapter 2, 'Specific characteristics of the middleground'). And more than that, Schenker attempts as far as possible to organise the discussion of particulars along parallel lines within parts II and III: there is an exact correspondence between sections 1–15 of chapter 2 of each part, except that one additional section (on voice exchange) is interpolated in part III. As was commonly the case with his analyses, however, the part concerning the foreground is considerably longer than the others, including additional chapters entitled 'Specific foreground events', 'Meter and Rhythm' and 'Form' (the last two being in most people's estimation the least developed parts of the book).

---

[9] The Oster Collection includes a large collection of papers in a wrapper marked 'Stifter' (OC 12/176–248), but only two pages appear to concern the novelist, the rest being on miscellaneous topics. I am not the only reader of Schorske to have been struck by the parallel between Stifter and Schenker: see Snarrenberg 1992: 124 and 1997: 150.

All this can be understood as charting a process of individual growth, similar to a *Bildungsroman,* but there is a further aspect to Schenker's abstract-to-concrete plan which can be illustrated in terms of the opening chapter, the first two sections of which are 'The concept of background in general' and 'The background in music'. Beginning this way has two advantages for Schenker. In the first place, it means that he can present the masterworks of music as the direct outcomes of ideal, first principles, and in this way the very structure of the book embodies Schenker's favourite analytical ploy of showing how the music had to be precisely as it is—a strategy which, in the context of art history, has been termed 'retrospective prophecy' (Lorda 2000: 120), and to which I shall return later in this chapter. It might not be too extreme to say that this operates as a kind of conceptual censorship: the contingencies of reality are admitted only to the extent that they can be derived from first principles (no more than in the Rosenhaus is there room in *Der freie Satz* for such 'counter-examples'—Schenker's term [*MM2* 106]—as Reger or Stravinsky). In the second place, it makes clear right from the start that, while at one level the book is about music, at another level its scope is far broader: within the first few pages Schenker has told us that 'music mirrors the human soul in all its metamorphoses and moods', that the motion of the fundamental line is 'a full analogy to our inner life', that 'music is *subject,* just as we ourselves are subject', and even that fundamental structure and foreground represent 'the celestial and the terrestrial in music'.[10] In this way *Der freie Satz* creates its vision of music as not just music but the emblem of an aristocratic world in which art and nature work together harmoniously, from which dissonance is, if not eliminated (as in the Rosenhaus), then harnessed firmly in the service of consonance, and in which the masterworks of the past live again. It is as much an evocation of the Vormärz as *Der Nachsommer,* which is also to say that it evokes a time when it was possible to be both Jewish and German.

The problematic or at least unproductive nature of Stifter's utopia is obvious enough, in its cultural elitism, its uncreative nature, its lack of concern for empirical reality. (Schenker himself made the last criticism: in a sheet of notes about *Der Nachsommer* from 1927 he writes, 'Stifter presents the most complete purity and chastity. . . . It is as if he fulfils our dreams of Paradise', and then adds 'everything is transferred into the inner life. . . . This inner life is so much in the foreground that in *Nachsommer* Stifter, immersed in it, even fails to give the artistic form its foreground.')[11] And the point is that all of these are accusations which have at one time or another been levelled against Schenker, and especially against the Schenker of *Der freie Satz.* The cultural elitism is perhaps the most obvious. Inherent from an early stage in Schenker's

---

[10] *FC* I xxiii, 4, 9, 160; the last remark, removed to app. 4 in *Free Composition,* would otherwise have come on p. 5.

[11] This sheet, headed 'Schenker über Stifter', is in the Jonas Collection (OJ 21/3).

theory, Schenker's obsession—no other word will do—with genius, and concomitant dismissal of nongenius, reaches a climax in the 'Vermischtes' section of the final volume of *Meisterwerk:* 'Verdi was only a talent', he proclaims, and as such 'contributed absolutely nothing to genuine art', while Debussy 'would not rate as a composer at all'. And he adds that the 'vanishing of the genius' this illustrates is 'very welcome to the commonplace man, for the spectacle of towering superiority disturbs his cosy self-complacency' (*MM3* 71–3). Schenker's tirades from this period retain the tone of passionate critique from 'Von der Sendung' but, instead of being to some extent focused—however unrealistically—around the politics of the First World War, they are now directed scattergun-style at any and all aspects of contemporary culture: despite their sometimes furious expression, they seem increasingly disengaged from the world about him, conveying the sense that Schenker no longer saw himself as a participant in the culture he was criticising—which is of course exactly the point Morgan was making about Schenker's later theory when he described him as 'on the outside looking in'. (When in *Tonwille* 8/9 Schenker refers to 'the sun-storm of synthesis which raged through German art for two centuries' [*T1* 106], he is presenting it as a historical event now receding into the past, and himself—like Risach—as a curator of the masterpieces it left behind.) And while much of the anger has gone under the surface in *Der freie Satz*—the polemics are sublimated or at least abbreviated, and the personal attacks have disappeared, apart from a few sentences on Riemann—the basic subject position remains.

As for the second and third criticisms—lack of creativity and concern for empirical reality—these were already being voiced during the later years of Schenker's life. As early as 1924, replying to a letter in which Schenker had used the derogatory term 'foreground music' (*Vordergrundmusik*), August Halm—who was an active composer as well as theorist—called this a 'good expression', adding that he would accept it as a characterisation of his own music 'with much modesty as well as some pride. That is, I have long since believed that the foreground, or surface, has been neglected at the expense of the background'.[12] Four years later, an article by Hans Mersmann complains about the 'rigidity and unproductivity' of Schenker's approach in general and the *Urlinie* in particular, while the more sympathetic Hermann Roth suggests in 1931 that Schenker's theoretical interest in the ubiquitous manifestations of the *Urlinie* now outweighs his analytical concern with the music.[13] But these criticisms were spelt out more fully in

---

[12] Letter of 6 May 1924 (OC 12/15–7), transcribed and translated by Lee Rothfarb, Schenker Correspondence Project website.

[13] Mersmann, 'Zur Erkenntnis der Musik', *Melos*, April 1928, p. 179 (OC 2/78); Hermann Roth, 'Bekenntnis zu Heinrich Schenker', *Hamburger Nachrichten*, 17 September 1931 (OC 2/84).

what might be termed a critical obituary published by the American composer Roger Sessions just before the appearance of *Der freie Satz* (though it is evident that Sessions had prepublication access to it). Sessions is at pains to recognise the value of Schenker's work: he ends his article by saying that 'the musicians of today and tomorrow . . . will derive much profit and help from the clear and profound conceptions in Schenker's earlier works'—and then adds, 'just as they will turn away from the Talmudic subtleties and the febrile dogmatism of his later ones' (1985/1935: 13–4). It is perhaps predictable that a composer would bridle at the ex-composer's claim to define the necessary attributes not just of classical composition but of all composition: Schenker, Sessions complains (12–3), 'envisages creation as the painstaking and meticulous embodiment of principles that were once vital and in process of development, but whose very definiteness and, so to speak, formulability proclaims either their insufficiency or their exhaustion'. (Had Schenker still been alive, the comment on formulability, echoing his own early critiques of the 'formalists' and 'classicists', would no doubt have particularly infuriated him.) And Sessions continues: 'It is precisely when Schenker's teachings leave the domain of exact description and enter that of dogmatic and speculative analysis that they become essentially sterile': as he puts it a couple of pages earlier, at such times Schenker's interpretations appear to be 'dictated by the impulse to find confirmation for an a priori assumption, even when one must admit that this assumption was arrived at only after years of painstaking research' (11). In short, the complaint is that Schenker's later theory goes too far: it represents theory for theory's sake.

This may sound like little more than the classic standoff between artist and theorist (itself a telling observation, given Schenker's concern at the time of *Harmonielehre* to style himself as an 'artist'). But Sessions's basic criticism—that Schenker's later theory is just too abstract—can be expressed in a more precise and technical manner. What makes possible the abstract-to-concrete approach of *Der freie Satz* is more than anything the development of the archetypal *Ursatz* as found from *Meisterwerk* on, that is to say as a predefined, a priori entity in one of its three forms (with the *Urlinie* descending from $\hat{8}$, $\hat{5}$, or $\hat{3}$ to $\hat{1}$). David Neumeyer (1987: 276–8) has traced the process of codification through which the idea of the *Urlinie* became more and more narrowly defined: whereas early *Urlinien* are as likely to ascend as descend, or to do both (as in the case of the *Tonwille* graph of the *Kaiserhymne* I mentioned in chapter 3), descending *Urlinien* become increasingly prevalent during the successive volumes of *Meisterwerk*, in the last of which Schenker states as a matter of established fact that the *Urlinie* falls from $\hat{8}$, $\hat{5}$, or $\hat{3}$ (1930: 7). And William Pastille (1990: 71–2) has chronicled the development of this archetypal concept of the *Urlinie*, via the intermediate concept of melodic fluency ('a principle . . . of shaping melodic lines so that successions of large leaps are avoided'), from what is in a sense its diametric opposite: the motif, conventionally understood as the most compact embodiment of what is characteristic or unique to a given piece of music. The difference emerges from a revealing annotation Schoenberg entered in his copy of 'Die Urlinie: Eine Vorbemerkung' (from the first issue of *Tonwille*, apparently the only one he acquired). It should be possible to say what the *Urlinie* is in one sentence, Schoenberg writes, and as Schenker has failed to do this he will attempt it himself:

> The *Urlinie* is the uniform reduction of all appearances to their simplest base and shows not only the characteristics of the ideas brought to their common unity, but also that it is in its entirety only a development of the basic idea. It is the real inspiration of the composer, that totality, seen all at once and yet containing everything of substance, through which a piece of music is conceived as a whole by its author.[14]

Schoenberg added that 'More could be said, but that would then be more by me than by Schenker'—yet he had already said enough to underline the difference between his own, essentially traditional, understanding of the motif and Schenker's concept of the *Urlinie*. (Perhaps the most striking feature they have in common is the apparent imprint of pseudo-Mozart.) Moreover, Schenker's development of the *Urlinie* concept resulted in a redefinition of the motif: by 1925 Schenker's use of the term no longer refers to characteristic melodic formations but rather to 'the constituent transformative elements of Schenker's method—that is, linear progressions, arpeggiations, octave transfers, and the like' (Cadwallader and Pastille 1992: 132). To paraphrase what I said earlier, characteristic melodic formations are recognised only to the extent that they can be derived via these transformations from the *Urlinie*, and so it is only logical that in *Der freie Satz* Schenker now adopts the term 'diminution', leaving 'motif' as a pejorative term associated with 'false theory'. Schenker's view is now that, as conventionally defined, there are no such things as motifs.

In fact, Schenker's theoretical development could be characterised as a progressive denial of the basic categories of conventional theory (and this is the key to the reputation for iconoclasm to which I referred). In a sense, this goes back as far as the attacks on the 'formalists' or 'classicists' of the 1890s—attacks directed ostensively at composers but equally denying the musical reality of the pedagogues' formal schemes. However, the tendency becomes much more striking

---

[14] Translated in Dunsby 1977: 32. Reporting on an interview with Hans Weisse, the American critic Irving Kolodin (1932: 51) defined what he transcribed as the '*Ear-line*' in very similar manner: 'a pattern which is inherent in the thematic germ of the music, and which can be traced through the composition from beginning to end, and to whose inner life the composer's life is inseparably linked'. Schenker's scrapbook contains a copy of this article (OC 2/86), together with a translation in which Schenker has picked out the phrase corresponding to 'a pattern which is inherent in the thematic germ of the music'.

with the appearance of the *Urlinie*. In 'Die Urline: Eine Vorbemerkung', Schenker writes that 'all the various divisions and classifications such as classical, Romantic, programmatic, absolute, and the like, disappear in the face of the Urlinie, since these are biased by personal feeling or historical understanding' (*T1* 21–2): the *Urlinie*, in other words, pertains to a higher, indeed timeless, domain of musical reality than individual response or historical contingency. The list has become longer by the second volume of *Meisterwerk*, where we find Schenker announcing: 'Triads and seventh chords, dissonances, passing notes, sequences, progressions, melodies, motives and motivic developments, imperfect and perfect cadences etc., as understood by conventional theory, are simply not present in music' (*MM2* 59). And by the time of *Der freie Satz* it has turned into a refrain. Paragraph 50 is headed 'Rejection of the conventional terms "melody", "motive", "idea", and the like'; elsewhere (*FC* I 131, 8) Schenker denies the reality of conventional categories of form ('I reject those definitions of song form which take the motif as their starting point and emphasize manipulation of the motif by means of repetition, variation, extension, fragmentation, or dissolution') or key ('the most baleful error of conventional theory is its recourse to *"keys"* when, in its lack of acquaintance with foreground and middleground, it finds no other means of explanation').

The example of key is particularly revealing because the theoretical basis—the idea that what are conventionally seen as subsidiary keys should instead be seen as the expansion of scale steps within a single structural key—is already present in *Harmonielehre*, but applied quite differently from in *Der freie Satz*.[15] In a section of *Harmonielehre* called 'Theory of modulation', Schenker writes:

> Modulation means a complete change from one key to another. This change must be so complete that the original key does not return. In this lies the only essential difference between modulation and those changes to chromatically simulated keys which are changes only apparently, while in reality they are a fuller elaboration of a strictly diatonic scale-step, whereby the diatonic system must be assumed to continue. (*H* 321)

The distinction between appearance and reality, between simulacrum and the real thing, is in place. But Schenker uses it to make fine distinctions between one context and another (he then goes on to subdivide true modulations into three categories, each separately discussed and illustrated), and recognises the psychological effect of chromatic simulation; one might say that it is in the tension between appearance and reality that the analytical work is done. And at least as late as the

---

[15] One difference, of course, is that the analytically crucial idea of linear motions generating 'surface' keys developed subsequent to *Harmonielehre*. But this does not affect my argument.

final issue of *Tonwille* one can find similar, contextually informed discussions of whether a particular key is to be regarded as apparent or
real.[16] But by the time of *Der freie Satz* all this pussyfooting has been
swept away, subsumed under the category of 'illusory keys at the foreground level'.[17] (Schenker cites bar 12 of the *Kaiserhymne* as an example.) He explains what is at issue as follows:

> The coherence of the whole, which is guaranteed by the fundamental
> structure, reveals the development of one single chord into a work of art.
> Thus, the tonality of this chord alone is present, and whatever else we may
> regard as a key at the foreground level can only be an illusory one. . . . The
> error in the viewpoint of present-day theory consists in its mechanical
> reading of the degrees at their face value. This can only obstruct the per-
> ceptions of coherence. (*FC* I 112)

The effect of this is that a discourse designed to make fine discrimina-
tions has been replaced by a dichotomous, totalising one: keys are illusory or real, surface or background, black or white.[18] As Carl Schachter
says (1999b: 150–1), in his very balanced discussion of this whole topic,
'Schenker minimizes possibly valid distinctions between large-scale,
structural modulations and smaller, local ones. . . . Between these large
structural key changes and the fleeting tonicizations that some authors
call modulations, there is a vast range of possibilities.' But the dichotomies of *Der freie Satz* do not make it easy to capture this range of
possibilities; the result is a discourse that might be described as ideological in the sense that, whatever is said, the effect is to assert the universal validity of the theory that informs it. And it is also in *Der freie Satz*
that Schenker makes what Richard Cohn (1992a: 9) has characterised
as 'wild attempts' to subsume hitherto untheorised aspects of music
such as orchestration and instrumentation under the 'complete control' of the *Urlinie*. (It was in the preceding *Meisterwerk* volumes that
Schenker had attempted the same in relation to dynamics and, however perfunctorily, rhythm.)[19] To say it again, the theory does not so

---

[16] See for instance Schenker's discussion of the modulations to E minor and C major
in Schubert's G Major Impromptu D. 899 (op. 90), no. 3 (*T2* 139).

[17] The 'simulated' keys of the *Harmonielehre* translation and the 'illusory' keys of the
Der freie Satz translation both correspond to the same word (*Scheintonarten*).

[18] Suzannah Clark (1999: 96–9) has made a related point in her discussion of the relation between the 'surrogate' keys of *Harmonielehre* (*H* 250) and the 'illusory' keys of *Der
freie Satz*; see also the discussion of Schumann's 'Wenn ich in deinen Augen seh'' below.

[19] See the dynamic markings in the foreground graphs of the Largo from Bach's
Sonata no. 3 for Solo Violin BWV 1005 and the Prelude from the Partita no. 3 BWV 1006
(*MM1* 35, 42–3): the markings above the stave represent dynamics generated at the surface, those below it dynamics generated at the middleground, with the performer's job
being to combine these in an appropriately balanced manner (*MM1* 37–8). Schenker's
urge to subsume dynamics within the overall synthesis goes back to his astonishing statement in the Ninth Symphony monograph that if that work had 'come down to us without explicit indications, a capable hand would have had to enter the dynamic markings

much register as define what counts as musical content; put crudely but not I think inaccurately, the counter-examples of Reger and Stravinsky are counter-examples because their music is not music, and it is not music because it doesn't fit the theory—so that, after showing the lack of adequate composing-out in a passage from Stravinsky's Concerto for piano and wind instruments, Schenker can conclude that 'My demonstration gives me the right to say that . . . Stravinsky's way of writing is altogether bad, inartistic, and unmusical' (*MM2* 18). And it is in this sense that one may talk of Schenker's final theory being unconcerned with empirical reality; in the end, Schenker decides what is music in the same sense that Lueger decided who was a Jew.

In referring to the dichotomies inherent in *Der freie Satz*, I meant to imply an affinity with the patterns of conservative thinking I described in chapter 3, in which one term of the dichotomy is always valorised at the expense of the other. Lubben has emphasised the way this happens in Schenker's writing even as early as *Tonwille*, for instance in the opposition of real (positive) versus apparent (negative): Lubben (1995: 56–7) cites such phrases as 'misled by . . . appearance', 'merely coincidental', 'nothing more than'. Cohn (1992b: 8–9) similarly quotes a passage from *Meisterwerk* which expands this into a principle: just picking out notes from the foreground is meaningless, Schenker says, unless the tones can withstand 'the test of counterpoint [*der Satzprobe*]! The only valid conclusion is that which can be verified through the voice-leading transformations'.[20] Anything that fails this test, Cohn comments, is 'illusory, apparent, false, and even nonexistent. . . . to fail the Satzprobe is to be denied any ontological status whatever'. (Schenker virtually says this in his Stravinsky analysis: 'the only surety even for dissonances—and this is the crux of the matter—is the cohesiveness of a well-organized linear progression: without cohesiveness, dissonances do not even exist!' [*MM2* 18]) The objection is obvious: something may be merely coincidental in terms of theoretical derivation while at the same time being highly striking in terms of moment-to-moment experience, in which case the substance of the analytical observation will lie in the tension between the one and the other. In *Der freie Satz*, for example, Schenker dismisses conventional ideas that sonata developments involve 'changing keys' or the '"working out" [of] "motivic" materials' (his quotes), adding that 'none of these . . . rooted as they are in the "motivic" concept, are pertinent for the development section' (*FC* I 136): but of course changing keys and the working out of motives are what listeners hear. However sophisticated the theoretical grounding,

---

exactly as Beethoven himself did'. For rhythm see *MM2* 68, with a further apparent reference in *FC* I 15 (para. 21).

[20] *MM1* 107; for obvious reasons Cohn quotes from the Kalib (1973: 2:140–1) translation.

such sweeping denials, prompted by the language of 'merely' or 'nothing more than', lead to an approach towards analysis that is careless, at best, about what people actually hear when they listen to music.

In *Tonwille*, as Lubben argues, the problem is more at the level of rhetoric than of substance: there is a dynamic interaction between empirical observation and theoretical explanation (and I shall come back to this), of a kind that is largely absent from *Der freie Satz*, with its constant motion *from* the theoretical *to* the empirical—and with the empirical being grasped only to the extent that it illustrates the theory. There is in *Der freie Satz* no obvious feedback mechanism that might enable an empirical counter-observation to result in modification of the theory, for how could mere appearances change reality? From the very beginning—from 'The concept of background in general'—the theory is presented as simply how music is. If there is no space for counter-examples in *Der freie Satz*, there is no room for doubt either. Cohn (1992b: 8) describes Schenker as a 'monist'—which is what prompted my comparison with Rabbi Boruch in chapter 4—and this quality is underlined by the prophetic tone as much as the overt content of an excluded exclusion from *Der freie Satz* that I quoted in chaper 2: in both art and religion, says Schenker, there is

> only *one prime cause* in the background . . . so-called heathens are those who, whether creative or re-creative, consider only the foreground of the work and lose themselves in its particulars, while confessors of a true divinity are those who worship the background. In the artwork, too, the one prime cause remains immutable in the background, and deviating toward the cravings of the foreground heathens is a sin against the spirit of monotheism.[21]

An argument might of course be made that all this is the case not because some reductive transformation had come over Schenker's thinking by the time of *Der freie Satz*, but because the purpose of *Der freie Satz* is to draw together the many theoretical threads dispersed through Schenker's earlier publications: it is a work of systematic exposition rather than analytical application, the argument goes, and the empirical justification of the theory is to be found in the *Erläuterungsausgaben*, the *Tonwille* and *Meisterwerk* analyses, and *Fünf Urlinie-Tafeln*. (Edward Laufer describes *Der freie Satz* as 'a compendium . . . a treatise to be assimilated continually, ever more sharply, in conjunction with making and remaking one's own sketches' [1981: 158].) The idea that *Der freie Satz* is, in effect, a reference manual for the Schenkerian system does not adequately explain the kind of monism Cohn refers to, which is not a matter of literary genre but a basic habit of thought; even if it did, though, the problem would simply resurface in terms of the way *Der freie Satz*, or at least *Free Composition*, has been treated by many subse-

---

[21] Translated in Snarrenberg 1997: 154.

quent theorists as the definitive model for a reified Schenkerian practice. (Recall what I said about Forte and Gilbert's *Introduction to Schenkerian Analysis*.)

Many interpretations of Schenkerian analysis are reductive. A case in point is the idea already anticipated in Schoenberg's interpretation of the *Urlinie* as the concentrated essence of a work, a kind of musical stock cube that results from boiling off everything that is merely routine. Some such conception underlies the complaints made by Joseph Kerman in his widely read *Contemplating Music:* Schenkerian analysis, Kerman says (1985: 81–2), 'repeatedly slights salient features in the music' (he cites the omission of the low A in Schenker's reduction of the 'Ode to Joy' tune)[22] and 'ignores rhythmic and textual considerations' (here Kerman cites the following note, the syncopated F#, also omitted by Schenker). The counter-argument is obvious: the substance of the analysis lies not *in* the analytical graph, on the stock cube model, but in the experience it prompts, in the shuttling back and forth between the actual music and the reduction—which is also to say between the obvious and the nonobvious, the particular and the general, the empirical and the theoretical. (As regards the A, there is an even more obvious counter-argument, which is that Kerman has ignored the context of Schenker's analysis: Schenker is saying that the 'Ode to Joy' is a kind of compound melody containing its own bass progression, so that the A actually *is* in the graph, the point being that it appears in the bass.) And Schachter (1999b: 148) makes a similar argument in the discussion of Schenker's concept of key to which I have referred: comparing graphs of the Allemande from J. S. Bach's French Suite no. 4 and the first movement development from Beethoven's Sonata op. 7, he writes that 'to a casual reader' they 'might look pretty much the same. But anyone reading the Beethoven graph correctly—with ears as well as eyes—will *hear* the difference'. Kerman's problem, then, is that he is not reading the graph correctly; he is using his eyes and not his ears. It is the same problem Schenker was complaining about in his 1894 essay 'Das Hören in der Musik', only translated to a new context.

Although I think Schachter's argument is valid (I have made the same argument myself),[23] it isn't the end of the story. Schachter continues, 'And of course the analyst could easily refer to the key plan in a text accompanying the graph', in this way anchoring the graph in the particularities of the music. But then, it was Schenker who, in 1933, initiated the practice of wordless analysis with *Fünf Urlinie-Tafeln:* 'The presentation in graphic form', Schenker wrote in his foreword, 'has now been developed to a point that makes an explanatory text unnecessary'.[24] (It would probably be misguided to see in this an echo of the

---

[22] *FC* II fig. 109 e3.
[23] See e.g. Cook 1989b: 131–5.
[24] Schenker 1969/1933: 9.

logical positivism promulgated by the Vienna Circle, or even a rejoinder to the last sentence of Wittgenstein's *Tractatus Logico-Philosophicus:*
'What we cannot speak about we must pass over in silence'.) What
Schenker says may be true for the experienced Schenkerian analyst,
but the wordless presentation does nothing to orientate the less experienced reader to the purpose of the analysis; it is perhaps unfortunate
that, because of the low-cost reprint edition by Dover Publications, *Five
Music Graphic Analyses* was for a long time the most widely disseminated
of Schenker's publications. And there are other contexts, too, in which
Schenker could display a distinct lack of regard for the legitimate interests of different readers.[25] At one point in the Ninth Symphony monograph, for instance, he quotes a passage from Hermann Kretzschmar's
Führer durch den Konzertsaal (1887) and comments witheringly:

> Kretzschmar would undoubtedly have fared better if, instead of the
> plethora of words—'brief moment', 'happy frolic', 'elements of weary
> longing', 'stifled', 'cheered on', 'forceful strokes'—, he had, while main-
> taining the same brevity, provided concepts of truly orientational value,
> such as 'modulatory theme', 'second theme', and so forth. (*BNS* 159)

Schenker's point is basically the one Hanslick argued in *Vom Musikalisch-
Schönen:* the basis of an understanding of music's expressive properties
must be an understanding of its musical properties. But Hanslick's argument was about the proper scope of aesthetic theory. When he wrote
reviews for the *Neue freie Presse*, as Peter Kivy (1993: 274–5) has pointed
out, he wrote quite differently, because he was writing in a different literary genre for a different public. In the same way, Kretzschmar's *Führer
durch den Konzertsaal* was written, like Hirschfeld's Vienna Philharmonic
concert programmes, for new audiences of inexperienced listeners
seeking means of engaging with unfamiliar music, and the publication
and dissemination history of Kretzschmar's book shows that it was successful in this role. Schenker seems incapable of appreciating that it
is legitimate for different readers to have different requirements, or
more likely he was ignoring it for the sake of a perhaps cheap rhetorical effect.[26]

---

[25] In a letter to Hertzka concerning the second (1908) edition of *Ornamentik,*
Schenker makes the telling remark that he is concerned 'always to offer the reader the
best that my knowledge and the truth have to offer, less perhaps out of regard for the
reader than in fulfillment of the subject matter itself' (letter of 26 August 1908, WSLB
16, transcribed and translated by Bent, Schenker Correspondence Project website).

[26] As it happens, two contemporary critiques pasted into in Schenker's scrapbook
make exactly this point: Hans Friedrich ('Über Musikkritik', *Der Merker,* 1 December
1917, p. 794) writes that hermeneutical approaches are appropriate to certain audiences,
adding that Schenker would have to adopt them if he were a newspaper music critic,
while a presumably slightly later and apparently derivative article by Eberhard Freiherr
von Waechter ('Von moderner Musik, modernen Musikern und moderner Musikkritik',
Das Neue Österreich 1, 62) claims that 'the music critic of a daily paper has no other choice

There is also a parallel case to which Snarrenberg has drawn attention, and where the problem runs deeper. This is in the *Meisterwerk* 1 (1925) essay on the Prelude from Bach's Partita for Solo Violin no. 3, where—in addition to experimenting with dynamic analysis—Schenker attacked Ernst Kurth's concept of linear counterpoint. (Here, incidentally, is a further point of contact with Schoenberg [1975: 289–97], who wrote two unpublished essays attacking Kurth's approach, while characteristically explaining that he had not read his book.) In essence, Kurth describes how the music's thematic contours generate and dissipate energy (his writing is full of words like 'highpoint', 'nadir', and 'culmination'). Schenker complains about Kurth's 'continual deliberate evasion of any precision in concept and word', ascribing this to 'his basic viewpoint that melodic construction . . . is an independent force' (*MM1* 51): motion, Schenker continues, is 'more than motion pure and simple', it is motion from somewhere to somewhere else, and these places are defined by the structural harmonies. Misled by false theory, Schenker continues, 'Kurth clearly failed to find the power of hearing necessary to comprehend those horizontal realizations of vertical chordal conceptions'; instead of reading the music in a musical sense, he just looked at it, observing that 'here the notes go upward, there they go downward (these being the only two possible directions)'. And against Kurth's literary evocation of the effects of the theme from the B Major Fugue from Bach's *Das Wohltempierte Klavier* (Book 2), Schenker sets his own, severely technical interpretation, consisting of a voice-leading graph together with a verbal commentary that succinctly identifies the tonal spaces traversed by the various linear motions, and points out that in order to accommodate the combination of a third- and a fourth-progression Bach has recourse to a 5–6 exchange (*MM1* 52–3).

It is at such moments as this that Schenker seems to draw closest to the 'positivist' (Kerman's term) theorists of postwar America—such as Milton Babbitt—who played such an important role in the afterlife of the Schenker project, and to whom I shall return in the next section. Snarrenberg's point, however, lies in what Schenker does *not* say. Unlike Kurth, Schenker specifies the contrapuntal origins of the theme. But having done so, as Snarrenberg observes (1997: 137), 'Schenker says nothing at all about the character of the melodic motion that he has charted. . . . He does not describe the effect of the line created by an unfolding of the contrapuntal complex, that synthesis of the effects of sustained harmony, passing motions, and unfolding'. And Snarrenberg continues: 'Ordinarily I would argue that this is not so much a failure as an oversight or simply the result of a limited purpose. But not

---

but to resort to hermeneutics', adding that 'hardly anyone else is so capable of inspired hermeneutical dreams as the sensitive and perceptive Heinrich Schenker!' (OC 2/53, 2/54).

here, where the content of the thematic line is precisely what is at issue in his critique of Kurth'. He points out that in this respect Kurth's description was in fact highly compatible with Schenker's own analysis, and suggests that Schenker may have stopped short because of 'the risk of sounding too much like Kurth'. That would of course tie in with the anxiety of influence I read into the Ninth Symphony monograph, where—in order to distance himself from Wagner—Schenker blatantly contradicted himself, refused to understand apparently self-evident musical issues, and passed in silence over perhaps the most baffling and frequently discussed moment in the entire symphony (the beginning of the *Alla Marcia* section of the finale).[27] But it may equally be seen as an early symptom of the more abstract, less empirical orientation of Schenker's thought in his final years. The problem, to bring this argument back to its starting point, may not after all lie only in how later theorists have read *Der freie Satz*.

In the next section I will pursue the story beyond Schenker's death by tracing both the subsequent development of the totalising tendencies I have identified in *Der freie Satz* and the reaction against them. But first I want to complete the job I started by comparing *Der freie Satz* to Stifter's *Der Nachsommer:* after all, denigrating the totalising tendencies in the final phase of Schenker's thought is a cheap gesture unless accompanied by a genuine effort to understand them as a product of historical circumstance. Stifter's novel exemplifies the nostalgic and escapist strand present in Viennese culture since the Vormärz, and the circumstances of Vienna in the interwar period help to explain its attraction at that time. I have said that the 1920s and 1930s were a time of growing chaos in Austria, with deep divisions between Vienna (from 1919 under a Social Democratic mayor, Jakob Reumann) and the rural areas dominated by the Christian Socialists; there were riots at the time of the Fourteenth Zionist Congress (1925) and again in 1927 (the 'Justizpalast' massacre). Both socialist and conservative factions formed their own armies; the Austrian Parliament was suspended in 1933 (the same year, of course, as Hitler's accession to power in Germany), and in 1934 the country slid into civil war. If Schenker's retreat, as Morgan put it, into a 'self-contained Utopia, safely sequestered from outside events, where the "great works" of the Western tradition . . . coexist in a perfectly ordered system' represented an act of escapism—what in the previous chapter I called an 'inner emigration' into a kind of musical Rosenhaus—then this is neither incomprehensible nor unparalleled: the same kind of creeping detachment from an intractable reality can be identified in, for example, Hans Kelsen, a Bohemian Jew who studied law at the University of Vienna (and subsequently at Heidelberg,

---

[27] Cook 1995: 94–8; see p. 86 above.

with Georg Jellinek) and taught there from 1911 to 1929, as well as being responsible for drafting the Austrian federal constitution in 1920.[28]

As with Jellinek and Ehrlich, whom I discussed in chapters 1 and 3, it is easy to find points of comparison between Schenker's thinking and Kelsen's. In particular, there is an obvious parallel between Schenker's hierarchical theory of music and Kelsen's analysis of the operation of Habsburg law, in which there were multiple levels of jurisdiction 'from *k. und k.* ministries down through Austrian ministries and those of individual crownlands to municipalities' (Johnston 1972: 97): Kelsen developed what he termed a 'pure theory of law' consisting of autonomous 'norms' against which actual laws were to be measured and evaluated, giving rise to a strict hierarchical system the topmost level of which Kelsen called the '*Urnorm*'. This abstract-to-concrete approach, similar to Schenker's in *Der freie Satz*, represents just the opposite of Jellinek's and Ehrlich's historical approach, according to which the starting point for any theoretical understanding of law must be detailed study of actual legislative systems in real social contexts, and which I compared to Schenker's early approach to music: if Kelsen's thought represented a reaction against Jellinek's and Ehrlich's, then perhaps *Der freie Satz* should be considered as much a reaction against Schenker's earlier thought as a continuation or summation of it. Johnston (98) continues, 'Against a welter of ideologies and maneuvers prevailing here below, Kelsen counterposed seamless unity in a higher world of norms', adding that 'he paralleled members of the Vienna Circle who elevated logic into a self-contained science while jettisoning whatever did not fit their premises'. He links Kelsen's way of thinking not only to the general influence of Plato, but more specifically to the tradition of Leibnizian idealism which Schenker's teacher Robert Zimmermann helped to disseminate throughout the Austro-Hungarian empire almost into the twentieth century (Zimmermann died in 1898)— and indeed, instead of Kelsen, I could have invoked others whom Johnston includes in his chapter entitled 'Last Exponents of the Leibnizian Tradition', such as Othmar Spann, whose reinstatement of *Gemeinschaft* values was accused of tending towards totalitarianism, and of whom Johnston (314) says that he 'shared political naiveté with countless other professors in Germany and Austria, for whom studying the history of ideas had obfuscated political reality'. This then is the tradition that underlies such characteristically Schenkerian pronouncements as 'tones, just like stars in the firmament . . . have but few primal laws which remain as immutable at their core the more mutable, indeed in their mutability the more bewilderingly they objectify them-

---

[28] Details from Johnston (1972: 95–8), on which the following draws; Alpern (forthcoming) refers to Kelsen only briefly, but explores the idea of what he calls Schenker's 'federalized bureaucracy of free counterpoint' in some detail.

selves in individual phenomena'[29]—and, if I am right, the basic conception of *Der freie Satz*.

But there is a problem here. In this book I have repeatedly emphasised the dependence of Schenker's thought on Hegelian principles, or at least generalised principles of German idealism that can be illustrated by reference to Hegel. Even something as basic as the controversy between Schenker and Schoenberg has to be understood in terms of competing Hegelian constructions of music history: Schoenberg does not just think in terms of progress towards an as yet not fully envisaged future, but explicitly invokes the Hegelian dialectic ('Even if our tonality is dissolving, it already contains within it the germ of the next artistic phenomenon'),[30] whereas Schenker—like Spengler—sees the contemporary world as one of decline, with the period from Bach to Brahms representing a singular and now irrecoverable event in human history. That is what I meant when, in chapter 1, I said that you need some awareness of idealist philosophy to understand the form the argument takes. But the problem is one I also mentioned in chapter 1: we are now on the verge of conflating two quite different philosophies of idealism. Michael Cherlin (1988: 130, 131) emphasises the foundational role of Hegelian historicism in Schenker's thought, and argues on this basis that to read Schenker 'in Platonic or Neoplatonic terms is . . . untenable': as he explains, 'a Platonic reading of a Schenkerian graph does violence to that graph by viewing it as a static, atemporal blueprint. Organicism, in order to include teleological organicism, requires that the process of unfolding in time be a necessary aspect of reality'. And from a philosophical point of view, Cherlin's argument is irrefutable: in Frederick Beiser's words (1993: 276), you cannot at the same time believe with Plato or Leibniz that 'the object of thought is an eternal form, complete in all its meaning prior to our reflection on it', and with Hegel that 'the meaning of ideas is never complete and given to us, as if it were only a question of our perceiving their transparent essence. Rather, they become clear and distinct and take on a determinate meaning only through our activity of thinking about them'.

But then, Schenker was not a coherent philosophical thinker, the reason being (as I argued in chapter 1) that he was not a philosophical thinker at all. Or perhaps a more generous way of putting it would be that Schenker encountered both strains of idealism as a student at the University of Vienna—most obviously from Zimmermann on the one hand and Jellinek on the other—but failed to resolve the tension between them.[31] Either way, the fact is that, despite the indisputable role in Schenker's thinking of idealism of the Hegelian type, the profoundly

---

[29] Draft letter dated 29 December 1916 from Schenker to Halm (OC 1/B9, version 1), transcribed and translated by Rothfarb, Schenker Correspondence Project website.

[30] Schoenberg 1978/1911: 97.

[31] It is evident from Alpern's thesis that the history of nineteenth-century German-

un-Hegelian idea that there exist such things as eternal, unchanging ideas, removed from the circumstances of the world, is scattered throughout his writings: its best known formulation may be the passage from *Der freie Satz* I quoted at the beginning of chapter 1 ('whoever has once perceived the essence of a pure idea—whoever has fathomed its secrets—knows that such an idea remains ever the same, ever indestructible, as an element of an eternal order'), but as early as the *Geist* essay of 1895 Schenker is claiming that 'the material of the art of music is imperishable' (p. 330). While we cannot save Schenker as a philosopher by arguing that he switched allegiance from one coherent version of idealism to another, then, it does seem as if the Platonic or Leibnizian version was particularly associated in Schenker's mind with the developing *Urlinie* concept. At all events, Schenker specifically invokes both Plato and Leibniz in relation to the *Urlinie:* in his first systematic explanation of it ('Die Urlinie: Eine Vorbemerkung') he writes that the composer 'assigns his tones a merciful fate full of agreement between the life of each individual tone and a life that exists above and beyond their being' and adds in parentheses 'like a "Platonic idea" in music' (*TI* 22),[32] while in *Meisterwerk* 1—as it happens just a few paragraphs after the passage about the *Satzprobe*—Schenker writes that 'the Urlinie, to apply Leibniz's concept, is the preestablished harmony of the composition' (*MM1* 109).[33] I shall come back to the contradiction at the heart of Schenker's thinking which this suggests when, in the next section, I discuss the posthumous reception of Schenker's theoretical ideas.

What then are we to make of Schenker's project by the time of his death? In chapters 1–2, I presented it as something more than (but also, in its early stages, less than) a theory: a comprehensive and integrated agenda for musical reform, encompassing composing, performing, listening, writing, teaching, and editing. And in subsequent chapters I suggested that the project was not only a musical one but also and at

---

language jurisprudence could be written largely in terms of these opposing principles: 'Legal Germanism', Alpern writes, 'represented a humanistic, pluralistic, and moralistic conception of law rooted in historical time and space, in opposition to the rational, systematic, universal, and dehumanized abstractions of natural law, Roman jurisprudence, and crystalline generalizations of the Napoleonic Code'. He also cites Rudolf von Jhering's satirical description of the latter as 'an abstract, insular, and logically consistent "heaven of juristic concepts"', a formulation reminiscent of Johnston's 'heaven of ideas' (see p. 32 above).

[32] This might be considered an update to the vision of the composer as 'jurist' (Alpern's term) in *Harmonielehre* (see p. 195 above).

[33] See p. 32 above. It might also be possible, though here I am being entirely speculative, to see one of the sources of Schenker's theory of levels in an attempt to combine Hegelian historicism with the Zimmermannian idea of timeless aesthetic norms, which I mentioned in chapter 2 in relation to Schenker's contemporaries Hirschfeld and Adler. Botstein writes (1985: 1105), with specific reference to Hirschfeld: 'The conceit that the musical text had an objective spirit rested on the notion that the proportions and essence of melodic shape and dynamics, genuine phrasing and tempi, which all created a sense

the same time a social one, with music functioning as both a symbol and a means of enacting *Gemeinschaft:* in this way a theory of music that shows how the interests of part and whole may be reconciled is also a theory of the organic society, a *Gemeinschaft* of the spirit rather than the blood (and that is where the anti-Semitic dimension comes in). But the whole fabric of the project as I have interpreted it begins to unravel after the First World War. The first symptom is the totalising tendency that appears in Schenker's hysterical panegyrics of Germany and fulminations against its enemies, possibly tending towards a susceptibility to 'strong man' solutions to political chaos. This totalising impulse then becomes progressively reflected in the theory, with the *Urlinie* being seen in an increasingly abstract manner, underpinned by a Platonic or Leibnizian concept of the timeless. Ironically, then, as the power of the theory to model the interaction of part and whole increases, so Schenker's own orientation seems to become more narrow and schematic, and as this happens the social dimension of the theory withers away: we end up not with the Schenker project as I have described it, but rather with what *Der freie Satz* has traditionally been seen as—a work of music theory, throughout which are scattered a large number of rather gratuitous remarks pertaining to philosophy, religion, society, or the individual.

More than anything, perhaps, this amounts to a transition from optimism to pessimism, and we have already encountered some of the principal milestones in this process (here I am developing what I said near the end of chapter 2). The *Geist* essay of 1895, as I interpret it, is a plan for action, even though much of what it promises is as yet undeliverable: it is future-oriented, as when Schenker explains the nature of properly critical listening and then adds, 'it is to be hoped that the majority of listeners will eventually experience music in this way' (p. 324). By the time of *Harmonielehre* (1906) the agenda has solidified, while the orientation to the future remains and has indeed become more urgent: logically it would have been better to present his planned work on counterpoint first, Schenker says in his preface, but 'Any delay, however small, in initiating the needed reforms seemed to me to be counterindicated' (*H* xxvi). Yet just two years later, in the first volume of *Kontrapunkt,* the agenda has become one of disaster management: 'our first task must be a real excavation before we can even begin work that

---

of form and narrative, were somehow constant elements beneath a surface of individual and time-bound historical musical conventions'. Seen in this light, Schenker's theory would be an elaboration of Botstein's 'somehow', with the background—the level of pure (or German) musical logic—corresponding to constant, timeless norms, and the foreground to changing historical styles. If there is anything in this—the most one can say is that Schenker and Hirschfeld were acquaintances and in 1907 actually discussed the influence of time on musical technique (Federhofer 1985: 301n.)—then the element of historical change increasingly dropped out of the equation as the theory developed.

will allow us to proceed (I do not say: "progress"!)' (*C1* xxv). And after a further two years, in the Ninth Symphony monograph, Schenker refers to the 'dark hour of crisis' (*BNS* 25), continuing: 'I fear that in the artistic life of the German nation the generation of those fathers who lived in the second half of the nineteenth century have played an all too fateful role! May their children succeed in averting the calamity!'

Even this gloomy prognosis can be presented in a more positive light: in a letter to Hertzka of the same year, Schenker writes, 'Only when it is all long gone—the Debussys, Korngolds, Schoenbergs, Rétis, etc.—will the time have come for me and what I represent.'[34] (This, predictably, is a prelude to discussion of fees.) And after the First World War, in 'Die Urlinie: Eine Vorbemerkung'—the first musically oriented essay of *Tonwille*—Schenker seems to outline a new plan for action when he writes that 'The nadir of musical art was already reached long ago' and speaks of performing a great service to the art 'in the foreseeable future. . . . The hour of turning back has tolled' (*T1* 24). Only a year later, however, in *Kontrapunkt* 2 (1922), we find the bleakest assessment of all, which I quoted in chapter 2: music has been 'utterly eradicated', Schenker writes, so that 'Today the task before us is more to transmit the essence of music to more distant eras, since we cannot expect it to be restored in the near future' (*C2* xii). In *Der freie Satz*, Schenker's prognosis has not really changed, but it is expressed more elegiacally: 'If, after centuries have passed, only one person is once more capable of hearing music in the spirit of its coherence, then even in this one person music will again be resurrected in all its absoluteness' (*FC* I xxiv). Despite the dangers of selective quotation, the broad picture is clear enough: by 1935 the vision of renewal belongs more to fantasy than reality, and Schenker has retreated into his Rosenhaus.

A paragraph away from that last quotation in the original edition of *Der freie Satz*, but now removed to appendix 4, Schenker wrote:

> But how strange it is: mankind is more interested in the most distant star in the universe than in music, the star of the spirit's heaven! May the light of that noble star shine on! It surely is captured and protected in my eyes, but what will happen when my eyes have closed for good? (*FC* I 158)

The Posthumous Schenker

In an unjustly neglected dissertation on the philosophical and music-theoretical background to Schenker's work, Barbara Whittle (1993: 321–2) suggests that it was because of his lack of success as measured in money, fame, or prestigious appointments that Schenker came to see himself in terms of the Romantic mythology according to which ge-

---

[34] Letter of 9 June 1912 (WSLB 120), transcribed and translated by Bent, Schenker Correspondence Project website.

niuses are unrecognised in their own time. 'To have endured the most extreme poverty was a blessing for me', he told von Cube in 1928, continuing: 'I am very proud to have thus been marked out by fate. For it became my happy duty to set a spiritual plus against the material minus. . . . Only by serving the spirit faithfully and selflessly was I able to find what was granted from above for me to find'.[35] (He even remarked in the same letter that his death would be the 'first precondition' for the wider success of his theories.) Schenker's followers were also inclined to see him this way, and the result is that—as William Drabkin (2002: 835) and Ludwig Holtmeier (2004: 248) have both noted—there is still a tendency to underestimate the extent of Schenker's impact while he was alive, not only in Vienna but beyond.

One way to dispel this impression is simply to flick, or rather scroll, through Schenker's scrapbook in the Oster Collection (OC 2): his compositions, arrangements, performances, editions, and publications received a significant amount of critical attention, mainly though not exclusively in Austrian and German newspapers and periodicals. (Contrary to Schenker's allegations against Universal Edition, the scrapbook contains some handsome display advertisements for his publications.) There were in the first place supporters who published sometimes extensive profiles of Schenker and his work, in particular Walter Dahms and Otto Vrieslander, with both of whom Schenker was in close personal contact. Dahms, who was the author of books on Bach, Schubert, Schumann, and Mendelssohn, is represented in the scrapbook by a series of articles and reviews published between 1913 and 1928: he is a proselytiser rather than an independent commentator, and the same might be said of Vrieslander, who is represented by publications from 1922 on. (As we saw in chapter 3, the one exception to this concerned Schenker's politics.) Then there are commentators who retain a greater critical distance from Schenker's work while at the same time strongly supporting its general thrust: the most obvious example is August Halm, who maintained an extensive correspondence with Schenker— they never met—but, unlike Dahms or Vrieslander, was a theorist of distinction in his own right. (In chapter 3 I also quoted his sharp criticism of Schenker's political views; he could be equally outspoken about Schenker's musical judgements, writing of Schenker's critique of Berlioz in *Tonwille* 5 that 'such derogatory condemnation is not permissible without specifying precisely what is meant. . . . And even then one should consider whether the same clarity cannot be achieved with less harsh language.')[36] Perhaps more telling, however, is the sheer num-

---

[35] Letter to von Cube dated 29 April 1928 (vC 14), transcribed and translated by Drabkin, Schenker Correspondence Project website.

[36] Letter of 1 April 1924 (OC 12/13–4, transcribed and translated by Rothfarb, Schenker Correspondence Project website); Schenker's remarks about Berlioz may be found in *T1* 189–90. This is a rare case of Schenker clearly respecting someone who dis-

ber of references to Schenker—often carefully underlined—in articles on a variety of general musical matters ranging from analytical method, performance, and the phenomenology of music to Beethoven, Schubert, Brahms, and more contemporary composers. There are even two instances of the word *Urlinie* finding its way into journalistic criticism: in 1925 'E.B.' praises a Philharmonic concert on the grounds that 'what Heinrich Schenker calls the *Urlinie* of an artwork, the unity of theme and compositional structure, was grasped by the conductor', while in 1928 a review of Krenek's *Jonny spielt auf* invokes the *Urlinie* as a symbol of the highbrow concerns of contemporary German culture ('here flowers still a knowledge of the *Urlinie* of all music, the secret of its origin').[37]

But it is the many reviews of his editions and theoretical works that give the fullest insight into Schenker's reputation during his lifetime. In some ways they are as variable and contradictory as the reviews of Schenker's compositions I consigned to a note in chapter 1, particularly in terms of the responses to Schenker's polemics. 'H.L.', writing in 1903 about *Ornamentik*, sees Schenker's attacks on Bülow and other virtuosos as 'healthy sideswipes' adding to the enjoyment of the work (and continues, 'seldom does a knight of the musical spirit, armed to the teeth with knowledge and true love, grasp his problem so well and with such daring'); a decade later, Bruno Schrader says that Schenker 'should be thanked for his bravery in taking a stance against the false teachings of the Leipzig music-prophet Riemann'.[38] For other critics, by contrast, Schenker's polemics are 'overly sharp'; Hermann Wetzel, who in 1909 complained of *Ornamentik* that the polemics are 'too heated' (adding 'he works himself up where only the driest, calmest presentation can convince'), explained five years later in a review of the op. 109 *Erläuterungsausgabe* that 'it is not the fact that Schenker criticizes which I dislike, it is rather the hurtful, personally agitated tone'.[39] At the same time, critics saw Schenker's unwillingness to recognise the value of others' work as the flip side of his deep personal commitment to music.

---

agreed with him: 'Each time I see a work of yours', he wrote in a postcard dated 22 January 1927, 'the feeling comes over me that we two, despite all, would find ourselves in close accord if only we could first speak with one another (instead of writing)' (DLA 69.930/14, transcribed and translated by Bent and Rothfarb, Schenker Correspondence Project website).

[37] E[lsa] B[ienenfeld], 'Philharmonisches Konzert', *Neues Wiener Journal*, 17 March 1925 (OC 2/64); H[ans] L[iebstöckl], 'Krenek spielt auf', *Die Stunde*, January 1928 (OC 2/74). In a 1920 review of Walter Niemann's *Johannes Brahms*, Bienenfeld (otherwise known as a supporter of Schoenberg) had called Schenker 'the most significant theorist of the present day' (*Neues Wiener Journal*, 20 June 1920, translated by Bent, Schenker Correspondence Project website).

[38] *Illustriertes Wiener Extrablatt*, 18 September 1903 (OC 2/5), *Die Zeit am Montag*, 25 March 1913 (OC 2/29).

[39] 'F.S.', in *Musikpädagogische Zeitschrift*, 1912 (OC 2/29); Wetzel, *Die Musik*, January 1909 (OC 2/4); and *Die Musik*, 15 March 1914 (OC 2/40).

I have already quoted Halm's statement (from 1917) that Schenker 'did not practice polemics out of personal inclination' but rather let himself be 'destined for such a duty by the crisis', and there are other, similar views: an unidentified reviewer of the 'Chromatic Fantasy and Fugue' edition complains about Schenker's dismissive attitude to artists whose Bach 'transcriptions' he does not like, but goes on to ask how one could hold this against someone who fights for his beliefs, and whose only reward is that others take what he has done and proclaim it as their own.[40] This review, undated but probably from 1910, is one of the first to present Schenker in the light of a missionary, a tendency that grows stronger with the passage of time, especially among his closest adherents: in 1926 Dahms justified Schenker's polemics by likening him to 'a lonely individual who hears no echo of his voice' and hence shouts louder and louder, going on to describe him as 'a spiritual leader' who 'moves towards the light',[41] while I have already cited the memorial article in which Viktor Zuckerkandl refers to the Schenkerian campaign against falsifications of art as 'almost a religious war'.

In any case, the disagreements mask basic responses to Schenker's work that are more or less ubiquitous. Even those who have serious reservations about Schenker's work recognise its seriousness of purpose and attention to detail—particularly in relation to the Bach editions, the *Erläuterungsausgaben,* and the Ninth Symphony monograph, which appear to have been the key works in the forging of his reputation. Indeed, an anonymous reviewer of the Ninth Symphony monograph, writing in 1913, goes as far as to say that it is high time the universities recognised Schenker and offered him an appointment: this anticipation of Furtwängler's letter to Karpath twenty years later, which I mentioned in the introduction, was no doubt prompted by general knowledge of Schenker's failure to obtain a position at the Conservatory.[42] As it happens, an article mentioning this, which dates from the previous year, appears on the preceding page of the scrapbook.[43] And the fact that this was reported in the German press strongly suggests that Schenker's profile was higher than his mythologisation as unrecognised genius would have it. At the same time, his exclusion from the academic establishment became an essential element of that myth. Equally characteristic then is the claim that, as Snarrenberg (1997: xvi) puts it, Guido Adler (who as I mentioned in chapter 2 occupied the chair in music at the University of Vienna from 1898 to 1927) 'did what he could to check Schenker's influence, even for a time keeping Schenker's writings out of his seminar reading-

---

[40] *Wiener Mode* (OC/21).

[41] Dahms, 'Schenkers "Meisterwerk in der Musik", *Allgemeine Musikzeitung,* 24 December 1926 (OC 2/72).

[42] 'Beethovens neunte Symphonie', *Neues Wiener Tagblatt,* 7 April 1913 (OC 2/29).

[43] Hugo Ganz, 'Die Wiener Woche', *Frankfurter Zeitung,* 3 July 1912 (OC 2/28).

room'; this is based on two of Schenker's diary entries for 1914, entries that might alternatively be read as reflecting Schenker's readiness to buy into conspiracy theories—or to contribute to the process of his own mythologisation.[44]

Ayotte's (2004) research guide lists twenty-four articles in German during the ten years after Schenker's death, as well as four in English. But the twenty-four articles in German are not evidence of broad dissemination: they were all published in *Der Dreiklang: Monatsschrift für Musik*, a short-lived journal coedited during 1937–38 by Schenker's former pupils Oswald Jonas and Felix Salzer.[45] Conceived in order 'to venerate Schenker's memory and interpret his work',[46] *Der Dreiklang* contained published and unpublished articles and extracts by Schenker, articles by members of the Schenker circle (but mainly Jonas), and—in several issues—'Aphorisms' culled from such writers as Goethe, Kant, Schopenhauer, and Schenker himself. If this last feature harks back to the *Vermischtes* section of the *Tonwille* and *Meisterwerk* volumes, the title of the first article in *Der Dreiklang* I makes an explicit link with *Tonwille* 1: written by Salzer, it is entitled 'Die historische Sendung Heinrich Schenkers' (The historical mission of Heinrich Schenker), and in some ways anticipates the postwar Americanisation of Schenker—to which I shall soon turn. Salzer presents Schenker as reformulating nineteenth-century musical insight in the form of twentieth-century theory (the word he uses is *Lehre* or teaching), and thus acting as a bridge between one artistic epoch and another: even if we live in a period of decline, Salzer argues, such periods can give rise to highly original artists, and there are those who have been inspired by Schenker's own work to anticipate a new flowering of tonality (Salzer 1989/1937: 8–11). Such relatively optimistic views were not exceptional even among Schenker's closest supporters: a 1914 article by Dahms, which lampoons the idea of musical 'progress', nevertheless concludes that 'our music of today . . . is only an episode. We shall gain a better music', while in 1920 Halm says that he does not share Schenker's pessimism, but adds that his views should be taken seriously and draws the obvious parallel with Spengler.[47]

[44] The diary entries, for 29 May and 24 October 1914, are transcribed in Federhofer 1985: 50–1: they record that Schenker's pupil Hans Weisse—who also studied in Adler's class—told him on two separate occasions that Adler was keeping Schenker's works from the students. Schenker adds that the reason was 'the comment in *Harmonielehre*', which according to Federhofer may relate to a passage on Reger omitted from the English translation.

[45] All nine published issues of *Der Dreiklang* (really seven, but two were double issues) were reprinted in 1989 by Georg Olms Verlag (Hildesheim).

[46] Letter of 9 March 1935 from Jonas to Jeanette Schenker (OJ 12/6 [43]), translated by John Rothgeb, Schenker Correspondence Project website.

[47] Dahms, 'Musikalischer "Fortschritt"', *Neue Preussische (Kreuz-) Zeitung*, 9 April 1914 (OC 2/41); Halm, 'Heinrich Schenkers "Neue musikalische Theorien und Phantasien"', *Der Merker*, 1 September 1920, p. 506 (OC 2/55). Schenker, characteristically, was less gen-

The conventional Schenkerian history has it that only in its Americanised form was it possible for Schenker's theory to enter the academy. Yet there was more penetration of German-speaking musical academia than the mythology allows, both during Schenker's lifetime and up to the Second World War. We know from the documentation of Schenker's dispute with Universal Edition that university music departments at Berlin, Bonn, Breslau, Frankfurt, Freiburg, Göttingen, Halle, Königsberg, Leipzig, and Munich all took out subscriptions to *Tonwille* during 1924–25 (*T2* viii). And as early as 1927, on the occasion of his pupil Reinhard Oppel's appointment to the Leipzig Conservatory, Schenker wrote to Felix-Eberhard von Cube that 'the effect continues to broaden: Edinburgh (also New York), Leipzig, Stuttgart, Vienna (myself and Weisse), Vrieslander in Munich (he is writing a long monograph about me), yourself in Duisburg, and Halm, etc., etc.'[48] (It is at this point that Schenker makes one of his most celebrated remarks, though usually only the first sentence is quoted: 'All this shows that, in spite of Schoenberg and Hindemith, the hour has struck for us, too, but this hour will last an eternity because it bears the truth, not merely a fashion. Oppel will receive 700 marks for twenty hours of teaching; the Vienna Academy certainly does not pay as well.') Then there was Jonas at the Stern Conservatory in Berlin between 1930 and 1934, while in 1931 von Cube and Moriz Violin established a private but short-lived Schenker-Institut in Hamburg.[49] A second Schenker-Institut was set up at the New Vienna Conservatory in 1935, the year of Schenker's death; it lasted until 1938, when Jonas, Salzer, and Violin all emigrated in the wake of Hitler's annexation of Austria.[50] (That was also why *Der Dreiklang* folded.)

The real issue, as Holtmeier (2004) has made clear, is not so much that Schenker's ideas never became established, but that they were eliminated during the Third Reich, along with so much of the rest of the predominantly Jewish music-theoretical tradition. In 1934 von Cube was forced out of his position at Hamburg, apparently by those who saw Schenker's theory as 'Jewish propaganda'.[51] In 1939 the the-

---

erous about Halm, describing his *Von zwei Kulturen der Musik* as 'a downright grotesque mixture of technical and the most far-flung aesthetics' (diary entry for 17 March 1914, transcribed and translated by Bent and Rothfarb, Schenker Correspondence Project website).

[48] Letter of 1 June 1927 (von Cube family collection, vC 10), transcribed and translated by Drabkin, Schenker Correspondence Project website). Vrieslander's monograph never appeared.

[49] For further details see Matthews 2001 (Jonas); Jackson 2001 (Oppel); and Drabkin 1985, where information on the Schenker-Institut may be found on pp. 187–8, Tepping 1982, and Tepping 1988 (von Cube).

[50] See Fink 2003, which is the main source for information on Schenkerian analysis in Vienna following Schenker's death.

[51] Letter of 7 June 1934 from von Cube to Schenker (OJ 9/34 [41]).

ory was held up as an example of Jewish intellectualism by the influential musicologist Wolfgang Boetticher, and—as I said—the following
year Schenker was listed in Stengel and Gerigk's *Lexicon der Juden in der
Musik,* with the comment that his 'basic ideas were widespread' (Berry
2004: 435–6); Schenker was named, too, in the 1944 book *Judentum
und Musik* by Karl Blessinger, who spoke disparagingly of his 'fabulous'
Urlinie (Holtmeier 2004: 251). And after the war, Schenker's rabid nationalism worked against the kind of rehabilitation Schoenberg en-
joyed: as Holtmeier puts it (249), 'Thanks to the Third Reich, Schenker
the politician was able to wipe out Schenker the theorist from public
awareness in Germany'. In Vienna, Franz Eibner put on seminars and
courses on Schenker during the 1950s and 1960s at both the old and
the new conservatories, while Jonas taught on a visiting basis up to the
1970s (Fink 2003). But in Germany, partly as a result of sustained hostility from the highly influential Carl Dahlhaus, there was a lengthy
hiatus in the study of Schenker. It would be fair to say that until 1991,
when Martin Eybl was appointed to the University of Vienna, the only
postwar Schenkerian scholars in the German-speaking countries to attract international attention were Hellmut Federhofer (a Jonas pupil
who started his academic career in Graz but later moved to Mainz), and
perhaps the less prolific Eibner and Karl-Otto Plum.[52] It is only very recently, under the influence of younger scholars such as Holtmeier, that
this situation has begun to change.

Although there was one Schenker adherent in the United Kingdom (John Petrie Dunn, who taught at Edinburgh University, was not
a pupil but had studied Schenker's writings), the exodus to the United
States prompted by the Anschluss meant that the story of the posthumous Schenker was an almost exclusively North American one—at
least until around 1980, when Schenkerian analysis first became established in other English-speaking countries, particularly the United
Kingdom, and after that in parts of continental Europe.[53] William Rothstein's 1986 article 'The Americanization of Heinrich Schenker' is the
classic overview of the story of the American reception—or transformation—of Schenker, while an ongoing series of studies by David Carson Berry (2002 and 2003) is filling in many of the details, so my summary of its externals can be brief. I mentioned that a connection had
been forged with America through Schenker's pupil (from 1912) Hans

---

[52] A polemical exchange between Dahlhaus, Federhofer, and Plum, which took
place in 1983–84 and was sparked off by Dahlhaus's review of Federhofer's 1981 book
*Akkord und Stimmführung in den musiktheoretischen Systemen von Hugo Riemann, Ernst Kurth
und Heinrich Schenker,* conveys the barricaded nature of Schenkerian debate in Germany
at this time (Federhofer puts Dahlhaus's hostility to Schenker down to his admiration for
Schoenberg): the exchange is summarised in Puffett 1984.

[53] And beyond: visiting Shanghai Conservatory in the late 1980s, I discovered to my
embarrassment that I had pitched a lecture on Schenkerian analysis at much too low a
level for my audience.

Weisse: while still in Vienna he taught a number of American students (including William Mitchell), but the beginning of Schenkerian analysis in North America is usually traced to 1931, when Weisse was offered a post at the David Mannes Music School in New York, since 1953 the Mannes College of Music.[54] (That explains why *Fünf Urlinie-Tafeln*—which Weisse used in his teaching—was copublished by the Mannes School.) Weisse would no doubt have had more influence on the subsequent history of Schenkerian theory had he not died in 1940, but he was replaced at the Mannes School by Felix Salzer, who had studied with both Weisse and Schenker (and also, like Weisse, with Guido Adler at the University of Vienna): Salzer's *Structural Hearing: Tonal Coherence in Music*, published in English in 1952, remained until the 1970s the principal English-language source for Schenkerian theory (or at least Salzerian theory, which was not always the same thing). Prior to this, in 1938, Oswald Jonas, himself the author of a German-language introduction to Schenker's theory,[55] had emigrated to the United States, teaching from 1941 at Roosevelt University (Chicago) and later at the Riverside campus of the University of California—as had Jonas's pupil Ernst Oster, who taught at the New England Conservatory and subsequently at Mannes College. (By this time Salzer had moved on to Queens College, since 1961 part of the City University of New York, which together with Mannes is the leading international centre for work on Schenker today.) And of course the fact that so many of these obtained positions in American higher education made it possible for them in turn to train the next generation: Weisse, who as I mentioned had taught Mitchell before leaving Vienna, taught Adele Katz, for example, while John Rothgeb studied with Jonas, Carl Schachter with Salzer, and Edward Laufer with Oster.

While this network of first- and second-generation pupils represented a strategic base for the development of Schenkerian theory in North America, a key role in its dissemination was played by Allen Forte, who himself taught at Mannes College from 1957 to 1959 before moving to Yale University; together with Milton Babbitt, of whom more shortly, it was Forte who was 'instrumental in bringing Schenker firmly into the Ivy League' (Rothstein 1990a: 199). And more than anyone else, it was Forte who transformed Schenkerian theory from something with the qualities of an at times embattled religious sect into

---

[54] Detailed information on Weisse's pedagogy may be found in Berry 2003. One of the not so familiar parts of the story is that Schenkerian ideas were already circulating in the United States prior to Weisse's arrival, as represented by the work of Victor Lytle, George Wedge, and Carl Bricken, who had also studied with Weisse in Vienna: Berry discussed this in '*Verborgene Wiederholungen?* Schenker's (Hidden) Influence in America before Hans Weisse and the Mannes Vanguard', paper presented at the annual meeting of the Society for Music Theory, Seattle, 11–14 November 2004.

[55] *Das Wesen des musikalischen Kunstwerkes: ein Einführung in die Lehre Heinrich Schenkers* (1934), translated into English as Jonas 1982/1934.

a contemporary American college subject, combining it with his own approach to atonal music to produce the still more or less standard 'Schenker and sets' conformation of academic music theory. As Patrick McCreless has argued (1997: 22), Schenkerian theory 'helped the theory teacher transform into a music theorist': one reason for its success, then, was its efficacy in furthering a post-war institutional agenda, the transformation of what had been seen as essentially service teaching into a research-based discipline. The integration of Schenkerian theory into American higher education also disposed of the traditional idea that it had to be taught through a one-to-one apprenticeship (hence the genealogies through which the older Schenkerians, like concert pianists, were identified by reference to their teachers—preferably with an unbroken line of succession going back to Schenker himself). Again this development is associated with Forte, culminating in the *Introduction to Schenkerian Analysis,* which I have already mentioned.

I referred to the 'external' story of the posthumous Schenker: it is the language of American Schenkerian theory that provides the 'internal' story. In his 'Americanization' article, Rothstein (1990a: 198) compared the rhetoric of the founding fathers of Schenkerian analysis: he characterised Schenker's own tone as that of an Old Testament prophet, Jonas's as poetic and philosophical, Salzer's as authoritative and kindly, and Forte's as that of the 'cool taxonomist'. (It is only fair to Rothstein to point out that he characterises his own characterisations as 'oversimplified'.) He also told the full, or nearly full, story of the notorious appendix 4 of *Free Composition,* consisting as I have already said of the polemical and mystical passages from *Der freie Satz* which Jonas and later Oster excised in order to protect Schenker's reputation in American academia, and which after much argument were finally included but not reinstated to their original locations—which, of course, meant that Schenker's critics could find all the most incriminating passages in one place, without the trouble of reading the rest of the book. (What Rothstein for some reason did not mention is the excluded exclusions.) Most telling, however, is the change that was wrought in Schenker's language by English and more particularly American translators—and specifically Oster, whose rendering of *Der freie Satz* comes complete with a two-way dictionary of terms (appendix 5) and is described by Drabkin as 'the ultimate court of appeal in disputes over Schenkerian terminology in the English language' (in *MM1* xiii). This story has been told by Robert Snarrenberg (1994, 1996): in a nutshell, Snarrenberg shows how, in the decade or so following his death, Schenker's own biologically oriented terminology, in which the central metaphor is one of procreating, was systematically replaced by a terminology closer to that of architecture or engineering, in which the central metaphor—a metaphor nowadays so familiar that we hardly recognise it as a metaphor at all—is that of structure. As Schenker's verbs turn into nouns, Snarrenberg (1996: 328) argues, so process is transformed into product:

the dynamic terminology of 'earlier' and 'later' that Schenker uses to characterise the layers of his analyses is replaced by a static vocabulary of 'higher' and 'lower', and the emphasis is transferred from synthesis (in essence an idealised compositional act) to analytical reduction.

But in linguistic terms, the most extreme appropriation of Schenkerian theory must be that which took place at Princeton University from around 1960 under the presiding genius of Milton Babbitt, who had taken private lessons with Roger Sessions—hardly the conventional route into the Schenkerian world—but was also a personal friend of such insiders as Jonas and Oster. (Despite this, Babbitt comments [2003: 478], he 'was necessarily an outsider, perhaps even a suspect outsider'.) Schenkerian theory formed a complement to Babbitt's theory of combinatorial serialism in much the same way as with Forte's Schenker and sets: the aim was to retain the central insights of Schenkerian theory, but to express them in a terminology that was both more rigorous and more internally consistent than Schenker's. Among the directions opened up by this agenda were computer implementation of the theory and generalising it beyond the specific repertory in terms of which Schenker had formulated it (Michael Kassler's and Benjamin Boretz's doctoral dissertations, completed respectively in 1967 and 1970, illustrate these approaches). Just to say this, of course, is to demonstrate the distance between Schenker's Vienna and Babbitt's Princeton. Perhaps predictably, the 'neo-Schenkerian' project of decoupling Schenker's system from the 'chord of nature' and the entire repertorial value system it supported met with a great deal of hostility from the first- and second-generation Schenkerians, who like most emigré communities proved fiercely loyal to their traditions: as may be seen from the way Oster (1960) responded to Roy Travis's (1959) application of the idea of prolongation to nontriadic harmonies, the dropping somewhere in mid-Atlantic of Schenker's biological language, metaphysics, and German suprematism might be one thing, but analysing *Le sacre du printemps* alongside the German masterworks was quite another. Yet there were distinct points of contact between Schenker's own approach and the academic milieu of post-1945 American music theory: precisely the tendencies I emphasised in my account of *Der freie Satz*—its concern with and indeed delight in autonomous systems, its willingness to subordinate empirical realities to a higher conception, as well as what Kerman calls its 'clear method with an objective feel to it' (1985: 82)—facilitated its assimilation within an extremely non-Schenkerian world in which the sciences were valued above the arts, and in which compositional authenticity was identified with a hard-core modernism based on systematic approaches sometimes unhampered by any concern for perceptual constraints.

Schenkerian theory might be said to have reached a fully comfortable accommodation with the American academy only as a new generation of native Schenkerians reached positions of academic power.

Or perhaps not a *fully* comfortable accommodation with the academy: Rothstein (who studied with both Oster and Forte) wrote in his 1986 article that while the academy might have accepted Schenkerian theory, its acceptance 'of Schenkerians themselves is still in part an uneasy one'[56] (it is at this point that he charts the evolution of Schenkerian rhetoric from Schenker to Forte, the point being that the tone of the 'cool taxonomist' is that of the academy). One symptom of this discomfort is the tension in editions and translations of Schenker's writings between the furtherance of a cause and accepted scholarly practice, as represented by the difference between Jonas's bowdlerised and teleologically annotated texts on the one hand and the editorially cutting-edge teamwork of Drabkin's *Meisterwerk* and *Tonwille* translations on the other; a small but telling sign of the transition from the former to the latter is the disappearance of the once obligatory (and selective) list of Schenker's works at the end of each volume, last seen in Irene Schreier Scott's 2000 translation of *Die Kunst des Vortrags*. More generally there is a tension between what is sometimes called 'Schenkerism,' the focus of a community of believers, and the scholarly practice of Schenker studies: even today, the Schenker symposia held at the Mannes School of Music retain a certain ritualistic quality uncharacteristic of other musicological conferences. But a particularly explicit demonstration of what is at issue was provided by the publication in a 1989 issue of the *Journal of Music Theory Pedagogy* of an article entitled 'A Schenker Pedagogy' by Gregory Proctor and Lee Riggins.

'It may well be that the production of a good Schenkerian analysis requires an artistic upbringing', Proctor and Riggins argued (1989: 21), 'but if the behaviour belongs to the academy, then it can be taught, it can be good, without requiring or eliciting metaphysical sensibilities. . . . What we are proposing is the demystification of Schenker'. In an uncharacteristically vitriolic letter to the journal, published the following year, Rothstein responded (1990b: 298): 'I believe—and this is really the point of my "Americanization"—that my kind of Schenkerian pedagogy is in conflict with the American university system as it is currently structured'. What matters to Proctor and Riggins, Rothstein complains (295), 'is how well a given analysis conforms to a predetermined theory, not whether it does justice to a piece of music'; Schenkerian theory is made to fit the educational system, in other words Americanised, through 'jettisoning all ambiguities, all internal inconsistencies, all that arises from analysis rather than from theory, and all that is not narrowly technical'. Judged by such standards, Rothstein adds, 'Mr Schenker himself was a woefully poor student of "Schenkerian analysis"', freely breaking his own rules when they contradicted his musical intuitions; by contrast, Proctor and Riggins's 'preconceived idea of what they will find easily blinds them to what *actually* occurs in

---

[56] Rothstein 1990a: 196.

the music. Theory wins, music loses' (295, 297). The point I want to make is the one I made in relation to Stifter's *Der Nachsommer:* these are in essence just the same objections as have been levelled against *Der freie Satz,* only now magnified to the nth degree. It is not surprising then that Rothstein (297) reserves study of *Free Composition* for advanced students, while the final sentence of Proctor and Riggins's article reads 'most of all, we recommend that *Free Composition* be not hidden from students'.

It is telling, though under the circumstances also rather ironic, that Rothstein characterises 'Americanization' in very much the way Schenker himself would have, or any other German cultural conservative of the period up to the Second World War: Rothstein's reference to turning Schenkerian analysis into 'a streamlined technology—very much in the American spirit' (1990b: 295) evokes precisely the *Gesellschaft* values of which America was seen as the epitome, as in the Bösendorfer/Steinway dichotomy I discussed in chapter 3. And it is the American assimilation of Schenker that gave rise to the idea of 'structural hearing' (the title of Salzer's 1952 book): a model of how music should be heard and understood that not only carries a great deal of ideological baggage with it (Subotnik 1988), but might also be seen as a musical equivalent to architectural modernism of the Bauhaus/Le Corbusier type. The ideal that inspires structural listening is transparency: heard right, a musical composition reveals its structure in the same way as a Bauhaus building. But nothing could be further from the Viennese modernism of Loos, the 'discreet' exterior of whose houses concealed rather than disclosed the private spaces that lay within, or of Schoenberg and Schenker, for both of whom truth lay concealed behind appearances.[57] The 'better listening' Schenker called for (*TI* 119)—what Furtwängler called 'long-range hearing'[58] . . . applied over great spans to fundamental relationships that often spread across many pages' (1985/1954: 3) —was less a matter of total disclosure than of orientation, as Schenker makes clear when he goes on to speak of the need to 'guide the ear down those paths along which our great masters have created such novel and ingenious varieties and prolongations of the fundamental laws'. For Schenker, the idea of concealment, which I traced in chapter 4, extended into broader aspects of interpretation and performance, as illustrated for example by his attacks in the Ninth Symphony monograph on the 'clarification-mania' which led Wagner to clarify through reorchestration what Beethoven had artfully camou-

---

[57] See p. 118 above. Holly Watkins has pursued this comparison between Loos and Schoenberg, concluding from it that structural hearing is an inappropriate approach to Schoenberg's atonal music, in 'Schoenberg's Interior Designs', paper presented at the annual meeting of the Society for Music Theory, Seattle, 11–14 November 2004.

[58] *Fernhören,* a term coined by Schenker by way of presumably ironic reference to the telephone receiver (*Fernhörer*); see Bent's explanation in *TI* 164n.

flaged (*BNS* 86, 70–1). This kind of clarity, whether Wagnerian, French,[59] or American, belongs to a tradition of modernism quite distinct from that of Loos, Schoenberg, and Schenker: the fact that there are such distinct traditions of modernism was one of the main points I was attempting to establish in chapter 2. And my purpose in providing this brief narrative of Schenker's posthumous assimilation to a very non-Viennese kind of modernism has been to provide a point of departure for what might be called postmodern approaches to Schenker—approaches that turn out be at least as close to the historical Schenker, or maybe I should say one historical Schenker, as the modernist orthodoxy of Schenkerian theory.

Korsyn's image, to which I referred in chapter 1, of a deconstructionist Schenker, who destabilises the opposition between the organic and the mechanical through a faultless application of Derridean technique, may be simply anachronistic (or not so simply, given Nietzsche's place in the genealogy of deconstruction). But then there is Morgan's image, which I have previously mentioned, of Schenker as 'the consummate cultural "Grenzjude"'—an image that evokes Jacques Le Rider's (1993: 204) characterisation of the assimilated Jew as 'the prototype of the postmodern self'. And Rothstein's reaction against Proctor and Riggins's Americanised modernism exemplifies an increasingly widespread image of Schenkerian analysis that might at least loosely be termed postmodern. Kofi Agawu (1989: 295), for instance, succinctly replicates Rothstein's complaints: 'neo-Schenkerian efforts . . . have reduced away the exciting tension in his analytical method. To put it crudely, we are being taught how to make grammatically correct statements rather than interesting or profound ones'. Writers such as Peter Smith (1995: 277) and Joseph Lubben (1995: chap. 2), too, have celebrated Schenker's inconsistencies, his self-contradictions, his preparedness to sacrifice neatness of graphing to the rich messiness of musical particularity. Nor is this just a matter of celebration: in the last few years there has been a movement, largely driven by Lubben, to model Schenkerian analysis more on *Tonwille* than *Der freie Satz*, in other words to substitute a diverse and less systematised analytical practice for the perfectly ordered, clockwork-precise world of Schenker's last work. If, as Rothstein complained, Schenkerian analysis of the Proctor-Riggins variety encourages a top-down approach where you know what you are going to find before you have looked for it, then it is more than anything the archetypal, multiple-choice *Ursatz* that encourages

---

[59] In 'Von der Sendung des deutschen Genies', Schenker lampooned the *Clarté* group and the very idea of French clarity: 'Clarity courtesy of French mediocrity? . . . The French language—the supreme rule of which is: effect, especially effect on others of the opposite sex—is intrinsically unsuited to accurately perceiving and promoting genuine clarities' (*TI* 14).

this. (Eugene Narmour [1977] said as much in his once influential book *Beyond Schenkerism*.) And the analytical focus on the *Ursatz* tends to direct attention to the most abstract and least audible—perhaps least useful—level of musical structure, that of an entire movement. In the late 1980s, David Neumeyer (1987a, 1987b) put forward a number of commonsense proposals for relaxing the archetypes—by allowing for ascending *Urlinien* or expanding the *Ursatz* to three parts—but it can be argued that these tinker with the problem, basically by introducing an additional remote middleground layer, rather than address it head on. In this section, then, I consider some proposals for postmodernising Schenker's system, so to speak, through overhauling and recategorising the archetypes, if not doing away with them altogether.

If this reaction against the particular kind of modernism represented by *Der freie Satz* (and even more so *Free Composition*) is not so much a reaction against Schenker as a siding with the middle-period Schenker against the late—by which I also mean posthumous—Schenker, then the same might be said of something that penetrates deep into the dynamics of Schenkerian analysis. As Richard Cohn (1992b) tells the story, I take some of the blame for what happened through an obvious misreading of the idea of 'tension' to which Schenker frequently refers. In a contribution to a 1989 colloquium entitled 'The future of theory', I cited Schenker's reference to 'the tension of musical coherence' (*FC* I 6) as evidence of what I saw as an analytical turn towards issues of tension, conflict, and disunity, adding 'maybe it has taken deconstructionism to sensitize us to phrases like this in Schenker's writings' (Cook 1989a: 72). As Cohn pointed out, and as anybody who knew anything about German idealist philosophy would have known, this is plain wrong: Schenker means 'tension' (*Spannung*) in the sense of overcoming conflict in order to create a higher synthesis, that is to say of the Hegelian dialectic. Cohn quotes another passage, this time from *Meisterwerk* 2, which makes it clear: 'The conceptual unity of a linear progression signifies a conceptual tension between the beginning and the end of the progression: the primary note is to be retained until the point at which the concluding note appears. This tension alone engenders musical coherence'.[60]

This is the basis of Schenker's theory of dissonance, the central means through which music is constituted as culture rather than nature. The hearing of a dissonance, Schenker says, is accompanied by 'the covert retention, by the ear, of the consonant point of departure. . . . It is as though the dissonance would always carry with it the impression of its consonant origin', and he adds that the consonance 'always stands at its [the dissonance's] cradle' (*C2* 57–9). To translate this into Husserlian terminology (and it is here that Schenker's thought

---

[60] *MM2* 1; Cohn, writing before the appearance of this translation, cited the passage in Sylvan Kalib's (1973) translation.

comes close to Husserl's), it is the unified consciousness of retention and protention that defines a musically meaningful entity, whether at the level of a single phrase or an entire movement. We are in fact talking about no more and no less than what in *Tonwille* 7, in the course of his analysis of Beethoven's Sonata op. 57, Schenker calls 'German synthesis—synthesis pure and simple!' (*T2* 54–5): he goes on to define this as 'the binding together of a tonal whole' by means of what he terms 'the lineage of a tone', the *Urlinie*, the *Ursatz* (then a very new term), prolongation, harmony, diminution, and registers. It comes as no surprise to find in this same passage the reference to the tonal body having 'boundaries that arise from within, from its soul, and are not given to it from without' which I quoted in chapter 3, as well as mention of the 'miraculous, secret way' in which the synthesis extends to the piano itself.

As this already makes clear, Schenker applied the same fundamental insight not only to the passage of time, or the relationship between consonance and dissonance, but more generally to the relationships between structural levels. Speaking of the act of composition, and echoing his earlier reference to the dissonance's cradle, Schenker writes in *Der freie Satz* that 'the fundamental structure . . . accompanies each transformation in the middleground and a foreground, as a guardian angel watches over a child'.[61] And there is no contradiction between my calling this the fundamental insight of Schenkerian theory and my saying the same of axial causality in chapter 1,[62] for they are in reality the same thing: prolongation, as I said there, works axially rather than laterally, or maybe one should say that for Schenker axial causes have lateral effects. All this, incidentally, explains why it is a mistake to place too much weight on apparent anticipations of Schenkerian analysis in terms of graphic reduction technique: what matters is the larger framework of axial causality or prolongation which informs such techniques. Indeed, Schenker implied as much when, in *Der freie Satz*, he emphasised the desirability of pursuing graphic analysis as far as the middleground or background, and added that in order to do this one 'need only employ the familiar method of reducing more extensive diminutions, as taught in textbooks and schools' (*FC* I 26).

It is then abundantly clear that the idea of tension, and everything Schenker draws from it, has nothing to do with postmodern celebra-

---

[61] *FC* I 18. Schenker goes on to speak of 'this "continual present" in the vision of the composer', characterising the composer's perception as 'the meeting of past, present, and future', so making explicit the association of axial causality with the pseudo-Mozart image of creation I discussed in chapter 1. This is one of the features of Schenker's theory strikingly anticipated in Louis and Thuille's *Harmonielehre* of 1907: quite extended passing-chord passages are explained on the principle of the 'ideal organ-point', according to which 'we retain the fundamental of the first chord in our memory unaltered' (translated in Wason 1985: 131).

[62] See pp. 70–1 above.

tions of conflict or difference. I was at least in good company—Agawu (1989: 290) quoted the same passage about 'the tension of musical coherence' a few pages before referring to the 'exciting tension' in his method—but Cohn's point was a larger one. Though what he called the 'paradigm of constructive conflict'—the idea of interplay between conflicting structural elements—was quite foreign to Schenker's way of thinking, Cohn argued, it is commonplace in many of the writers who make up the contemporary Schenkerian orthodoxy: Cohn cited David Beach, John Rothgeb, and Carl Schachter as theorists making use of this paradigm (and if he had been writing more recently, he could have cited any number of others, from Leslie Blasius [1996: 55] to Lawrence Kramer [1992]). To illustrate the point from an article I have already quoted, after Schachter criticises the later Schenker's catchall category of 'illusory keys at the foreground level', he sets out a taxonomy of key types and criteria for identifying structural modulations which he then applies to Cherubino's arietta 'Voi che sapete' from Mozart's *Le Nozze di Figaro:* 'To concentrate on background continuity to the exclusion of foreground disruptions', he concludes, 'is to produce a skewed picture of a piece or passage' (Schachter 1999b: 157). What Schachter is advocating, then, is the theorising of conflict between different layers of the music, and in this way he shows—as he had already written elsewhere, with specific reference to *Der freie Satz*—that Schenker's concept of coherence is not one 'that results from uniformity but one that is based on the interaction between contrasting elements' (1981: 120).

That is a telling remark, linking with the way I characterised Schenker's project in chapters 2 and 3: as a quest for unity through the reconciliation, or sublation, of contrasting elements, in contrast to the standardised approach 'that understands unity only as uniformity' (as Schenker put it in 'Weg mit dem Phrasierungsbogen').[63] Perhaps the most intriguing statement of this idea comes in the op. 101 *Erläuterungsausgabe,* the work in which the *Urlinie* first appears: 'no idea can come naked into life', Schenker proclaims, explaining that 'even if everything . . . derived from a single, all-fundamental reason for being, it nonetheless has a life of its own which we immediately confront in the veiled, illusive present, and which is there to drive the fundamental idea, so to speak, into the background'.[64] (This is as much as to say that there is an inherent tension between the idea and its realisation.) And it is easy to multiply references on Schenker's part to this more dynamic kind of kind of unity. In *Harmonielehre,* for instance, he writes that 'the independence of different counterpoints results in the creation of a superior kind of complex. This very friction, which is caused by independent voice-leading, and the psychological labor required to overcome it reveal to our mind the goal of unity' (*H* 160). In *Kontra-*

---

[63] See p. 130 above.
[64] Schenker 1972/1921: 41, translated in Goldman 1990: 81–2.

punkt 2, referring to the combination of species, he expresses it more concisely: 'unity is revealed only through the act of conquering the contrast' (*C2* 191). Indeed, one might see the dialectical conception as built into the very structure of *Neue Musikalische Theorien und Phantasien:* first the 'independent spheres' of harmony and counterpoint are outlined in succession, and then their synthesis in the higher unity of free composition.[65] But before coming back to the role Schenker may have played in Cohn's paradigm of constructive conflict, I want to consider the area in which it has perhaps been most influential: the analysis of musical form.

What is at issue here is essentially the rehabilitation of certain aspects of what Schenker saw as 'false theory' and hence attempted to eliminate from *Der freie Satz*. I have already quoted Schenker's rejection of 'those definitions of song form which take the motif as their starting point', but his denial is a much more general one: 'All forms appear in the ultimate foreground', he writes, 'but all of them have their origin in, and derive from, the background' (*FC* I 130). In short, though Schenker refers to chapter 5 of *Der freie Satz* as setting out a 'new theory of form' (*FC* I 130), his basic position appears to be that there can in reality be no such thing. What are traditionally called forms are epiphenomena, simply the outcomes of deeper processes, the projection of background and middleground on the foreground: you cannot theorise them in their own right. 'It is precisely because I derive the forms from the background and middleground', says Schenker, 'that I have the advantage of brevity in presentation'—and this way, Schenker adds, he has delivered 'the "Essay on a New Theory of Form" which I have promised for decades'. (This was no exaggeration: Schenker's first reference to it, in the Ninth Symphony monograph [*BNS* 4], went back more than thirty years.) The brevity of his presentation has not, however, satisfied his critics, starting with Oster, who inserted a four-column footnote to amplify what he saw as Schenker's 'sketchy and in a number of ways incomplete' account of sonata form (*FC* I 139).

If, as I have argued, it is not helpful to see *Der freie Satz* as the summary and culminating point of Schenker's life's work, then it might be better to think of it rather like the broken watch in a detective story: the trace of an ongoing process, frozen in time by Schenker's death. How might the ideas in *Der freie Satz* have developed if Schenker had died not at sixty-six but at seventy-eight (as Charles Rosen once said he did [1998: 163])? Bent speculates that if Schenker had lived longer he might have 'come forward with a new conceptualization of total struc-

---

[65] In one of its several versions, the opening sentence of the 'Freier Satz' section intended for *Kontrapunkt* 2 reads 'Two independent spheres begin to bear a relationship to each other for the first time in free composition: the scale degrees and voice leading' (quoted in Siegel 1999: 16).

ture—a formulation that eradicated the old formal constructs, the formal models, just as it had earlier eradicated the old phraseological terminology' (1991: 33). That would be consistent with the position I put
forward in the previous paragraph, and Gianmario Borio concurs
(2001: 271): one might argue, he says, that 'the centrality of the *Ursatz*
and its prolongations renders superfluous the need for a theory of form
as a discipline distinct from counterpoint and harmony'. But then Borio
makes the essential point: the fact is that Schenker nevertheless included
a chapter on form in *Der freie Satz* (just, Borio adds [272], as did Salzer
and Federhofer in their textbooks published shortly after the war). In
this way, Borio concludes, however Schenker's theoretical claims
might suggest the contrary, in practice he 'did not consider the question of form to have faded away *sic et simpliciter* thanks to the theory of
structural levels'. Borio accordingly sees the *Der freie Satz* chapter on
form not as a kind of vestigial remnant of false theory, but rather as 'a
first draft (and not the definitive version) of a structural morphology'.

What might the definitive version of Schenker's structural morphology have looked like? This is probably not a sensible question, but
recent Schenkerian debate about form has tended to revolve around
the question of how far formal patterns—like modulation a significant
component of perceptual experience—can be accommodated within
voice-leading structure. Perhaps the most substantial contribution to
this debate is Charles Smith's (1996) proposal for a comprehensive re-
formulation of Schenker's theory as expressed in *Der freie Satz*, the basic
objective of which is an analytical practice that 'complements and en-
hances our formal intuitions instead of contradicting and replacing
them' (Smith 1996: 242). In reality, Smith argues, Schenker didn't ig-
nore what Smith calls taxonomic form in the way that his theoretical
formulations claimed: he used it as a criterion for the identification of
the fundamental structure, but covertly and inconsistently ('Regrettably', Smith remarks [239], 'Schenker's formal instincts were irregular at best'). But Smith's central point is not the importance of taxonomic
form for identifying the fundamental structure: it is that the fundamental structure should itself embody the essential features of taxonomic form, thereby reconciling what have up to now been paradoxically seen as 'two disconnected types of musical form' (280). And he
sets about this through a systematic analysis of the background structures found in *Der freie Satz*, showing how in practice such features as
the three archetypal forms of the *Ursatz*, patterns of division, patterns
of openness and closure within divided forms, and even major versus
minor mode are all interrelated: many theoretically possible combinations are nonexistent or inherently contradictory. By eliminating the
redundant combinations and classifying the others, Smith arrives at an
expanded range of background structures, a new set of archetypes in-
corporating all these features: this gives rise to a modified Schenkerian
practice in which 'structural analysis consists of invoking a repertoire

of fundamental structures, each of which is derived from and signalled by a formal pattern—so that pieces with similar forms have similar structures' (270).

Perhaps the most iconoclastic of Smith's proposals is the incorporation within the fundamental structure of keys other than tonic and dominant, such as the form-defining cadence in the subdominant at bars 7–8 of 'Wenn ich in deine Augen seh'', the fourth song of Schumann's *Dichterliebe:* figure 5.1 shows the relevant passage, while figures 5.2 and 5.3 respectively show Schenker's sketch from *Der freie Satz*, in which the subdominant is reduced to a surface feature, and Smith's (1996: 208) resketching 'to reflect formal shape'. One might of course argue, as I did in relation to the 'Ode to Joy' tune, that the substance of Schenker's analysis lies in the discrepancy between graph and song. But that seems like sophistry in the face of Smith's obviously plausible argument that Schenker's downgrading of the subdominant cadence is not in reality a response to the music, but the consequence of an unnecessarily restrictive dogma: as Suzannah Clark (1999: 96–9) has explained, while in the terms of *Harmonielehre* such a feature might be seen as a 'surrogate' for the normative dominant, in those of *Der freie Satz* (*FC* I 112) it must be consigned to Schenker's catchall category of 'illusory keys at the foreground level'. (The elimination of all structural

Figure 5.1 Schumann, 'Wenn ich in deinen Augen seh', bars 4–9.

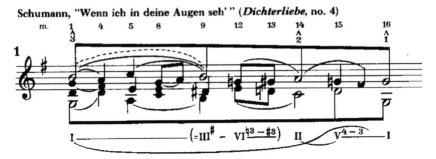

Figure 5.2 Schenker, sketch of 'Wenn ich in deinen Augen seh' (*Der freie Satz*, vol. 2, fig. 152, 1).

harmonies except tonic and dominant, then, takes its place alongside that of the ascending *Urlinie* as Schenker's theory reaches its final, most reductionist form.) How, after all, can it make sense to pass over so self-evidently emphatic a cadence (especially if the singer takes the alternate line with its climactic g^2), in a way that would be inconceivable if it were a dominant one? Doesn't this represent a relapse into the kind of denial of the musical facts that motivated Schenker's and his contemporaries' own reaction against the dogmatic rules of the Sechter-Bruckner tradition in the first place? Isn't it in short a perfect illustration of Neumeyer's (1989: 13) maxim that 'when an established theory conflicts with the musically most satisfying or stylistically most appropriate analysis, the theory should be examined and changed where necessary'?

Of course, things are never quite this simple, and in the hands of someone like Carl Schachter the archetypal backgrounds can prove

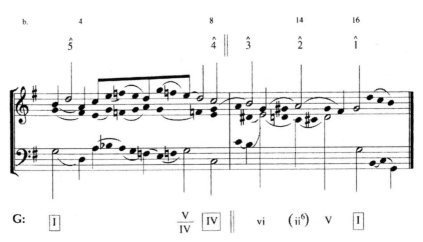

Figure 5.3 Smith, sketch of 'Wenn ich in deinen Augen seh' (1996: ex. 5b). Used by permission of Blackwells Publishing Ltd.

themselves capable of accommodating extraordinary flexibility and subtlety of interpretation. An object lesson in this is Schachter's (1999a: 299) contribution to *Schenker Studies 2*, in which he writes, 'often the foreground's ellipses, transformations, and multiple meanings can complicate the inference of an underlying structure so that the relation between perceived surface and inferred structure becomes problematic; and it is the problematic character that brings the background up to the front of the stage'. (That is as much as to say, again, that Cohn's 'paradigm of constructive conflict' plays a central role in Schachter's analytical practice.) It can be argued—I think rightly—that the possibility of virtuoso deployment isn't in itself a good argument for sticking to a framework if it tends to constrain rather than encourage sensitive response to the particularities of individual musical works. And yet, in the case of 'Wenn ich in deine Augen seh" at least, Smith's argument is not quite as self-evident as it might seem. What is characteristic about the cadence at bars 7–8, I would argue, is the way it almost instantly evaporates, slipping through the g^2–a^2–b^2 rise in the piano onto the V of E minor chord that will eventually lead through an unbroken cycle of fifths to the final tonic. The effect is to undercut the subdominant cadence in the most striking manner, and with it the idyllic picture of love the entire song paints—until the ending of Heine's text, which reveals it as a lie: 'doch wenn du sprichst: Ich liebe dich, / so muss ich weinen bitterlich' (but when you say, 'I love you', I must weep bitterly). Schumann's music, however, has already made this revelation at the subdominant cadence, and Schenker's graph explains how: the ever so emphatic cadence is a facade, no more real than the song's profession of love. One might even claim that, by contrast, Smith's literal reading of the cadence is a music-analytical equivalent of Eric Sams' misreading of the song, according to which 'Heine means that "Ich liebe dich" was a lie. But Schumann is innocent of innuendo'.[66]

My aim here is not on the basis of a single, perhaps untypical, example to construct a general argument against the extension of Schenkerian structures to incorporate so-called exotic keys, but to suggest that the attempt to integrate the different elements of the music within a single summative representation may not necessarily be the most productive way in which to deploy Schenkerian techniques. In the case of 'Wenn ich in deinen Augen seh", the issue might be seen as turning on the distinction between the standard, dominant-oriented expectation modelled by Schenker's analysis and the idiosyncratic (Schenker might have said 'artificial') subdominant structure modelled by Smith's. But the point is a more general one, and for once it is Adorno who expresses what is at issue most lucidly. Near the beginning of his 1969 radio talk 'On the Problem of Musical Analysis', Adorno

---

[66] The quotation is from Sams 1969: 111; I am here condensing an argument from Cook 1998: 135–40.

makes the familiar argument that analysis is not a matter of simply
mapping music onto formal schemata: rather it involves what is going
on *'underneath* these formal schemata'. For contrary to widespread belief, Adorno says,

> even that which is going on underneath is not simply a second and quite
> different thing, but is in fact mediated by the formal schemata, and is
> partly, at any given moment, *postulated* by the formal schemata, while on
> the other hand it consists of deviations which in their turn can only be at
> all understood through their relationship to the schemata. (2002: 164–5)

The framework of this remark is, obviously, the Hegelian dialectic.
Yet Adorno is not attempting to push through towards a resolution of
the conflicted relationship between taxonomic and unique form: his
concern seems to be with keeping the different elements mobile, keeping them in play. One might say that Adorno is interested in the interactive rather than the integrative dimension of sublation. (Or one
might invoke Bakhtin and characterise this as a dialogical rather than
dialectical relationship.) To borrow Cohn's word, Adorno's approach is
not monist, in the way that Schenker's approach in *Der freie Satz* often
seems to be—and certainly that Bent's predicted trajectory, if Schenker
had lived longer, would have been. On the other hand, Adorno's description is very much in line with Schenker's earlier analytical practice,
such as the *Tonwille* analysis of the *Kaiserhymne*. Lubben's readings of
the *Tonwille* analyses in general might be described as antiteleological—
that is, he focuses on precisely those aspects that were not carried over
into *Der freie Satz*—and they revolve in particular around the interaction between voice-leading structure and other parameters such as motivic organisation, melodic design, and rhythm: 'The final configuration
of the musical surface', Lubben writes (1995: 25), is 'seen as the result
of the composer's arbitration of the conflict between these independent tendencies'. And on this basis he distinguishes two distinct senses
in which Schenker used the term 'synthesis' in *Tonwille:* when he is
analysing particular pieces, Lubben explains, it means this interaction
between largely autonomous parameters (in the *Tonwille* 2 analysis
of Beethoven's Sonata op. 2 no. 1 Schenker writes that 'in the world
of synthesis, the sense of interaction, of relationship, is decisive'),[67]
whereas when he is talking in more general theoretical terms it means

---

[67] *TI* 90; in the next issue of *Tonwille* Schenker spells out the 'constant interaction of
the operative forces' more explicitly, writing that 'sometimes the constraint of repeating
a motive impels new harmonic degrees and Urlinie tones to appear, while at other times
the Urlinie and harmonic degrees, with their own constraint, make a new motive credi-
ble' (*TI* 112). And in the first volume of *Meisterwerk*, Schenker writes of the seventh of
Bach's Twelve Little Preludes that 'each separate attribute of the voice-leading does not
pertain to itself alone; it exists not only for itself but contributes to all the others' (*MM1*
61).

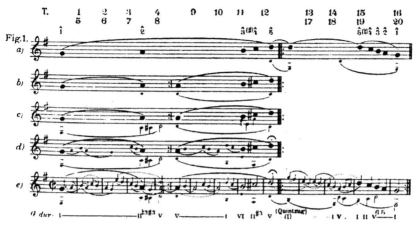

Figure 5.4 Schenker, first sketch of *Kaiserhymne* (*Tonwille* 2: 135, fig. 1).

the incorporation of all other musical elements within the *Urlinie*. It is basically the latter meaning which is carried over into *Der freie Satz*.

We can return to the *Kaiserhymne* in order to make the point more concretely. As Lubben says (1995: 38–9), the main graph in the *Tonwille* analysis (fig. 5.4) does not look too different from Schenker's final practice, in particular because linear and harmonic structures are fully coordinated with one another (unlike in the 1923 analysis of the fifth of Bach's Twelve Little Preludes, which I referred to in chapter 1 and which Lubben analyses immediately before the *Kaiserhymne*). But as Lubben goes on to explain (44), Schenker had a different story to tell in the rest of his article, which 'skewed his derivation graphs in an ad hoc manner, and included mutually contradictory descriptions of structure within a single analysis'. Lubben details the way Schenker describes motives, melodic design, and rhythm as independently converging on the highest note (the g² which elicited Schenker's comparison between royal and artistic justice):[68] this represents an arbitration between or coordination of autonomous elements. The mutual contradiction is evident in Schenker's second graph (fig. 5.5), the purpose of which is to show the functioning of what Schenker calls 'superelevations', that is rising and falling motions from one note of a triad to another. But the words above the stave (*Brechung des G-Klanges: Grundton—Terz—Quint—Oktav—Quint—Terz—Grundton*) spell out an arpeggiation from g¹ to g² and back again which cannot be seen as deriving in any way from the analysis in the first graph: as Lubben puts it (42), this is 'an alternative reading of the middleground'. Schenker, in short, is explaining the particular force of the g² in terms of the interaction of two individually salient but mutually incompatible structural processes, as

---

[68] See p. 196 above.

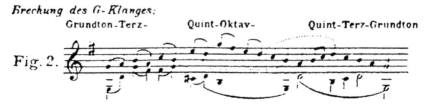

Brechung des G-Klanges:
Grundton-Terz-
Quint-Oktav-
Quint-Terz-Grundton
Fig. 2.

Figure 5.5 Schenker, second sketch of *Kaiserhymne* (*Tonwille* 2: 135, fig. 2).

well as of the separate parameters to which I have referred. If one can speak here of unity, it is not unity as uniformity: it is unity that results 'only through the act of conquering the contrast', to repeat Schenker's words. And so Lubben (43) concludes that the real focus of the *Kaiserhymne* essay is the way 'a variety of musical parameters cooperate to achieve a coherent and compelling result'. That is the definition of what Lubben describes as Schenker's 'early *Synthese*' (82), his first kind of synthesis—the kind that in chapter 3 I characterised as musical *Gemeinschaft.*

Schenker came back to the *Kaiserhymne* in *Der freie Satz,* and his analyses there illustrate Lubben's second kind of synthesis: all aspects of the music are as far as possible coordinated with the *Ursatz*—and where this is not possible, Schenker is inclined to pass over the offending feature in silence. As in the case of the 'Ode to Joy' and 'Wenn ich in deinen Augen seh'', then, what is striking about the *Der freie Satz* graphs of the *Kaiserhymne* is what is absent from them, even the most detailed one (fig. 5.6). That the arpeggiated approach to the g^2 from figure 5.5 has been eliminated will occasion no surprise. In its place is a series of asterisks outlining a series of 'peak tones' which, Schenker insists, must 'under no circumstances' be read as a genuine linear progression (*FC* I 101); this caution seems so gratuitous that one wonders whether Schenker intended it as an oblique cancellation of his earlier interpretation, even though the notes do not entirely coincide. The g^2—in terms of both structural and social meaning the nub of Schenker's *Tonwille* analysis—appears in figure 5.6, but only as local detail; in the other graphs from *Der freie Satz* it appears in brackets, or not at all. In short, however we read it, figure 5.6 embodies a coherence

Haydn, "Emperor Hymn" (Qt. op. 76 no. 3) (cf. Figs. 39,3; 119,3)
m. 1 2 3 4 12 12 13 14 15 16
6a)
(div.)
(n.n.)
I
(I II V)
-I6 I
I6 II V I

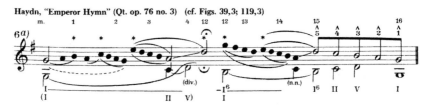

Figure 5.6 Schenker, sketch of *Kaiserhymne* (*Der freie Satz,* vol. 2, fig. 120, 6).

achieved through the imposition of a single, authorised code: different elements are brought in relationship with one another to the extent, and only to the extent, that all conform to the *Ursatz*. If it made sense, in light of Schenker's own parallel in the *Tonwille* analysis between political and musical justice, to compare his early synthesis to the devolved operation of the Habsburg empire,[69] then it is not wholly unreasonable to compare the synthesis of *Der freie Satz* to the structures— and even perhaps the eliminationist tendencies—of the authoritarian regimes which were coming into being in the 1930s; in this way there turn out, after all, to be musical grounds for Martin Eybl's distrust of Schenker's authoritarian impulse.[70] And it is in this context that we might see the analytical system of *Der freie Satz* as tending towards precisely the kind of uniformity or standardisation that Schenker had himself lampooned in 'Weg mit dem Phrasierungsbogen'. If he had been on the other side of the argument, one could easily imagine Schenker railing about 'a huge *Urlinie* encircling the entire world'.

In the previous section I referred to the tension between dialectical thinking predicated on historical change and the unknowability of reality on the one hand and a Platonic or Leibnizian world of eternal ideas on the other. We can now see that this maps onto the tension between Schenker's two kinds of synthesis, between coherence as dynamic interaction and as static uniformity, between pluralism (again Cohn's word [1992b: 6]) and monism. A particularly telling example of such tension is a passage from 'Rameau or Beethoven?' in the final volume of *Meisterwerk*, where Schenker begins by setting out a dialectical point of view but then overrules it. He begins by explaining that 'From the moment counterpoint entered into music . . . a tension between the horizontal and vertical axes has pervaded the history of musical composition' (*MM3* 2), and goes on to complain that Rameau 'reduced all musical phenomena to fundamental basses and the progressions proper to them'. But then, instead of showing how the horizontal and vertical axes may be thought together—instead of setting out his own approach to interaction and synthesis—he argues a position that is just as reductive, just as monist, as Rameau's, only the opposite one: '*It is the temporal-horizontal axis of musical motion,* however one may otherwise explain its laws, *that alone generates musical content and guarantees the latter's cohesiveness*'.[71] And it is the same monist compulsion that informs such rhapsodic tirades as the one that concludes 'Das organische der Fuge' (The organic nature of fugue): 'there is only one path to progress,

---

[69] See p. 196 above.

[70] See p. 153 above.

[71] Schenker's emphases. Compare his related, but pluralist, reference in *Kontrapunkt* 2 to 'a constant interaction between the demand for triadic completeness and the laws of voice leading, so that in truth it is only the act of reconciling the two forces that represents the essence of three-part counterpoint' (*C2* 4).

leading into the depths, the blue depths!' Schenker exclaims. 'Return to the fathers, I cry, back to the masters, but now, finally, with an ear attuned to the depths! . . . With eyes and ears focused on the depths, let us bind eternity to eternities!' (*MM2* 54)

There is something impossible about this monist compulsion, a point at which it begins ineluctably to unravel. In terms of logic, there is a basic contradiction within Schenkerian theory as embodied in *Der freie Satz*. It is a matter of principle that features of surface 'design'—motives, themes, taxonomic forms, and the rest—can only be properly apprehended on the basis of the fundamental structure (that is what they are designs *of*, so to speak), yet in practice, as Smith pointed out, it is only on the basis of such features that you can decide what the fundamental structure is.[72] In principle, that is to say, there can be no such thing as Schenkerian analysis, because there is no discovery procedure for the *Urlinie*. In terms of Schenkerian practice this is clearly an absurd position. Yet even in the 1920s, when his analytical practice embraced interaction and contradiction, Schenker had a weakness for fantastically sweeping pronouncements along such lines, as when he wrote of Beethoven's Sonata op. 2 no.1 that 'nothing in the outward existence of the tones betrays the mysterious relationships that rule within, which no ear has yet received, no tongue named' (*T1* 83). At such times the disconnect between a compulsively monist theory and a relatively pluralist practice seems complete. It is as if Schenker the theorist was in denial about Schenker the analyst.

And Lubben makes a telling observation that ties in with this. Even in *Der freie Satz*, he says, Schenker cannot avoid making occasional reference to the constructive impact of foreground features within the synthesis, as in the following two passages, both of which Lubben cites (and the second of which I have already quoted in part):

> The content of the second and subsequent levels is determined by the content of the first level, but at the same time it is influenced by goals in the foreground, mysteriously sensed and pursued. (*FC* I 68)

> It is impossible to present in specific and perceptible forms all the events which occur through the miraculous rapport of fundamental structure with foreground—especially in forms which would satisfy the superficial interest of the curious. A wonder remains a wonder and can be experienced only by those blessed with special perception. (*FC* I 27)

Even after making allowances for Schenker's usual profligacy with words like 'mysterious' and 'miraculous', there is something curiously Delphic about these utterances: why, Lubben asks (1995: 25), does Schenker insist on assigning this kind of interaction 'to the realm of the

---

[72] I originally set out the critique I am now developing in my *Guide to Musical Analysis* (Cook 1987: 60–1); Cohn 1992a advances a related and more detailed argument with specific reference to motives.

unfathomable'? I hope the answer is now obvious. These points of awkward mystification, of conceptual embarrassment, mark the fault-lines between two incompatible modes of thought: on the one hand the dialectical thinking conveyed by the quotation from Adorno, which is predicated on an interaction between foreground and background; on the other the idealism of a Platonist or Leibnizian type that pervades *Der freie Satz*, according to which ideas are abstract and eternal, removed from the generations and their times.

There is in this way a double mismatch in Schenkerian theory: on the one hand between the monism of Schenker's theoretical proclamations and the relative pluralism of his analytical practice, and on the other between the relative monism of Schenker's analytical practice in the last phase of his work and his earlier, more pluralist practice. Schachter (1999b: 149) has observed that Schenker was in the habit of using the same word at different times to mean different things, usually without warning his readers of this (as just illustrated by his use of the term 'synthesis', and earlier of 'prolongation' and 'motif'); there is a similar sense in which, as Lubben suggested in relation to the *Kaiser-hymne*, the graphic representations in *Tonwille* and *Der freie Satz* can mean essentially different things even when they look the same. In this way, the paradigm of constructive conflict is not as foreign to Schenker's way of thinking as Cohn suggested. Cohn (1992b: 12–3) put it down to the influence of more recent theorists such as Meyer, Berry, Narmour, Epstein, or Lerdahl and Jackendoff, suggesting that Schenkerians were influenced by these theorists' approach to cross-parametrical interaction even as they often criticised them: 'Schenkerian theory has given way to post-Schenkerian theory', he writes (18–19), and for this reason 'tonal theory cannot proceed in good health if it continues to be executed under the watchful eye of Schenker's ghost'. Given the extent to which the paradigm of constructive conflict is in fact anticipated in Schenker's analytical practice of the 1920s, however, it can be argued that what is needed is not so much exorcism as winding the clock back.

By itself, however, that may not be enough. The commentary in Schenker's *Tonwille* analysis of the *Kaiserhymne* makes it clear that the analysis revolves around the interaction of different parameters—Lubben's first kind of synthesis—but the main graph, at least, does not, and that is why Schenker's meaning has failed to communicate. As early as the 'Eroica' analysis from *Meisterwerk* 3, Drabkin has remarked, 'The text functions more as an aid to understanding the graphs, rather than the other way round' (*MM3* x), and in the wake of *Five Graphic Music Analyses* a practice of Schenkerian reading developed for which the graph *is* the analysis. A Schenkerian—or post-Schenkerian—analytical practice predicated on the interaction of different parameters or structural principles needs ways of representing such interaction more explicitly than the traditional Schenkerian graph, whether through the incorporation of different elements within a single representation or through the use of complementary representations. For this reason, Smith's graph of 'Wenn ich in deine Augen seh'' need not be seen as a replacement for Schenker's, but can rather stand alongside it as a construal of the music from an alternative perspective, with difference between the two representing—to use Schenker's phrase once again—the tension of musical coherence.[73] Rethinking the *Ursatz*-dominated synthesis of *Der freie Satz*, in short, has opened up possibilities within a broadly Schenkerian practice, and in its relationship to other analytical approaches, that were progressively foreclosed during the final decade of Schenker's life. It seems somehow fitting to be arguing such a position in 2006, the year when, in much of the world, copyright in Schenker's writings expired.

The difference between monism and pluralism, to repeat Cohn's catchwords, is in part an epistemological one. In one of the passages Cohn quotes from *Der freie Satz*—a passage that stands wholly opposed to the alternative development of Schenkerian practice I have just outlined— Schenker writes: 'The fundamental structure represents the totality. It is the mark of unity and, since it is the only vantage point from which to view that unity, prevents all false and distorted conceptions. In it resides the comprehensive perception' (*FC* I 5). But this is 'perception' in a strongly idealist sense, as far removed as could possibly be from the kind of experimental psychology to which Korsyn tried to assimilate the Schenker of the 1890s:[74] as Ruth Solie says (1980: 150), Schenker 'predicated his notion of totality not upon perceptual mechanisms in the observer, but upon the work of art itself'. He says how the music *is*, not how it is heard (though, to repeat Rehding's phrase, from this follows the 'implicit "ought"' embodied in long-range hearing). As we have seen, however, in order to defend Schenker's method against crass misunderstanding, present-day Schenkerians such as Schachter have resorted to explanations that are perceptual in the quite different sense that they revolve round aural-imaginative experiences, 'hearings' of the music prompted by analysis. So there is clearly another mismatch here, which I shall address by reference to a principled approach to Schenker's writings that might be considered postmodern in its ascription of meaning not to the music but rather to the act of interpreting it.

Earlier I presented Babbitt as the presiding genius of the neo-Schenkerian project, based as it was on the translation of Schenker's insights into a rigorous and internally consistent metalanguage. It was Babbitt who famously, or infamously, wrote: 'there is but one kind of language, one kind of method for the verbal formulation of "concepts", whether in music theory or in anything else: "scientific" language and

---

[73] See Kielian-Gilbert 2003 for a development of the idea of 'oscillating' between different readings.

[74] See p. 60.

"scientific" method'.[75] But in some way that I suspect is fully intelligible only to those who have been long enough at Princeton, Babbitt simultaneously acted as godfather to an ostensively quite different analytical epistemology based on the construction of meaning through experience. In a review of Salzer's *Structural Hearing*, published in 1952, Babbitt raised and dealt with the familiar complaint that nobody hears Schenkerian backgrounds as follows:

> the test of the validity of Schenker's conceptions is not whether 'one hears that way' but whether, after having become aware of these conceptions, the listener does not find that they may not only codify his previous hearing but extend and enrich his perceptive powers by making listening more efficient and meaningful, by 'explaining' the formerly 'inexplicable', and by granting additional significance to all degrees of musical phenomena.[76]

This is a rationale for the Schenkerian practice which, to misquote Schachter, mght be called hearing with eyes as well as ears.

The most searching development of this idea, however, may be found in a 1990 article by Joseph Dubiel (who took his doctorate at Princeton), entitled '"When You Are a Beethoven": Kinds of Rules in Schenker's *Counterpoint*'; Dubiel's thinking is in turn developed in Robert Snarrenberg's 1997 book *Schenker's Interpretive Practice*, though I do not need to pursue the story that far. In essence, Dubiel reads *Kontrapunkt* as providing a systematic training in hearing the qualities of different note combinations—qualities which are not simply inherent in the musical sound, but result from the relationship between the sound and an appropriately constituted act of hearing. Accordingly, Dubiel says (1990: 316), we should 'interpret the study of species counterpoint not as the introduction of fundamental truths about "the tonal material", but as a field in which to practice making attributions which, in Schenker's (not ungrounded) opinion, it will be useful to make consistently and fluently'.[77] Seen from this point of view, Schenker's characteristic way of talking about music—in terms of the tones acting of their own volition, so that the music had to be the way it is—is revealed

---

[75] Babbitt 1972/1961: 3.

[76] Babbitt 2003: 24.

[77] Botstein (1997: 16) comes close to ascribing just such a model of musical meaning to Schenker, arguing that the unpredictable interactions between combined musical effects result in 'the potential for the attachment of changing emotional and extramusical meaning. . . . The classical masters . . . created musically coherent works that possessed an infinitely differentiated and individual opportunity for the ascription of emotional meaning'. The idea that combinations of effects might be (in Douglas Dempster's [1998] term) 'semantically compositional' seems to me at least compatible with Schenker's thinking, if nowhere actually stated by him. But to move from this to an attributional model—in which meaning is constructed through the act of ascription—is to move from what Schenker might have said to something he would never have said: for Schenker, meaning (of whatever sort) is always inherent in the music and the listener's job is to recognise it for what it is.

as a rhetorical sleight of hand: it smuggles agency from the analyst or listener into the music itself, thereby creating an impression of objectivity and inevitability. Despite what I just said, I shall quote Snarrenberg (1997: 133) at this point, since he puts it particularly clearly: 'The habit of investing tonal entities with subjectivity . . . minimizes the role of the perceiver's subjectivity in constituting content and thereby promotes the illusion that content is out there in the world, objective, eternal, immutable'.

There is a strong resonance between Dubiel's argument and Schenker's presentation, as early as the *Geist* essay, of counterpoint as a means of disciplining the aural imagination—an idea which underlies both volumes of *Kontrapunkt*, sometimes close to the surface and sometimes deeply buried. As for the rest of Dubiel's explanation, however, Schenker would have had no truck with it. What is at issue becomes clear when Dubiel cites a passage from *Kontrapunkt* 1 in which Schenker quotes Riemann's much more modest contention that consonance or dissonance are not inherent properties of chords but depend on the relationship of the chord to its context. Schenker then snorts: 'isn't the thing we call a "relationship" in truth merely a mode of our way of conceptualizing . . . and in no way an objective reality? But why should a "mode of thought" have such power over the natural phenomenon of consonance as to alter its innermost nature?!' (*C1* 282; recall what I said earlier in this chapter about appearances changing reality.) The standoff between Riemann and Schenker is ontological and intractable: Riemann sees consonance as a cognitive construction, whereas Schenker sees it as an objective reality, a fundamental truth, an absolute—out there in the world, objective, eternal, immutable.

And there is an even sharper example of such a standoff in 'Musikkritik' (Music criticism), an article written for the second issue of *Tonwille* but 'censored' (Schenker's word) at proof stage by Hertzka.[78] Here the target is Paul Bekker, who had excited Schenker's ire by, among other things, comparing Schenker's writings unfavourably with those of Kurth and Halm. In one of the many passages Schenker quotes, Bekker sets out the standard hermeneutical epistemology deriving from Dilthey:[79] 'The special art of criticism', he says, 'lies in making judgments based on feeling understandable and believable from the material penetration of the artistic substance' (*T2* 162–3). And because of this, Bekker continues, it is

in no way desirable that critical statements agree with one another. Such a result would turn criticism into what it always has been for the lazy

---

[78] Actually much of the material was doubly 'censored', having been written for the op. 101 *Erläuterungsausgabe* but deleted, again at proof stage (*T2* xv–xvi, 161n.).

[79] See p. 69 above.

thinkers among the reading public: the inviolable expression of 'the way it was'. In truth, however, every piece of criticism is invisibly headed by the words: 'the way I see it'.

But the whole *raison d'être* of Schenker's theory was of course to say 'the way it was' and not 'the way I see it': one of Schenker's *Meisterwerk* critiques, directed this time at Walter Engelsmann, concludes each of its four main arguments by intoning 'That is the way it is, not otherwise' (*MM1* 100–103), while in a later *Meisterwerk* passage on the masses and genius Schenker expands this into the positively liturgical 'Thus it was, thus it is, and thus it shall ever remain' (*MM2* 46). And so his response to Bekker's position is predictable enough: 'God save us then', he remarks acidly, 'from ultimately discovering who Bach is, who Beethoven is, how Beethoven differs from Wagner, and how these two are in turn utterly different from the symphonic illiteracy of, for instance, a Berlioz or a Mahler'. Further aspersions follow regarding Bekker's 'singular lack of objectivity' and 'hermeneutical misguidedness' before Schenker relapses into more or less personal abuse. In the face of such an epistemological gulf, there can be no basis for reasoned debate.

Perhaps the reason for Schenker's extreme sensitivity is that this again represents a fault-line in his own thinking. In chapter 1, I emphasised Schenker's insistence—despite his suspicion of scientific approaches—that music must be explained in terms of strict causality, which is to say according to the criteria associated by Dilthey with the natural rather than the human sciences; I quoted his rhetorical question from *Harmonielehre* ('Is it not true that a system must be strong enough to explain, without exception, all phenomena within its range?'), while later in the same work he proclaims that 'from the point of the view of the artist, each note must be heard in its artistically immanent cause and effect' (*H* 121). It was this concept of what it means to explain music, I argued, that led to the impasse embodied in the *Geist* essay, as well as—eventually—Schenker's solution to it in terms of axial causality. This solution allowed him to develop his theory beyond the self-evident absurdity of strict note-to-note determinism and incorporate within it the idea of freedom within the law to which I referred in chapter 2—but without forcing a rethinking of his epistemological assumptions, as may be seen from his exclamation in the last of the *Tonwille* pamphlets (*T2* 152): 'How wonderfully one force leads to another, each step becomes an event that embeds itself in the ordered succession, everywhere there is cause and effect, pattern and copy'. (Maybe the image of causality flowing from the background to the foreground was a further impediment to Schenker's conceiving of a two-way, interactive relationship between levels.) And seen from the perspective of such an epistemology, Schenker's exasperation with Bekker is easy enough to understand.

But the version of what Schenker meant by explaining music that

I have just set out is diametrically opposed to the one Wayne Alpern presents on the basis of his study of Schenker's legal education, as may be seen from a series of brief quotations from his thesis:

> Schenker's musical laws are modelled upon *nomos*, the civil laws of society, and not *physis*, the physical 'laws of nature' like the laws of thermodynamics or gravity. They are normative and prescriptive rather than objective and descriptive. . . . Schenker's musical legislation imposes normative obligations upon free agents like the laws of society or morality. Unlike the laws of physics or the logical dictates of mathematics, legal and moral obligations can be broken by free agents. Even so, the law remains. . . . Schenker presents music not as a logical construct or unalterable causal process, but as a social drama invoking an expressive internal dynamic offering critical means of adjudication and resolution within an overall framework.

And as evidence for this, Alpern cites Schenker's claim in the *Geist* essay that music lacks any principle of causation. Now it would be tempting for me to respond that you cannot characterise Schenker's thinking as a whole in terms of the *Geist* essay, and that this is just another example of the misinterpretation that results when quotations from different periods of Schenker's work are mixed together. But I do not think that would be right, for Alpern's image of the jurisprudential Schenker does indeed capture much of the tone and process of Schenker's analytical practice at least up to the mid-1920s. Yet the kind of musical explanation this embodies is quite incompatible with the idea of a natural-scientific mode of explanation based on causality: aiming at persuasion rather than proof, it stands much closer to Dilthey's model of the human sciences, or indeed to the kind of hermeneutical approach Schenker was condemning in Bekker. Schenker's views about what it means to explain music are, in short, as conflicted as his understanding of philosophical idealism. The most generous construction, which is probably too generous, is that he insisted on strict causality as a matter of principle, but in practice was more flexible, more humanistic than his principles should properly have allowed.

All the same, to bring back this argument to its starting point, it is inconceivable that Schenker would have accepted Dubiel's claim (1990: 332) that in *Kontrapunkt* he was formulating 'rules determining the content of possible attributions (and thereby roughly constraining the making of these attributions)'. Yet Dubiel makes an irresistible case that it would have been better all round if Schenker *had* framed his theory this way, and not in terms of supposed absolute laws the unavoidable—one sometimes feels intended—effect of which is to undercut the possibility of reasoned debate. Dubiel (307) professes himself perplexed as to 'why anyone would want to respond to a highly esteemed composition by telling a story of how it *had to be* exactly as it was', and wonders if this doesn't suggest some kind of character defect. But it is perhaps more productive to see it as an example of what I referred to as retrospective prophecy, the deeply conservative pattern of thought by which you explain empirical phenomena through positing ideal (eternal, immutable) entities that correspond to them, and then deriving the former from the latter, the actual from the ideal. This is what Schenker does in the Ninth Symphony monograph: as Snarrenberg puts it (1997: 34), Schenker explains what Beethoven wrote by setting out the effects that Beethoven intended, then 'takes the intention as given and specifies the "necessities that caused the tonal content to arise in just this way and not otherwise"'. It is a way of thinking that makes it necessary—inevitable—that everything should be precisely as it is (which is why I called it deeply conservative). And, as Schenker's continued rhetoric of inevitability shows, it is a way of thinking that survived the transition from the effects/means model to the axial causality one: indeed, as I suggested in the course of my comparison with *Der Nachsommer,* is it built into the very structure of *Der freie Satz.* It is also the conceptual mechanism that lies behind the exasperatingly normative and exclusive quality of Schenker's thought, the slippage from the demonstration of how (Viennese classical) music is to the claim that all music must be so—what Babbitt called 'an illicit derivation of a "should" from an "is" or—given that the analyses are exegetic wakes—of a "should" from a "was"'.[80]

Are we then to understand Schenker's theory on his own terms, however flawed or unacceptable we may consider his epistemology, or on ours, as illustrated by Dubiel's creative misreading of it? Is it defensible to pick and choose what we want from his work? Can it make sense to adopt his analytical methods while ignoring his aesthetic, political, and philosophical beliefs? The first two questions seem straightforward enough: in the United Kingdom at least, the term for authors' moral rights is identical to that for copyright, and in any case it is less a question of morality than of trades description, as when in his critique of Proctor and Riggins's 'Schenker pedagogy' Rothstein complains that 'in the interests of honesty, they should call theirs a Proctor-Riggins pedagogy and leave the name of Schenker out of it' (1990b: 295). But the last question is a hardy perennial of Schenker studies, and one that has become increasingly pressing as more and more work has been done on setting Schenker in his period context: work that has tended to roll back the modernist assumptions of Schenker's postwar reception, or— perhaps better expressed—to replace those assumptions with a more realistic, more conflicted, messier conception of Viennese modernism itself.

At one extreme is the position set out by Bent, which I quoted at the very beginning of this book: 'where his world of ideas is concerned, there are no margins: there is only a single, integrated network of thought'. At the opposite extreme is the position expressed by Rothgeb, which emanates from the first-generation followers and their editorial

---

[80] Babbitt 2003: 480.

policies: 'however much Schenker may have regarded his musical pre-
cepts as an integral part of a unified world-view, they are, in fact, not
at all logically dependent on any of his extramusical speculations. Indeed, no broader philosophical context is necessary—or even relevant—to their understanding'.[81] (1987 may have been a little late in
the day to be saying this, but it is only fair to note that this passage follows on Rothgeb's justification of his and Jürgen Thym's decision, as
editors and translators, not to abridge the text of *Kontrapunkt*.) The classic statement of this position, however, has to be the one Allen Forte
gave in his introduction to *Free Composition* (*FC* xviii):

> The modern-day English language reader may be somewhat puzzled, or
> perhaps even offended, by the polemical and quasi-philosophical material
> in Schenker's introduction and elsewhere. . . . In part, this material is typ-
> ical of many other German language authors of an older period; in part, it
> is characteristic of Schenker, and must be placed in proper perspective. Al-
> most none of the material bears substantive relation to the musical con-
> cepts that he developed during his lifetime and, from that standpoint, can
> be disregarded; it is, however, part of the man and his work.

As Schachter has said (2001: 10), the truth of this magisterially diplo-
matic formulation, with its recognition but at the same time marginal-
isation of context, would have at one time seemed self-evident but is
nowadays less so. All the same, Schachter's own views are essentially
the same, though expressed in a characteristically irresistible manner:
of course the polemical and quasi-philosophical material is important
for an understanding of the development of Schenkerian theory, he
concedes, but it is irrelevant when it comes to analytical practice—to
making specific interpretive decisions in particular musical contexts. 'I
must confess', he says, 'that I never think about Schenker's politics, religion, or philosophy when engaged in analyzing a piece or refining a
theoretical concept' (13). There isn't really an answer to that. There are
however two comments that can be made, one short and the other
longer.

The short comment is that to separate practice too cleanly from
theory is to encourage a practice that is unreflective—in which skills
are acquired and procedures gone through without consideration of
why they might be the appropriate skills or procedures, why the ques-

---

[81] *CI* xiv; see also Laufer's comments on *Free Composition*, quoted in note 8 above. Actually this view might be traced back as far as Schenker's original publishers, for as
Drabkin and Bent write with specific reference to *Tonwille*, 'Universal Edition never
seems to have grasped Schenker's conception of the Miscellenea as integral to their volumes: they viewed this section as an appendix (*Anhang*), while referring to the remainder of an issue as its content (*Inhalt*)' (*TI* xi). There is indeed a sense in which it might be
ascribed to Schenker, who at one time considered publishing his polemics—the preface
to the Ninth Symphony monograph, the forewords to the two volumes of *Kontrapunkt*,
extracts from the *Erläuterungsausgaben*, the 'Vermischtes' sections from *Tonwille* and *Meisterwerk*—as a separate, stand-alone volume (*MM3* 69n.); mercifully he never did so.

tions they are designed to address are the right questions, what indeed the questions are and where they have come from. In McCreless's words (1997: 31), Schenkerian theory (like atonal theory) is based on 'an aesthetic ideology whereby analysis validates masterworks that exhibit an unquestioned structural autonomy'. Or as Benjamin puts it (1981: 164), 'the theory encourages certain conceptions of what it means to "know music" and resists others'. Through the very act of practising, or teaching, Schenkerian analysis in the twentieth-first century, we work to an agenda built on such assumptions as that the moment-to-moment diversity of music represents a problem to be overcome through encompassing it within a larger unity (or, better, a reciprocal understanding of the local in terms of the global, and vice versa); that music is an ultimately cognitive entity which cannot be reduced to a series of sounds, gestures, or emotions; that what is most important about music is concealed (or, better, that what is overt needs to be understood in terms of what is not), meaning that a deep understanding of music entails special, indeed specialist skills; and so on. None of these assumptions is self-evident; there are always alternatives. That does not necessarily mean that there is anything wrong with working to these assumptions—depending on the repertory in question and the kind of understanding aimed at, they may be indispensable—but the point is that decisions have been made. They are built into the method. (As Neumeyer puts it [1990: 25], 'When you pick up the tool that is Schenker analysis, much of this comes with it.') And a knowledge of the context within which Schenker formulated his theory—of its social, political, religious, or philosophical dimensions—is important not just if one is to understand why these particular decisions have been made, thereby taking ownership of them, but if one is to understand that decisions have been made at all; the danger otherwise is of an analytical practice that has all the answers but none of the questions. (Rothstein comes near to saying that of Proctor and Riggins.) This is not to claim that Schenker's view of democracy, for instance, has any relevance at the moment of deciding whether the primary tone is $\hat{3}$ or $\hat{5}$, much less that one needs to condone it—but if you have *never* worried about Schenker's elitist conception of culture, never wondered what Schenker saw as the point of analysis, never asked what Schenker's project was, then there is an odds-on chance that you are doing analysis because it is there to be done, because it is doable, rather than on the basis of any more critical or personal investment. Analysis can mean more than that.

The second and longer comment has to do with the particular argument that Schachter invokes to justify his position. Schenker believed firmly in the autonomy of music, Schachter says, and so did his friends and pupils who accepted his musical insights while deploring his politics, and in this way 'the removal of political ideology from Schenker's approach—a trend that developed in full force here in the

United States—actually began early on in Austria and Germany'
(Schachter 2001: 12). That is undoubtedly true: after the comment I
quoted in chapter 3 that not all Schenker's friends supported his political statements, for instance, Vrieslander continued: 'Art may indeed be
kept free of all that serves the present day, and all political grumbles belong to that'.[82] Yet the autonomy of music is not the straightforward
and self-evident concept for which the postwar music-theoretical establishment took it, as is evident from the highly contested role it plays
in Schenker's writings. The statement by Richard Wallaschek I quoted
in chapter 3 ('German music in fact has no national-characteristic element in its artistic works; it is pure beauty') illustrates what is at stake,
as does Neumeyer's characterisation of the Americanisation of Schenker
(1990: 25): 'the analytic method was in fact detached from Schenker's
ideology, but only to be plugged into another kind of ideology appropriate to the American academy'. (He adds: 'post-structuralist analysis
of texts to uncover the exact components of this ideology would be
very welcome'.) Perhaps predictably, the problem goes back to Hanslick, or rather the misreading of Hanslick to which I referred in chapter 1. I can make the point in terms of a passage from 'Die Urlinie: Eine
Vorbemerkung' which Schachter himself quotes:

> The so-called poetic idea is also given the lie by the Urlinie. Although ever
> so many analogies may be swept from human life into music (how should
> humanly conceived art *not* embody the human?), the poetic idea may be
> relied upon all too often by all those muscle-men of 'expression' who do
> not grasp that it is only possible for them to dissolve themselves in art and
> not art in themselves; or by certain hermeneutical babblers of 'affect'
> whose inability compels them to see rather than hear their way about in
> music, as in the rest of the objective world, and thereby compels them to
> debase music to a cinema for the ears. Above and beyond all that, music
> with the Urlinie remains a world of its own, unto itself, comparable to the
> Creation in the sense that it rests only in itself, operating with no end in
> sight. (*TI* 21)

Schenker is marshalling against those who ascribe poetic ideas to
music the same argument he used to attack Kretzschmar and Kurth
(whose observations of the notes going upwards or downwards, 'these
being the only two possible directions', illustrate the 'cinema for the
ears' that Schenker refers to here). It is only because musical ideas are
specifically musical, Schenker is saying, only insofar as they are governed by the *Urlinie*, that they possess specific expressive meaning: the
hermeneutic babblers misunderstand musical meaning because, like
Kurth, they do not realise that it is generated by specifically musical
processes, and that is why their descriptions of it are otiose and redundant. Or as Schachter puts it (2001: 11), 'For Schenker the symbolic
connections between music and the world take on validity only when

---

[82] Vrieslander, 'Heinrich Schenker und sein Werk (see chapter 3, note 31), p. 78.

the music is heard and understood in its autonomy'. But that of course is precisely Hanslick's central argument in *Vom Musikalisch-Schönen*— the argument which, as I said, has since Hanslick's own time been persistently misrepresented as a denial that music can be anything except autonomous, that it can convey feelings, moods, or emotions. Peter Gay sees Hanslick as having brought this misreading on himself through his 'memorable, but far too simple, sentence: "The contents of music are sounding moving forms". . . . Once Hanslick had launched it, he had launched the myth of his formalism'.[83] If that is so, then perhaps Schenker brought the same misunderstanding on himself, for in the preface to *Harmony* he came close to quoting Hanslick's phrase ('the theory of harmony presents itself to me as . . . a system of ideally moving forces').[84] Either way—to repeat it once more, but it seems to be something one has to keep repeating—the essential point is that neither Hanslick nor Schenker are seeking to deny that music has meaning in more than a technical sense: their argument is that you need first to understand music as music ('as an autonomous domain', as Schachter puts it [11]), for only then are you in a position to understand it as the bearer of expressive or social meaning.

It might be said that Schachter—like the larger postwar music-theoretical project to which he has made so distinguished a contribution— has turned the claim that it is necessary to understand music as an autonomous domain into an assumption that it is sufficient to do so: that is what underlies his distinction between Schenkerian theory, for which an understanding of context is important, and Schenkerian practice, for which it isn't (Schachter 2001: 13). And Schachter reads a parallel distinction into Schenker's own work: 'The polemical statements', he writes, 'are only rarely attached to the analytical monographs or the theoretical explanations; they appear as separate essays, as introductory material (perhaps in a foreword), or as aphorisms placed in a section of miscellaneous remarks' (12). That is often true, of course, for instance in *Kontrapunkt*, where the polemical material is basically restricted to the prefaces, or *Der freie Satz*, where it comes mainly in the introduction—which actually includes a section called 'Aphorisms'—or the first chapter, 'The Background' (these are the source of ten of the seventeen passages in appendix 4 of *Free Composition*). But it is not so true of other writings, as illustrated by several of the 1890s essays, or by the Ninth Symphony monograph (where analytical and polemical materials roughly alternate), or the *Meisterwerk* essay 'Weg mit dem Phrasierungsbogen', which—as I have repeatedly said—presents

---

[83] Gay 1978: 271–2. Payzant translates Hanslick's phrase as 'The content of music is tonally moving forms' (Hanslick 1986/1854: 29).

[84] *H* xxv; the similarity is however in part an artefact of translation (Hanslick's phrase is 'tönend bewegte Formen', Schenker's 'eine Welt von ideell treibenden Kräften').

an argument that is about music and politics at the same time. And in these latter cases, any straightforward categorisation of Schenker's writing into the technical and the polemical, the musical and the extramusical, ceases to be tenable: the domains of the musical and the extramusical become coextensive.

As so often, the problem comes from trying to read Schenker's work as a whole through *Der freie Satz*, where the passages on music's broader social and cultural meaning no longer seem fully thought into the work. Sometimes they have an obvious source in one of Schenker's earlier writings (as in the case of the comments on Scarlatti, which as I said in chapter 4 come from *Meisterwerk* 1). At other times they have the appearance of ideas or quotations Schenker has previously stockpiled and now applies decoratively, as Rytting said;[85] this is most obviously the case in the 'Aphorisms' section, which is exactly what its title suggests—an unordered sequence of observations that did not find a home anywhere else. The disorganised impression may be just the result of the circumstances under which *Der freie Satz* was completed, or maybe it would be better to say brought to a halt. But it may be that, by 1935, many of the basic impulses that had motivated the Schenker project in the 1890s had lost their hold on Schenker, or perhaps it was just the certainty that they would not be given realisation in his lifetime; either would explain the way in which the aphorisms have taken on the quality of fossils, vestigial remains of a more broadly imagined project. And if so, there is, after all, a sense in which the editors of *Free Composition* knew what they were doing when they removed those passages to appendix 4.

---

[85] See p. 45 above.

Conclusion

Music Theory as Social Practice

If bad news makes good copy, then good news makes no copy at all. This is not just a journalistic adage: it is a basic principle that affects the interpretation of historical documents. The problem is not simply that contemporary commentators wax eloquent on what is bad without telling us what is good, though this is certainly a problem in the study of period performance (we are told that modern musicians do too much of this or not enough of that, but cannot get a clear impression of the norm against which 'too much' or 'not enough' are measured). It is that commentators do not tell us what was taken for granted, what was considered self-evident or more likely not considered at all, and the result is that we can sometimes reconstruct a great deal of detail about a particular practice and yet lack a basic understanding of what it meant, what made it meaningful, what it felt like. In this sense, the situation of Schenkerian theory today is rather like that of a performing tradition that has been lost, or to make the analogy more accurate, a tradition that has developed into something quite different from what it used to be, so that its original form needs to be reconstructed on the basis of the available evidence. The specifically theoretical content of Schenkerian theory remains intact: no significant bridging of historical distance is necessary in order to understand what Schenker meant by unfolding or obligatory register. The historical gap is in our understanding of what the theory as a whole meant to Schenker and his contemporaries, and what we call his 'polemics' flag up an entire dimension of meaning absent from Schenkerian theory and practice in their present-day, Americanised form. Rectifying this is partly a question of situating Schenker's thought in its contemporary philosophical context, although as I complained in chapter 1, this has often been done by treating Schenker as if he was a philosopher, rather than a music theorist working in a milieu with basic intellectual assumptions different from our own. But other contexts play an equally important role in bringing to light connotations, or rather whole systems of signification, that in *fin-de-siècle* Vienna were self-evident, taken for granted, and accordingly absent or at best incompletely presented in what Schenker wrote, and it is a selection of such contexts that I have presented in this book.

What might it mean to embody this knowledge of Schenker's contexts within a new, or reconstructed, practice of reading his work? At the most basic level, it is a matter of becoming aware of the broader cultural or social resonances of apparently straightforward technical terminology, and the way what is ostensively an argument about music may be as much motivated by the cultural or social values it articulates or—more problematically—does not articulate. A good example is the network of terms connected with harmonic rootedness, terms which have a technical musical meaning yet at the same time carry the imprint of the political and racial discourses of *fin-de-siècle* Vienna. These political and racial connotations tend to be spelt out more explicitly in Schoenberg's theoretical writings than Schenker's, and the term Schoenberg uses in his *Harmonielehre* to describe chords that lack rootedness immediately reveals what is at issue: they are 'vagrant' chords. It is not just the term that creates the meaning: Schoenberg retained it in his textbook *Structural Functions of Harmony,* but in that auto-Americanised text[1] (completed in 1948) the idea of vagrancy functions as little more than a piquant but isolated metaphor, the vestige of a meaning Schoenberg elaborated much more fully in *Harmonielehre.* Circumstances can turn any chord into a vagrant, he says there;[2] perhaps he was thinking of the displaced *Ostjuden* (later he might have thought of himself). But there is one class of chords that are vagrant 'by nature': those that lack perfect fifths (the obvious example is the chord of the diminished seventh), and so are artificial in the sense that they have been generated by 'logical development of the tonal system'. Schoenberg may or may not have been thinking of literary models of the artificial man—Frankenstein, the golem—but at all events he assigns a range of equally dubious attributes to his vagrants: they are 'the issue of inbreeding', their character 'indefinite, hermaphroditic, immature'. It is possible for them to be assimilated (Schoenberg's phrase is 'fit into the environment'), but when they appear in large numbers they will 'join forces',

---

[1] If it was: that depends on the role of Leonard Stein (see the 'acknowledgment' in Schoenberg 1969/1954: vii).
[2] Schoenberg 1978/1911: 196.

and 'through accumulation of such phenomena the solid structure of tonality could be demolished'; elsewhere Schoenberg says that vagrant chords have 'led inexorably to the dissolution of tonality'.[3]

The resonances with contemporary conservative discourse are almost too obvious to point out: the dangers posed by a large unassimilated underclass, especially if they 'join forces'; the idea that vagrancy can be inherent rather than the product of circumstances; the theme of inbreeding (elsewhere Schoenberg refers to incest and emasculation)—all these are shared, as Julie Brown points out (1994: 68), with the ideology of Houston Chamberlain and later the Third Reich, where the vagrants will be identified as gypsies and Jews. But this is just part of a wider discourse concerned with the idea of roots and rootedness. When in 1925 Schoenberg was appointed to the Prussian Academy of the Arts in Berlin, fourteen years after the publication of *Harmonielehre*, the conservative musicologist and critic Alfred Heuss attacked the 'specifically Jewish spirit' of Schoenberg's music, which he saw as resulting from a 'ruthless tendency to draw the very last consequences from a narrow premise'; this, he said, 'has nothing in common with German attitudes. . . . The Jew who relies only on himself, is no longer rooted in any soil, and consciously defies tradition—that kind of Jew as fanatic leader means nothing else than the road to perdition'. That kind of Jew is quite different from the 'genuine' ones who 'have made themselves truly at home in a culture and are in their way capable of contributions of great importance', Heuss continues, and he concludes: '*Rooted and rootless Jews,* that is the principal issue in this matter'. The idea of roots or origins is also a heavily invested one in Jewish writing of the period, whether in Roth's nostalgic evocation of the rootedness of the Galician shtetl (in contrast to the 'sterilized anonymity of urban bourgeois existence with all its superficial cleanliness, comforts, and technological appliances'),[4] or indeed in Schoenberg's own Zionist proclamation in 1933 that 'our essence is not Western: the latter is only an external borrowed one. We must return to our origins, to the source of our strength, to the place where our toughness originates and where we shall discover our ancient fighting spirit'.[5]

Quite what one is meant to make of Schoenberg's appropriation of these discourses in *Harmonielehre* is another matter. At some points, it seems as if he is making a rather grim kind of fun of racist stereotypes, as when he speaks of vagrant chords as 'homeless phenomena, unbelievably adaptable and unbelievably lacking in independence; spies, who ferret out weaknesses and use them to cause confusion; turncoats, to whom abandonment of their individuality is an end in itself; agitators

---

[3] Schoenberg 1978/1911: 247, 196.

[4] Wistrich 1989: 658.

[5] Letter of 13 June 1933 to Dr Jakob Klatzkin, translated in Lazar 1994: 105 (partly quoted in chapter 4, p. 243n. above).

in every respect, but above all: most amusing fellows'.[6] At all events, Schoenberg's argument ends up undermining the conservative discourses from which it borrows, and it does so in a manner unmistakably reminiscent of Wagner. In chapter 4, I mentioned how, in the postscript he added in 1869 for the republication of 'Das Judenthum in der Musik', Wagner called on 'intelligent and high-minded Jews' to act as the redeemers of German music (there is an echo of this in Heuss's 'genuine' Jews). Schoenberg achieves a similar inversion when he talks of vagrant chords bringing about the destruction of the tonal system: 'the consequence', he writes, 'is not necessarily disintegration and formlessness. For the chromatic scale is a form, too. It too, has a formal principle, a different one from that of the major or minor scale, a simpler and more uniform principle. Perhaps it is an unconscious striving for simplicity that leads musicians here'—just, he adds, as the seven church modes were simplified into the major and minor scales.[7]

And this links up with the passage I have already quoted from earlier in *Harmonielehre,* where Schoenberg writes, 'even if our tonality is dissolving, it already contains within it the germs of the next artistic phenomenon.'[8] He continues: 'Nothing is definitive in culture; everything is only preparation for a higher stage of development, for a future which at the moment can only be imagined, conjectured'. Here the Hegelian frame of reference is self-evident. But the way Schoenberg turns a conservative argument against the archetypal Other into an affirmation of the role of the Other in the future of German culture might be seen as representing something more than an invocation of the Hegelian dialectic to legitimise atonality. It is, if the word can be used without anachronism, a deconstruction of the conservative discourse of hybridity. And it works by taking a political stance, translating that into musical terms, developing the musical argument, and then translating (or leaving the reader to translate) the conclusion back into political terms. In other words, it uses music to create an assertion about something other than music—in rather the same way, to draw an analogy which is perhaps not as distant as it might appear, that television commercials use musical logic to make a point about hair dye or financial products.[9]

Schenker does not talk about vagrancy, nor does he use the terminology of roots, origins, and sources in the blatantly political manner that Schoenberg does in *Harmonielehre,* and yet such concepts are an integral part of his system. There is no better way of making the point than to quote (again) the opening sentences of *Der freie Satz:*

[6] Schoenberg 1978/1911: 258.
[7] Schoenberg 1978/1911: 247.
[8] Schoenberg 1978/1911: 97.
[9] For the claim about television commercials see Cook 1998: 3–23.

The origin of every life, whether of nation, clan, or individual, becomes its destiny. Hegel defines destiny as 'the manifestation of the inborn, original predisposition of each individual'.

The inner law of origin accompanies all development, and is ultimately part of the present.

Origin, development and present I call background, middleground, and foreground: their union expresses the oneness of an individual, self-contained life. (*FC* I 3)

Though there is no explicit mention of roots here, the reference to 'the oneness of an individual, self-contained life' might be read against the stereotype of the Jew as a purely relational being, defined not by what he or she is but by the sum total of what he or she is not: in Leo Pinsker's words, the Jew 'is not a native in his own home country, but he is also not a foreigner; he is, in very truth, the stranger par excellence. He is regarded as neither friend nor foe, but as an alien, of whom the only thing known is that he has no home'.[10] Indeed, the idea of the individual—and particularly the 'complete' individual—was a trope of German conservative discourse at this time (Reiter 2003: 143). But the mention of the 'origin' (*Ursprung*) takes us much deeper into Schenkerian theory, while at the same time being one of the most resonant terms of both Jewish and gentile discourse at the Viennese *fin de siècle:* on the one hand invoking Hegel (whom Schenker explicitly mentions), the term when read in its period context also conveys a nostalgic sense of lost wholeness (a sense in which it is particularly associated with Kraus). It carries the latter connotation in the third paragraph, where Schenker defines 'the oneness of an individual, self-contained life' in terms of the linkage of origin and present, background and foreground: seen from this point of view, Schenker's theory, at one level a theory of music, is at the same time a discourse on rootedness in general. And the second paragraph, again connecting the origin with the present, represents a one-sentence summary—although this time not expressed in specifically musical terms—of what in chapter 5 I referred to as the fundamental insight of Schenkerian theory, that prolongation subsists in the retention of the consonant point of departure.[11]

Actually there is another contemporary discourse which is relevant here, and the fact that I am bringing it up so late in the book demonstrates what I said in chapter 1 about there always being one more context to be adduced. This is what Alexander Rehding refers to as the phi-

---

[10] Quoted in Lazar 1994: 27. The similarity to anti-Semitic stereotypes such as Heuss's characterisation of Schoenberg illustrates the well-known interdependence of anti-Semitism and Zionism (Pinsker was a Russian Jew who proposed the idea of a Jewish state fifteen years before Herzl).

[11] See chapter 5, p. 283. There is a distinct echo here of Rameau's idea (derived from the canonist tradition) of notes returning to their source; as I said earlier, Schenker vilifies those theorists on whom he draws the most.

losophy of origins (2000: 346–7), the conservative discourse—reflected in the academic discipline of philology—based on the following idea:

> While the origin of an object, invariably imagined to be pure and simple, may become overlaid with complex layers of historical meanings so that the initial simplicity is obscured—or perhaps refined—over time, it can never be fully abandoned: the origin was understood as that which is consistent in the face of change. Knowledge of the point of origin of an object . . . can afford insights into this once pure and authentic state.

While this resonates with the Hegelian history and archaeological metaphors we have already encountered, it goes further than that. I called it a conservative discourse because it affords a rationale not only for doctrines of racial purity but also for the narratives of decline so pervasive in Schenker's lifetime. If, as Rehding goes on to say, the philosophy of origins constructs identity through opposition to a nonoriginary Other, then cultural decline can be attributed to adulteration: the striking similarity between Riemann's account of the collapse of the tonal tradition through the pernicious effect of Berlioz[12] and the one Schenker had put forward several years earlier in his unpublished *Niedergang* can only be attributed to a common framework of thought. (This discourse of musical purity, linked to the claim that 'in the final analysis, the decline of German tonality was caused from without' [378], is what Schoenberg was mocking in *Harmonielehre*.)[13] It is also a conservative discourse because, to quote Rehding again, 'in the philosophy of origins the point of departure does not legitimize the tradition emerging from it, contrary to its own claims, but conversely, it is the tradition being legitimized that determines the identification of its origin' [349]). This is exactly the pattern of thought I have been describing as retrospective prophecy.

And to say that is to establish the link with Schenker's analytical practice. One of the drawbacks of Oster's translations of *Urlinie* and *Ursatz* as 'fundamental line' and 'fundamental structure' is that the English terms lack the connotation of the primordial which Schenker's coinages convey, and which links them to the philosophy of origins. To

---

[12] Rehding 2000: 378, quoting Riemann's *Handbuch der Musikgeschichte*: 'It is beyond dispute that Hector Berlioz gave the first initiative to the anti-formalist tendencies of the post-Beethovenian age, seeking novelties *à tout prix*'; he goes on to comment, 'Strauss and Schoenberg in his wake became the metaphorical executioners in the destruction of the tonal legacy', perhaps fortuitously echoing Schenker's description of Wagner as 'the hangman of German music' (*TI I* 24). Two further comments might be made: first, of the principal protagonists in Rehding's account of the philosophy of origins, two were resident in Vienna (Richard Wallascheck and Guido Adler); second, Rehding's statement that 'the origin was understood as that which is consistent in the face of change' might be linked with my speculation in chap. 5, n. 33 concerning the time-based and the timeless in Schenker's theory.

[13] Hence his claim that 'It is not that the war *was lost*, rather that *we lost it*' (see p. 155 above).

be sure, Schenker is not saying the *Ursatz* came first in a historical sense, but then, as Rehding says (2000: 347), 'The origin, as it is constructed in musicology, refers back beyond a historical "first cause", connoting rather an essence'. It is in this sense that Schenker's model of axial causality represents a specifically music-theoretical formulation of the way, to quote it yet again, 'The inner law of origin accompanies all development, and is ultimately part of the present'. And that is just the point. In itself, the idea that prolongation subsists in the retention of the consonant point of departure might be said to amount to little more than Schoenberg's facetious remark about harmonies that always carry with them 'a certificate of domicile and passport carefully indicating country of origin and destination'.[14] But the connotations of rootedness as against homelessness, or of original purity as against adulteration, remain as Schenker develops the idea into the basis of a theoretical system that might be said, in the most general way, to articulate the relationship between the centrifugal—the urge towards individual identity (whether as tone or person), towards difference—and the centripetal, the urge towards collectivity or dependence on the whole. One would hardly expect someone who had invested as heavily as Schenker in the ideal of cultural assimilation to adopt Schoenberg's picturesque and provocative—not to say racy—vocabulary; it is characteristic that he favours legal terminology when he says of the finale from op. 101, 'Beethoven metes out justice in fitting proportion to each individual note, as we see here; he places them all at the service of an idea, and creates the super- and substructure required for its realization . . . and achieves the euphony of an organic whole'.[15] But as I have now explained several times, the point about the Hegelian framework in which I have attempted to situate Schenker is that it presents issues of whole and part, centre and periphery, unity and difference, in such a stripped-down, abstracted manner as to be equally and simultaneously applicable to politics, the law, or music.

A practice of reading Schenker in context will not understand the social or political references in his writings as simple metaphors, that is to say figurative language that draws certain connotations into the music-theoretical discourse but leaves it otherwise unchanged. Nor is it just a matter of alternating between musical and social or political discourse, in the manner of Schoenberg's deconstruction of hybridity. The idea of the community of tones is at the same time a musical and a social one, so that when at the end of 'Weg mit dem Phrasierungsbogen' Schenker draws conclusions about the state of the world, he is translating his argument into a different terminology rather than changing the subject. If, to make the point, Schenker's analytically based stric-

---

[14] Schoenberg 1978/1911: 129.
[15] Schenker 1972/1921]: 85–6, translated in Goldman 1990: 166–7 (the ellipses denote a passage omitted in Jonas's edition).

tures about unity as uniformity are applied to Adler's comparison between music and the 'higher unity' of the Habsburg empire,[16] the result is a forewarning of what happened in the post-1918 nation-states
that took its place: they defined political unity as ethnic uniformity, and
ethnic cleansings continue to this day.

Yet even if the musical and the social represent different dimensions of a single discourse, one can still ask just what the relationship
between these domains of signification is meant to be. The most familiar answer to this question, not least because it was the one adopted by
the 'New' musicologists of the 1990s, is that music represents society.
When Adorno—on whom some at least of the 'New' musicologists drew
heavily at this point—described middle-period Beethoven as encoding
the values of Vormärz Vienna, in which there was fleetingly a balance
between the interests of the individual and the state,[17] he was implying that music reflects society: in some more or less mysterious way, a
musical score bears within it the traces of the society that gave rise to
it. Adorno's most concise statement of this principle is that music 'presents social problems through its own material and according to its own
formal laws—problems which music contains within itself in the innermost cells of its technique'.[18] Though this is a characteristically cryptic formulation, one element in the relationship is clearly homology:
significant social patterns are reproduced in musical terms, as in the
balance Adorno saw in middle-period Beethoven between the individuation of the parts—local keys, characteristic passages—and the formal
demands of the whole. By contrast, he interpreted the fragmentation
of Beethoven's late style, what he saw as the failure of synthesis between part and whole, as representing the alienation inherent in a society in which the relationship between individual and state was no
longer in balance. 'New' musicologists' appropriations of Adorno's approach equally drew on the principle of homology, most obviously in
the parallel pursued by Susan McClary (1991: chap. 5) between the
teleological drive inherent in Beethoven's music and a highly gendered
construction of subjectivity (between the two senses of 'climax', to put
it crudely).

What did Schenker think? It seems likely that for him the interrelationship of music and social meaning was self-evident; at all events,
he never presented a systematic exposition of it. There are however a
number of statements relating to the topic, some of which I have already quoted, within a few pages of one another in *Der freie Satz*, and
from these it is evident that homology plays a part in his thought. That
is the principle underlying the parallels between music and emotional

---

[16] See p. 12 above.

[17] See p. 190 above.

[18] Quoted from Adorno, "On the Social Situation of Music", *Telos* 35 (1978) in Martin 1995: 100.

life Schenker frequently draws, most explicitly when he writes that 'we perceive our own life-impulse in the motion of the fundamental line, a full analogy to our inner life' (*FC* I 4)—an idea which we nowadays associate particularly with Suzanne Langer, but which was advanced in chapter 2 of Hanslick's *Vom Musikalisch-Schönen*, and was old even then. And on other occasions, Schenker speaks of reflection ('music mirrors the human soul') or simulation (music 'may simulate expectation, preparation, surprise, disappointment, patience, impatience, and humor').[19] But there are times when he seems to be saying not that the music reflects or simulates the phenomena of emotional life, but rather that it *enacts* them: just a few lines before his reference to simulation, he comments that 'In the art of music, as in life, motion toward the goal encounters obstacles, reverses, disappointments, and involves great distances, detours, expansions, interpolations, and, in short, retardations of all kinds' (his intention at this point is to establish the psychologically foundational role of prolongation), while a page later he writes that 'as a motion through several levels, as a connection between two mentally and spatially separate points, every relationship represents a path which is as real as any we "traverse" with our feet' (*FC* I 6). The clearest expression of this idea, however, comes from the 'Vermischtes' section of *Tonwille* 4: to the great masters, Schenker writes, 'was given what was denied even to the religious institutions: namely, to grant mankind actual fulfillment, not merely a recipe for fulfillment' (*T1* 160).[20]

That music is a powerful means of creating or transforming identity, an arena within which different identities can be lived out or imagined, is well known to ethnomusicologists and popular music scholars. Mark Slobin writes that people 'may try to wish themselves out of their class' (in the case of *fin-de-siècle* Vienna one might substitute 'race'), and he continues: 'music is a good way to imagine you are somewhere else' (1992: 29). (That takes us back to the account I offered in the introduction of music in Galicia.) And this performative orientation is consistent with the Hanslick/Schenker approach to musical meaning to which I have repeatedly referred. Snarrenberg explains it like this, with reference to Schenker's suggestion that the performer should create an effect of swooning at a certain point in Beethoven's Sonata op. 110:

> There is no body swooning in bar 9 of the *Arioso dolente*. There is only swooning. Swooning is not what bar 9 means, as if the tones somehow pointed to the concept of swooning. Quite the contrary: 'swooning' points to the tones and the complexion of their effects. (1997: 119)

---

[19] *FC* I xxxiii, 5.

[20] A similar idea is found in Walter Dahms's (1925) article 'The Biology of Music', which is based throughout on Schenker's ideas though his name appears only once in it (on p. 45): Dahms argues that whereas representational art 'depicts Nature and Life in their own semblance . . . music in any shape is also a bit of life'. There is an article entitled 'Musikalische Biologie' in Schenker's scrapbook (OC 2/38, from the *Ostdeutsche Rund-*

Rather than representing swooning, that is to say, the musical effect is so configured as to prompt an imaginative enactment of swooning, and in that enactment the tones will be understood. What I am suggesting is that we might see—and that Schenker himself may have seen—music's social meaning in the same way: music is not, or not just, a reflection or simulation of social reality, but the enactment of it. This is what I meant when I spoke of the chamber music concerts in the Bösendorfer-Saal as an enactment of *Gemeinschaft*, a reliving through music of the aristocratic culture of the Vormärz, or at least of that culture as it was remembered, or misremembered, in the nostalgically modernist Vienna of the *fin de siècle*. It is also in this light that I would read one of those fantasising passages from *Der freie Satz* I have already quoted: 'If, after centuries have passed, only one person is once more capable of hearing music in the spirit of its coherence, then even in this one person music will again be resurrected in all its absoluteness' (*FC* I xxiv).

The listener to op. 110 does not swoon but enacts swooning in his or her imagination; the quotation about the 'path which is as real as any we "traverse" with our feet' continues 'a relationship is to be "traversed" *in thought*' (my emphasis). From as early as the *Geist* essay, Schenker locates the core of music in spirit rather than technique, and so—like Hanslick—understands it not as a titillation of the ears and nerves but as an object of thought, a system of ideally moving forces, a community of tones. And that, of course, places what we see as analysis but what Schenker (who detested the word)[21] saw as the only fully adequate form of aesthetic experience at the heart of musical culture. For Schenker, whose gravestone reads 'Here lies the man who perceived the soul of music, and who proclaimed its laws as the masters understood them, as no one had done before',[22] it was a matter of experiencing music correctly: of hearing the masterworks for what they really are, and conveying that practice of hearing to others so that—in Snarrenberg's words—they may 'participate re-creatively in the tradition and so nourish their spirits with the products of music's world-historical individuals' (1997: xvi). (It is in order to emphasise this performative dimension of Schenker's theory that Snarrenberg entitles the final chapter of his book 'Participation'.) For us, to whom Schenker is

---

schau, 16 October 1913), but it is a much briefer and less developed piece than the *Musical Quarterly* one.

[21] In *Meisterwerk* 3 Schenker refers to 'that much used and abused term "analysis"', adding 'a new concept or form of expression needs to be coined for the extrapolation of foreground relationships from the background and middleground. But on no account should it be called analysis' (*MM3* 68).

[22] Drabkin 2002: 831; the German text, together with a photograph of the tombstone, may be found in Chiang 1996: 47. This epitaph was specified in the codicil to Schenker's will (see Chapter 5, n. 6).

one theorist among many, analysis is rather a matter of making choices, of deciding what there is to hear, of construing music as an object of thought. Either way, it is a process inevitably informed by our experiences of the personal, social, and cultural world in which we live, and so analysis becomes a site for the construction of music as socially meaningful. And because the process of signification works in two directions, it is also a vehicle for the feeding back of musical meaning into the world beyond music.

McClary's project was to establish correlations between music and social meaning: she identified homologies between the patterns of music and those of society, and saw them as conduits for the flow of signification. But in reality her homologies were not established directly with the music: they were mediated by conventional notions of cadential direction, harmonic rhythm, formal plan, and so forth, for it is only insofar as the music is construed in these terms that the patterns which support the homologies can be said to exist. As Kofi Agawu pointed out, among others, McClary did not thematise these analytical constructions: 'The props of insight-formation are considered self-evident', he complained (1997: 302), in other words they are presented as just the way the music is. The point Agawu wanted to make was that analysis, attacked by 'New' musicologists for its complicity in the ideology of musical autonomy, was in fact ubiquitous in the 'New' musicologists' interpretations, but concealed, and hence not open to critique. The point I want to make is that any attempt to read direct from music to society, or vice versa, is problematic in two ways: first, it involves an illegitimate distinction between music and society, in that music is one of the dimensions within which social relations are performed; and second, it attempts to short-circuit the interface between music and the rest of society, which is precisely the process of critical reflection on what music is—or might be—that we call analysis. Of course, nobody would want to claim that music has meaning only because of analysis in the academic sense, let alone that it has meaning only for analysts. But if the social meaning of music depends on the correlation of musical and other social patterns, then it is based on those construals of music as thought that are presented in an explicit and discussable manner in music theory, and internalised in the experiences of all who participate in musical culture: it is in this sense that, as Goethe wrote and as Schenker quoted him in the inscription of chapter 1 of *Der freie Satz*, 'one can say that with every intent glance at the world we theorize' (*FC* I 3). To be sure, this is not a matter of *Urlinien* or unfoldings, but it is certainly a matter of such basic ontological constructions as the idea of music being a system of ideally moving forces or a community of tones.

And if analysis presents musical meaning in the making, then it is not enough to understand it in purely technical terms, as we might understand the development of the internal combustion engine. It must rather be understood as imbued with worldly meaning, as drawing its signification from the multiple contexts within which we live, as funnelling our experiences, hopes, and fears into music and back from music into the world we inhabit. The aim of this book was to show how that might be.

Appendix

Heinrich Schenker,
'The Spirit of Musical Technique'
(Der Geist der musikalischen
Technik)

Translated by William Pastille

1. Melody

Since every organ of the human body strives innately to fulfill its specific characteristics and drives, it is quite possible that the larynx and the vocal chords themselves may have compelled the first humans to voice the first musical tone. Just as songbirds use mere rasps and screeches for the commonplace urge to squabble and bicker, but lend the poetry of song to the urge for sex and procreation as well as to the closely related hunger drive; just as they greet the shimmering profusion of the sun's rays with bright, shimmering tones; so too in the first humans the vocal chords could have been set in motion innately by every elevated condition of the soul whose essence was joy, and by every elevated sensation, whereas plain speech without musical tones—saturated as it is with concepts and actualities—sufficed for humdrum emotions and other routine functions.

The first singing was probably a sudden, spontaneous outburst of accumulated emotional or physical delight, as one sees nowadays in children and shepherds when they convert instinctive joy into instinctive exultation. Soon, however, the joy of singing must have become an end in itself, dissociating singing from its immediate stimuli and establishing it as an independent, specialised field. This was song for song's sake. Much later, humans eventually learned how to excite and inspire the musical imagination with mere mental representations, with images of objects and emotions. In this situation, the resulting emotional vibrations derived not from an intrinsically musical cause, but rather from a mediated external cause. From that point onward, these creative prin-

This translation was originally published in *Theoria* 3 (1988), 86–104, but has been completely revised.

ciples governed the art of music, and these alone will continue to govern it until the end of time. None of these principles is so egotistical, however, that it desires to exclude the participation of the others; in the vast majority of cases, rather, the content of a musical artwork is based on the interaction of these principles.

The most underrated of these principles—even ridiculed nowadays for a variety of reasons—is no doubt that which separates music from an actual or imagined emotion or sensation, and establishes it instead on the footing of a purely internal desire for activity. I should like to call this the formal principle of creation. It is perhaps most difficult to make music according to this principle alone, for how quickly the activity degenerates into randomness and incoherence, into excess and aimlessness! Does one not still hear shepherds piping tunes that seem to lack coherence, but which nevertheless satisfy the musical and emotional needs of their creators?

In the earliest times, the greater part of such musical needs may have been satisfied in this way. But how much progress, how many new and lasting advantages were obtained by the art of music when it was able to rein in this naive impulse, and to intensify it greatly at the same time—as, for example, in Bach's Toccatas and Fugues for organ!

It follows, then, that the aimless and self-indulgent musical impulse of early times must have been relieved to shelter itself under the protection of language and its laws. In those times, music strove to liken its cadences to the cadences of language, and in order to do so, it first had to learn to imitate, in its own fashion, the most distinguishing feature of language; that is to say, it had to learn to suggest convincingly the impression of self-contained thought. Through its association with language, music learned to mimic accurately all of thought's vicissitudes—its striving, its self-organisation, its closure—and through habituation over what was perhaps many centuries, the art of music eventually began to fancy that it possessed an intrinsic logic similar to that of language. Be that as it may, music became an art only when a series of tones arose that demanded to be understood and felt as a whole, as a self-contained idea. *This first whole composed of musical tones was given the honorific title of Melody.* Nevertheless, the impression of completeness rested more on the unstable principles of tradition than on a sure and permanent foundation. In speech, that which is to be considered a complete thought is not subject to one person's arbitrary judgment, and a logical idea too, like a mathematical theorem, holds its own against unenlightened criticism; but music, since it is fundamentally ignorant of causality or logic, may never represent a whole so convincingly that it can coerce everyone's sensibilities and allay the doubts of skeptical auditors. Consequently, different means of fashioning a musical whole have been employed among different peoples at different times, right down to the present day. And for this reason alone I believe that the proper approach to the concept of melody has not yet been discovered.

2. Repetition

Our understanding of musical technique would have advanced much further if only someone had investigated the questions of where, when, and how its most striking and most distinguishing feature—namely, the feature called repetition—incorporated itself into the art of music. Clearly, all the arts that relate or represent a story have no reason to repeat individual motives. Every story has, of course, an ultimate goal toward which all its operative and logical forces strive in accordance with the laws of causality, as it were, once and for all. Just as every act and every event takes place only once, so too their depictions can occur only once. The question is: Where did music get the idea of subjecting portions of melodies—some short, some long—to repetition, when language, its model, prefers exactly the opposite—namely, a continuous, non-recurring flow? Well, when music entered into the service of language, it paid close attention at first to the natural intonation of language. Only later did it summon up the courage to sail out from the shores of language into the free, open sea of more distant musical intervals; in the process, however, she must have noticed that a new melodic advance, a collection of tones wholly independent of language, needed to present itself to the ear and to the mind more than once in order to make itself in any way comprehensible. For a musical motive, unlike a verbal phrase, does not possess the good fortune of being able to represent objects or concepts by itself. If a word is only a sign for something—that is, for an object or for a concept in which objects are assimilated—then the musical motive is only a sign for itself; or, to put it more accurately, it is nothing more and nothing less than itself. People must have become thoroughly convinced of this deficiency on the part of music as soon as instrumental music began to arise. For as long as music clung to language, it believed itself to be comprehensible, although it was only language that ensured comprehensibility; but when it ventured out alone into the world, it must have realised its self-deception rather quickly and recognised its inability to solicit understanding in any other way than by clarifying individual motives and tonal successions through repetition and imitation. Repetition, this ancient and original musical discovery, probably provides the best evidence that even millennia ago music *carried in its own womb a unique and reliable principle of organisation,* and, following this line of thought, *was emancipated from language much earlier* than music historians suppose. It also shows, in my opinion, the great antiquity of instrumental music, which had been operating according to purely musical principles long before the beginning of the sixteenth century, when musicians began that epochal cultivation whose fruits we enjoy today.—That the purely musical impulse in music could never be silenced, and could not be muffled even by the language of the church, is perhaps demonstrated most clearly by, among other things, the melismas that ecclesiastical singing used from the earliest times in the most diverse circumstances. One need only call to mind the neumes of Gregorian chant. But organisation according to purely musical principles was not readily sanctioned, for one sensed in them (however one might otherwise express it) the self-indulgence of an entrancing sensuality, and musicians repeatedly had to remind the selfish tones of their sober model, language, and of the explicit responsibilities imposed by it. And in fact, the struggle between language and music extends throughout the entire history of music, right up to the present day. Sometimes music, when it could no longer tolerate its indentured servitude to language, felt compelled toward excess, toward license in all its elements; but sometimes, weary of being wild and reprobate, music returned repentantly to the ideal proportions and limits recommended by language. This is also the case, though it is usually overlooked, even in purely instrumental music. Although instrumental music appears to be unfettered by language, it nonetheless observes laws analogous to those governing language, and its effect is the more powerful the more it makes use of the idea-associations and operative principles of language.—I will only add here that when music was borrowing its laws from language, it often put its own distinctive feature of repetition at the disposal of language, as if out of gratitude. One can see this in the oldest epic and lyric poems, which repeat brief or even lengthy verbal motives in a musical manner. I also consider the refrain to be originally a musical principle.

3. Polyphony

Polyphony entered western music as a purely musical principle, working with its own distinctive material toward its own distinctive ends. It is the one artifice that music, having understood its appeal and its usefulness, can no longer forego. I do not believe that the appearance of this artifice was brought about by ninth- and tenth-century theory, since I am of the general opinion that practical music almost never concerns itself with those things which theory either ascribes to it or derives from it. If fifths and fourths were used predominantly when people first began to sing in two and three parts, this happened, as I am convinced, not because these intervals make consonances according to theory, but because by singing in that way it was possible for everyone to sing the melody as he knew it, even if he had to sing it at a different pitch level. Is it not both poignant and natural that in the beginning no one would willingly agree merely to accompany the pitches of the other singers, that it did not even occur to anyone to relinquish the melody, which was, so to speak, everyone's personal property? In this way it came about that singers could practice polyphony while at the same time each of them could sing the melody to his own satisfaction. But soon other intervals besides fourths and fifths began to occur in polyphony—the need for novelty may have led to this—and theorists began to ascribe to the short-lived phenomena of a groping imagination, or often even to an unimaginative capriciousness, rules that pretended to be valid for all time. Apart from all the natural charm that must have emanated elementally from polyphony, revolutionary changes began to insinuate themselves into the realm of sensibility through this new artifice. Would feeling alone not suffice to tell everyone that the slightest alterations in those voices that served merely to counterpoint the melody had an affect on the very heart, so to speak, of the melody? Thus the sensibilities learned to follow faithfully even the tiniest alterations, they adapted to the new spirit of artifice and complexity, and educated themselves to appreciate the innumerable variations that were, and still are, possible in music.—Even when the new keys arrived and brought with them what seemed to be a completely new kind of counterpoint—for one could no longer, to use the charmingly ingenuous expression of Josef Haydn, 'decide to let one's ears remain empty'—the spirit of counterpoint remained the same. Counterpoint was and is an utterly unique, historically conditioned, and continually evolving method of training, not only for the creative imagination, but also for the receptive sensibilities. The imagination sees how infinitely many perspectives there are from which to develop a given idea, and it learns to recognise how an alteration in one element brings with it a corresponding change in expression; and, most important of all, through such a prolific education it develops the ability to select, from the infinite multitude of developments that it envisions, precisely the one that best suits the artist's disposition at a particular time. The imagination's adaptability grows so vast that, for the most part, it creates from the outset not a simple melody, but one that is in some provisional manner conceived contrapuntally. The sensibilities, on the other hand—as I have already said above—learn to adapt to each and every change in contrapuntal perspective. I want to make a crude but illuminating comparison here between the discipline of counterpoint and the discipline of independent, mechanical finger-dexterity that every performing artist must acquire if he is to meet the technical and mechanical challenges of an artwork. In the same way that the discipline of purely mechanical finger-dexterity prepares the fingers—once they have been trained for mobility, independence, and strength—to meet the mechanical challenges of any artwork (and in this connection one should not forget that, under the best circumstances, the performing artist's inspiration can coincide felicitously with that of the composer), the discipline of counterpoint likewise enables the imagination to see countless different dispositions and transformations of a theme, in order ultimately to determine the disposition best suited to the emotional compass of the artwork being contemplated. But once all of the work's contrapuntal techniques have been fixed permanently, they become just as subjective as the work's emotional character. For this reason, I believe, J. S. Bach's counterpoint is the generative soul of his artworks, wide-ranging and magnificently idiosyncratic, acquired, undoubtedly, from long and difficult intellectual discipline and certainly also from a special natural talent; but since its use in his compositions is subjective, one ought not to confuse it with the training he had previously completed. And one does indeed confuse the two when one maintains that his contrapuntal technique is merely mechanical. This confusion may be caused precisely by the astonishment and admiration that one must have for the unprecedented abundance and cleverness of his contrapuntal vigor. Since the listener may well be unable to comprehend Bach's expansive spirit in terms of his own more limited spirit, he assumes, merely because his own interest wanes, that the heart of Bach's artistry is also exhausted; at the point where his own inspiration leaves off, he begins to imagine that the music too has become a mechanical formula. The strangest thing of all is that even those composers and theorists who wrote about counterpoint and fugue, and who, in their creative activity, were certainly aware of the subjective significance of these techniques, were unable to communicate clearly the spirit of counterpoint. (See in this regard the works of Fux, Marpurg, Cherubini, Albrechtsberger, Bellermann, and so forth.) Let me cite here, however, as typical evidence for my interpretation of this matter, the opinion shared by Albrechtsberger and Salieri about their student Beethoven: 'Beethoven was always so obstinate and willful that he had to learn through harsh experience many things which he had previously refused to accept as the object of a lesson.' From this one can see that Beethoven tried repeatedly to force the subjective technique that he envisioned as his ultimate goal into the cold, objective system of instruction imparted to him by his teachers. Albrechtsberger could surely have spared him all these disconcerting exertions if only he could have explained the spirit of counterpoint from the first in a manner that would have promoted straightforward understanding and assent on Beethoven's part. But even in his published textbook Albrechtsberger was unable to provide this sort of explanation; as a consequence, Beethoven had to strive for the understanding on his own, and he submitted as soon as he saw that his teacher was right to demand this or that, even though he was unable to say why. No wonder, then, that Beethoven, in a letter to his pupil Archduke Rudolf (1 July 1823), was clearer than Albrechtsberger and the others (in so far as language was able to convey his thoughts): 'It is also necessary to compose away from the keyboard, and working out a simple chorale melody from time to time, first with simple, then with more elaborate figurations in accordance with the counterpoint, then going even a bit beyond that, will surely not give your royal highness a headache, but on the contrary will cause a great pleasure when, while thus engaged, you suddenly catch yourself involved in creating art.—*Little by little the ability arises to represent precisely what we want, what we feel— a basic necessity for the nobler man.'*

To put it frankly here, I intend to make a detailed attempt at explaining harmonic and contrapuntal prescriptions and proscriptions. And I hope to be able to bring forward evidence for the fact that every prescription and pro-scription is essentially relative, serving only to advocate a particular *musical stimulus*—nothing more or less that this—and what is more, only so long as a more compelling interest in another musical stimulus does not come into play. The less compelling interest in the one stimulus then yields to the more com-pelling one in the other. The totality of all these interests constitutes the piece. Of course, the spirit of the mood hovers over the totality of the interests, but the composer's interest is demonstrable to everyone, whereas the mood ap-pears to each according to his own taste. This is a very important distinction. Only after one has heard and understood all of the composer's interests and all of the objective materials in the artwork is it permissible—either at the same moment, or sometime later on—to submit the artwork to one's own sensibility for mood, and then to make a final 'judgment' about it. No one can object to this way of 'recreating' an artwork; on the contrary, it is to be hoped that the majority of listeners will eventually experience music in this way.

Because I will explain the nature of harmonic and contrapuntal prescrip-tions almost solely in terms of their psychological origins and impulses, I also hope to bring what are called the 'disciplines of harmony and counterpoint' into a welcome proximity to free composition, that is, to the actual life of music. And these disciplines, once clarified, would be able both to explain the expressions of free composition and to prepare students to express themselves, just as the grammar of language explains all verbal phenomena, both in art and in ordinary life. And students would not, as is usually the case nowadays, have to spend years contemplating material that seems irrelevant and unproductive, without receiving any insight into free composition; they would all, I think, be able to express their precise understanding more clearly and easily than Mas-ter Cherubini himself, who was able to express his perfectly correct sentiments only with these appallingly pedantic and inarticulate phrases: 'The young com-poser who has carefully followed the instructions contained in this course of study, once he has attained to the fugue, will no longer need lessons. He will be able to write with purity in all styles, and it will be easy for him, in practis-ing the forms of the different genres of composition, to express his ideas ap-propriately and to produce the effect he desires.'

4. Harmony

It is said that the Greeks were ignorant of harmony, and they are excused for this, one might say, on the grounds that Pythagoras reckoned the third and the sixth as dissonant, without which intervals, of course, the triad, the basis of harmony, is inconceivable. Now it seems to me that Pythagoras was not so much at fault as is generally believed, and for that reason I am prepared to restore to the word 'harmony' (which the Greeks were the first to use) what was and still is its original and finest meaning. By 'harmony' the imaginative Greeks understood *the melody itself,* that is, the succession of tones as a whole, together with all the particular elements at work in that succession. In this broad sense, the concept of harmony ceased to exist quite some time ago, yet even today the concept seems to strive innately toward the broad significance that it had for the Greeks at the start of its existence. All too often we forget that every succession of tones, every melody, carries its own harmonic credo within itself, and that it expresses this conviction autonomously. That which the plan of the melody imparts directly to Feeling can be easily interpreted by Reason, which always strives to articulate what it sees, from the melody's focal points. *In this sense, every melody possesses a harmony of its own, and so Greek melody too must have had its own sort of harmony.* It is unfortunate that this primal, proper, broad, and beautiful conception of harmony has disappeared from the province of theory. It is still an essential element in the province of creative practice, however, where it appears as the dominant harmonic perspective in which a melody is first able to appear on the imagination's horizon. No matter how much ingenuity, diversity, or variety one may subsequently employ in reinterpreting harmonically the relations among the several melodic tones, the spirit of the original harmony, foreshadowed by the melody itself, hovers above all the profuse variations and above all the new relationships established by harmonic regrouping.

One would suppose that a new spirit of harmony arose spontaneously with the introduction of polyphony, one that drew its specific character expressly from polyphony. For is it not the case that several vocal lines sung together simultaneously also bring harmonies into being? And yet, at that time, and even much later, people were entirely fascinated by the independence of the voices, so much so that they overlooked the simultaneous and inevitable phenomenon of harmony while focusing solely on the attraction produced by the new, independent vocal lines, and they believed that all the enchantment was due to the vocal interactions alone, when in fact harmony was working its own wonders. If the relation of those generations to harmony was indeed as it is often described—and there is more than enough room for doubt here, in my opinion—then the remarkably constrained hearing of that period bears a certain similarity to the natural science of earlier generations, who no doubt saw nature for themselves, and yet did not understand how to draw from it sharply attuned natural sensibilities. Later on, of course, they did begin to hear the harmonies rustling even in polyphony, and the new, non-hellenic conception of harmony then came into being.

The most recent and narrowest conception of harmony dates from the time of Rameau, however, and it still casts its spell over the entirety of contemporary music. According to this conception, as is generally known, it is the function of harmony to interpret melody; that is, to provide the motivation, as it were, for the relationships among the individual tones of the melody.

It seems to me, though, that harmony, however we conceive of it, performs an even deeper, more necessary function: harmony helps music to deceive both itself and its listener about its lack of logic and causality, because harmony behaves as though it possesses the force of logic. Harmony too acts as if it contains within itself the force of logic. Tradition and habit, enthralled, go along with this self-deception, and they concede to harmony a logic that it has no more than melody does. And if harmony now enters into the service of melody, then it only adds its own ability to deceive to the deceptive ability of melody. Harmony and melody seem to espouse the principles of necessity and logic, and they feign both, but when they do so at the same time the subterfuge is very much greater, and the music's end is attained, as it were, with twice the intensity and twice the subterfuge.

5. Moods, Forms, and the 'Organic'

In our own time, if one listens to very primitive dance music in places where highly developed musical artistry does not exist (and there are certainly more than enough such places), one can come very close to solving the conundrum of musical moods and forms. It is noteworthy that village musicians, when they intend to create a mood for dancing, play the same dance-melody in the same manner several times in succession. Consequently, many composers have portrayed this sort of thing realistically enough in artworks, and even in the Ninth Symphony Beethoven alludes to it with a realism that is only partially disguised. This way of creating a mood accords simultaneously both with music's intrinsic need for repetition, and with its need for mood. For it seems that it is the same with mood as it is with pitch. Physicists assert that it takes two or three double oscillations to produce a pitch, and even though all 435 vibrations do not have to be present in order to produce the tone A, for example, a single oscillation alone is in no way sufficient. Similarly, it takes two or three mood-waves to establish a mood, and a single wave will not suffice. Mood, therefore, requires some duration, or, from a compositional standpoint, it requires a piece to have a certain length. But precisely at this point composer and listener seem to go their separate ways. When the composer is writing, he is more or less in the middle of a mood, and while he is creating, he is carrying that mood forward, one might say. Fundamentally, therefore, the extent of the composer's mood is longer than the listener's, for whom the mood (whatever he takes it to be) certainly cannot begin to establish itself before he hears the first notes of the completed artwork. As a consequence, the composer may deceive himself terribly about the duration of the mood—and thus about the effect of his piece—if he ignores this factor. When, in some of his Bagatelles, Beethoven discloses to us only the first burst of the melody that, for him, had quite naturally been a product of the mood, and withholds the more extensive treatment that, for us, seems necessary, it really has to be called extraordinary, especially for Beethoven, who surely knew the old proportions used to establish moods and was quite capable of creating new ones. On the other hand, this choice on Beethoven's part is accounted for by the humour with which he endowed these musical ideas. He put both seriousness and lightheartedness in the Bagatelles, but the precise source of his humour consisted in his whimsical foreshortening of those moods. The humour, one might say, lies outside of the piece, and is not communicable to third parties who cannot fully discern the composer's intent. A concert-hall audience is bound to find the moods too short, mere suggestions, and will not be able to sense the humour that is trying to express itself not so much through the content of the piece as through the whimsical foreshortening.

But not all cases in which a piece's foreshortening comes at the expense of the mood can be interpreted in this way. It seems to me that in the other cases the solution is rather the following: it is incumbent on the performer or listener to approach the piece more than just once. Each time he does so, his memory will send out in advance, so to speak, a prologue to proclaim the mood— namely, the impression it formed quickly upon first exposure or previous hearings, and as a result the durational proportions of the mood will appear to the listener (allowing for subjective differences) almost exactly as they appeared to the composer himself. The mood-waves are present before the piece starts, and when it does begin, one has only to continue on in the same mood. This is also the path that leads most reliably to the composer, not only in these, but in nearly all cases. This facility of artificially extending a mood by means of the mood already deposited in memory provides, I think, the most persuasive justification of the fundamental axiom that we should only 'judge', as we say, an artwork when we have listened to it more than once.

In all cases where language joins together with music, it is language, thanks to its exceptional ability to produce associations of ideas, that immediately reveals the mood and plainly defines its character. Whether, as is the case in most recitatives, the tones merely act as a buskin for the text and place their more extensive undulations at the text's disposal, or whether they possess in addition a purely musical effect, it is simply never the case that they have the power to induce and to develop the mood *as assuredly* as the text with which it has combined. Now if music knows how to take advantage of the assistance of language, then it does not need to extend its content to such lengths as it does otherwise, when it stands by itself without the help of language. If I am not mistaken, the musical content of liturgical melodies has to be considered the most diminutive of all, and yet what moods can radiate from them!

Long before music knew the ways to generate content of considerable extent using only its own resources, it came face-to-face with the problem of supporting poems of fairly substantial length, both sacred and secular, and inasmuch as music was able to solve that problem, it conceived from this new artifice, which it had to develop under the influence of language, an intimation, I think, of how it could also erect analogous time-spans in the realm where it could indulge its own free will—that is, in pure instrumental music. Serendipitously, other elements that were more inwardly decisive for music also shared the same goal. For example, music's need for repetition was now in a better position to be able to extend its influence over a longer duration. Repetition satisfied itself, and contributed at the same time to the extension of content. And it goes without saying that a longer content was also more compatible with music's need to establish moods. Thus different causes cooperated to drive instrumental music toward an artifice that soon gathered together similarities and broke up dissimilarities, giving birth to the conceptions of the so-called 'forms'. Since I can think of no more appropriate word than 'artifice' to describe the opposite of music's intrinsic nature (which consists, in my opinion, of creating melodies individually), I will use it here in that sense, though at the same time I must ask that the term be divested of the derogatory connotation that adheres to it in common opinion.

There were very many resources available to artifice. Thus modulation, for example, played a very important role by carrying a melody back and forth industriously through the so-called related keys, and in this way did great service

for the extension of content, as well as for the intelligibility of relationships and
for the establishment of mood. One could also construct transitions that served
as transitions in the true sense of the word, since they led from one principal
section to another.

Composers saw to it, however, that they did not betray the intent of
artifice blatantly; they concealed it and dressed it up, in order to keep the sensibilities entirely in that instinctive state which would be most likely to hear
and accept the artificial whole as something generated naturally. And while
they were expanding tonal content for the sake of the already expanded
melodies (and concatenations of several melodies), they never missed an opportunity to promote the feeling of a 'whole', using every means available at
the time. By association, the feeling of rounding, of closure, habitually simulated the nature of conceptual thought, which distinguishes itself precisely by
an unmistakable beginning and an unmistakable ending. And in this way an illusory halo of rational logic began to shine over all the structures elaborated by
the artificial designs of the imagination, and it did not take long before people
even began to believe that the artificial constructs had the same sort of necessity possessed by natural organisms. This belief still exists today, at a time when
artifice threatens to overwhelm the receptive capacities of our generation. The
highest praise that can be rendered to a musical artwork nowadays is to say that
it is constructed 'organically'.

In deference to those who use the word 'organic', I am more than content
to believe that, when they use the term, they have no intention at all of calling
into question the scientific concept, and that they instead believe themselves to
be paying music a supreme compliment with this simple analogy.

But the simple analogy leads to errors, just as it originated in an error, and
before long the inconsistent use of the term maligns one artwork or another to
which the term has been applied in the ordinary sense. For the first thing to
note is the very striking fact that artworks are never said to be organic when
their content displeases us. And yet, is there any reason why content that is unpleasant to our taste could not also be organic? But right here is part of the solution. For if we only bestow the honour of the scientific conception on works
to which we can listen without upsetting our own abilities, capacities, and enjoyment, then it is all too clear that we are here transferring the supposed
charm of the organic to the content that has imparted that sort of charm. It is
for this reason that an exceptionally fine piece is held to be organically constructed, and the error is made even worse by the fact that people possess little
understanding about the fundamental nature of what is commonly called
'form'. As a matter of fact, no musical content is organic. It lacks any principle
of causation, and a contrived melody never has a determination so resolute
that it can say, 'Only that particular melody, and none other, may follow me'.
Indeed, it is part of the work of shaping content for the composer to obtain
from his imagination a variety of similarities and contrasts, in order ultimately
to select his best option. Because he has selected only one option, we cannot
know what other materials were available for him to choose from (the rejected
options can often be elicited from his studies and sketches), but only the one
that was most agreeable to him personally.

Now it can happen that the imagination of the composer (and also the
imagination of an extraordinary listener) surveys the entire content, despite its
consecutive nature, from a bird's-eye view, so to speak, arranging and balanc-

ing against one another the characteristics and proportions of all the different moods contained in it; and yet this process, as much as it appears to be a logical operation, is neither logical nor organic in origin, but rather, the moods and proportions of the different parts, as well as of the entire content, reveal most plainly the personal disposition of the composer and his intense determination to win the listener over to the particular order of moods and proportions that he himself had constructed, sneaking them in by manipulating the listener's own perspective. But the capacity to respond to these proportions with or without impediment lies within us; the ordering of moods either pleases us or does not, and our receptivity to moods and proportions is just as relative and subjective as the composer's arranging of them.

And though one might be tempted to consider at least the sequence of moods to be strictly organic, there are arguments to be made against it: for instance, that the mood in which the first theme of a sonata is engendered never recurs in exactly the same way over the entire course of the piece; and, much more important, that any sort of necessary connection must be denied to a sequence of moods that is not rooted in the world of ideas and experience. The causality of life's events governs and disposes the moods of life, but musical representations of moods, unfamiliar with the tendency of ideas and experience to drag things earthward, are governed only by a deceptive appearance of life's causality. It is also not right, I think, to assume that mood B follows mood A organically just because B was directly appointed to follow A directly at a certain point, regardless of whether this was the outcome of careful consideration on the part of the composer. That would be to sanction the conclusion that the second follows the first 'organically' merely because it follows it in fact. The consequence is this, therefore: strictly speaking, the material of musical content never arises organically, but rather, the composer's teleological intent is to bring it about that the arrangement of proportions and the order of moods, which were generated and ultimately cast in final form by him, should be judged from the perspective of the organic. But the inorganic origin of the musical material simply scoffs at the composer's resolute intention, and that is why it can happen, as I mentioned, that we resist the composer's arrangement, even if his intent was focused very directly on producing something 'organic'.

Nevertheless, I do recognise one phenomenon of the musical imagination to which the scientific sense of the 'organic' seems to apply quite strictly. This is a phenomenon that can only be verified with great difficulty, but I myself consider it to be a fact. I find that the imagination, after it has generated a particular pattern, is positively besieged by many patterns similar in nature, and that the influence of these similar patterns on the composer is often so irresistible that he includes them in the developing content without having become aware at all of their similarity. Often—and one can discover this only by an extremely painstaking study of the artwork—the composer would have preferred to conjure up a completely different pattern, but behold! the imagination refuses to change its original direction, and compels him to accept a similar pattern instead. Is this case not a perfect example of the old adage, 'Omnis natura vult esse conservatrix sui?!'[1]

But this organic element remains organic only so long as it does not become contaminated by consciousness, and the moment the composer directs

---

[1] Every natural thing wants to preserve itself.

his imagination toward the hunt for similarities, then that which otherwise could easily have seemed organic to us devolves into the merely *'thematic'*— that that is, into *intentional similarity*. To be circumspect, then, we can only discuss that which is organic hypothetically: a particular similarity has actually arisen *organically* in the imagination only inasmuch as the composer has *not intended* it.

Besides this significant object lesson about artifice, I perceive, coming from deep within the evolutionary history of music, yet another lesson that is just as important, a lesson about the imperishability of musical content.

Each and every content that was fresh at one time was also endowed, self-evidently, with its own distinctive expressiveness. After this content has passed through the heads of many subsequent imitators and auditors, it degenerates into a familiar idiom, because one no longer needs to concentrate on its novelty or attend to it carefully. (In a similar way, our day is swarming with musical idioms brought into the world by the many ruminators on Wagner and Brahms.) In conjunction with these idioms, which seem to bring about a depreciation of expressive value, the preconception arises that content routinely loses expressiveness over time, and people become accustomed to saying, metaphorically, that contents expire and pass away. But I think differently. Each and every content retains the power which it had originally, and it is up to us to perceive this vitality anew. Even if there were a hundred and one factors hindering us from granting some expressiveness to contents that have allegedly expired, then just a single case in which we are able to reinvigorate a lifeless content with active and youthful vitality demonstrates the triviality and inefficacy of all those factors. And how often do we actually manage, in an unexpectedly receptive mood, to build a bridge to ancient contents despite the long history of our musical impressions! And since, therefore, we *do not have to be estranged* from the contents of earlier times, I believe I am able to say that the material of the art of music is imperishable. This material never contradicts itself anywhere, no more than we contradict ourselves when we are captivated by Brahms today, but by Palestrina or by another pre-modern composer tomorrow.

Also related to the question of musical idioms is the evaluation of unoriginal composers, a subject on which I may be permitted a few words here. Although it is true that the original composer always exhibits his newly created content more simply and more distinctively than his imitators, it would still remain quite inexplicable why we would not be happy to embrace a content which is, after all, akin to the content that is recognised by us as being original and engaging. Now it is clear that, in this instance, we momentarily confuse our personal evaluation of the derivative composer with our impression of the content itself, and the content—which we could otherwise have welcomed with pleasure had we not known the original source—leaves us cold as soon as we know that its creator's abilities were purely derivative. This very question is undergoing a remarkable clarification due to the evaluation of the very recently discovered remains of Greek music that have come down to us. Who can say whether in these remains we really have the most original Greek music? And yet, delighted with the ancient art, we justifiably disregard all this, because these remains are still Greek music, and they transmit information about it, whether or not they were once representative and original.

Now since it is apparent that I reject the notion of rigor mortis in relation to musical content and that I cannot accept the notion of the organic in regard to musical content (for the hypothetical character of the organic ultimately does not suffice for constructing integrated content), it goes without saying that I am also an adversary of the term 'formalism'. 'Formalism' is either everywhere or nowhere in music. The only thing that determines this is the perspective from which one considers the content. Even though it might be highly desirable for the term to have a firm and unqualified definition, the only definition it could acquire would be one fits together with the proper meaning of 'form'. The only fruitful significance of 'form' seems, in my opinion, to be this: that the mere notion of a 'form' can influence the creative imagination, and that from the perspective of a model—let us say, for instance, any of Beethoven's sonatas—the imagination can do its work. And this only proves, as I said at the beginning, that musical creation can receive both its seed and its sustenance from an external stimulus. If someone believes he has evidence that a composer has clearly used a model as a stimulus for his imagination, then let him accuse that composer of 'formalism'!

Despite the fact that the majority of unoriginal composers (and even the masters themselves, often enough) take this creative path, I nevertheless consider it pointless and unproductive always to account for and identify the form before the content. In the strict sense, each and every content ultimately has its own form, just as every human has his own form despite familial, national, and racial similarities. *In complex constructs, however, one hears only the content, never the form.* What is called form is an abstraction, a representation that is not rooted in the ear. In fact, form is a comparative study that extracts its representations from the evidence supplied by the senses. It never discloses anything that can stand on its own; the content supports and accounts for everything. It is all the more necessary to stress this today, when a rather large part of the literature on music history has subjected only the external element of form to scrutiny and has spurned the inner technique of content. On this path, however, they arrived at mere platitudes and inanities, to put it quite bluntly. How ridiculous one would seem, both to himself and to others, if he decided to classify, for instance, works of poetry according to the number of themes they contain—say, three themes make a sonnet, four an ode, and so forth. But in music—just think of it!—the number of themes is still counted up diligently and the form characterised accordingly. Centuries ago, some composer was inclined to give a piece he composed the title 'Sonata'. Perhaps he even had it in mind that the title really signifies nothing and its relation to the content does not extend beyond the simple and economical declaration that something would soon be 'sounding'. But no harm done, since the piece, as he evidently thought, had to have a title. Then came others who dragged his content through their imitative contents. And so one began to imagine that the meaningless term possessed a determinate formal significance. Then, when content began to expand and several themes were conjoined in a single movement, people still continued to say—and here is where it becomes ridiculous—that the sonata has grown to encompass two or three themes, two, three, or four movements; and in a similar vein, Liszt is praised for having reconfigured the sonata into a single movement. Now I ask, Is Liszt's sonata the same as Beethoven's, Beethoven's the same as Kuhnau's, and so forth? Or does it not appear more likely here that the empty, meaningless term 'sonata' is a terrible *medium comparationis?!* Nowadays composers write a great many 'intermezzi'. The term means just as little as 'sonata'. And yet there is reason to fear that, by

virtue of its externality, it will soon be elevated to the status of a formal category by those who study and identify externals. It is indeed curious that composers do not prefer to act like lyric poets, for example, who do not provide all
their lyric poems with headings, and pass them off nonetheless as lyrics.—To
be sure, there are also titles that betoken the mood of a work aptly, such as 'fantasy', 'capriccio', and so on.—But to my way of thinking, the external indexing
of themes described above demonstrates beyond a shadow of a doubt how
powerful, even at the present time, is the musical instinct that seems to say *the
intrinsic nature of music is to create melodies* which live together peaceably, like
folksongs, like familial relations, and which, like the first humans in paradise,
can frolic naked and unclothed in the paradise of music. But, of course, when
music donned fig leaves and became Art, people began to keep track of how
large a structure one can actually weld together; one melody established a
homestead, as it were, and then whole families came along, and a dense population that, unfortunately, is not subject to the law of Malthus!—It is only because of this, I think, that people today, as in the past, turn their awareness of
externals toward the artificial proliferation of melodies in a single movement,
and yet feel themselves drawn above all and most intensely to the melodies
themselves, which seem to be the intrinsic nature of music.

References

Adorno, Theodor. 1976/1962. *Introduction to the Sociology of Music.* Trans. E. B. Ashton. New York: Seabury.

———. 1992/1963. *Quasi una Fantasia: Essays on Modern Music.* Trans. Rodney Livingstone. London: Verso.

———. 1998. *Beethoven: The Philosophy of Music.* Ed. Rolf Tiedemann. Trans. Edmond Jephcott. Cambridge: Polity.

———. 2002. *Essays on Music.* Ed. (with commentary) Richard Leppert. Berkeley: University of California Press.

Agawu, Kofi. 1989. 'Schenkerian notation in theory and practice'. *Music Analysis* 8, 275–301.

———. 1997. 'Analyzing music under the new musicological regime'. *Journal of Musicology* 15: 297–307.

Almén, Byron. 1996. 'Prophets of the decline: The worldviews of Heinrich Schenker and Oswald Spengler'. *Indiana Theory Review* 17, 1–24.

Alpern, Wayne. 1999. 'Music theory as a mode of law: The case of Heinrich Schenker, Esq'. *Cardozo Law Review* 20, 1459–1511.

———. Forthcoming. *Schenkerian Jurisprudence: Echoes of Schenker's Legal Education in his Musical Thought.* Ph.D. diss., City University of New York.

Applegate, Celia, and Pamela Potter. 2002. 'Germans as the "people of music": Genealogy of an identity'. In Celia Applegate and Pamela Potter, eds., *Music and German National Identity.* Chicago: University of Chicago Press, 1–35.

Ayotte, Benjamin. 2004. *Heinrich Schenker: A Guide to Research.* London: Routledge.

Babbitt, Milton. 1972/1961. 'Past and present concepts of the nature and limits of music'. In Benjamin Boretz and Edward T. Cone, eds., *Perspectives on Contemporary Music Theory*. New York: Norton, 3–9.

———. 2003. *The Collected Essays of Milton Babbitt*. Ed. Stephen Peles. Princeton, N.J.: Princeton University Press.

Babbitt, Milton, et al. 1977. 'Ernst Oster (1908–1977) in memoriam'. *Journal of Music Theory* 21, 340–54.

Barford, Philip. 1975. 'Music in the philosophy of Schopenhauer'. *Soundings* 5, 29–43.

Barnouw, Dagmar. 1999. 'Wiener Moderne and the tensions of modernism'. In Bryan Simms, ed., *Schoenberg, Berg, and Webern: A Companion to the Second Viennese School*. Westport, Conn.: Greenwood Press, 73–127.

Beiser, Frederick. 1993. 'Hegel's historicism'. In Beiser, ed., *The Cambridge Companion to Hegel*. Cambridge: Cambridge University Press, 270–300.

Beller, Steven. 1989. *Vienna and the Jews, 1867–1938: A Cultural History*. Cambridge: Cambridge University Press.

Beller-McKenna, Daniel. 2005. *Brahms and the German Spirit*. Cambridge, Mass.: Harvard University Press.

Bent, Ian. 1986. 'Heinrich Schenker, Chopin and Domenico Scarlatti'. *Music Analysis* 5, 131–49.

———. 1991. 'Heinrich Schenker e la missione del genio germanico'. Trans. Claudio Annibaldi. *Rivista italiana di musicologia* 26, 3–34.

———. 1994. *Music Analysis in the Nineteenth Century*. Cambridge: Cambridge University Press.

———. 2005. '"That bright new light": Schenker, Universal Edition, and the origins of the Erläuterung series, 1901–1910'. *Journal of the American Musicological Society* 58, 69–138.

Berkley, George. 1988. *Vienna and Its Jews: The Tragedy of Success, 1880s–1980s*. Cambridge, Mass.: Abt Books.

Bernstein, David. 2002. 'Nineteenth-century harmonic theory: The Austro-German legacy'. In Thomas Christensen, ed., *The Cambridge History of Western Music Theory*. Cambridge: Cambridge University Press, 778–811.

Berry, David Carson. 2002. 'The role of Adele T. Katz in the early expansion of the New York "Schenker school"'. *Current Musicology* 74, 103–51.

———. 2003. 'Hans Weisse and the dawn of American Schenkerism'. *Journal of Musicology* 20, 104–56.

———. 2004. *A Topical Guide to Schenkerian Literature: An Annotated Bibliography with Indices*. Hillsdale, N.Y.: Pendragon Press.

Blasius, Leslie. 1996. *Schenker's Argument and the Claims of Music Theory*. Cambridge: Cambridge University Press.

Bohlman, Philip. 1991. 'Of *Yekkes* and chamber music in Israel: Ethnomusicological meaning in Western music history'. In Stephen Blum, Philip Bohlman, and Daniel Neuman, eds., *Ethnomusicology and Modern Music History*. Urbana: University of Illinois Press, 254–67.

Borchmeyer, Dieter. 1992/1986. 'The question of anti-Semitism'. In Ulrich Müller and Peter Wapnewski, eds., *The Wagner Handbook*. Cambridge, Mass.: Harvard University Press, 166–85.

Boretz, Benjamin. 1970. *Meta-Variations: Studies in the Foundations of Musical Thought*. Ph.D. diss., Princeton University. Rev. edn., Red Hook, NY: Open Space, 1995.

Borio, Gianmario. 2001. 'Schenker versus Schoenberg versus Schenker: The difficulties of a reconciliation'. Trans. Laura Bassini. *Journal of the Royal Musical Association* 126, 250–74.

Borsi, Franco, and Ezio Godoli. 1986. *Vienna 1900: Architecture and Design*. Trans. Marie-Hélène Agüeros. London: Lund Humphries. First published 1985.

Botstein, Leon. 1985. *Music and its Public: Habits of Listening and the Crisis of Musical Modernism in Vienna, 1870–1914*. Ph.D. diss., Harvard University.

———. 1992a. 'Cinderella, or, music and the human sciences: Unfootnoted musings from the margins'. *Current Musicology* 53, 124–34.

———. 1992b. 'Listening through reading: Musical literacy and the concert audience'. *Nineteenth-Century Music* 16, 129–45.

———. 1992c. 'Arnold Schoenberg: Language, modernism and Jewish identity'. In Robert Wistrich, ed., *Austrians and Jews in the Twentieth Century*. New York: St. Martin's Press, 162–83.

———. 1997. 'Music and the critique of culture: Arnold Schoenberg, Heinrich Schenker, and the emergence of modernism in *fin-de-siècle* Vienna'. In Juliane Brand and Christopher Hailey, eds., *Constructive Dissonance: Arnold Schoenberg and the Transformations of Twentieth-Century Culture*. Berkeley: University of California Press, 2–22.

———. 2002. 'Schenker the regressive: Observations on the historical Schenker'. *Musical Quarterly* 86, 239–47.

———. 2003. 'Gedanken zu Heinrich Schenkers jüdischer Identität'. In Evelyn Fink, ed., *Rebell und Visionär: Heinrich Schenker in Wien*. Vienna: Verlag Lafite, 11–7.

Bouillon, Jean Paul. 1987. *Klimt: Beethoven: The Frieze for the Ninth Symphony*. Trans. Michael Heron. New York: Rizzoli. First published 1986.

Brown, Julie. 1994. 'Schoenberg's early Wagnerisms: Atonality and the redemption of Ahasuerus'. *Cambridge Opera Journal* 6, 51–80.

———. Forthcoming. 'Otto Weininger and musical discourse in turn-of-the-century Vienna'. In Brown, ed., *Western Music and Race*. Cambridge: Cambridge University Press.

Burnham, Scott. 1992. 'Musical and intellectual values: Interpreting the history of tonal theory'. *Current Musicology* 53, 76–88.

Cadwallader, Allen, and William Pastille. 1992. 'Schenker's high-level motives'. *Journal of Music Theory* 36, 119–48.

Cascelli, Antonio. 2003. *A Study of Schenker's Unpublished Analyses of Chopin in the Oster Collection*. Ph.D. diss., University of Southampton.

Celenza, Anna. 2004. 'Music and the Vienna Secession: 1897–1902'. *Music in Art* 29, 203–12.

Chatterjee, Ranjit. 1992. 'Judaic motifs in Wittgenstein'. In Robert Wistrich, ed., *Austrians and Jews in the Twentieth Century*. New York: St. Martin's Press, 142–61.

Cherlin, Michael. 1988. 'Hauptmann and Schenker: Two adaptations of Hegelian dialectics'. *Theory and Practice* 13, 115–31.

Chiang, Yu-ring. 1996. 'Heinrich Schenkers Wiener Gedenkstatten: Gedanken zu seinem sechzigsten Todesjahr'. *Mitteilungen der Österreichischen Gesellschaft fur Musikwissenschaft* 30, 41–51.

Christensen, Thomas. 1982. 'The *Schichtenlehre* of Hugo Riemann'. *In Theory Only* 6/4, 37–44.

Clark, Suzannah. 1999. 'Schenker's mysterious five'. *Nineteenth-Century Music* 23, 84–102.

Cohn, Richard. 1992a. 'The autonony of motives in Schenkerian accounts of tonal music'. *Music Theory Spectrum* 14, 150–70.

———. 1992b. 'Schenker's theory, Schenkerian theory: Pure unity or constructive conflict?' *Indiana Theory Review* 13, 1–19.

Cook, Nicholas. 1987. *A Guide to Musical Analysis.* London: Dent.

———. 1989a. 'The future of theory' (colloquium contribution). *Indiana Theory Review* 10, 70–72.

———. 1989b. 'Music theory and "good comparison": A Viennese perspective'. *Journal of Music Theory* 33, 117–41.

———. 1989c. 'Schenker's theory of music as ethics'. *Journal of Musicology* 7, 415–39.

———. 1991. 'Heinrich Schenker and the authority of the Urtext'. In Tokumaru Yoshiko et al., eds., *Tradition and Its Future in Music.* Osaka: Mita Press, 27–33.

———. 1995. 'Heinrich Schenker, polemicist: A reading of the Ninth Symphony monograph'. *Music Analysis* 14, 89–105.

———. 1998. *Analysing Musical Multimedia.* Oxford: Clarendon Press.

———. 2002. 'Epistemologies of music'. In Thomas Christensen, ed., *The Cambridge History of Western Music Theory.* Cambridge: Cambridge University Press, 78–105.

Dabrowska, Danuta, Abraham Wein, and Aharon Weiss, eds. 1980. *Pinkas hakehillot Polin: Entsiklopedyah shel ha-yishuvim ha-Yehudiyim le-min hivasdam ve-'ad le-ahar Sho'at Milhemet ha-'olam ha-sheniya.* Vol. 2. *Ukraine.* Jerusalem: Yad Vashem. English translation by Shlomo Sneh and Francine Shapiro available at the JewishGen '"Podhajce"—Encyclopedia of Jewish Communities in Poland, Volume II (Ukraine)' website (Francine Shapiro, project coordinator), at www.jewishgen.org/yizkor/pinkas_poland/pol2_00410.html (accessed June 2006).

Dahlhaus, Carl. 1987. *Schoenberg and the New Music: Essays.* Trans. Alfred Clayton and Derrick Puffett. Cambridge: Cambridge University Press.

———. 1989/1978. *The Idea of Absolute Music.* Trans. Roger Lustig. Chicago: University of Chicago Press.

Dahms, Walter. 1925. 'The biology of music'. *Musical Quarterly* 11, 36–54.

Dempster, Douglas. 1998. 'Is there even a grammar of music?' *Musicae Scientiae* 2, 55–65.

DeNora, Tia. 1995. *Beethoven and the Construction of Genius: Musical Politics in Vienna, 1792–1803.* Berkeley: University of California Press.

Drabkin, William. 1973–74. 'The new Erläuterungsausgabe'. *Perspectives of New Music* 12/1–2, 319–30.

———. 1985. 'Felix-Eberhard von Cube and the North-German tradition of Schenkerism'. *Proceedings of the Royal Musical Association* 3, 180–207.

———. 2002. 'Heinrich Schenker'. In Thomas Christensen, ed., *The Cambridge History of Western Music Theory.* Cambridge: Cambridge University Press, 812–43.

———. 2005. 'Schenker's "Decline": An introduction'. *Music Analysis* 24, 3–32.

Dubiel, Joseph. 1990. '"When you are Beethoven": kinds of rules in Schenker's *Counterpoint*'. *Journal of Music Theory* 34, 291–340.

Dunsby, Jonathan. 1977. 'Schoenberg and the writings of Schenker'. *Journal of the Arnold Schoenberg Institute* 2, 26–33.

Eigeldinger, Jean-Jacques. 1986/1970. Ed. Roy Howat. Trans. Naomi Shohat. *Chopin: Pianist and Teacher as Seen by His Pupils.* Cambridge: Cambridge University Press.

Erwin, Charlotte, and Bryan Simms. 1981. 'Schoenberg's correspondence with Heinrich Schenker'. *Journal of the Arnold Schoenberg Institute* 5, 22–43.

Eybl, Martin. 1995. *Ideologie und Methode: Zum ideengeschichtlichen Kontext von Schenkers Musiktheorie.* Tutzing: Schneider.

Federhofer, Hellmut. 1982. 'Fux's *Gradus ad Parnassum* as viewed by Heinrich Schenker'. Trans. Alfred Mann. *Music Theory Spectrum* 4, 66–75.

———. 1985. *Heinrich Schenker, nach Tagebüchern und Briefen in der Oswald Jonas Memorial Collection, University of California, Riverside.* Hildesheim: Georg Olms Verlag.

Field, Frank. 1967. *The Last Days of Mankind: Karl Kraus and His Vienna.* London: Macmillan.

Fink, Evelyn. 2003. 'Analyse nach Schenker an Wiener Musiklehranstalten. Ein Betrag zur Schenker-Rezeption in Wien'. In Evelyn Fink, ed., *Rebell und Visionär: Heinrich Schenker in Wien.* Vienna: Verlag Lafite, 18–34.

Franke, Lars. 2005. *Music as Daemonic Voice in Late Eighteenth- and Early Nineteenth-century German Culture.* Ph.D. diss., University of Southampton.

Franklin, Peter. 1997. *The Life of Mahler.* Cambridge: Cambridge University Press.

Friedenreich, Harriet Pass. 1991. *Jewish Politics in Vienna, 1918–38.* Bloomington: Indiana University Press.

Furtwängler, Wilhelm. 1985/1954. 'Heinrich Schenker: A contemporary problem'. Trans. Jan Emerson. *Sonus* 6: 1–5.

Gay, Peter. 1978. *Freud, Jews, and Other Germans: Masters and Victims in Modernist Culture.* New York: Oxford University Press.

Geshuri, Me'ir Shim'on. *Sefer Podhajce: Memorial Book of Podhajce. Podgaytsy, Ukraine.* Tel Aviv: Podhajce Society, 1972. Partial English translation by Jerrold Landau et al. available at the JewishGen 'Memorial book of Podhajce (Podgaytsy, Ukraine)' website (Jean and Mervin Rosenbaum, project coordinators), www.jewishgen.org/Yizkor/Podhajce/Podhajce.html (accessed June 2006).

Goldhagen, Daniel. 1997. *Hitler's Willing Executioners: Ordinary Germans and the Holocaust.* London: Abacus.

Goldman, David. 1990. *Heinrich Schenker: The "Erläuterungsausgabe" of Beethoven's Sonata Opus 101.* M.A. thesis, Queens College, New York.

Gottheil, Richard, and Wilhelm Bacher. 1904. 'Ibn Ezra, Abraham Ben Meïr (Aben Ezra)'. In Isidore Singer, Cyrus Alder et al., eds., *The Jewish Encyclopedia: A Descriptive Record of the History, Religion, Literature, and Customs of the Jewish People from the Earliest Times to the Present Day.* Vol. 6. New York: Funk and Wagnalls, 1904, 520–4. Available at www.jewishencyclopedia.com (accessed 2006).

Gravagnuolo, Benedetto. 1982. Trans. C. H. Evans. *Adolf Loos.* Milan: Idea Books Edizioni.

Hanisch, Ernst. 1992/1986. 'The political influence and appropriation of Wagner'. In Ulrich Müller and Peter Wapnewski, eds., *The Wagner Handbook.* Cambridge, Mass.: Harvard University Press, 186–201.

Hanslick, Eduard. 1986/1854. *On the Musically Beautiful: A Contribution towards the Revision of the Aesthetics of Music.* Trans. Geoffrey Payzant. Indianapolis: Hackett. (Translation based on the 1891 edition.)

Helsby, Nathan. 2001. *Schenker's Brahms: Analyses in the Oster Collection of the New York Public Library.* 2 vols. Ph.D. diss., University of Southampton.

Henisch, Meir. 1967. 'Galician Jews in Vienna'. In Josef Fraenkel, ed., *The Jews of Austria: Essays on their Life, History and Destruction.* London: Vallentine, Mitchell, 361–73.

Hepokoski, James. 1991. 'The Dahlhaus project and its extra-musicological sources'. *Nineteenth-Century Music* 14, 221–46.

Hindemith, Paul. 1952. *A Composer's World: Horizons and Limitations.* Cambridge, Mass.: Harvard University Press.

Holtmeier, Ludwig. 2004. 'From *"Musiktheorie"* to *"Tonsatz"*: National Socialism and German music theory after 1945'. *Music Analysis* 2004, 245–66.

Iversen, Margaret. 1993. *Alois Riegl: Art History and Theory.* Cambridge, Mass.: MIT Press.

Jackson, Timothy. 2001. 'Heinrich Schenker as composition teacher: The Schenker-Oppel exchange'. *Music Analysis* 20, 1–115.

Janik, Allan. 1987. 'Viennese culture and the Jewish self-hatred hypothesis: A critique'. In Ivar Oxaal, Michael Pollak, and Gerhard Botz, eds., *Jews, Antisemitism and Culture in Vienna.* London: Routledge and Kegan Paul, 71–88.

Janik, Allan, and Stephen Toulmin. 1973. *Wittgenstein's Vienna.* New York: Simon and Schuster.

Johnston, William. 1972. *The Austrian Mind: An Intellectual and Social History, 1848–1938.* Berkeley: University of California Press.

Jonas, Oswald. 1963. 'Schenker, Heinrich'. In Friedrich Blume, ed., *Die Musik in Geschichte und Gegenwart.* Kassel: Bärenreiter, 11:1670–2.

———. 1982/1934. *Introduction to the Theory of Heinrich Schenker: The Nature of the Musical Work of Art.* Trans. John Rothgeb. New York: Longman.

Kalib, Sylvan. 1973. *Thirteen Essays from the Three Yearbooks Das Meisterwerk in der Musik by Heinrich Schenker: An Annotated Translation.* 3 vols. Ph.D. diss., Northwestern University.

Karnes, Kevin. 2001. *Heinrich Schenker and Musical Thought in Late Nineteenth-century Vienna.* Ph.D. diss., Brandeis University.

———. 2002. 'Another look at critical partisanship in the Viennese *fin de siècle:* Schenker's reviews of Brahms's vocal music, 1891–92'. *Nineteenth-Century Music* 26, 73–93.

Kassler, Michael. 1967. *A Trinity of Essays: Toward a Theory That Is the Twelve-Note-Class System, Toward Development of a Constructive Tonality Theory Based on Writings by Heinrich Schenker, Toward a Simple Programming Language for Musical Information Retrieval.* Ph.D. diss., Princeton University.

Kater, Michael. 2000. *Composers of the Nazi Era: Eight Portraits.* New York: Oxford University Press.

———. 2002. 'Culture, society, and politics in the cosmos of "Hans Pfitzner the German"'. In Celia Applegate and Pamela Potter, eds., *Music and German National Identity.* Chicago: University of Chicago Press, 178–89.

Keiler, Allan. 1989. 'The origins of Schenker's thought: How man is musical'. *Journal of Music Theory* 33, 273–98.

———. 1996. 'Melody and motive in Schenker's earliest writings'. In John Knowles, ed., *Critica Musica: Essays in Honor of Paul Brainard.* Amsterdam: Gordon and Breach, 169–191.

Kerman, Joseph. 1985. *Musicology.* London: Fontana Press.

Kimel, Alexander. [Accessed] 2006. 'My world collapses'. On Alexander Kimel's 'Online Holocaust Magazine' website, www.kimel.net/collaps.html (accessed June 2006).

Kivy, Peter. 1993. *The Fine Art of Repetition: Essays in the Philosophy of Music.* Cambridge: Cambridge University Press.

Knittel, K. M. 1995. '"Ein hypermoderner Dirigent": Mahler and anti-Semitism in *fin-de-siècle* Vienna'. *Nineteenth-Century Music* 18, 257–76.

Kobler, Franz. 1967. 'The contribution of Austrian Jews to jurisprudence'. In Josef Fraenkel, ed., *The Jews of Austria: Essays on Their Life, History, and Destruction.* Londo: Valentine, Mitchell, 25–40.

Kolodin, Irving. 1932. 'Music'. *Arts Weekly,* 26 March 1932, 51.

Korsyn, Kevin. 1988. 'Schenker and Kantian epistemology'. *Theoria* 3, 1–58.

———. 1993. 'Schenker's organicism reexamined'. *Integral* 7, 82–118.

Kosovsky, Robert. 1990. *The Oster Collection: Papers of Heinrich Schenker. A Finding List.* New York: New York Public Library.

———. 1999. 'Levels of understanding: An introduction to Schenker's *Nachlass'.* In Carl Schachter and Hedi Siegel, eds., *Schenker Studies* 2. Cambridge: Cambridge University Press, 3–11.

Kramer, Lawrence. 1992. 'Music and representation: The instance of Haydn's Creation'. In Steven Paul Scher, ed., *Music as Text: Critical Inquiries.* Cambridge: Cambridge University Press, 139–62.

Kravitt, Edward. 2002. 'Mahler, victim of the "new" anti-Semitism'. *Journal of the Royal Musical Association* 127, 72–94.

Lang, Robert, and Joan Kunselman. 1994. *Heinrich Schenker, Oswald Jonas, Moriz Violin: A Checklist of Manuscripts and Other Papers in the Oswald Jonas Memorial Collection.* Berkeley: University of California Press.

Laufer, Edward. 1981. Review of *Free Composition (Der freie Satz),* by Heinrich Schenker. *Music Theory Spectrum* 3, 158–84.

Lazar, Moshe. 1994. 'Arnold Schoenberg and his doubles: A psychodramatic journey to his roots'. *Journal of the Arnold Schoenberg Institute* 17, 8–150.

Le Rider, Jacques. 1993. Trans. Rosemary Morris. *Modernity and Crises of Identity: Culture and Society in Fin-de-Siècle Vienna.* New York: Continuum. First published 1990.

Loewenberg, Peter. 1992. 'The pagan Freud'. In Robert Wistrich, ed., *Austrians and Jews in the Twentieth Century.* New York: St. Martin's Press, 124–41.

Loos, Adolf. 1982/1921. *Spoken into the Void: Collected Essays 1897–1900.* Trans. Jane Newman and John Smith. Cambridge, Mass.: MIT Press.

Lorda, Joaquin. 2000. 'Problems of style: Riegl's problematic foundations'. In Richard Woodfield, ed., *Framing Formalism: Riegl's Work.* Amsterdam: G and B Arts International, 107–34.

Lubben, Joseph. 1995. *Analytic Practice and Ideology in Heinrich Schenker's* Der Tonwille *and* Cantata Harmonia Mundi. Ph.D. diss., Brandeis University.

Magee, Bryan. 2001. *Wagner and Philosophy.* London: Penguin Books.

Mandell, Eric. 1967. 'Salomon Sulzer 1804–90'. In Josef Fraenkel, ed., *The Jews of Austria: Essays on Their Life, History, and Destruction.* London: Vallentine, Mitchell, 221–30.

Mann, Michael. 1949. 'Schenker's contribution to music theory'. *Music Review* 10, 3–26.

Mann, Thomas. 1983/1918. *Reflections of a Non-political Man.* Trans. Walter Morris. New York: Ungar.

Martin, Peter. 1995. *Sounds and Society: Themes in the Sociology of Music*. Manchester: Manchester University Press.

Masheck, Joseph. 2000. 'The Vital Skin: Riegl, the Maori and Loos'. In Richard Woodfield, ed., *Framing Formalism: Riegl's Work*. Amsterdam: G and B Arts International, 151–82.

Mast, Paul. 1980. 'Brahms's study, Oktaven u. Quinten u.A., with Schenker's commentary translated'. *Music Forum* 5, 1–196.

Matthews, Ramona. 2001. 'Oswald Jonas'. In Stanley Sadie and John Tyrrell, eds., *The New Grove Dictionary of Music and Musicians*. 2nd ed. 13:186–7.

McCagg, Willliam, Jr. 1989. *A History of the Habsburg Jews, 1670–1918*. Bloomington: Indiana University Press.

McClary, Susan. 1991. *Feminine Endings: Music, Gender, and Sexuality*. Minneapolis: University of Minnesota Press.

McColl, Sandra. 1996. *Music Criticism in Vienna, 1896–1897: Critically Moving Forms*. Oxford: Clarendon Press.

Miller, Daniel. 1987. *Material Culture and Mass Consumption*. Oxford: Blackwell.

Miller, Patrick. 1991. 'The published music of Heinrich Schenker: An historical-archival introduction'. *Journal of Musicological Research* 10, 177–97.

Morgan, Robert. 1978. 'Schenker and the theoretical tradition: The concept of musical reduction'. *College Music Symposium* 18, 72–96.

———. 2002. 'Schenker and the twentieth century: A modernist perspective'. In Andreas Giger and Thomas Mathiesen, eds., *Music in the Mirror: Reflections on the History of Music Theory and Literature for the Twenty-First Century*. Lincoln: University of Nebraska Press, 247–74.

Münz, Ludwig, and Gustav Künstler. 1966. *Adolf Loos: Pioneer of Modern Architecture*. Trans. Irene and Harold Meek. London: Thames and Hudson. First published 1964.

Narmour, Eugene. 1977. *Beyond Schenkerism: The Need for Alternatives in Music Analysis*. Chicago: Chicago University Press.

Neumeyer, David. 1987a. 'The ascending Urlinie'. *Journal of Music Theory* 31, 275–303.

———. 1987b. 'The three-part Ursatz'. *In Theory Only* 10/1–2, 3–29.

———. 1989. 'Fragile octaves, broken lines: On some limitations of Schenkerian theory and practice'. *In Theory Only* 11/3, 13–30.

———. 1990. 'Responses to Beach and Rothgeb'. *In Theory Only* 11/5, 19–26.

Notley, Margaret. 1993. 'Brahms as liberal: Genre, style, and politics in late nineteenth-century Vienna'. *Nineteenth-Century Music* 17, 107–23.

———. 1997. 'Bruckner and Viennese Wagnerism'. In Paul Hackshaw and Timothy Jackson, eds., *Bruckner Studies*. Cambridge: Cambridge University Press, 54–71.

———. 1999. 'Musical culture in Vienna at the turn of the twentieth century'. In Brian Simms, ed., *Schoenberg, Berg, and Webern: A Companion to the Second Viennese School*. Westport, Conn.: Greenwood Press, 37–71.

Osborne, Charles. 1973. *Richard Wagner: Stories and Essays*. London: Owen.

Oster, Ernst. 1960. 'Re: A new concept of tonality (?)'. *Journal of Music Theory* 4, 85–98.

Ostrow, Saul. 2000. 'Introduction: Aloïs Riegl: History's deposition'. In Richard Woodfield, ed., *Framing Formalism: Riegl's Work*. Amsterdam: G and B Arts International, 1–10.

Oxaal, Ivar. 1988. 'The Jews of young Hitler's Vienna: Historical and sociological aspects'. In Ivar Oxaal, Michael Pollak, and Gerhard Botz, eds., *Jews, Antisemitism and Culture in Vienna*. London: Routledge and Kegan Paul, 11–38.

Paddison, Max. 1993. *Adorno's Aesthetics of Music*. Cambridge: Cambridge University Press.

Painter, Karen. 1995. 'The sensuality of timbre: Responses to Mahler and modernity at the *fin de siècle*'. *Nineteenth-Century Music* 18, 236–56.

Pastille, William. 1984. 'Heinrich Schenker, anti-organicist'. *Nineteenth-Century Music* 8, 28–36.

———. 1990. 'Music and morphology: Goethe's influence on Schenker's thought'. In Hedi Siegel, ed., *Schenker Studies*. Cambridge: Cambridge University Press, 29–44.

Pekacz, Jolanta. 2002. *Music in the Culture of Polish Galicia, 1772–1914*. Rochester, N.Y.: University of Rochester Press.

Peles, Stephen. 2001. Review of *Schenker's Argument and the Claims of Music Theory*, by Leslie D. Blasius'. *Journal of Music Theory* 45, 176–90.

Pevsner, Nicholaus. 1966. Introduction to Münz and Künstler, *Adolf Loos: Pioneer of Modern Architecture*, 13–22.

Pollak, Michael. 1987. 'Cultural innovation and social identity in *fin-de-siècle* Vienna'. In Ivar Oxaal, Michael Pollak, and Gerhard Botz, eds., *Jews, Antisemitism and Culture in Vienna*. London: Routledge and Kegan Paul, 59–74.

Potter, Pamela. 1998. *Most German of the Arts: Musicology and Society from the Weimar Republic to the End of Hitler's Reich*. New Haven, Conn.: Yale University Press.

Proctor, Gregory, and Herbert Riggins. 1989. 'A Schenker pedagogy'. *Journal of Music Theory Pedagogy* 3, 1–24.

Puffett, Derrick. 1984. [Contribution to] 'Article guide'. *Music Analysis* 3, 289–92.

Rather, L. J. 1990. *Reading Wagner: A Study in the History of Ideas*. Baton Rouge: Louisiana State University Press.

Rechter, David. 2001. *The Jews of Vienna and the First World War*. London: Littman Library of Jewish Civilization.

Rehding, Alexander. 2000. 'The quest for the origins of music in Germany circa 1900'. *Journal of the American Musicological Society* 53, 345–85.

———. 2001. 'August Halm's two cultures as nature'. In Suzannah Clark and Alexander Rehding, eds., *Music Theory and Natural Order from the Renaissance to the Early Twentieth Century*. Cambridge: Cambridge University Press, 142–60.

———. 2003. *Hugo Riemann and the Birth of Modern Musical Thought*. Cambridge: Cambridge University Press.

Reich, Willi. 1971/1968. *Schoenberg: A Critical Biography*. Trans. Leo Black. London: Longman.

Reiter, Andrea. 2003. '"Von der Sendung des deutschen Genies": The music theorist Heinrich Schenker (1868–1935) and cultural conservatism'. In Rüdiger Görner, ed., *Resounding Concerns*. Munich: Iudicium Verlag, 2003, 135–59.

Ridley, Hugh. 1988. 'The culture of Weimar: Models of decline'. In Michael Laffan, ed., *The Burden of German History 1919–45: Essays for the Goethe Institute*. London: Methuen, 11–30.

Riegl, Aloïs. 1992/1893. *Problems of Style: Foundations for a History of Ornament*. Trans. Evelyn Kain. Princeton, N.J.: Princeton University Press.

Riethmüller, Albrecht. 2002. '"Is that not something for *Simplicissimus?!"* The belief in musical superiority'. In Celia Applegate and Pamela Potter, eds., *Music and German National Identity.* Chicago: University of Chicago Press, 288–304.

Ringer, Alexander. 1990. *Arnold Schoenberg: The Composer as Jew.* Oxford: Clarendon Press.

Robertson, Ritchie. 1992. '"Jewish self-hatred"? The cases of Schnitzler and Cannetti'. In Robert Wistrich, ed., *Austrians and Jews in the Twentieth Century.* New York: St. Martin's Press, 82–96.

Rockmore, Tom. 1993. *Before and after Hegel: A Historical Introduction to Hegel's Thought.* Berkeley: University of California Press.

Rosen, Charles. 1998. *Romantic Poets, Critics, and Other Madmen.* Cambridge, Mass.: Harvard University Press.

Rothfarb, Lee. 1996. 'Beethoven's formal dynamics: August Halm's phenomenological perspective'. *Beethoven Forum* 5, 65–84.

———. 2002. 'Energetics'. In Thomas Christensen, ed., *The Cambridge History of Western Music Theory.* Cambridge: Cambridge University Press, 927–55.

Rothgeb, John. 1990. Letter. *In Theory Only* 11/4, 43–4.

———. 2001. Review of *Heinrich Schenker, nach Tagebüchern und Briefen in der Oswald Jonas Memorial Collection, University of California, Riverside,* by Hellmut Federhofer. *Journal of Music Theory* 45, 151–62.

Rothstein, William. 1984. 'Heinrich Schenker as an interpreter of Beethoven's piano sonatas'. *Nineteenth-Century Music* 8, 3–27.

———. 1990a. 'The Americanization of Heinrich Schenker'. In Hedi Siegel, ed., *Schenker Studies.* Cambridge: Cambridge University Press, 192–203. First published 1986.

———. 1990b. 'The Americanization of Schenker pedagogy?' *Journal of Music Theory Pedagogy* 4, 295–300.

———. 2001. Review of articles on Schenker and Schenkerian theory in *The New Grove Dictionary of Music and Musicians,* 2nd ed., ed. Stanley Sadie and John Tyrrell. *Journal of Music Theory* 45, 204–27.

Rozenblit, Marsha. 1984. *The Jews of Vienna, 1867–1914: Assimilation and Identity.* Albany: State University of New York Press.

———. 2001. *Reconstructing a National Identity: The Jews of Habsburg Austria during World War I.* Oxford: Oxford University Press.

Rufer, Josef. 1962/1959. *The Works of Arnold Schoenberg: A Catalogue of His Compositions, Writings and Paintings.* Trans. Dika Newlin. London: Faber.

Rumph, Stephen. 1995. 'A kingdom not of this world: The political context of E. T. A. Hoffmann's Beethoven criticisim'. *Nineteenth-Century Music* 19, 50–67.

Rytting, Bruce. 1996. *Structure versus Organicism in Schenkerian Analysis.* Ph.D. diss., Princeton University.

Salzer, Felix. 1986. 'The significance of the ornaments in Carl Philipp Emanuel Bach's keyboard works'. Trans. Mark Stevens. *Theory and Practice* 11, 15–42.

———. 1989/1937. 'Die historische Sendung Heinrich Schenkers'. *Der Dreiklang: Monatsschrift für Musik* 1, 2–12. Reprint, Hildesheim: Georg Olms Verlag.

Sams, Eric. 1969. *The Songs of Robert Schumann.* London: Methuen.

Samson, Jim. 1994. 'Chopin reception: Theory, history, analysis'. In John Rink and Jim Samson, eds., *Chopin Studies 2*. Cambridge: Cambridge University Press, 1994, 1–17.

Schachter, Carl. 1981. 'A commentary on Schenker's *Free Composition*'. *Journal of Music Theory* 25, 115–42.

———. 1999a. 'Structure as foreground: "Das Drama des Ursatzes"'. In Carl Schachter and Hedi Siegel, eds., *Schenker Studies 2*. Cambridge: Cambridge University Press, 298–314.

———. 1999b. *Unfoldings: Essays in Schenkerian Theory and Analysis*. Ed. Joseph Straus. New York: Oxford University Press.

———. 2001. 'Elephants, crocodiles, and Beethoven: Schenker's politics and the pedagogy of Schenkerian analysis'. *Theory and Practice* 26, 1–20.

Schenker, Heinrich. 1931. 'Ein verschollener Brief von Mozart und das Geheimnis seines Schaffens'. *Der Kunstwart* 44, 660–66.

———. 1972/1921. *Beethoven: Die letzten Sonaten, Sonate A dur Op. 101: Kritische Einführung und Erläuterung*. Ed. Oswald Jonas. 2nd ed. Vienna: Universal Edition.

———. 1988. 'Three essays from *Neue Revue* (1894–97)'. Trans. Jonathan Dunsby and Horst B. Loeschmann. *Music Analysis* 7, 133–41. Essays first published 1894, 1897.

———. 1991/1897. 'Johannes Brahms'. Trans. William Pastille. *American Brahms Society Newsletter* 9/1, 1–3.

Schoenberg, Arnold. 1964. *Letters*. Ed. Erwin Stein. Trans. Eithne Wilkins and Ernst Kaiser. London: Faber.

———. 1969/1954. *Structural Functions of Harmony*. 2nd ed. London: Ernest Benn.

———. 1975. *Style and Idea: Selected Writings of Arnold Schoenberg*. Ed. Leonard Stein. Trans. Leo Black. London: Faber.

———. 1978/1911 *Theory of Harmony*. Trans. Roy Carter. London: Faber and Faber.

Schor, Naomi. 1987. *Reading in Detail: Aesthetics and the Feminine*. New York: Methuen.

Schorske, Carl. 1980. *Fin-de-Siècle Vienna: Politics and Culture*. New York: Knopf.

Sedlmayr, Hans. 2000. 'The quintessence of Riegl's thought'. In Richard Woodfield, ed., *Framing Formalism: Riegl's Work*. Amsterdam: G and B Arts International, 11–32.

Sessions, Roger. 1985/1935. 'Heinrich Schenker's contribution'. *Modern Music* 12, 170–8. Reprint, *Sonus* 6, 6–14.

Shamsai, Peri. 1997. *The Case of Beethoven: Aesthetic Ideology and Cultural Politics in Fin-de-siècle Viennese Modernism*. Ph.D. diss., Columbia University.

Siegel, Hedi. 1999. 'When "Freier Satz" was part of *Kontrapunkt*: A preliminary report'. In Carl Schachter and Hedi Siegel, eds., *Schenker Studies 2*. Cambridge: Cambridge University Press, 12–25.

Simms, Edwin. 1977. 'New documents in the Schoenberg-Schenker polemic'. *Perspectives of New Music* 16/1, 110–24.

Singer, Peter. 1983. *Hegel*. Oxford: Oxford University Press, 1983.

Slobin, Mark. 1992. 'Micromusics of the West: A comparative approach'. *Ethnomusicology* 36, 1–87.

Smith, Charles. 1996. 'Musical form and fundamental structure: An investigation of Schenker's *Formenlehre*'. *Music Analysis* 15, 191–297.

Smith, Joan Allen. 1986. *Schoenberg and His Circle: A Viennese Portrait.* New York: Schirmer.

Smith, Peter. 1995. 'Structural tonic or apparent tonic? Parametric conflict, temporal perspective, and a continuum of articulative possibilities'. *Journal of Music Theory* 39, 245–83.

Snarrenberg, Robert. 1992. 'Schenker's senses of concealment'. *Theoria* 6, 97–133.

———. 1994. 'Competing myths: The American abandonment of Schenker's organicism'. In Anthony Pople, ed., *Theory, Analysis and Meaning in Music.* Cambridge: Cambridge University Press.

———. 1996. 'The art of translating Schenker: A commentary on *The Masterwork in Music,* vol. 1'. *Music Analysis* 15, 301–42.

———. 1997. *Schenker's Interpretive Practice.* Cambridge: Cambridge University Press.

———. 2001. 'Heinrich Schenker'. In Stanley Sadie and John Tyrrell, eds., *The New Grove Dictionary of Music and Musiciains,* 2nd ed., 22:478–81.

Solie, Ruth. 1980. 'The living work: Organicism and musical analysis'. *Nineteenth-Century Music* 4, 147–56.

Solomon, Maynard. 1980. 'On Beethoven's creative process: A two-part invention'. *Music and Letters* 61, 272–83.

Spiel, Hilde. 1987. *Vienna's Golden Autumn, 1866–1938.* London: Weidenfield and Nicolson.

Sponheuer, Bernd. 2002. 'Reconstructing ideal types of the "German" in music'. In Celia Applegate and Pamela Potter, eds., *Music and German National Identity.* Chicago: University of Chicago Press, 36–58.

Stern, Fritz. 1961. *The Politics of Cultural Despair: A Study in the Rise of the Germanic Ideology.* Berkeley: University of California Press.

Stern, J. P. 1979. *A Study of Nietzsche.* Cambridge: Cambridge University Press.

Subotnik, Rose Rosengard. 1976. 'Adorno's diagnosis of Beethoven's late style: Early symptom of a fatal condition'. *Journal of the American Musicological Society* 29, 242–75.

———. 1988. 'Toward a deconstruction of structural listening: A critique of Schoenberg, Adorno, and Stravinsky'. In Eugene Narmour and Ruth Solie, eds., *Explorations in Music, the Arts, and Ideas: Essays in Honor of Leonard B. Meyer.* Stuyvesant, N.Y.: Pendragon Press, 87–122.

Taruskin, Richard. 1995. *Text and Act: Essays on Music and Performance.* New York: Oxford University Press.

Taylor-Jay, Claire. 2004. *The artist-operas of Pfitzner, Krenek, and Hindemith: Politics and the Ideology of the Artist.* Aldershot, England: Ashgate.

Tepping, Susan. 1982. 'A lesson in analysis: An account of the study of Bach's E Major Invention with Felix-Eberhard von Cube'. *Indiana Theory Review* 9, 63–74.

———. 1983. Interview with Felix-Eberhard von Cube. *Indiana Theory Review* 6, 77–100.

Thieberger, Richard. 1988. 'Assimilated Jewish youth and Viennese cultural life around 1930'. In Ivar Oxaal, Michael Pollak, and Gerhard Botz, eds., *Jews, Antisemitism and Culture in Vienna.* London: Routledge and Kegan Paul, 174–84.

Tournikiotis, Panayotis. 2002/1991. *Adolf Loos.* New York: Princeton Architectural Press.

Travis, Roy. 1959. 'Towards a new concept of tonality?' *Journal of Music Theory* 3, 257–84.

Vergo, Peter. 1975. *Art in Vienna, 1898–1918: Klimt, Kokoschka, Schiele and Their Contemporaries.* London: Phaidon Press.

Wagner, Richard. 1892. *Prose Works.* Vol. 1. *The Art-Work of the Future.* Trans. William Ashton Ellis. London: Routledge and Kegan Paul.

———. 1894. *Prose Works.* Vol. 3. *The Theatre.* Trans. William Ashton Ellis. London: Routledge and Kegan Paul.

———. 1970. *Wagner on Music and Drama: A Selection from Richard Wagner's Prose Works.* Trans. Willam Ashton Ellis. Arr. Albert Goldman and Evert Sprinchorn. London: Gollancz.

Waissenberger, Robert. 1985. *Wien 1890–1920.* New York: Rizzoli. First published 1984.

Wason, Robert. 1985. *Viennese Harmonic Theory from Albrechtsberger to Schenker and Schoenberg.* Ann Arbor, Mich.: UMI Research Press.

Watkins, Holly. 2004. 'From the mine to the shrine: The critical origins of musical depth'. *Nineteenth-Century Music* 27, 179–207.

Weitzmann, Walter. 1988. 'The politics of the Viennese Jewish community'. In Ivar Oxaal, Michael Pollak, and Gerhard Botz, eds., *Jews, Antisemitism and Culture in Vienna.* London: Routledge and Kegan Paul, 121–51.

Whittle, Barbara. 1993. *The Cultural Context of the Theories of Heinrich Schenker.* Ph.D. diss., Open University.

Wicks, Robert. 1993. 'Hegel's aesthetics: An overview'. In Frederick Beiser, ed., *The Cambridge Companion to Hegel.* Cambridge: Cambridge University Press, 348–77.

Wistrich, Robert. 1987. 'Social democracy, antisemitism and the Jews of Vienna'. In Ivar Oxaal, Michael Pollak, and Gerhard Botz, eds., *Jews, Antisemitism and Culture in Vienna.* London: Routledge and Kegan Paul, 111–20.

———. 1989. *The Jews of Vienna in the Age of Franz Joseph.* London: Littman Library of Jewish Civilization.

Wolf, Hans. 1989/1937. 'Schenkers Persönlichkeit im Unterricht'. *Der Dreiklang: Monatsschrift für Musik* 7, 176–84. Reprint, Hildesheim: Georg Olms Verlag.

Index

abbreviation, law of, 168
Abraham a Sancta Clara, 188
Abraham, Karl, 209
Adler, Guido, 12–3, 60 n. 60, 79,
    107, 230, 267 n. 33, 272, 276,
    312 n. 12, 314
Adorno, Theodor, 13, 15, 36, 39,
    157, 190–7, 207 n. 15, 232, 247,
    289–90, 295, 314
Agawu, Kofi, 281, 284, 317
Akademischer Wagner-Verein, 230
Albrechtsberger, Johann Georg, 210
Almén, Byron, 44 n. 20
Alpern, Wayne, 6, 14, 42–3, 134,
    158 n. 33, 193–4, 197, 212 n. 27,
    216, 225, 266 n. 31, 300
Alt-Wien, 184–5, 187
Anschluss, 23, 275
anti-semitism, 6, 22, 54, 87–8,
    150–1, 159–60, 175, 199, 201,
    205, 217–23, 226, 229–43, 268,
    311 n. 10; 'new' anti-semitism
    (defined), 217–20. See also Dreyfus
    Affair

Auspitz, Lazar, 206–7
autonomy of music, 303–6
axial causality, 71, 76, 166, 283, 299,
    313
Ayotte, Benjamin, 273

Babbitt, Milton, 263, 276, 278,
    296–7, 301
Bach, Carl Philipp Emanuel, 19, 83,
    84 n. 94, 90–2, 105, 129, 132–3,
    149, 188, 189 n. 89, 233
Bach, David Josef, 247
Bach, Johann Sebastian, 28, 31,
    51, 52 n. 38, 71, 90, 92, 187,
    189 n. 89, 238, 248, 258 n. 19,
    261, 263, 270, 272, 290 n. 67,
    291, 299
Bahr, Hermann, 39, 98–9, 186
Bakhtin, Mikhail, 290
Barford, Philip, 47
Baudelaire, Charles, 135
Bauer, Karl, 174
Bauhaus, 127, 280
Beach, David, 284

Beethoven, Ludwig van, 9, 13, 35, 40 n. 12, 52–3, 65–6, 77, 96, 137, 142, 148, 156, 185, 190–1, 193–4, 197, 207, 211 n. 25, 213–4, 222, 229, 234, 238–9, 244, 252, 271, 290, 299, 313–5; Ninth Symphony, 51, 86, 90, 103, 156, 174, 258 n. 19, 261, 264, 280, 301

Beethoven exhibition, 99–102

Beiser, Frederick, 288

Bekker, Paul, 173, 298–300

Beller, Steven, 201, 204–7, 210, 214–6, 220–1, 229, 247

Bellermann, Heinrich, 210

Ben-Gurion, David, 244

Benjamin, William, 148, 234 n. 71, 243, 303

Bent, Ian, 3, 5–6, 19, 22, 25, 69, 87, 118, 143–4, 152, 210, 289–90, 301

Berg, Alban, 190

Berkley, George, 203

Berlioz, Hector, 74–5, 233, 270, 299, 312

Berry, David Carson, 275

Berry, Wallace, 295

Bienenfeld, Elsa, 271 n. 37

Billroth, Theodor, 184, 218

Binswagner, Ludwig, 208–9

Blasius, Leslie, 5, 45 n. 21, 47, 62, 85, 93, 284

Blessinger, Karl, 275

Boethius, Anicius Manlius Severinus, 67

Boetticher, Wolfgang, 275

Bohlman, Philip, 247

Bolzano, Bernard, 32

Borchmeyer, Dieter, 231, 236–7

Boretz, Benjamin, 278

Borio, Gianmario, 171, 286

Borsi, Franco, 125

Boruch, Rabbi, 206, 260

Bösendorfer, Ludwig, 183–7, 192, 229

Bösendorfer-Saal, 183–4, 186, 192, 246, 316

Bösendorfer pianos, 180–3, 185, 280

Botstein, Leon, 14–15, 56, 102, 156, 181–2, 184, 186, 192, 204, 210, 246, 267 n. 33, 297 n. 77

Bouillon, Jean-Paul, 102

Brahms, Johannes, 18, 52–5, 77–78, 85, 87–88, 127, 137, 139, 142, 178, 184, 207, 231, 233, 242–3, 248, 271

Breitkopf & Härtel, 239

Breyl, Marie, 240

Bricken, Carl, 276 n. 54

Broch, Hermann, 138, 222, 251

Brown, Julie, 237–8, 243, 309

Bruch, Arthur Moeller van den, 143

Bruckner, Anton, 17, 52–4, 60–1, 64, 69, 70, 72, 77 n. 81, 78–9, 88, 160, 170, 178–9, 184, 211, 288

Brüll, Max, 18

Brzeżany, 9–10, 17, 202

Bülow, Hans von, 91–2, 94–6, 106, 207

Burke, Edmund, 129

Burnham, Scott, 137, 167, 192

Busoni, Ferruccio, 18, 82 n. 89, 83, 99, 181 n. 79, 185, 225

Butler, Judith, 134

causality. *See* logic, musical

Chamberlain, Houston, 231, 233, 309

Charles VI, Emperor, 189

Chatterjee, Ranjit, 211, 213, 226

Cherlin, Michael, 197, 266

Cherubini, Luigi, 210

Chopin, Frédéric, 52 n. 38, 144, 154, 182, 223, 238–9, 241–2

chord of nature, 168, 278

Christensen, Thomas, 6

Christian Socialists, 22–3, 150, 186, 229

Clark, Suzannah, 171, 258 n. 18, 287

classicism, classicists, 7, 54–5, 58, 94–5, 121–7, 137–8, 255–6

clavichord, 91, 106, 185

Cohn, Richard, 258–60, 282, 284–5, 289–90, 293

concealment, 212, 225–7, 280

conservatism, 53–4, 128–9, 140–1, 151, 158–75, 215, 310–2

Conservatory, Vienna, 11, 14, 17, 23, 25, 60, 108, 115–6, 164, 186, 209, 272

conversion, 202, 219, 242

Corbusier, Le, 127, 280

Cotta Verlag, 76, 82, 83 n. 93
Cracow, 11
Cube, Felix-Eberhard von, 149, 249, 270, 274
cyclic form, 74, 84

Dahlhaus, Carl, 170–1, 275
Dahms, Walter, 157, 163 n. 141, 270, 272–3, 315 n. 20
d'Albert, Eugen, 18, 37, 69, 82, 83 n. 93, 181 n. 79
Darwin, Charles, Darwinism, 33, 143, 195
Debussy, Claude, 176, 254, 269
deconstruction, 39, 62, 64, 281–2
democracy, 8, 43, 145–6, 150–1, 161–5, 168
Dempster, Douglas, 297 n. 77
DeNora, Tia, 15
Derrida, Jacques, 281
Deutsch, Sophie, 22
Deutsche Zeitung, 219
Deutsches Volksblatt, 88
Dilthey, Wilhelm, 69, 298, 300
diminution, 256, 283
Dolchstoß, 143, 147, 174
Dollfuss, Engelbert, 149–51
Drabkin, William, 76, 78 n. 81, 143, 146, 152, 209 n. 20, 250, 270, 277, 279, 295, 301 n. 81
Dreiklang, Der, 85, 273–4
Dreyfus Affair, 41, 220, 227
Dubiel, Joseph, 297–8, 300
Duesberg, August, 246 n. 1
Dühring, Eugen, 223
Dunikowski, Emil, 9–10
Dunn, John Petrie, 275
Dunsby, Jonathan, 133
Dvořák, Antonín, 79, 81, 239, 241
Dvořák, Max, 107, 152
dynamics, Schenker's theory of, 27, 258

editing, 90–7
Ehrlich, Eugen, 43, 47, 161, 193, 265
Eibner, Franz, 275
Eitelberger, Rudolf von, 97, 103, 104
Elias, Angi, 22, 85 n. 96
Ellis, William Ashton, 231
emotion, expression of, 35, 50–1, 92

Engelsmann, Walter, 299
epigonism, 54–5, 79, 98, 128
Epstein, Julius, 18
Erlach, Fischer von, 112–3, 115, 189
Erwin, Charlotte, 225
ethics, 8, 128, 205–7, 215. *See also* freedom
Eybl, Martin, 6, 146, 148, 152–3, 275, 293

Fackel, Die, 136, 205
Federhofer, Hellmut, 6, 15, 21, 23, 40, 45, 49, 224 n. 54, 275, 286
fingering, 93–4, 106, 134, 183 n. 81
First World War, 6, 23, 137–8, 140, 142–7, 159, 199, 217, 246, 254, 268–9
Fleiss, Wilhelm, 213
Flesch, Karl, 17
form, analysis of, 285–9
formalism, formalists, 48–62, 66, 74, 107, 255–6
Forte, Allen, 250, 260, 276–9, 302
Fraktur type, 30
Frank, Hans, 175
Frankfurter Zeitung, 152
Franklin, Peter, 115, 164
Franz Josef, Emperor, 10–11, 22, 87, 115, 150–1, 231
Franzos, Karl-Emil, 223
freedom, 93–6, 128, 133–5, 299. *See also* ethics
Freud, Sigmund, 21, 72, 131, 207–9, 211, 213–4, 216, 224, 231, 247
Friedenreich, Harriet Pass, 150
Friedrich, Hans, 262 n. 26
Fuchs, Johann Nepomuk, 17
Fuchs, Robert, 54, 84 n. 94
Furtwängler, Wilhelm, 25, 156, 224, 272, 280
Fux, Johannes, 189, 210

Galicia, Galician Jews, 9–11, 15–7, 154, 166, 173, 199–202, 204, 207, 216–8, 225, 227–30, 232, 242, 244, 309, 315
Gay, Peter, 128, 151–2, 205, 247, 305
Gemeinschaft/ Gesellschaft (defined), 161
gender imagery, 177–9

Genée, Rudolph, 82 n. 92
genius, 53, 65–7, 72–3, 87, 93, 141,
  143–4, 146, 148, 174, 241
Gerigk, Herbert, 209, 275
Geshuri, Me'ir Shim'on, 200, 218
Gilbert, Steven, 250, 260
Godoli, Ezio, 125
Goebbels, Joseph, 17
Goehr, Lydia, 7
Goering, Hermann, 175, 223
Goethe, Johann Wolfgang von, 5,
  7, 32, 44–5, 47, 68, 204, 229,
  233 n. 69, 273, 317
Goldhagen, Daniel, 217
Goldmark, Karl, 18
Gomperz, Theodor, 206
Goodman, Nelson, 211 n. 25
Grädener, Hermann, 54
Graf, Max, 58 n. 53, 222 n. 46
Gravagnuolo, Benedetto, 123, 126,
  134
Grieg, Edvard, 81
Grove, George, 58
Gründerzeit, 97
Grzegorzewska, Sabina, 10

Hagen, 53, 231, 241
Hahn, Albert, 8, 96
Halm, August, 13, 44–5, 60, 61 n. 62,
  149, 153, 156, 158, 194 n. 101,
  211, 254, 270, 272–4, 298
Hammer, Viktor, 224
Handel, George Frideric, 90, 241
Hanisch, Ernst, 163–6, 221, 229
Hanslick, Eduard, 11–2, 18, 38–9,
  48–62, 64, 68, 70, 75, 82 n. 89, 96,
  104, 107, 165, 171 n. 60, 197–8,
  202, 229, 262, 304–5, 315–6
harmonic dualism, 6–7
Hassler, Hans Leo, 30
Hausegger, Friedrich von, 48
Haydn, Joseph, 9, 31, 67, 79–80, 82,
  196
Hazlitt, William, 129
Hegel, Georg Wilhelm Friedrich,
  13–4, 30, 32–4, 39, 43, 44 n. 20,
  46–7, 50, 78, 104–6, 131–2, 135–7,
  164–5, 180, 190–7, 237, 266–7,
  282, 290, 310–3; Hegelian State,
  193–6. *See also* sublation

Heine, Heinrich, 289
Helm, Theodor, 53, 108, 180
Helmholtz, Hermann von, 53 n. 39,
  60 n. 60, 62
Hepokoski, James, 6
Herbart, Johann Friedrich, 59
Herder, Johann Gottfried, 166 n. 48
Hertzka, Emil, 19, 31, 76, 156–7,
  224 n. 54, 243, 269, 298
Herzl, Theodor, 87, 151 n. 14,
  202 n. 6, 220, 223, 227, 244–5,
  311 n. 10
Hesse, Hermann, 251
Heuss, Alfred, 309–10, 311 n. 10
Hindemith, Paul, 172, 274
Hindenburg, Paul von, 157, 173, 175
Hinterberger, Heinrich, 41 n. 16
Hirschfeld, Robert, 48, 53, 56, 58,
  107–8, 175–7, 180, 262, 267 n. 33
Hitler, Adolf, 22–3, 147, 149–50,
  160, 175, 222, 224, 264; *Hitler
  Jugend,* 146, 152–3, 175
Hoboken, Anthony van, 22, 249
Hoffmann, E. T. A., 166 n. 48,
  193 n. 98, 215
Hoffmann, Josef, 99, 122
Hofmannsthal, Hugo von, 163–4,
  211–2
Hollein, Hans, 99
Holtmeier, Ludwig, 270, 274–5
homology, 314–5, 317
Horn, Camillo, 52
Hume, David, 38–9
Husserl, Edmund, 282

Ibn Ezra, Abraham, 210, 216
idealism, German (defined), 32
impressionism, Viennese, 39, 57,
  985
influence, ascriptions of, 39–47
inner emigration, 244, 264

Jabotinsky, Ze'ev, 244
Jackendoff, Ray, 295
Jahn, Otto, 49 n. 29
Janik, Allan, 44, 188
Jellinek, Adolf, 202–3, 216, 229
Jellinek, Georg, 42–3, 47, 134–5,
  164, 193–4, 196, 216, 264–6
Jesus, 208

Jews, Jewish identity, 11–2, 14, 22–3, 88, 138, 146, 150, 154, 199–245, 253, 308–11. *See also* anti-semitism
Jhering, Rudolf von, 267 n. 31
Johnston, William, 32, 39, 43, 161, 246, 265, 267 n. 31
Jonas, Oswald, 5, 21, 147, 158, 182, 208–9, 224, 237, 249–50, 273–9
Jonas Collection (Riverside), described, 40
Jung, Carl, 208–9

Kabala, 210
Kahl, Willi, 156–7
Kaiserhymne, 71, 196–7, 258, 290–3
Kalbeck, Max, 11, 17–8, 54 n. 43, 180, 184, 202
Kalmus, Alfred, 224 n. 54
Kandinsky, Wassily, 152
Kant, Immanuel, 5, 31–2, 38–9, 44–6, 47 n. 24, 73, 87, 132, 190, 273
Karnes, Kevin, 35, 53, 56, 64, 69, 86 n. 101, 105 n. 22, 140, 203 n. 6, 240
Karpath, Ludwig, 25, 82, 272
Kassal-Mikula, Renata, 116
Kassler, Michael, 278
Kater, Michael, 173
Katz, Adele, 276
Kauders, Albert, 180
Keiler, Allan, 5, 37–9, 44, 48, 58, 64, 77, 86
Kelsen, Hans, 264–5
Kerman, Joseph, 4, 261, 263, 278
keys, 257–8, 284
Kivy, Peter, 67, 262
Klimt, Gustav, 100, 103
Klinger, Max, 99–101
Knittel, K. M., 221
Koczalski, Raoul, 183 n. 81
Kolodin, Irving, 256 n. 14
Korngold, Julius, 269
Korsyn, Kevin, 5, 38–40, 42, 44, 48, 57, 60, 64, 70–1, 163 n. 40, 281, 296
Kosovsky, Robert, 40, 77, 78 n. 81
Kralik, Richard, 52, 202, 231
Kramer, Lawrence, 284

Kraus, Karl, 9, 56, 102, 128, 136, 151, 156, 186, 204–5, 207, 215–6, 222, 237 n. 78, 247, 311
Kravitt, Edward, 159, 217, 221 n. 46
Krenek, Ernst, 271
Kretzschmar, Hermann, 56, 58, 92, 192, 262, 304
Kultur/Zivilisation (defined), 161
Kultusgemeinde, 203, 216, 221
Künstler, Gustav, 126
Kunstwart, Der, 248
Kunstwollen, 104–6
Kurth, Ernst, 13, 263, 298, 304

Langer, Suzanne, 315
language and music, 35–6, 55–9, 64, 77–8, 210
Laufer, Edward, 251 n. 8, 260, 276, 302 n. 81
law, 14, 17, 42–3, 75, 134–5, 193–6, 265, 293, 300, 313; Roman, 17, 193–4, 202, 214, 267 n. 31
Lazar, Moshe, 215, 244
Le Rider, Jacques, 156, 186, 281
Leibniz, Gottfried, 32, 46, 48, 265–8, 293, 295
Lemberg. *See* Lvov
Leppert, Richard, 190
Lerdahl, Fred, 295
Levi, Hermann, 54 n. 4, 236
liberalism, 22, 54, 150, 159
Liszt, Ferenc, 74, 83, 233
Loewenberg, Peter, 214
logic, musical, 36–8, 46, 57, 62, 63–81, 85, 87, 167–8
Loos, Adolf, 78 n. 83, 98, 102–6, 111–29, 137, 139, 156, 178, 180, 186, 205, 229, 244 n. 97, 280–1
Lorda, Joaquin, 105
Lothar, Rudolph, 177
Lothlórien, 190
Louis, Rudolf, 41 n. 17, 54, 60–1, 223, 233, 283 n. 61
Lubben, Joseph, 27, 46, 196, 251, 259–60, 281, 290–2, 294–5
Ludwig, Ernst, 17
Lueger, Karl, 54, 87, 150, 159, 231, 259
Lvov, 9, 11, 15, 18, 200, 202
Lytle, Victor, 276 n. 54

Mach, Ernst, 39–40, 42, 48, 57, 60, 62
Magee, Bryan, 32
Magris, Claudio, 206
Mahler, Gustav, 85, 101, 115, 175–7, 179–80, 207 n. 15, 219, 222 n. 46, 223, 233, 299
Makart, Hans, 97
Mann, Michael, 182 n. 80
Mann, Thomas, 144, 161–4
Mannes College of Music, 276, 279
Marr, Wilhelm, 217, 220
Marx, Adolf Bernhard, 56, 92
Marx, Carl, Marxism, 106, 137, 145, 148–9, 185, 192, 214
Mattsee incident, 242
Mayer, Sigismund, 215
McCagg, William, 9, 159, 200–1, 218
McClary, Susan, 15, 314, 317
McColl, Sandra, 52–3, 180, 184
McCreless, Patrick, 277, 303
mediators, 207, 213
melodic fluency, 26, 255
Mendelssohn, Felix, 9, 52 n. 38, 231, 233–4, 270
Menger, Anton, 43
Menger, Carl, 161
Mersmann, Hans, 254
Messchaert, Johannes, 18–9, 93
Meyer, Leonard B., 295
Mikuli, Karol, 9–10, 182, 239
Milch, Baruch, 200
Milch, Erhard, 223
Miller, Patrick, 83
Mitchell, William, 5, 276
monarchy, 151, 164, 193, 196
Morgan, Robert, 61 n. 62, 106, 138–9, 242, 247, 251, 254, 264, 281
Morgen, Der, 112, 122, 125
Moses, 207–8
motif, 105–6, 256–7, 295
Mozart, Wolfgang Amadeus, 9, 26, 75, 84 n. 94, 90, 181, 197, 208, 229, 284. *See also* pseudo-Mozart
Münz, Ludwig, 126
Musik, Die, 156
Musikalisches Wochenblatt, 17, 33
Musil, Robert, 138, 222, 250
Mussolini, Benito, 23, 149–150

Nachlass, Schenker, 40
Narmour, Eugene, 282, 295
National Socialism. *See* Nazism
nature, 8, 33, 65–7, 73, 77 n. 81, 80, 86, 164–5, 168–74, 252, 278
Nazism, National Socialism, 22, 140–1, 148, 150–1, 172; 160, 209, 223. *See also* Hitler, Adolf
Nestroy, Johann, 128
Neue freie Presse, 11, 102, 112, 114, 151 n. 14, 262
Neue Revue, 18, 81, 139
Neues Wiener Journal, 83
Neumeyer, David, 255, 281, 288, 303–4
Niemann, Walter, 176–7
Nietzsche, Friedrich, 39, 47 n. 24, 177, 214, 222, 238, 281
Niloff, Artur, 90
nonpolitical (defined), 163–4
Notley, Margaret, 107, 246 n. 1

Offenbach, Jacques, 128, 148
Olbrich, Josef, 99, 107
Oppel, Reinhard, 150, 274
orchestration, Schenker's theory of, 258
organicism. *See* logic, musical
ornamentation, 90–137, 179, 207
Osten, Heinrich, 81
Oster, Ernst, 5, 40, 147, 249–50, 251 n. 8, 276–9, 285, 312
Oster Collection (New York), described, 40
overtone series, 67, 168–9

Paddison, Max, 191
Paderewski, Ignacy Jan, 181 n. 79
Painter, Karen, 175–6, 180, 221
Pastille, William, 5, 37–8, 47 n. 24, 65–6, 71, 255
Paul, Jean, 68, 72
Payzant, Geoffrey, 48, 59, 305 n. 83
Pekacz, Jolanta, 9–11, 204
Peles, Stephen, 32, 44, 47
performers, performance, 18, 62, 90–7, 130, 181–2, 234, 280–1, 307
Pevsner, Nikolaus, 116, 126
Pfitzner, Hans, 173–5, 222
philology, 214, 312

philosophy of origins, 311–2
Pinsker, Leo, 311
Plato, 31, 265–8, 293, 295
Plum, Karl-Otto, 275
Podhajce, 200–1, 217–8, 225
Potemkin, Grigori Aleksandrovich, 98, 111
Praetorius, Michael, 93
Proctor, Gregory, 279–81, 301, 303
programme music, 51, 54–5, 58, 74, 247
prolongation, 26, 34, 53, 71, 76, 166, 283, 295, 313
pseudo-Mozart, 49, 57, 67–8, 116, 256, 283 n. 61
psychology, 7, 33–5, 59–63, 105, 296–7
Puchstein, Hans, 241

Queens College (New York), 276

Rameau, Jean-Philippe, 63, 137, 192, 236 n. 74, 293, 311 n. 10
Ratz, Erwin, 40
Rechter, David, 12, 218, 248
Reger, Max, 253, 259, 273 n. 44
Rehding, Alexander, 7–8, 33, 60, 172 n. 61, 296, 311–3
Reinecke, Carl, 181
Reisnerstrasse, 108–11
Reiss, József, 11, 166
Reiter, Andrea, 144, 153
repetition, 33–5, 57, 64
Réti, Rudolph, 134, 269
retrospective prophecy, 253, 301, 312
Reumann, Jakob, 264
Reynolds, Joshua, 129–30
Richardson, Henry, 119
Ridley, Hugh, 151
Riegl, Aloïs, 104–7, 127, 137, 152, 166, 171, 185, 229
Riemann, Hugo, 6–8, 58, 92, 96, 298, 312
Riethmüller, Albrecht, 167
Riggins, Lee, 279–81, 301, 303
Rimsky-Korsakoff, Nikolai, 81
Ringer, Alexander, 214–5, 225
Ringstrasse, 97–8, 102, 104, 108, 111
Robertson, Ritchie, 222–3
Rochlitz, Friedrich, 49, 67

Rockmore, Tom, 135
Röntgen, Julius, 18, 51, 75, 82, 84 n. 94, 181 n. 79
roots, rootedness, 308–13
Rosen, Charles, 285
Roth, Hermann, 181, 229, 254
Roth, Joseph, 200, 216, 227, 309
Rothfarb, Lee, 13 n. 9, 59 n. 56, 212
Rothgeb, John, 5, 250, 276, 284, 301–2
Rothschild, Alphons von, 22, 25, 91, 225 n. 59
Rothstein, William, 4, 60 n. 60, 181–2, 275, 277, 279–81, 301, 303
Rousseau, Jean-Jacques, 163
Rozenblit, Marsha, 11–2, 154, 202, 247
Rubinstein, Anton, 37, 181 n. 79
Rumph, Stephen, 194 n. 98
Ryle, Gilbert, 134
Rytting, Bruce, 45–6, 64, 73, 306

Sachs, Melchior, 8, 96
Salzer, Felix, 5, 21, 133, 135, 209, 273–4, 276–7, 280, 286, 297
Sams, Eric, 289
Samson, Jim, 239
Saussure, Ferdinand de, 249
Scarlatti, Domenico, 241–2, 306
Schachter, Carl, 6, 147–50, 158, 258, 261, 276, 284, 288–9, 302–5
Schalk, Josef, 60
Schenker, Heinrich, compositions of, *Drei Gesänge für Frauenstimmen a capella,* 83 n. 94; *Fantasie,* 18, 82, 83–4; *Fünf Klavierstücke,* 18, 82, 85 n. 96; *Ländler,* 18, 82; *Sechs Lieder,* 18, 82; *Syrische Tänze,* 18, 81–2, 84 n. 94, 99, 170, 225; *Vorüber,* 18, 84 n. 94; *Zwei Clavierstücke,* 18, 82; *Zweistimmige Inventionen,* 18, 82
Schenker (Kornfeld), Jeanette, 21, 27, 40, 78 n. 81, 108, 147, 216, 227, 232 n. 67, 249–50
Schering, Arnold, 12
Schiele, Egon, 152
Schiff, Victor, 236 n. 75
Schiller, Friedrich, 44, 100, 168, 204, 229, 244

Schmitz, Oskar, 207, 227
Schnabel, Artur, 82 n. 89
Schneider, Ernst, 231
Schnitzler, Arthur, 237 n. 78
Schoenaich, Gustav, 202
Schoenberg, Arnold, 42 n. 17, 70, 72, 81–2, 102, 127–8, 133–4, 136–7, 139, 151–2, 155, 157, 166, 169–73, 175, 180, 184, 186, 188, 194–5, 202, 205, 207 n. 15, 208, 210, 215–6, 219, 221–2, 229–33, 236, 242–4, 247, 252, 256, 263, 266, 269, 271 n. 37, 274, 280–1, 308–10, 311 n. 10, 312–3; arrangement of *Syrische Tänze*, 18, 81–2, 170, 225; Society for Private Musical Performances, 155, 186
Schönerer, Georg von, 54 n. 43, 88, 159, 219, 231
Schopenhauer, Arthur, 47 n. 24, 72, 86, 173, 214, 273
Schor, Naomi, 129–31, 135
Schorske, Carl, 97, 100, 104, 124, 150, 159, 204–5, 251–2
Schrader, Bruno, 271
Schubert, Franz, 51, 75, 81, 239, 258 n. 16, 270–1
Schumann, Robert, 51, 75, 185, 239, 270, 287–9, 296
Schuschnigg, Kurt, 23
Scott, Irene Schreier, 158, 279
Secession, Vienna, 99
Sechter, Simon, 12, 60–1, 70, 72, 215, 288
Semper, Gottfried, 106, 166, 171
Sessions, Roger, 255
Shamsai, Peri, 102, 115, 134
shtetl (defined), 200–1
Siegel, Hedi, 232 n. 67
Simms, Bryan, 225
Singer, Peter, 193
Slobin, Mark, 315
Smetana, Bed_ich, 79–80, 86, 239–41
Smith, Charles, 286–9, 294, 296
Smith, Joan Allen, 152
Smith, Peter, 281
Snarrenberg, Robert, 5–6, 67, 195–6, 211, 251, 263, 272, 277, 297–8, 301, 315–6

Social Democrats, 8, 23, 151, 229, 264
Solie, Ruth, 296
Spann, Othmar, 24
Spengler, Oswald, 44 n. 20, 95, 157, 161–3, 173, 211, 266, 273
Sperber, Manès, 206, 216
Spiedel, Max, 54
Spiel, Hilde, 78 n. 83
St Germain, Treaty of, 23, 54 n. 43, 145, 152, 159
Stefan, Paul, 119
Stein, Leonard, 308 n. 1
Steiner, George, 205
Steinsaltz, Adin, 212
Steinway pianos, 182–3, 186, 280
Stengel, Theophil, 209, 275
Stern, Fritz, 143
Stern, J. P., 214
Steuermann, Eduard, 190
Stifter, Adalbert, 251–3, 264, 280, 301
stoicism, 205–7, 214
Stolzing, Josef, 55 n. 43
Strauss, Richard, 26, 74, 312 n. 12
Stravinsky, Igor, 253, 259, 278
Stufen, 6, 26
Stumpf, Carl, 33
sublation, 13, 131–2, 135, 179–80, 195, 237
Subotnik, Rose, 190–1, 193
Sulzer, Salomon, 213
synthesis, 38, 75–6, 106, 132, 142–3, 172, 179, 196–7, 207, 263, 283, 285, 290–3, 295

Talmud, 209–10, 214–6, 226, 250, 255
Taruskin, Richard, 72
tension, 282–5, 296
Teuber, Oscar, 184
Thuille, Ludwig, 60–1, 283 n. 61
Thym, Jürgen, 302
Tönnies, Ferdinand, 161, 163
Toulmin, Stephen, 44
Tovey, Donald, 56
Trakl, Georg, 222
Travis, Roy, 278
Truman, Harry, 244

unity vs uniformity, 130, 135–6, 284–5, 292, 314
Universal Edition, 19–21, 31, 157, 224 n. 54, 302 n. 81. *See also* Hertzka, Emil
University of Vienna, 12, 14, 17, 32–3, 42–3, 93, 104, 107, 160, 193, 202, 214, 220, 223, 232, 264, 266, 270, 272, 274, 276
Urgesetz, 43
Urlinie, 7, 26–7, 32, 49, 66, 71, 87, 177–8, 188, 212, 241, 249, 254–7, 260, 267–8, 271, 275, 282–4, 288, 293–4, 304, 312
Ursatz, 27, 43, 214, 255, 281–3, 286, 292, 296, 312–3

Verdi, Giuseppe, 254
Vergo, Peter, 126
Versailles, Treaty of, 23, 152, 159
Victor Emmanuel III, 150
Vienna Circle, 262, 265
Vierkandt, Alfred, 172 n. 61
Viertel, Sasha, 152
Vincent, Heinrich, 8, 96
Violin, Moriz, 82, 203, 274
virtuosos, 93–6, 106–7, 141, 185–6, 230, 234 n. 70
Vischer, Robert, 165
Vormärz, 128, 190–1, 197, 252–3, 264, 314, 316
Vrieslander, Otto, 25, 157, 224 n. 54, 270, 275, 304

Wackenroder, Wilhelm, 166 n. 48, 187 n. 85
Waechter, Eberhard Freiherr von, 262 n. 26
Wage, Die, 81
Wagner, Cosima, 231
Wagner, Otto, 106
Wagner, Richard, 54 n. 43, 74, 76, 77 n. 81, 85–7, 91, 130, 155, 160–2, 164, 177, 218–9, 222, 229–42, 264, 280, 299, 310, 312 n. 12

Wagnerians, Wagnerism, 52–3, 87–8
Walker, Ernest, 156 n. 22
Wallaschek, Richard, 164, 202, 239, 304, 312 n. 12
Waniek, Piotr, 10
Warfield, Gerald, 147, 250
Wason, Robert, 61
Wassermann, Jakob, 236 n. 75
Watkins, Holly, 166 n. 48
Weber, Carl Maria von, 9
Webern, Anton, 125, 243
Wedge, George, 276 n. 54
Weininger, Otto, 222, 238
Weisse, Hans, 21, 25, 256 n. 14, 273 n. 44, 274–6
Weizmann, Chaim, 244
Wetzel, Hermann, 271
Wey, Francis, 132
White, Harry, 189–90
Whittle, Barbara, 269
Wickhoff, Franz, 104
Wiener Werkstätte, 184
Wisniowczyk, 200
Wistrich, Robert, 202, 208, 222
Wittgenstein Ludwig, 15, 151, 205, 207, 211, 213, 222, 226, 236, 249, 262
Woerz, Johann Georg, 202
Wolf, Hans, 83, 89, 243
Wolf, Hugo, 160
Wood, Abigail, 225 n. 57

Zeit, Die, 18, 164
Zeitgeist, 141
Zenck, Claudia, 173
Zerner, Henri, 105
Zhismann, Joseph, 43
Zimmermann, Robert, 32, 42, 48, 59, 104–5, 265–6, 267 n. 33
Zionism, 6, 87, 201 n. 4, 220–1, 227, 229, 231, 242–5, 248, 264, 309, 311 n. 10
Zohn, Harry, 202 n. 5
Zuckerkandl, Victor, 209, 272
Zukunft, Die, 18